Crossing Boundaries

The Center for Renaissance and Baroque Studies at the University of Maryland sponsors programs in all disciplines of the arts and humanities as well as in such allied fields as the history and philosophy of science. Designed primarily for faculty and graduate students, the Center's scholarly programs include conferences and colloquia, lectures, an annual interdisciplinary symposium, and a wide variety of outreach programs for secondary school teachers and their students. Programs in the arts include concerts, lecture-demonstrations, performances, and exhibitions. The Center is administered by its director in conjunction with an advisory board of outside consultants and a faculty advisory committee.

Crossing Boundaries: Attending to Early Modern Women

Edited by
Jane Donawerth and Adele Seeff

with the assistance of Sharon Achinstein,

Susan Dwyer Amussen, Richard Chapman, Sheila ffolliott,

Joan E. Hartman, Susan Jenson, Carole Levin,

Margaret Mikesell, Karen Nelson, Jaime Osterman,

Anne Lake Prescott, Betty S. Travitsky,

and Lee Vedder

DELAWARE

Newark: University of Delaware Press
London: Associated University Presses

Associated University Presses
440 Forsgate Drive
Cranbury, NJ 08512

Associated University Presses
16 Barter Street
London WC1A 2AH, England

Associated University Presses
P.O. Box 338, Port Credit
Mississauga, Ontario
Canada L5G 4L8

The paper used in this publication meets the requirements of the American National Standard for Permanence of Paper for Printed Library Materials Z39.48-1984.

**Library of Congress Cataloging-in-Publication Data
is available from the Library of Congress**

PRINTED IN THE UNITED STATES OF AMERICA

CENTER FOR RENAISSANCE AND BAROQUE STUDIES

Other titles available from the University of Delaware Press

The Public and Private in Dutch Culture of the Golden Age (forthcoming)
Edited by Arthur K. Wheelock, Jr. and Adele Seeff

In Iberia and Beyond: Hispanic Jews Between Two Cultures
Edited by Bernard Dov Cooperman

Attending to Women in Early Modern England
Edited by Betty S. Travitsky and Adele F. Seeff

Attending to Early Modern Women
Edited by Susan Amussen and Adele F. Seeff

The Picaresque: A Symposium on the Rogue's Tale
Edited by Carmen Benito-Vessels and Michael Zappala

Action and Reaction: Proceedings of a Symposium to Commemorate the Tercentenary of Newton's Principia
Edited by Paul Theerman and Adele Seeff

Settlements in the Americas: Cross-cultural Perspectives
Edited by Ralph Bennett

The French Academy: Classicism and Its Antagonists
Edited by June Hargrove

Urban Life in the Renaissance
Edited by Susan Zimmerman and Ronald F. E. Weissman

Print and Culture in the Renaissance: Essays on the Advent of Printing in Europe
Edited by Gerald P. Tyson and Sylvia S. Wagonheim

Contents

Part Four: Keynote Address

Part Five: Pedagogy

Part Six: Performance

Director's Preface

THE CENTER FOR RENAISSANCE AND BAROQUE STUDIES was established in 1981 through the vision of Dr. Shirley S. Kenny, then provost of arts and humanities at the University of Maryland, and the beneficence of the Maryland legislature during an all-too-familiar period of retrenchment in higher education. It held its inaugural conference on 11–12 March, 1982. From the outset, the university has envisaged the center as multidisciplinary. Music and the visual arts, literature in several modern European and Asian languages, philosophy, and history—indeed all the appropriate disciplines in the humanistic pantheon—come within the center's domain. Throughout the academic year, the center engages the university community, the wider educational community in Maryland, and area cultural institutions with a continuing program of interdisciplinary symposia, public lectures, and colloquia. In addition, the center has ongoing partnerships with many Maryland school districts and offers statewide and national programs for secondary school teachers of literature, drama, and the performing arts. These secondary school teachers are always included in the audience of other events as well.

This volume is the third to take up questions relating to the lives and production of early modern women. The first and second volumes, *Attending to Women in Early Modern England* and *Attending to Early Modern Women*, published by the University of Delaware Press in 1994 and 1997 respectively, recorded the dynamic scholarly exchanges that took place at symposia sponsored by the Center for Renaissance and Baroque Studies at the University of Maryland in 1990 and 1994. The present volume, too, had its genesis at a symposium held in College Park on 6–8 November, 1997. The formal plenary papers, conversations, and workshops that filled two crowded days are recorded here. An expanded geographical range, explicit in the title, and a consequent focus on diversity and comparative explorations distinguish this third volume from its predecessors; breaching physical, legal, and cultural borders–materially and fancifully–proved evocative, as these papers illustrate. The commitment to an interdisciplinary framework, however, remains unchanged. The essays collected here, contributed by scholars of literature, (including Chinese literature), history, history of science, music, classics, and art history raise crucial interdisciplinary questions about the shaping of the female self through gendering the body, the relation of legal codes to gender, and female travel, often experienced vicariously through imaginative literature. The symposium also offered opportunities to (re)consider teaching strategies for students in this field.

As with previous symposia, a distinguishing feature was the inclusion of workshops convened by scholars from different fields. They explored such topics as salons and coteries in seventeenth-century France and England, domestic texts and objects in modern Europe, the Elizabeth Canning case, the relationship between gender and persecution, aged women in European art and Japanese Noh drama, women and travel, and the teaching opportunities afforded by the Brown Women Writer's Project Textbase. Many of these workshops appear in this volume in summary form accompanied by reference bibliographies, where they add to the broad range of topics addressed, and serve, perhaps, as generative of future courses.

Thanks go to the members of the symposium planning committee, whose sustained attention to early modern women continue to shape a vital field. The planning committee have contributed to these symposia for close to a decade now and friendship can now be counted with the thanks. Thanks also to Lee Vedder who has left the center for the Henry E. Huntington Library. Her successor, Jaime Osterman, is to be commended for her excellent proofing. Thanks, too, to Richard Chapman for his patience, good humor, and impeccable sense of design. The greatest debt is owed to Jane Donawerth: colleague, co-editor, and center board member.

Introduction

ANNE LAKE PRESCOTT
English and French Literature

> . . . Poor female sex, you are forever troubled
> With evil fortune, held in base subjection
> And forced to live deprived of liberty!
> This does not come from any fault of ours,
> Because, though we fall short of men's robustness,
> We are the same in mind and intellect.
> For virtue does not lie in strength of body,
> But in soul's vigor and the force of genius
> By which anything known can be possessed.
> And I am certain that in such endeavors,
> Women are not in any way less worthy,
> But often show a greater aptitude.
>
> —Veronica Franco, 1575*

The time having come, Mademoiselle, that men's severe laws no longer forbid women to apply themselves to the arts and sciences, it seems to me that those who have the opportunity ought to use the honorable liberty for which our sex has longed to study them, and to show men the wrong they have done us by depriving us of the good and honor that may come to us through them.

> —Louise Labé, 1555†

> the muses ffemalls are
> and therfore of Vs ffemales take some care
> Two Vniuersities we haue of men
> o thatt we had but one of women then
> O then thatt would in witt, and tongs surpasse
> All art of men thatt is, or euer was.
>
> —Martha Moulsworth, 1632‡

THIS VOLUME offers essays on early modern women that derive from papers presented at the interdisciplinary conference on "Attending to Women: Crossing Boundaries," held at the University of Maryland, College Park, in the fall of 1997. It offers, as well, reports on the many workshops that gave participants an opportunity for interdisciplinary conversation, the exchange of

11

helpful information or questions, and the start of friendships and collaborations. Those workshops, the Planning Committee believes, are the heart of our
"Attending" conferences as both sites of productive talk and a reminder that
the study of early modern women is at this stage of its development especially
open to various modes of collaborative teaching and learning.

This was the third conference in the "Attending to Women" series. The first
had concentrated on early modern Englishwomen; the second had broadened its
focus so as to include women on the continent of Europe. As the organizing
committee made plans for the third, we wondered how we might expand our
view yet further. The intellectual issues involved in such expansion would not be
insignificant. Periodization in any given culture is problematic to begin with.
How, for example, does the "Renaissance" relate to the "early modern"? What
are the relevant dates, and do they work equally well for all geographical areas of
Europe? Were some people less modern than others? If some women probably
did have a Renaissance, did all European women have an early modern period?
Did they do so in quite the same ways as did men? Everywhere? In all classes?

Even trickier, we realized, was when and how to apply "early modern" to
areas beyond Europe. It goes without saying that the world of "early modern"
Europe affected and was affected by other cultures and ecologies as European
exploration, trade, and conquest proceeded. We thought of having a conference
on "Early Modern Women East and West," but we soon realized that we did
not want to impose a European chronology on all humanity. Yet, early modern European women did not exist apart from the rest of the globe: in one way
or another all were influenced by contact with it, and in a few cases women
actually set foot outside their ancestral territory. Some non-European cultures, moreover, had their own early modernity, however different their
"modern" was from Europe's. It would be helpful, the committee thought, and
especially so in view of our interdisciplinary emphasis, for those studying
early modern Europe to hear more about those cultures.

As the Planning Committee wondered how to move our purview beyond
Europe's confines, it occurred to us that we could have a conference on just that
theme—why not call the conference "Crossing Borders"? The borders would
not be merely geographical, for women can cross borders in many ways, not all
of them requiring literal movement. Even the perimeters of the female body
have often seemed (and to both sexes) shifty, leaky, mysterious, inviting or
repelling various sorts of border crossing. Clearly a plenary session on bodies
would be in order. Those bodies have to live somewhere, though, and where they
live inevitably limits what they can do or say, if only because one way in which
all human beings maintain order and create cultural space is by laying down
rules. Needless to say, the disconcertingly mobile confines of rules and laws, both
religious and secular, are defined and policed by what happens when somebody

strays across them. How, when, and why did women negotiate such crossings? What made women suspect or criminal—"made" in the sense that authorities can criminalize certain acts simply by making them illegal and "made" in the sense that some women were impelled to break them? Desperation? Malice? The "wrong" faith? Anger? Delusion? Greed? Love? Being in the wrong place at the wrong time? Then, because some border crossings are indeed actual, we also wanted a plenary session to take account of the mostly European women who traveled (or fled) from one place to another or who lived in the "New World" while still belonging, in part, to the "Old." So, we agreed, we would arrange plenary sessions on women and law, and travel and settlement. Finally, as in previous "Attending to Women Conferences," the Planning Committee wanted to facilitate sharing materials and thoughts relevant to the classroom: a fourth plenary session would consider pedagogy.

We would, we agreed, continue to encourage each other to cross the frontiers of our own disciplines as we explored how early modern women worked, loved, thought, aged, wrote, felt, believed, created, sang, bonded, suffered, talked, imagined, and lived—or refused to live, or could not live—within their prescribed physical or cultural spaces. Of course, we would not ignore how the men in their lives imagined, treated, constructed, and in several ways "attended to" these women. The conference, we hoped, would again give many scholars the pleasure of comparing notes, engaging in mutual exploration and discovery, encouraging each other, offering amicable correction, and suggesting new perspectives. We had found our first two conferences enjoyable, instructive, and moving in large part because of their tone: so much sharing, so little cock-of-the-walk strutting, spotlight hogging, or self-positioning in a pecking order. No academic scene is without its hierarchies and egotisms, but we hoped to make this conference, too, as free as possible from cant, self-promotion, and stubborn insistence on being right. We hope, too, that readers of this volume will sense the conference's friendly atmosphere and will find in it material for their own explorations, collaborations, and border crossings.

Readers of the following essays will notice just how fruitful the notion of border crossing turned out to be, producing valuable observations on our main topics—bodies, laws, travel—and providing one more way to conceive of or describe a range of social phenomena, practices, developments, and energies.

The first three essays, from the plenary session on bodies, explore several ways in which the female body was attended to, not always pleasantly. Most of us live our lives sure that we know where the physical "me" ends and the physical "not me" starts, and we are usually equally sure that we know what lies tucked inside the body and what is on or beyond its visible surface. Yet, it is not news to the thoughtful that bodies, which seem to their owners so solid and natural and their perimeters so clearly demarcated, are subject to cultural shaping and definition. Judith T. Zeitlin describes a set of male-authored literary texts from early modern (alternatively, "late imperial") China in which a dying woman orders her portrait or, in one significant case, paints it herself, thus preserving the beauty that illness has wasted. However, because the portrait both represents her individual body and literally captures her interior animating spirit, her *qing*, it can also behave like a ghost. A portrait can even, in some cases, restore the woman and her body to life. In such cases the permeable borders between life and death, inwardness and exterior, original and representation, illusion and reality, image and memory, are crossed and recrossed. Sometimes, though, the woman is dying just because there is not *enough* movement within her: she is obstructed by "static congestion," the somatic correlative of blocked longing in which her inner vitality, her *qi*, cannot circulate and therefore congeals. Readers of this volume will be intrigued to learn that, in addition to maidens and widows suffering from frustrated sexual desire, those most subject to static congestion are scholars who fail their examinations.

Zeitlin notes that the playwright Wu Bing can make his painter a doctor because both medicine and portraiture require close observation (require, we might say, "attending to" the subject with alert sympathetic understanding). Such observation, says Zeitlin, was medically necessary in a culture that did not privilege anatomy or dissection. The European Renaissance, by contrast, saw an increased interest in just those enterprises. Katharine Park's essay explores a particularly problematic aspect of dissection: the eroticized penetration and dismemberment of female interiority. Exploring a woman's insides, read as something ordinarily occult and deliberately kept secret from men, can look disturbingly like a sexual violation.

Park illustrates this curious mixture of medical investigation and prurience by analyzing the frontispiece to an anatomy book by Vesalius and locating one source of its imagery in an appalling if doubtless apocryphal story of how the emperor Nero ordered his still living mother split open so that he could see where he came from. Medieval images of this episode, or even of Nero doing the job himself, strikingly anticipate that of the woman lying open to Vesalius, emperor of dissection and anatomy, and a large crowd of rowdy men. The emperor not only wanted to *see* a woman's insides, Park's account suggests; he also in some ways wanted to *be* a woman. In an extraordinary demonstration of what some would call womb envy and everybody would call misplaced curiosity, he insisted that his doctors make him pregnant. The doctors slip a frog into his belly, give him an emetic, and tell him that the creature is his deformed and premature fetus. (In another version of the legend, I might add, Nero has a palace built for his horrific newborn frog-baby, calling it the "Late*ran*," from *ranus*, Latin for frog.[1]) This story and the title page to Vesalius's book, Park shows, accompany the common, if hardly universal, understanding of the female body as secret and transgressive, containing a mysterious womb that can nevertheless be cut open and revealed as empty.[2] The womb, in such a view, is a place of faithless imaginings, a source of interruptions or detours in patrilinear descent. A woman's interior is less and less subject to female expertise when science becomes, as it did for writers like Francis Bacon, a masculine enterprise with a male lineage and when the female body becomes the province of male doctors.

That female body, however often enjoined to silence, has a voice. Suzanne G. Cusick's essay shows the complexity of gendering that physical voice when it issued as soprano song from the throat of the Italian performer and composer Francesca Caccini (1587–after 1641). What gave Caccini such success? Cusick locates the answer in the combination of the singer's family background (her father was an important composer), the protection and patronage of the Medici *famiglia,* her own talents, a fashion for expressive singing that required tight control of the throat and airstream, and her age's theories about voice and physiology. All these gave her a power that was unusual in her own age and that was denied the opera sopranos who soon followed her. Explaining the culture's views on the physiology of sound, power, and gender, Cusick argues that, because a high but flexible and controlled voice bespoke rhetorical and physical energy (produced, it was thought, by a fiery overflowing spirit or anima), and because energy and power were gendered male, the new styles and techniques that Caccini's father helped invent gave this soprano a paradoxical subjectivity that mingled masculine and feminine qualities and the authority to become a composer. In her case, "crossing borders" took place inside a single body. Her impressive control of air shaped by trained yet inevitably resistant muscles in her throat gave her a cross-gendered rhetorical and symbolic power that helped authorize her prowess as a composer. As a diva, says Cusick, Caccini ruled the minds and bodies of her listeners, for although a subject, she was also a sovereign—at least while singing. Because her throat was heated by anima, however, and because heat was thought to be sexual and the throat was associated in medical theory with the cervix, Caccini's voice also resituated her in dubious erotic territory by giving her a disturbing sexual agency. These and later divas, though, Cusick reminds us, were to play roles that combined vocal power with images of subjugation in their theatrical roles, allowing male listeners the titillation of crossing over into an alien subjectivity that was at once erotic and bound.

The workshops that followed the papers by Zeitlin, Park, and Cusick extended and enhanced many of the themes laid down in this plenary session on bodies. Covering England, Scotland, France, Italy, Germany, the Low Countries, and Japan, these workshops focused on women embodied as queens consort and regnant, as writers and ballad singers, as domestic managers and domestic servants, as needleworkers, spinners, and weavers, as wives and frequenters of alehouses. Whatever their social status and whatever their age, early modern women shared an irreducible female body drawn and dissected in anatomy illustrations, described in medical treatises and midwifery manuals, and subjected to interrogation and discipline by secular and church authorities.

Workshops reviewed the ways women's bodies were constrained by clothing and architecture, examined in legal situations, and eroticized for fashion. Participants examined the material presence of women in domestic paraphernalia—caskets, needlework, dressing tables, and spinning tools that mediate or establish domestic femininity. Several workshops explored the too frequent definition of women in terms of their reproductive and sexual functions. Participants discussed maternal bodies, childbirth, and nursing in European art and literature; the queen's body as an instrument of foreign policy and that body's relation to dynastic marriage and national identity; and early modern debates about virginity and its bodily signs. Other workshops sought explanations for early modern women's agency as they performed with their bodies in popular culture—selling and singing ballads; playing games and music; dancing; acting in festival drama; voicing desires in the food they prepared, the gardens they designed, or the clothing they chose. Discussants asked what strategies of care and healing women used to address physical and emotional vulnerability, how they coped with the physical effects of childbirth, depression, or spousal abuse.

Workshop organizers crossed many boundaries. For example, one workshop compared the frequent negative European representations of old women to the positive depiction of such women in Japanese Noh drama, where a background of Buddhist philosophy encouraged celebration of old women as exemplifying the pleasures of change and surprise. Some organizers performed and embodied their views of early modern women, with one workshop serving marchpane, pretzels, and shortbread, and another acting out the alehouse fellowship of ordinary wives. Even as workshop organizers attended to the historical and cultural framing of bodies, the material female body kept emerging to link early modern women with us.

Our volume's next essay derives from the plenary session on law and criminality.[3] The eloquent and often personal meditation on historiography by Anne Llewellyn Barstow examines the law's response to women who crossed social and religious borders, or were thought to have done so, in ways that got them accused of witchcraft. Barstow argues that, although in recent years some have preferred not to study this horrifying topic in the context of women's studies, the witchcraft craze remains inescapably a part of women's history. In what ways should it matter to us that, in the sixteenth century, more women appeared in court, whether as the accused, accusers, or witnesses?

Or that those courts were extending their reach further into private lives, including sexual behavior, even as the law saw a shift from restitutive to punitive justice? How did the many convictions for witchcraft affect the position of women in general? And how are we to answer what Barstow calls "the challenge of writing about the violence in this material, and of naming the misogyny that underlay it" without indulging in sometimes subtle forms of denial or, by sliding over the torture and sexual sadism, committing a "censorship that distorts history"? Citing modern historians who, in her view, do censor the story of how the law hunted down women and killed them, Barstow insists that these women really were "victims," not independent-minded figures suitable for turning into heroines. Historians should deal with their anguish without evasion and with the victims' gender in mind.

The workshops that followed the plenary session on law and criminality probed the boundaries that both separated and articulated women's transgressive and "legitimate" behaviors—in the most literal legal sense, in social and religious custom, and as represented in literature and art. Some of the workshops focused intensively on the two major axes of the plenary session, law and gender, as they studied the criminalization of traditionally female skills or the shifting lines between law and its actual application to women. More often, the workshops gathered larger issues into what became multidimensional discussions. Some workshops explored the occasionally nurturing but often hostile relations between women and Islam, Judaism, or Christianity and the attentive presence of those religions' established authorities in women's lives. Other workshops examined the portrayal of crime and gender in the arts—exploring, for example, literary texts' images of sexual violence, interactions between male protagonists and lesser female characters, trial scenes, and the like. Those reporting on the workshops regularly find discussions "lively," with participants taking up such topics as the trove of information about women's lives in court records; the importance of nation and class in understanding women's "innocence" and "culpability" in legal or religious spheres; the consequences of male power to codify female "crime" and enforce its "punishment"; the weight of convention in the representation of women, crime, and gender in literature and court documents; and the way female agency and authority function within these legal and social entanglements. In the workshops as a group, the conference's commitment to interdisciplinarity showed in the range of countries under study (most commonly England, France, Holland, and Italy); in the extraordinary diversity of sources (depositions, inquisition records, laws, canonical literature, and art, but also ballads, wills, pornography, letters, didactic and instructional treatises, portraits of criminals, and polemics); and, perhaps most powerfully, in the diversity of perspectives and methods that enabled this exchange.

The next group of essays engages the topic of our third plenary session: travel. Some borders are, of course, quite literal—not just national and hence cultural, but made of water separating Europe from what Europeans had come to call the "New World."

Jodie Bilinkoff's "Navigating the Waves (of Devotion)" is part of an effort to travel "toward a Brave New World," a "gendered analysis" of Catholic culture from around 1450 to 1750. Bilinkoff thus hopes "to cross or even blur several conceptual boundaries, of chronology, geography, gender, and genre." She focuses on two early modern biographical texts, Francisco Losa's *Life* of the devout Spanish layman Gregorio López, who died in Mexico in 1596, and Paul Ragueneau's *Life* of Catherine de Saint Augustin, a mystic and hospital sister who died in Québec in 1668. Because many people associate saints' lives with the Middle Ages, argues Bilinkoff, and because charismatic spirituality is often associated with women, it is fruitful to remember that early modern Spain in fact saw a golden age of saints and of hagiography praising them. Whether or not women had a Renaissance, they certainly had a Counter Reformation. In 1742, Bilinkoff notes, long after the Council of Trent supposedly put a stop to charismatic female behavior, the controversial Colombian nun Madre Castillo wrote a spiritual autobiography that fits a tradition of ecstatic female mysticism we are wrong to think exclusively "Medieval." Are these texts from Spain and the Americas also "colonial"? Bilinkoff shows how each *Life* notices the native inhabitants as well as offering scholars evidence for the age's thought on gender, exemplarity, and identity.

Among the most famous Catholic figures living in the Americas was Sor Juana Inés de la Cruz, who among her other works wrote the "plan, libretto and explanation" of a ceremony at the portal of the Cathedral of Mexico on November 30, 1680. Electa Arenal's essay examines the text and the ceremony itself, which included a large arch, an "elegant, silent set design" for an allegory representing the transfer of the Spanish viceroy's power to Spain's northern territories in "the so-called new world." Unlike earlier printed accounts of entries and arches—those splendid liminal structures so favored by European cities and rulers when they wanted to commemorate a new royal status or to welcome a VIP across an urban border—Sor Juana's text is also, says Arenal, a "feminist political treatise." The allegorical arch, five stories tall and splendid with hieroglyphs and fourteen paintings showing both European and Aztec figures, has a subtext, a "secret": the conflict between Sor Juana and her less-than-sympathetic Jesuit confessor. Sor Juana resolves this conflict, at least in her imagery, by reworking "inherited cosmographic and cosmological concepts" so as to recognize more fully the female half of humanity. To be sure, Baroque art includes many a female figure, yet Arenal demonstrates that Sor Juana gave figures such as Isis and Sophia new power and meaning. As for male figures, she can also allegorize Neptune and his trident in ways that defend women against what she saw as Tridentine and Jesuit injustice. Sor Juana was not entirely a "gender essentialist," though, for Arenal also shows that in the nun's view both "feminine" and "masculine" are "in great part fluid and figurative." The feminism that Sor Juana found so "plausible," says Arenal, has "barely begun to be appreciated in the twentieth century," and one suspects that readers of this volume in the twenty-first century will find Sor Juana in many ways liberated and liberating. It is poignant to reflect that her face can be seen on modern Mexican money—if not borne on Neptune's currents, she circulates as currency.

In workshops following the plenary session on travel, participants considered the ways early modern women participated in real and fictional travel. One workshop took on the task of theorizing travel as a gendered activity, suggesting that domestic travel be considered as well as foreign travel. Insisting that the category "travel" include women who moved aristocratic households from one estate to the next, wives who accompanied their husbands on diplomatic missions or into exile, and slaves and indentured servants forced from their homelands, the panel examined the differences between voluntary and coerced travel. Other workshop participants explored women's assimilation into New World culture, asking whether their new situations opened up possibilities for the emancipation of women, as in the narratives of colonial women captured or living with Native Americans and the evangelical travel that the African-Caribbean Hart sisters pursued. Discussing the journeys of women to the New World during the Catholic Reformation, the church's encouragement of Spanish women's emigration, and the attraction of women to the Jesuit missionary model of spirituality, participants considered the travel of women to the New World in the light of religious commitments. Colonial travel was also central to another workshop, which compared two famous historical figures—Malintzin/Dona Marina ("La Malinche," translator and mistress to Cortés) and Elizabeth I—in order to examine the relationships between early colonialism, and the role of these figures in national fantasy. Further broadening the definition of travel, participants queried the nature of space for women of the European Renaissance, looking at itineraries in connection with Catherine de' Medici's building program, French and Italian paintings commissioned by women, and music as "invasion" of women's bodies.

Women traveled across imaginary as well as geographical borders. In a workshop on armchair travel by women who wrote or translated plays and travelogues, discussants followed Margaret Cavendish to a woman-ruled utopia in her *Blazing World*, Aphra Behn to a New World with fluid class and gender lines, and to the coast of Florida where shipwrecked passengers lost their European norms and morals with their boat. How, they wondered, did the royalism of Behn and Cavendish connect to empire building? Workshops explored other imaginary worlds by contrasting Aemilia Lanyer's Cookeham, Cavendish's Blazing World, and Madeleine de Scudéry's utopian Land of the New Sauromates.

The workshops following the plenary session on travel thus opened up an important set of questions for gender analysis by considering how the various borders that constrained and defined women's lives were changing in the early modern period. Borders may have been opening up through opportunities offered by conquest—or, on the other hand, closing down along national and class lines. Female utopian space may have been an outlet for overtly feminist protest, or it may have been the site for a withdrawal of political energy into the private realm of the imagination. Religion may have provided women with opportunities for transnational contact and for escaping restrictive spaces within nations, but religion may also have challenged notions of ethnic or cultural difference. Because early modern women created spaces and invested spaces with meaning, attending to the organization of space also elucidates their epistemology.

Women may, however, cross such borders without leaving their own houses or even standing up. Karen Newman's essay, based on her keynote address to the conference, explores the value for women of "armchair travel." Europeans had recently seen a rapid increase of exploration, conquest, foreign trade, imported commodities, and early instances of what would become the "Grand Tour" for young men who wanted to build up their cultural capital. As Newman notes, even the popular Renaissance word "method," so important for early modern ventures in new ways of knowing, derives from the Greek *hodos*, or "way, road." Some moralists found literal travel problematic—too fascinated by fashion, too productive of vanity, in sum too feminine—yet they, too, resorted to travel metaphors when describing their own intellectual development. To discourage women from travel, says Newman, was to deprive them of "the cultural capital travel proffered."

For the most part excluded from literal trips abroad, however, some women could at least turn to books. Many such books were romances, a genre especially likely to launch characters into spatial motion. That these texts were often criticized as unrealistic, too apt to uproot or displace the reader's imagination, would have made them all the more appealing—and valuable as another form of cultural capital—to those forced by their culture to stay put. In such texts the characters' spatial movement, Newman argues, figures emotional and psychological change. Educated women may have been more sedentary than the men in their lives, but Newman ends with delicious statistics on chairs in seventeenth-century Paris, chairs whose elegant legs could propel those who sat and chatted on them to many a new world.

The next three essays concern pedagogy. How do we guide our students to paths and explorations of their own? The speakers on the fourth plenary panel explored ways to teach materials by women or relevant to them. When these materials are written texts with implied voices, how are those voices gendered and how does it matter? Barbara McManus's essay asks, "Whose Voice Is It Anyway?" It suggests a range of possibilities for students to think about and, after they have pondered texts that raise such issues, to come to a more profound and theoretically sophisticated understanding of gender, authorship, and subjectivity.

McManus suggests that even without assigning samples of "Theory" teachers can juxtapose texts—classical, early modern, contemporary—that are ascribed to various subject positions, including those that deliberately or implicitly cross gender lines. They can assign works by writers who are, for example, anonymous, male, male masquerading as female, male temporarily adopting a female subjectivity, female, and off-the-shelf-neuter because unidentified and hence default-male. Then teachers can help students see how performing gender relates to performing class, race, and situation. (I would add nationality, for Italian and French women found it easier than Englishwomen to write erotic poetry. It is thus instructive to see how Englishmen translated Marguerite de Navarre and Louise Labé. When Robert Greene's 1588 translation of Labé's "Débat" identifies the author as French, but conceals her gender, does her female self-mockery mutate into his banal male misogyny? What happens to voice when an Englishwoman such as Mary Sidney translates the Israelite David, or the French Robert Garnier?) Traditional and nontraditional assignments that take up such matters without preempting students' own voices can make them better readers. They can become less obsessed than many of us used to be with identifying a writer's actual sex and certainly more alert, McManus ruefully confesses, than she was herself when she wrote a whole dissertation on Vergil, of all people, without paying the slightest attention to gender. Anyone over a certain age, one suspects, can make similar or indeed far more embarrassing confessions.

Frances E. Dolan records a rather different confession, one that she makes to her students: seldom, if ever, can we determine the truth about the early modern or any other historical period. But, disconcerted students often respond, "If we can't know what 'really' happened, why should we study the past?" As teachers, she points out, the more we in fact know, the more we also understand just how ignorant we are, and the less readily we will be to deliver "canned mini-lectures." Students, however, often prefer professorial certitude and a sturdily framed "Elizabethan World Picture." Dolan dryly notes, "When you stick to hegemony, it's easier to prepare for the final." Yet, the fact-hungry can understand, thanks to such recent courtroom events as the trial of O. J.

Simpson, that even such seemingly solid evidence as DNA and videotape is subject to interpretation. The new topics that feminist scholars study, their increased awareness that historical documents are as representational as are ballads and plays, the impact on scholars' answers of the ways they frame their questions, the interplay of cultural expectations and human behavior—all these make narratives and conclusions about early modern women problematic. So, how do professors answer the question that Dolan's students put to her? Dolan has seven convincing answers—and would be the first to suggest that her readers think of more. She also makes the entertaining but pedagogically intriguing suggestion that we ask students to jot down their teacher's "narrative interruptions, and pauses for reflection" in their class notes: such doubts and silences "are where the intellectual action is." Students, she points out, do not always believe her on this. (Imagining such notes is a pleasure, though: "Prof. Dolan scratches head and thinks"; "Prof. Prescott grasps lectern and turns pale"; "Prof. Donawerth falls silent and looks out window.")

Narratives are useful vehicles for getting somewhere interesting; the big ones, after all, lead to our fascinating selves. They can, however, lead us into the delusion of smooth certainty. As we study early modern materials, do they in fact make a story we might tell students? In her essay, "Directly from the Sources: Teaching Early Modern Women's History without the Narrative," Martha Howell traces a shift in her classroom techniques. The impulse to tell stories is so powerful, and students' hunger for narrative and collecting those hard little pebbles of information called "facts" is likewise so strong that it is tempting to line up the little pebbles into a path that seems to lead somewhere—to create a tale with a plot. Preferably the tale has a usable conclusion about, say, the effects for women of the Reformation or their status in early modern marriages, and the professor can make the story even more compelling by identifying the good guys and the bad guys. Yet, argues Howell, by changing our methods a little we can strengthen students' understanding of how the evidence and facts we use in shaping narratives about the past come to us already shaped by their cultures' own narratives. To do so would both incorporate poststructuralist insights into our pedagogy and also empower even reluctant students by giving them the opportunity to see what meanings they can derive from evidence that they will notice is contradictory, multiple, slippery, unstable. Howell concedes that some students remain uncomfortable with her method of juxtaposing—for example—a fabliau, sumptuary legislation, and a Dutch still life as commentary on early modern consumption, and she acknowledges that not all modern historians would adopt such methods when practicing their craft. However, students will learn through the conflicts inherent in such varied pieces of evidence to "respond more critically to what they read or are told."

Participants in the workshops after the plenary session on pedagogy approached questions of classroom method and politics from widely divergent directions. As Merry Wiesner-Hanks points out in her summary of workshop 37, these sessions allowed participants to "articulate concerns and feel less isolated" as they work across the many boundaries confronting teachers in these new territories. How might scholars and teachers grapple with new technology in the classroom? How might they maximize the potential of new technologies to collapse traditional disciplinary boundaries? How does the present moment of technological change allow us to rethink "publication" in both the early modern period and in our own rapidly changing time? As teachers expand their syllabi to incorporate women's works and to encompass world cultures more extensively, how do they serve as authorities in the classroom for disciplines or areas in which many may not have been formally trained? What impact do the economic realities of the academy have upon research and teaching, when disproportionate numbers of junior instructors are challenged with expanding the curriculum, or when small institutions unable to afford microform archives also cannot afford access to online databases, hardware and software for faculty, students, and staff, or professional development funds for training in the new technologies? Workshop conveners approached these questions using foci ranging from portraits and holograph letters of Mary Sidney to representations of female prostitutes in fiction and in statutory records. They explored women's philosophy, poetry, painting, educational tracts, and music from China, Italy, England, France, New England, and New Spain. They agreed, finally, that only an interdisciplinary approach could serve to frame these multiple concerns.

We also offer an essay, unconnected with any plenary session, in which Alison Findlay, Stephanie Hodgson-Wright, and Gweno Williams discuss the productions of plays by early modern women that they have staged—*The Tragedy of Mariam* by Elizabeth Cary, *The Concealed Fancies* by Elizabeth Brackley and Jane Cavendish, and *The Convent of Pleasure* by Margaret Cavendish—and give us tantalizing glimpses of the performances with photographs from the videos shown at the conference. Criticism, they argue, has too often encased such plays in the category of "closet dramas"; their productions bring these plays across the genre's border and into performance.

Those who enjoy tales of the supernatural know that ghosts, those liminal and unsettled remnants of other lives, are especially likely to show themselves at temporal or spatial borders: at crossroads, on battlements, in attics or cellars, and during times of stress or passage. Crossing borders can be hazardous, not least for those who become stuck midway, like ghosts with work left undone or messages still to deliver. Yet, borders, whether natural or socially created, also allow for new perspectives, for that double vision that Shakespeare in *A*

Midsummer Night's Dream calls seeing "with parted eye." Perhaps, as we study the boundaries and borders of the past and attend to the women who crossed them or whose own boundaries were violated or pondered, we, too, may see with parted eye and find ways to depict the past in something like its full complexity. If we also arouse some ghosts, Judith Zeitlin has reminded us that ghosts, like depictions, need not remain such but can, if well attended to, reanimate dead women into speech and motion. The three clever women whose words make up this introduction's epigraphs would have enjoyed our conference. In a way they, too, like so many of those to whom we attend, were invisible participants.

*Veronica Franco, *Terza Rima* 23, trans. Laura Anna Stortoni and Mary Prentice Lillie, in *Women Poets of the Italian Renaissance: Courtly Ladies and Courtesans,* ed. Laura Anna Stortoni (New York: Italica Press, 1997), 204–5:
> Povero sesso, con fortuna ria
> sempre prodotto, perch'ognor soggetto
> e senza libertà sempre si stia!
> Né però di noi fu certo il diffetto,
> che, se ben come l'uom non sem forzute,
> come l'uom mente avemo ed intelletto.
> Né in forza corporal sta la virtute,
> ma nel vigor de l'alma e de l'ingegno,
> da cui tutte le cose son sapute:
> e certa son che in ciò loco men degno
> no han le donne, ma d'esser maggiori
> degli uomini dato hanno piú d'un segno.

†Louise Labé, *Oeuvres Complètes,* ed. Enzo Giudici (Geneva: Librarie Droz, 1981), 17, my own translation:
> Estant le tems venu, Madamoiselle, que les severes loix des hommes n'empeschent plus les femmes de s'apliquer aus sciences et disciplines: il me semble que celles qui ont la commodité, doivent employer cette honneste liberté que notre sexe a autre fois tant desiree, à icelles aprendre: et montrer aus hommes le tort qu'ils nous faisoient en nous privant du bien et de l'honneur qui nous en pouvoit venir.

‡Martha Moulsworth, "My Name Was Martha," *A Renaissance Woman's Autobiographical Poem,* ed. Robert C. Evans and Barbara Wiedemann (West Cornwall, CT: Locust Hill Press, 1993), ll. 31–35.

Notes

1. Gérard Walter, *Nero,* trans. Emma Craufurd (London: Allen and Unwin, 1957), 264–65.

2. To be sure, at least one scholar of the Renaissance thinks that a male writer, in this case François Rabelais, could find the codpiece paradoxically empty; see Terence Cave, "The Cornucopian Text," in *Problems of Writing the French Renaissance* (Oxford: Clarendon Press, 1979).

3. We were unable to obtain for this collection two other papers from this plenary session, one on English women, criminality, and pamphlet literature, and the other on the painter Artemisia Gentileschi and her female subjects.

Crossing Boundaries:
Attending to Early Modern Women

Part One
The Body and the Self

Dissecting the Female Body: From Women's Secrets to the Secrets of Nature

KATHARINE PARK
History

IN HIS *New Organon* (1620), Francis Bacon sketched the outlines of a new logic, to replace the old Aristotelian organon—what he called "the vulgar logic"—with an intellectual tool capable of "dissecting nature [*ut ... naturam revera persecet*], and discovering the virtues and actions of bodies, with their laws as determined in matter."[1] This image, of nature under the knife of the reforming Baconian philosopher, reappears in various forms throughout the work. "It is better to dissect nature than to reduce her to abstractions," Bacon wrote in Book I, and to this end the human understanding must equip itself to "penetrate into the inner and more remote recesses of nature."[2] For, he argued, "there is much ground for hoping that there are still hidden [*recondita*] in the innards [*sinu:* literally, fold] of nature many things of excellent use ..., which have not yet been found out."[3]

This image—of the reforming natural philosopher as anatomist, probing the body of nature to discover the secrets hidden there—did not stand alone in Bacon's work, as Sarah Hutton has emphasized, but formed part of a larger and more diverse set of gendered metaphors meant to capture the complicated relationship between the scientist and nature.[4] Nor was the image of nature under the naturalist's knife unique to Bacon: it was taken up by some of Bacon's followers, and it eventually inspired a popular subgenre of nineteenth- and early twentieth-century paintings that showed the male anatomist ruminating on a dissected, or soon to be dissected, female corpse.[5]

Here, however, I am concerned less with Bacon's successors than with his antecedents, for he did not invent this image. Its most renowned expression appeared eighty years earlier, on the title page of Andreas Vesalius's famous *On the Fabric of the Human Body* (1543). There, Vesalius embodied his own vaunted reform of anatomy in a scene that shows him exposing the entrails of a female cadaver to an unruly band of male colleagues and students (fig. 1). But if the anatomist's opening of the female body functioned in these works

29

Figure 1. Title page of Andreas Vesalius, *De humani corporis fabrica* (Basel: Johannes Oporinus, 1543).

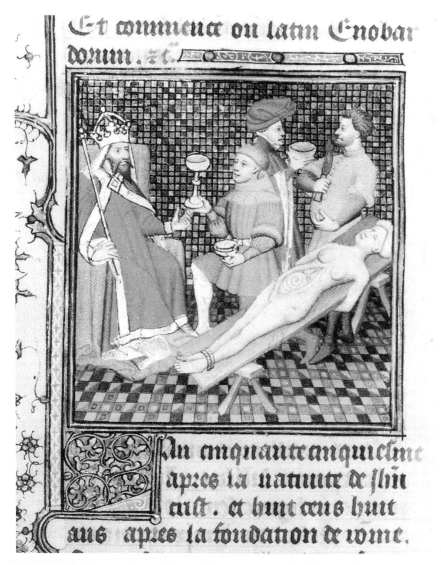

Figure 2. Nero's opening of his mother Agrippina, in Giovanni Boccaccio, *Des cas des nobles hommes et femmes*, trans. Laurent de Premierfait (French, ca. 1410). Paris, Bibliothèque de l'Arsénal, Ms. 5193, fol. 290ᵛ.

as a metaphor for scientific innovation—for the natural inquirer's penetration of the secrets of nature—what exactly were those secrets, and why were they to be sought in the entrails of women in particular? I approach this question by considering an even earlier body of images—at least twenty are still extant—that appear in a number of fourteenth- and fifteenth-century manuscripts and printed books. These images illustrate an apocryphal episode from the life of the Roman emperor Nero (fig. 2): the opening of his mother Agrippina, in order to see "the place where he was conceived," in the words of Jean de Meun.[6] In this essay, I trace the transformations of this trope, from its roots in medieval accounts of the Nero story to its use by Vesalius and Bacon; I argue that the preoccupation of some early modern scientific writers with exploring the "secrets of nature," imagined in anatomical terms, grew in part out of a late medieval concern with what were often called the "secrets of women" and that their use of this image continued to reflect those origins.

One of the most frequently illustrated versions of Nero's opening of Agrippina appears in Jean de Meun's section of the *Romance of the Rose* (ca. 1275). While enumerating the emperor's myriad cruelties—his torching of Rome and his murder of its senators—Jean turned to the following scene:

> Indeed, he had a heart harder than stone . . . when he had his mother dismembered [*desmembree*] so that he might see the place where he was conceived. After he saw her dismembered, he judged the beauty of her limbs. Ah, God! What a criminal judge she had! According to the story no tear issued from his eyes, but, as he was judging the limbs he commanded that wine be brought from his rooms, and he drank for his body's pleasure.[7]

Nero's command to have his mother's body opened, so that he might see the womb that bore him, does not appear in Roman sources. It seems rather to have been a medieval invention, an elaboration of the accounts of Agrippina's death by Tacitus, Suetonius, and Dio Cassius.[8] The first known versions of this story appear in German sources, in the long twelfth-century poems known as the *Kaiserchronik* and *Moriz von Craûn*, but it spread quickly and over the next three centuries made its way into French, Italian, English, and Scottish works as well.[9] Of the numerous medieval texts that describe this scene, the three most frequently illustrated were those of Jean de Meun, the German chronicler Enikel (ca. 1380), and Laurent de Premierfait's early fifteenth-century French translation of Giovanni Boccaccio's *On the Falls of Illustrious Men* (fig. 2).[10] In addition, Premierfait's version of Boccaccio inspired another type of visual representation: a scene in Eustache Marcadé's French play *The Revenge of Jesus Christ* (ca. 1415), which graphically staged Nero's dissection of his mother. This play enjoyed such success that it appeared in seven editions from five different Parisian printers between 1491 and 1539.[11]

In order to appreciate the broader implications of Nero's dissection of Agrippina, however, it is necessary to consider the second half of the story, which does not appear in Jean de Meun or Laurent de Premierfait, but which circulated widely in other versions, most notably Jacobus de Voragine's influential *Golden Legend* (ca. 1260), a collection of saints' lives that was translated into various European vernaculars over the course of the fourteenth and fifteenth centuries. "Obsessed by an evil madness," Jacobus writes,

> [Nero] ordered his mother killed and cut open so that he could see how it had been for him in her womb. The physicians, calling him to task over his mother's death, said, "Our laws prohibit this, and divine law forbids a son to kill his mother, who gave birth to him with such pain and nurtured him with so much toil and trouble." Nero said to them: "Make me pregnant with a child and then make me give birth, so that I may know how much pain it cost my mother!"... They said to him: "That is not possible because it is contrary to nature, nor is it thinkable because it is contrary to reason." At this Nero said to them: "Make me pregnant and make me give birth, or I will have every one of you die a cruel death!" So the doctors made up a potion in which they put a frog and gave it to the emperor to drink. Then they used their skills to make the frog grow in his belly, and his belly, rebelling against this unnatural invasion, swelled up so that Nero thought he was carrying a child.... At last, unable to stand the pain, he told the doctors: "Hasten the delivery, because I am so exhausted with this childbearing that I can hardly get my breath!" So they gave him a drink that made him vomit, and out came a frog horrible to see, full of vile humors and covered with blood. Nero, looking at what he had brought forth, shrank from it and wondered why it was such a monster, but the physicians told him that he had produced a deformed fetus because he had not been willing to wait the full [nine-month] term.[12]

This longer version of the Nero story begins to reveal the full import of Agrippina's dissection. The story concerns more than incestuous desire and a narcissistic search for origins; at its heart lies Nero's own wish to conceive and bear a child. The medieval texts explain this wish in various ways. For Jacobus de Voragine, in the passage above, it reflected both a kind of idle curiosity and a power struggle with his physicians—an attempt to justify his opening of his mother against their advice. More commonly, it was ascribed to Nero's own notoriously disordered sexuality and his sodomitical desire for other men, which medieval writers equated with effeminacy. "He had himself treated like a woman," according to *Moriz von Craûn*, "and indeed preferred men's to women's bodies. Listen how one day he lay there thinking how a woman must feel when she carries and bears a child."[13] Yet another explanation appears in the *Imperial Book*, an early fourteenth-century Italian chronicle of the Roman emperors, which attributes Nero's actions to his mistrust of his wife's fidelity and his concerns about the legitimacy of his issue: "he commanded the philosophers to make him pregnant, so that he might bear a male child that resembled him, because he doubted that his wife would bear legitimate children."[14]

Nero's suspicion of his wife in this version recalls a highly influential contemporary text, *Women's Secrets,* a late thirteenth- or early fourteenth-
century natural philosophical treatise attributed (falsely) to Albertus Magnus,
which, like the *Golden Legend,* came out of a Dominican environment. This
work circulated in many fourteenth- and fifteenth-century manuscripts, most
notably in France and Germany, and appeared in roughly fifty Latin incunab-
ula, as well as numerous editions during the following three centuries.[15] This
treatise specifically identifies women's "secrets" with generation and reproduction, and it characterizes these not merely as incidentally "hidden"
(*occulta*) in the sense of pertaining to the internal organs, or "secret" (*secreta*)
because of the shameful nature of the sexual parts, but also as powerful and
important knowledge available to women and purposely kept from men.
Women's secret knowledge includes, for example, how to provoke miscarriages
(in order to free themselves for promiscuous sex); how to determine whether
they are pregnant; how to know the sex of the child they are carrying; and how
to judge whether other women are still virgins.[16]

One of the most fundamental secrets of generation concerns the degree to
which the mother can influence the form and nature of her offspring, at the
expense of the influence of the father. Quoting Aristotle, the author of
Women's Secrets notes that "the most natural operation is for each thing to
generate something similar to itself so as to participate in the divine and the
immortal."[17] If one ascribes, with Aristotle, primary agency in generation to
the father, the logical conclusion is that "nature always intends to produce a
male," in the words of one of the text's commentators, "and thus it has been
said that woman is not human, but a monster in nature."[18] Yet this ideal tra-
jectory, the generation of a son identical to his father, meets with frequent
obstacles and as a result often falls short of its goal. The child may be female
or otherwise defective—*Women's Secrets* treats both in its section on monsters—or it may be rendered sickly in its mother's womb. The author does not
deny the father's contribution to these conditions; he indicates the importance
of appropriate times and forms of intercourse, the contribution of the father's
diet to the conformation of his children, and the fact that a penis that bends to
the left may project the seed to the part of the uterus where females are conceived.[19] But here and elsewhere he emphasizes to a much greater extent the
role of the mother: her provision of too much or too little menstrual matter,
the poor disposition of her uterus, and the like. Thus his discussion (in the section on infertility) on how to help a woman conceive a male child—no corresponding section exists for daughters—consists of a remedy to be administered to the mother alone.[20]

Indeed, one of the recurring themes of the treatise, both implicit and
explicit, is the vulnerability of the fetus to its mother's physical and psycho-

logical states: nourished by maternal matter, it can be harmed by her consumption of strong drink, her frustrated cravings for particular kinds of food, and her fears.[21] Yet, even when her diet and emotions are closely regulated, the fetus finds itself in a profoundly hostile environment, since the menstrual matter that nourishes it, and from which its body is constructed, is itself corrupt and poisonous. (The most widely circulated commentary notes that "since women are naturally poisoned they do not poison themselves," while another cites Avicenna's comparison of the womb to a "sewer situated in the middle of a town where all the waste materials run together and are sent forth.")[22] Most disturbing of all, however, are the intentional measures women take to provoke abortions, in order to avoid the consequences of lust:

> For this reason harlots, and women learned in this art [*docte mulieres vel helene in hac arte*], engage in a good deal of activity when they are pregnant. They move from place to place, from town to town: they lead dances and take part in many other evil deeds. Even more frequently they have a great deal of sex, and they wrestle with men. They do all these things so that they might be freed from their pregnancy by the excessive motion.[23]

The unusually misogynistic tone of *Women's Secrets* does not characterize all late medieval works on generation. Many medical writers in particular adopted a more positive view of women and their contribution to conception, in contrast to the Aristotelian ideas that underlie works, like *Women's Secrets,* in the philosophical tradition.[24] However, the paranoid view of the process of generation in this treatise was by no means unique. The extraordinary popularity of the work testifies to its wide appeal, and its fantasies illuminate many contemporary literary creations, including the Nero story.

According to the version of this story in the *Imperial Book,* Nero's principal concern was his wife's fidelity: the only way he felt able to guarantee his child's legitimacy was to eliminate all female participation in the act of generation, producing a "male child that resembled him," in the words of the passage cited above. Here, the child's legitimacy is established by its resemblance to its father, guaranteeing its lack of contamination, through the mother, by any alien seed. Yet, the child's maleness suggests an even stronger set of identifications; it is uncorrupted even by the influence of his wife. As the author of *Women's Secrets* notes, "every human being who is *naturally* conceived is generated from the seed of the father and the menses of the mother, according to all philosophers and medical authorities."[25] The highly unnatural nature of Nero's parthenogenetic act of conception, which his physicians so emphasize in the account by Jacobus de Voragine, ensures him the perfect child: a faithful reproduction of its father, uncompromised by the effeminizing influence of a mother or by any of the other birth defects and weaknesses

that it might have acquired in her womb. As Janet Adelman writes, apropos
of Posthumus's anxious musings on his own conception in *Cymbeline,*

> the parthenogenesis fantasy . . . makes bastardy contingent not on the mother's
> infidelity but on her mere participation in the act of procreation. . . . Bastardy is the
> sign of the mother's presence in the child: only the pure lineage of the father,
> uncontaminated by the mother, would guarantee legitimacy. The rational concern
> with patriarchal lineage thus covers a fantasy in which maternal sexuality *per se* is
> always infidelity, always a displacement of the father and a corresponding contam-
> ination of the son; in effect, through her participation in the procreative act, the
> mother makes the son in her own image.[26]

Against this background, the meanings of Nero's dissection of his mother
take shape. In part, it is a punitive act: by violating her body—a number of the
versions emphasize that Agrippina was in fact vivisected—Nero can revenge
himself on her as the source of his own shortcomings and vulnerabilities. In
part, it is an attempt to probe the secrets of women: to understand the mysteries of the uterus in order to appropriate its function. In part, it may even be
Nero's attempt to identify himself with his illustrious predecessor Julius
Caesar, whose eponymous caesarean section, like that of the invulnerable
Macduff in Shakespeare's *Macbeth,* could be read as a "fantasy of self-birth."[27]
Caesar's birth, in fact, marked the beginning of the Roman imperial line; the
fact that emperors like Nero, beginning with Julius Caesar's son, Augustus,
succeeded each other by the all-male process of adoption, further emphasized
the irrelevance of the maternal role.

In the end, however, Nero's experiment with parthogenesis was a failure, as
the conclusion of Jacobus de Voragine's account makes clear. The emperor was
unable to bring the child to term, and after he had vomited up the bloody frog,
his immediate reaction was one of horror: "Is this what I was like when I came
out from my mother's womb?"[28] His fantasy of perfect reproduction was
forced to yield to an intolerable realization: either men without women can
give birth only to unnatural monsters, or he was himself as loathsome as the
frog. Unable to countenance either alternative, "he commanded that the fetus
be fed and kept in a domed chamber with stones in it." Finally, however, both
Nero and his "son" came to loathsome ends:

> the Romans could tolerate his insanity no longer, so they rose up against him and
> drove him out of the city. Seeing that no escape was possible, he sharpened a stick
> to a point with his teeth and drove it through his middle, thus putting an end to his
> life. . . . When the Romans came back into the city, they found the frog hiding in
> its nest, hurried it out beyond the walls and set it afire.[29]

Considered against this background, Vesalius's title page (fig. 1) assumes a
host of new meanings. Indeed, the parallels between the Nero images and the

VIGESIMAQVARTA QVINTI LIBRI
FIGVRA.

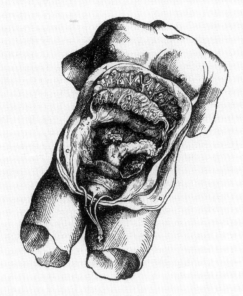

A,B, C,D Peritonæi anterioris sedis interior superficies.

E,E Mesenterij pars tenuia intestina dorso connectens.

F, F Altera mesenterij membrana notatur, ab altera quam G & G insigniui diuulsa. Vtraq; au-
G,G. tem membrana uasorum per mesenterium seriem, et glandularum uasorum distributionibus in
terpositarum naturam indicat,

H,H Hac mesenterij parte colon intestinum, quà recto erat proximum, committebatur.

I Hac mesenterij parte, coli intestini initium, seu ipsius cum tenuibus intestinis continuitas, dein
cæcum quoq; intestinum consistebant.

K Rectum intestinum inibi præsectum ubi colon desinit, quæ sedes est è regione connexus sacri os
sis cum infima lumborum uertebra.

L Anterior uteri fundi sedes, à qua nihil prorsus auulsum cernitur.

M Dexter mulieris testis.

N Mulieris sinister testis. atq; huius anterior pars hic tota oculis subijcitur, quum interim dextri
testis modica uideatur portio: idq; ideo accidit, quod dextrum testem ita delineauerimus, quem
admodum uterque testis membrana tegitur seminaria mulieris uasa deducente, atque à perito-
næo nata: sinistrum uerò testem illa membrana deteximus, quod solius manus, nullo adhibito cul
tro, sit beneficio. Hæc namque membrana anteriori testis sedi nulla ex parte adnascitur, sed
incumbit solum.

O,O Membrana à peritonæi dextra sede pronata, & testem dextrum unà cum huius lateris semi-
nalibus uasis, ac illis quæ uteri elatiorem sedem implicant uasis, dorso committens, uterumq; pa
riter continens, & deniq; cum alterius lateris membrana secundam uteri tunicam constituens.

P Hac in nuper dicta membrana carneæ excurrunt fibræ, dextrum uteri constituentes musculū.

His

Figure 3. The uterus and other female organs of generation, in Andreas
Vesalius, *De humani corporis fabrica*, 5, fig. 24 (Basel: Johannes Oporinus,
1543), 377.

title page are striking: the central cadaver is female, and she is presented in the unusual oblique position of most of the manuscript illustrations of Agrippina—features that almost never appear in other representations of academic dissections, where the male cadaver is almost always displayed parallel to the front of the image.[30] Similarly, Vesalius's stance, with pointed finger, clearly echoes that of Nero in the manuscript and woodcut images. Furthermore, the organ under examination on Vesalius's title page is the womb: the internal view is identical to that in the image of Book V of the *Fabrica* that shows the position of the uterus in the abdominal cavity (fig. 3).[31]

But why would Vesalius, who we know supervised the minutest details of the illustrations of the *Fabrica*,[32] choose as a model the Roman emperor who had long been a standard exemplum of cruelty, madness, and disordered sexuality? This evocation of Nero challenges the dominant recent interpretation of the *Fabrica* illustrations, which argues that they were conceived to legitimize Vesalius's work by neutralizing its transgressive aspects: the source of his cadavers, mainly executed criminals fresh from the gallows or bodies stolen from local tombs; the violence implicit in human dissection; and the violation of putative "taboos" against opening the body.[33] On the contrary, I would argue that the allusion to Nero aimed not to neutralize but to underscore the violent and transgressive elements in anatomical dissection. This kind of emphasis required special work, because there was in fact no generalized taboo against opening human bodies in late-medieval and Renaissance Italy, and the practice was quite common, as part of private elite medical and funerary practice, as well as of civic and academic culture.[34] Thus, in order to shock and horrify, Vesalius had artificially to pump up the sense of social and moral violation through various unprecedented iconographical strategies: by choosing a female cadaver for his frontispiece; by placing that single female body in the middle of an unusually large and rowdy male crowd (the carnivalesque atmosphere reminiscent of Nero's own drunken debauchery); and by placing it, and himself, in a position calculated not only to magnify the sexual element, but also to suggest powerful parallels with Nero and Agrippina.

These visual strategies were echoed by numerous passages in the text of the *Fabrica*, in which Vesalius obviously aimed to shock. Unlike other sixteenth-century anatomical authors, who for the most part obscured the provenance of cadavers obtained illegally, he included detailed accounts of robbed gibbets, violated tombs, burgled ossuaries, and manhandled corpses, that would have shaken even mid-sixteenth-century readers, whose experience with and tolerance for violence against persons was considerably higher than their modern counterparts. Why this repeated need to horrify or shock? In part, it seems a pedagogical strategy that aimed to produce homosocial bonding between male teachers and students through rough or exaggeratedly "masculine" or misog-

ynist behavior. Additionally, however, Vesalius seems to have expressly culti-
vated his violent and transgressive image as a source of special authority, setting himself up, like Nero, as a heroic—or rather antiheroic—figure, not
bound by the usual social and moral norms.

Rather than simply identifying himself with Nero, however, Vesalius established himself in the *Fabrica* as the man who succeeded where Nero had failed.
Nero was unable to realize his dream of male parthenogenesis; he could torture and murder Agrippina, but even his dissection of her uterus failed to
reveal the secrets of her undeniable generativity. Vesalius, in contrast, proposed a spectacle of masculine reproductive autonomy, and a corresponding
denigration of the woman's part.

Though Vesalius, in line with most contemporary medical writers, considered female seed necessary for generation,[35] his title page implicitly problematized the female role in procreation. First of all, he identified the woman whose
body was represented on the title page as a condemned criminal who
attempted to avoid execution by falsely claiming to be pregnant; her deception
was exposed by midwives consulted by the court and confirmed by Vesalius's
dissection.[36] Thus the only thing we know about this woman is that she was
emphatically *not* pregnant. Indeed, she is one of the first (and few) non-
pregnant female figures in the early history of European anatomical illustration; the traditional representations of female anatomy inevitably focused on
the reproductive system and privileged the fetus inside the womb.[37] By placing an empty uterus at the center of his title page, Vesalius suggested that its
mysteries were illusory, just as he rejected *Women's Secrets* as an "ignorant
book" in his chapter on that same organ.[38] The principal secret of women was
that the uterus held no secrets at all.

In contrast, Vesalius made the title page into a celebration of his own creativity, elaborated in terms of the fantasized male capacity for reproduction
without the mediation of a living woman. The title page represents this capacity in two separate and perhaps not wholly conscious ways. On the one hand,
representing himself as a matricide allowed Vesalius to appropriate for himself
his dead "mother's" generativity, lodged no longer in her destroyed womb, but
in the phallic objects—a scalpel, a razor, possibly a pen—on the table at her
side. On the other hand, Vesalius surrounded himself with a huge throng of
students and disciples, which university ideology and rhetoric would identify
as his "sons."[39] The father of not one or two, but a hundred or so male children, he became the exemplum of prodigiously generative masculinity—the
ultimate expression of manly *virtù*. In contrast to Nero's abortive offspring,
they were legitimate grounds for the anatomist's pride.

But Vesalius's parthenogenetic progeny were not confined to the students
who surrounded him: the most dazzling of his sons was certainly the *Fabrica*

itself, dedicated to yet another emperor, the great Charles V. In his preface, Vesalius positioned himself as the restorer of the lost empire of medicine, as Charles was the restorer of the Roman Empire. As he put it in his dedicatory preface,

> In the great felicity of this age—which the gods desire to be controlled by your sagacious Majesty—with all studies greatly revitalized, anatomy has begun to raise its head from profound gloom, so that it may be said without contradiction that it seems almost to have recovered its ancient brilliance. . . . And lest all others should successfully accomplish something for the sake of our common studies while I alone remain idle, and lest I achieve less than my ancestors, I decided that this branch of natural philosophy ought to be recalled from the region of the dead.[40]

Thus Vesalius implicitly set himself up as the analogue of the emperor in the field of medicine, his absolute pre-eminence in that field reflecting imperial political sovereignty. In the process, he assigned himself the same providential role claimed by the Hapsburg dynasty in the political realm.[41] He accomplished this refoundation, as he repeatedly emphasized, by rejecting the conventional division of labor between the bookish anatomist and the hands-on surgeon, performing his own dissections in the context of both teaching and research. In this way, too, he outdid Nero, who could only look on as others dissected his mother (fig. 2), whereas Vesalius, in the ultimate spectacle of masculine autonomy, could conduct the procedure all by himself.

Thus the *Fabrica*'s title page assembles a variety of what Jonathan Goldberg has called "patriarchal formulas" in the world of early modern portraiture:[42] the elision of women from the male world of anatomical investigation, except as objects of investigation;[43] the extreme disempowerment and subordination of the woman's body; and her identification with the natural (as opposed to masculine social) order, here represented by the monkey and dog in the foreground, which, like the female cadaver, were present as objects of comparative study and potential dissection.[44] This identification of women with nature and the other is reinforced by the presence immediately behind the cadaver of the articulated skeleton, which functions not only as a prop to demonstrate osteology, but also as a personification of death.[45] In the same way, anticipating Bacon, the woman's naked body on Vesalius's title page functions both as the object of a particular dissection and as a personification of nature, whose secrets will be laid bare by the new methods of the reformed science.[46]

Bacon's vision of scientific reform was more radical than that of Vesalius. Whereas the anatomist saw himself in humanist terms, as reviving his discipline from the "death" in which it had languished since the time of Galen, Bacon rejected even ancient achievements and called for a wholly new natural philosophy based on principles never dreamed of by the Greeks. His use of the dissection metaphor reinforced this goal; using his new methods, he proposed to reveal secrets to that point wholly hidden in what he called the "innards of Nature" (*naturae sinu*).[47] In elaborating this metaphor—by substituting nature's secrets for the secrets of women—he was drawing on two traditions: a set of medieval tropes personifying nature as a veiled goddess, whose form was only dimly discernible to human eyes;[48] and an explosion of interest in the "secrets of nature."[49] One sign of the association between these two sorts of secrets is the fact that, beginning in the later sixteenth century, the most commonly reprinted version of *Women's Secrets* included the text of Michael Scot's *Physiognomy*, now retitled *On the Secrets of Nature*.[50] As William Eamon has argued,

> the continual appearance of that well-worn phrase indicates a fundamental shift in the direction of natural philosophy. The concept of nature's "secrets"—that is, the idea that the mechanisms of nature were hidden beneath the exterior appearances of things—was the foundation of the new philosophy's skeptical outlook, and of its insistence upon getting to the bottom of things through active experimentation and disciplined observation. The Scholastics had been too trusting of their senses, the new philosophers asserted. Their naive empiricism was responsible for the erroneous belief that nature exhibits her true character on the outside. . . . In reality, the new philosophers declared, nature's workings are hidden. The unaided, undisciplined senses do not reveal reliable information about what makes nature tick any more than observing the hands of a clock reveals how the clock works.[51]

Bacon was one of the first to formulate this set of ideas explicitly, using the metaphor of dissection in terms that recall Vesalius's title page. Although there is no evidence that he was drawing on Vesalius, Bacon used tropes of scientific innovation as generation that closely paralleled the parthenogenetic fantasy described above. His most extreme expression of this view appears in *The Masculine Birth of Time* (ca. 1603). In this early fragment, the "masculine birth" (*partus masculus*) referred both to the sex of the (male) scientist's metaphorical offspring—a new, virile natural philosophy, replacing the weak and effeminate theory of the ancients—and to a patriarchal model of generation that largely elided the role of the mother in the creation of a lineage of males. First of all, the work takes the form of a father's monologue to his son, while the title of its first chapter, "the legitimate method of transmission" (*tradendi modus legitimus*), underscores the imagined genetic links between teacher and student. Bacon explicated this "mode of transmission" in a later work, *On the Growth of the Sciences* (1623), naming it the "initiative method," for the true adepts of natural philosophy, in contrast to the "magistral method," for the common herd: "The one transmits knowledge to the crowd of learners; the other to the sons, as it were, of the sciences [*tanquam filiis scientiarum*]."[52]

Bacon did not completely eliminate the feminine element in this process of intellectual generation. Elsewhere, for example, in *The Wisdom of the Ancients,* he elaborated his ideal of male parthogenesis using the myth of Athena's birth from the head of her father Jupiter—who had previously eaten his pregnant wife Metis—thereby gendering the new natural philosophy (if not the new natural philosophers) as female.[53] He also did not completely deny the maternal role in the process of intellectual generation; even in *The Masculine Birth of Time,* he acknowledged a female presence, which was Nature herself. Still, Nature was dominated by the natural philosopher/father: as Bacon wrote to his imagined disciple, "I am come in very truth leading to you Nature with all her children to bind her to your service and make her your slave."[54] This passage echoes the subordination of the mother in the Feast of the Family as described in Bacon's utopia, the *New Atlantis* (comp. 1624). Accorded to every man with thirty living descendants over the age of three, the Feast culminates in a family procession and banquet, during which the mother of his children sits separate and invisible in a "loft . . . with a privy door."[55] No longer the one to hide secrets from others, the woman herself is now hidden from view.

Bacon's work thus contains a powerful rejection of the tradition of women as the knowers of secrets, and of generation as a natural process controlled by knowledge at which men could only guess. This tradition was codified in *Women's Secrets* and ratified in the medieval version of the Nero story, which emphasized Nero's own failure to conceive and carry a child to term. Vesalius rejected this tradition on his title page, portraying himself as having appropriated not only the knowledge of women's secrets, but also the generative power that they expressed, as exemplified in his lineage of male students and admirers. Bacon extended this act of appropriation to the secrets of Nature herself, proposing the new natural philosopher as the progenitor not only of an all-male lineage of disciples, but of a "masculine" science, capable eventually of penetrating even the most puzzling of natural phenomena to arrive at their true causes and to reproduce their effects. In each case, the exposed uterus and the dissected female body figured this attempt at appropriation of female-identified knowledge and power: Nero's "anatomization" of Agrippina, which failed to provide the necessary information; and Vesalius's contrasting success on the title page of the *Fabrica.*

Bacon portrayed his own victory as deferred; he believed that the full mastery of nature and exposure of her secrets lay in the future. Indeed, it would be centuries before men did more than dream of controlling the processes of birth and generation, and even then it was hardly under Baconian auspices. However, the victory he promised was definitive. Addressing his "son" in the *Masculine Birth of Time,* he proposed to wed him to the "things themselves":

"from this association," he assured him, "you will secure, beyond all the vows of ordinary marriages, a blessed race of Heroes who will overcome the infinite needs of the human race, which are more destructive than all giants, monsters, and tyrants, and will make you peaceful, happy, prosperous, and secure."[56]

Notes

1. Francis Bacon, *Novum organum*, 2.52, in *The Works of Francis Bacon*, ed. and trans. James Spedding, Robert Leslie Ellis, and Douglas Denon Heath, 14 vols. (London, 1857–74; rpt. New York: Garrett Press, 1968), 4:246 (Latin on 1:363). In this, as in other translations of Bacon's Latin, I have revised the English translation for accuracy and precision.

2. Bacon, *Novum organum*, 1.51, in *Works*, my translation (Latin on 1:168); Bacon, *Novum organum*, 1.18, in *Works*, 4:50 (Latin on 1:159).

3. Bacon, *Novum organum*, 1.109, in *Works*, 4:100 (Latin on 1:208).

4. Sarah Hutton, "The Riddle of the Sphinx: Francis Bacon and the Emblems of Science," in *Women, Science and Medicine, 1500–1700: Mothers and Sisters of the Royal Society*, ed. Lynette Hunter and Sarah Hutton (Stroud, England: Sutton Publishing, 1997), 7–28. Hutton adds important nuance to the less modulated claims of Carolyn Merchant, *The Death of Nature: Women, Ecology, and the Scientific Revolution*, 2nd ed. (San Francisco: Harper and Row, 1989), 168–72. See also Evelyn Fox Keller, "Baconian Science: The Arts of Mastery and Obedience," in her *Reflections on Gender and Science* (New Haven: Yale University Press, 1985), 33–42. For a somewhat overstated revisionist reading of this topic, see Peter Pesic, "Wrestling with Proteus: Francis Bacon and the 'Torture' of Nature," *Isis* 90 (1999): 81–94. Keller explores broader issues of visibility, secrecy, and science in "Making Gender Visible in the Pursuit of Nature's Secrets," in *Feminist Studies, Critical Studies*, ed. Teresa de Lauretis (Bloomington: Indiana University Press, 1986), 67–77.

5. On these images, see Ludmilla Jordanova, *Sexual Visions: Images of Gender in Science and Medicine between the Eighteenth and Twentieth Centuries* (Madison: University of Wisconsin Press, 1989), 88–93; and Elisabeth Bronfen, *Over Her Dead Body: Death, Femininity and the Aesthetic* (New York: Routledge, 1992), ch. 1. For an inventory of such images, see G. Wolf-Heidegger and Anna M. Cetto, *Die anatomische Sektion in bildlicher Darstellung* (Basel: S. Karger, 1967), figs. 88–89 and 285–88; documentation and explication on 182–83 and 335–37. I stress that only *some* of Bacon's successors took up this trope: it should in no way be seen as the originary moment for the gendered nature of modern science as a whole, as argued, for example, in Merchant (1989). On this point, see Dorinda Outram, "The Gendering of Science and Nature," in *The Cambridge History of Early Modern Science*, ed. Katharine Park and Lorraine Daston (Cambridge: Cambridge University Press, forthcoming).

6. Guillaume de Lorris and Jean de Meun, *The Romance of the Rose*, l. 6196, trans. Charles Dahlberg (Hanover, N.H.: University Press of New England, 1983), 122; French text in Guillaume de Lorris and Jean de Meun, *Le Roman de la rose*, ed. Daniel Poirion (Paris: Garnier-Flammarion, 1974), 191. For reproductions, documentation, and discussion of twenty such images, see Wolf-Heidegger and Cetto, nos. 9–28 and pp. 132–42.

7. Jean de Meun, *Romance of the Rose*, ll. 6192–6206, p. 122. The speaker is Reason, describing the power of Fortune to reward evil.

8. The principal ancient sources were Suetonius, *Lives of the Caesars,* 6.34 (which describes Nero's handling of Agrippina's limbs and his call for drink); Tacitus, *Annals,* 14.9 (which indicates that he had her stabbed in the womb, but not that he had her body opened); Dio Cassius, *Roman History,* 61.14 (which offers an account similar to that of Tacitus); and the brief reference in Boethius, *Consolation of Philosophy,* 2.m6. On the ancient accounts and their possible literary models, see B. Baldwin, "Nero and His Mother's Corpse," *Mnemosyne: Bibliotheca Classica Batava,* ser. 4, 32 (1979): 380–81; and Tamsyn Barton, "The Invention of Nero," in *Reflections of Nero: Culture, History, and Representation,* ed. Jas. Elsner and Jamie Masters (Chapel Hill/London: University of North Carolina Press, 1994), 55–57 and, especially, 96 n. 68.

9. *Der keiser und der kunige buoch oder die sogenannte Kaiserchronik,* ed. Hans Ferdinand Massmann, 3 vols. (Quedlinburg/Leipzig: Gottfried Basse, 1849–54), 1:324–27; *Moriz von Craûn,* ed. and trans. Stephanie Cain Van D'Elden (New York/London: Garland, 1990), 12–15. On the various medieval versions of this story, see Massmann, *Der keiser,* 3:682–90; Arturo Graf, *Roma nella memoria e nelle immaginazioni del Medio Evo,* 2 vols. (Turin: Ermanno Loescher, 1882), 1: 334–44; Ernest Langlois, *Origine et sources du Roman de la rose* (Paris: Ernest Thorin, 1891), 128–29; and Langlois, "Notice du manuscrit ottobonien 2523," *Mélanges d'archéologie et d'histoire* 5 (1885): 34–36.

10. Giovanni Boccaccio, *Des cas des nobles hommes et femmes,* trans. Laurent de Premierfait (Paris: Vérard, 1494), 7.6, cited in Wolf-Heidegger and Cetto, *Die anatomische Sektion,* 138: "Et affin que neron veist sa mere ainsi tuee, il vint de la cite brayes au village de beyoles et si grant fut la cruaulte de neron que sans larmes sans soupir sans signes de douleur il regarda et tint desireement toutes les membres de sa mere gesant morte descoulouree et *ouverte*" (my emphasis). The last word was inserted by Premierfait, since Boccaccio's own account makes no reference to the opening of Agrippina.

11. Graf, *Roma,* 335 n. 10; Stephen K. Wright, *The Vengeance of Our Lord: Medieval Dramatizations of the Destruction of Jerusalem* (Toronto: Pontifical Institute of Medieval Studies, 1989), 7, 11. This play seems to be the one described by Wolf-Heidegger and Cetto, *Die anatomische sektion,* 138–39, as *La vengeance et déstruction de Hiérusalem.*

12. Jacobus de Voragine, Life of St. Peter Apostle, in *The Golden Legend: Readings on the Saints,* trans. William Granger Ryan, 2 vols. (Princeton: Princeton University Press, 1993), 1:347; Latin text in Graf, *Roma,* 1:339–40.

13. *Moriz von Craûn,* ed. D'Elden, ll. 143–49, p. 10.

14. Cited in Graf, *Roma,* 1:342. On this work and its manuscript and printed versions, see also 1:84 n. 13.

15. On this work, see Lynn Thorndike, "Further Consideration of the *Experimenta* or *Speculum astronomiae,* and *De secretis mulierum* Ascribed to Albertus Magnus," *Speculum* 30 (1955): 427–43; Brigitte Kusche, "Zur 'Secreta mulierum'–Forschung," *Janus* 62 (1975): 103–23; Kristian Bosselmann-Cyran, *"Secreta mulierum" mit Glosse in der deutschen Bearbeitung von Johann Hartlieb* (Hanover: Horst Wellm Verlag Pattensen), 9–14; and the introduction to Helen Rodnite Lemay, *Women's Secrets: A Translation of Pseudo-Albertus Magnus's De secretus mulierum with Commentaries* (Albany: State University of New York Press, 1992).

16. Pseudo-Albertus Magnus, *Women's Secrets,* trans. Lemay, chs. 5, 7, 8, 9–10, pp. 102, 120–22, 123–26, 126–31. In this essay, I have used Lemay's translation and chapter divisions, checking her translation against the Latin text of both the work itself and the commentary she designates as Commentary A, in [ps.-]Albertus Magnus, *De*

secretis mulierum et virorum (Leipzig: Melchior Lotter, 1505). Lemay's translation is based on two printed editions, those of Lyons 1580 (text and commentary A) and Venice 1508 (text and commentary B); as Thorndike (1955) indicates, the printed editions of the work represent a significant reworking of the earlier manuscript versions, which did not, among other things, include chapter divisions.

17. Pseudo-Albertus Magnus, trans. Lemay, preface, 60; *De secretis mulierum et virorum* (1505), sig. aiiᵛ. Cf. Aristotle, *De anima*, 2.4; 415a28–b1.

18. Pseudo-Albertus Magnus, trans. Lemay, ch. 6, p. 117 (Lemay's commentator B); ch. 5, p. 106 (commentator A). Note that there are five known commentaries on *Women's Secrets*, of which Lemay has partially translated only two; see Thorndike, "Further Considerations," 427–28, n. 26. On women as monsters, see Ian Maclean, *The Renaissance Notion of Women: A Study in the Fortunes of Scholasticism and Medical Science in European Intellectual Life* (Cambridge: Cambridge University Press, 1980), 12, 30–31.

19. See also Pseudo-Albertus Magnus, trans. Lemay, ch. 12, p. 143. See Joan Cadden, *Meanings of Sex Difference in the Middle Ages: Medicine, Science, and Culture* (Cambridge: Cambridge University Press, 1993), 130–34.

20. Pseudo-Albertus Magnus, trans. Lemay, ch. 12, pp. 139–40.

21. E.g., Psuedo-Albertus Magnus, trans. Lemay, chs. 5 and 12, pp. 109–110, 141–42, and 103. Although this particular treatise does not mention it, the power of the imagination of a pregnant woman to deform her fetus was also widely credited.

22. Pseudo-Albertus Magnus, trans. Lemay, ch. 10, p. 130; ch. 11, p. 134.

23. Pseudo-Albertus Magnus, trans. Lemay, ch. 5, p. 102 (translation emended for accuracy; cf. *De secretis mulierum et virorum* 1505, sig. dir).

24. Some of the vernacular translations of *Women's Secrets* were also rewritten to be more woman-friendly than their Latin originals; see, e.g., Margaret Schleissner, "A Fifteenth-Century Physician's Attitude toward Sexuality: Dr. Johann Hartlieb's *Secreta mulierum* Translation," in Joyce E. Salisbury, ed., *Sex in the Middle Ages: A Book of Essays* (New York: Garland, 1991).

25. Pseudo-Albertus Magnus, trans. Lemay, ch. 1, p. 63 (my emphasis).

26. Janet Adelman, *Suffocating Mothers: Fantasies of Maternal Origin in Shakespeare's Plays*, Hamlet to The Tempest (New York: Routledge, 1992), 212; cf. William Shakespeare, *Cymbeline*, 2.5.1–28, in *The Riverside Shakespeare*, ed. G. Blakemore Evans (Boston: Houghton Mifflin, 1974), 1535–36.

27. Adelman, *Mothers*, 143. The birth of Julius Caesar was another favorite subject of fourteenth- and fifteenth-century manuscript illumination; see Renate Blumenthal-Kosinski, *Not of Woman Born: Representations of Caesarean Birth in Medieval and Renaissance Culture* (Ithaca: Cornell University Press, 1990).

28. Jacobus de Voragine, *Golden Legend*, 1:347.

29. Jacobus de Voragine, *Golden Legend*, 1:347–48.

30. The Nero illustrations might also be adjusted, conversely, to reflect the contemporary iconography of anatomical dissection; see, for example, Wolff-Heidegger and Cetto, *Die anatomische sektion*, fig. 21.

31. Andreas Vesalius, *De humani corporis fabrica*, 5, fig. 24 (Basel: Johannes Oporinus, 1543), 377. The images are reversed, as one would expect, if one were copied from the other. What makes these similarities particularly compelling is the fact that the image of Nero and Agrippina had evidently already served as the model for an earlier title page in at least one edition of the *Anatomy of Mondino*, the textbook that was standard when Vesalius was studying medicine at Paris in 1533–36: Wolf-Heidegger and Cetto, *Die anatomishe sektion*, fig. 116. The connection between Vesalius and Nero

has been noted by Jerome J. Bylebyl, "Interpreting the *Fasciculo* Anatomy Scene," *Journal of the History of Medicine* 45 (1990), 303–4; and Sander L. Gilman, *Sexuality, An Illustrated History: Representing the Sexual in Medicine and Culture from the Middle Ages to the Age of AIDS* (New York: John Wiley, 1989), 71.

32. The *Fabrica* was the product of close collaboration between the anatomist and the artists (draftsman or draftsmen and woodblock cutters), and it is clear that Vesalius was involved at every stage in the preparation of the drawings that served as the basis for the book's woodcuts, including producing some of them himself. There is no doubt that he was largely responsible for the *Fabrica's* iconography, including its striking title page. On the illustrations of the *Fabrica*, see, e.g., J.B. de C.M. Saunders and Charles D. O'Malley, *The Illustrations of the Works of Andreas Vesalius of Brussels* (New York: Dover, 1950), 22–29; Martin Kemp, "A Drawing for the *Fabrica* and Some Thoughts upon the Vesalius Muscle-Men," *Medical History* 14 (1970): 277–88; and David Rosand and Michelangelo Muraro, *Titian and the Venetian Woodcut* (Washington, D.C.: International Exhibitions Foundation, 1976), esp. Section VI.

33. E.g., Glenn Harcourt, "Andreas Vesalius and the Anatomy of Antique Sculpture," *Representations* 17 (1987): 28–61; Jonathan Sawday, *The Body Emblazoned* (London: Routledge, 1995), especially 84.

34. Katharine Park, "The Criminal and the Saintly Body: Autopsy and Dissection in Renaissance Italy," *The Renaissance Quarterly* 47 (1994): 1–33; Park, "The Life of the Corpse: Division and Dissection in Late Medieval Europe," *Journal of the History of Medicine and Allied Sciences* 50 (1994): 111–32. See also Giovanna Ferrari, "Public Anatomy Lessons and the Carnival: The Anatomy Theatre at Bologna," *Past and Present* 117 (1987): 50–106.

35. Vesalius, *Fabrica*, 5.15, pp. 535–36.

36. Vesalius, *Fabrica*, 5.15, p. 539.

37. See, for example, Karen Newman, *Fetal Positions: Individualism, Science, Visuality* (Stanford, Calif.: Stanford University Press, 1996)

38. Vesalius, *Fabrica*, 5.15, p. 531.

39. Jole Agrimi and Chiara Crisciani, *Edocere medicos: Medicina scolastica nei secoli XIII–XV* (Naples: Guarini, 1988), 219–23.

40. Vesalius, *Fabrica*, preface, trans. in C.D. O'Malley, *Andreas Vesalius of Brussels, 1514–1564* (Berkeley: University of California Press, 1964), 320.

41. See Marie Tanner, *The Last Descendant of Aeneas: The Hapsburgs and the Mythic Image of the Emperor* (New Haven: Yale University Press, 1993).

42. Jonathan Goldberg, "Fatherly Authority: The Politics of Stuart Family Image," in *Rewriting the Renaissance: The Discourses of Sexual Difference in Early Modern Europe*, ed. Margaret W. Ferguson, Maureen Quilligan, and Nancy J. Vickers (Chicago: University of Chicago Press, 1986), 22.

43. The only figure in the title page that could be read as female is the hooded person between the columns in the last row on the right; sometimes identified as a midwife, she is marginalized both by position and by occupation.

44. For Vesalius's use of animals in his anatomical demonstrations, see, *Andreas Vesalius' First Public Anatomy at Bologna, 1540: An Eyewitness Report*, ed. and trans. Ruben Eriksson (Uppsala: Almqvist & Wiksells, 1959), passim, especially 209–11, where Vesalius uses a pregnant dog to stand in for a woman's cadaver.

45. See Sawday, *Body*.

46. Although Vesalius does not write specifically of the secrets of Nature in the chapter on the uterus, he repeatedly personifies Nature, writing her name with a capital "N," e.g., Vesalius, 5.15, pp. 532, 535, 537.

47. Bacon, *Novum organum*, 1.109, in *Works*, 4:100 (Latin on 1:208); translation revised for accuracy.

48. See, e.g., George Economou, *The Goddess Natura in Medieval Literature* (Cambridge, Mass.: Harvard University Press, 1972); F. J. E. Raby, "*Nuda Natura* and Twelfth-Century Cosmology," *Speculum* 43 (1968): 72–77.

49. William Eamon, *Science and the Secrets of Nature: Books of Secrets in Medieval and Early Modern Culture* (Princeton: Princeton University Press, 1994), chs. 6–8; on Bacon's place in this tradition, see esp. 285–91.

50. E.g., *Alberti Magni de secretis mulierum libellus, scholiis auctus et a mendis repurgatus. . . . Adjecimus et ob materiae similitudinem Michaelis Scoti philosophi de secretis naturae opusculum* (Strassburg: Heirs of Lazarus Zetzner, 1625).

51. Eamon, *Science*, 297.

52. Bacon, *De augmentis scientiarum*, 6.2, in *Works*, 4:449 (Latin on 1:663). On Bacon's vision of the scientist as progenitor of a male lineage, see Keller, "Baconian Science," 41–42.

53. See Hutton, "Riddle," 17–21.

54. Bacon, *The Masculine Birth of Time*, 2, trans. Benjamin Farrington, in Farrington, *The Philosophy of Francis Bacon: An Essay in its Development from 1603 to 1609 with New Translations of Fundamental Texts* (Chicago: University of Chicago Press, 1964), 62 (Latin in *Works*, 3:528).

55. Bacon, *New Atlantis*, in *Works*, 3: 148–49.

56. Bacon, *Masculine Birth*, 3, in Farrington, 72 (Latin in *Works*, 3:539); translation revised for accuracy.

Making the Invisible Visible: Portraits of Desire and Constructions of Death in Sixteenth- and Seventeenth-Century China

Judith T. Zeitlin

East Asian Languages and Civilizations

In Chinese fiction or drama, for a young woman to commission a portrait of herself or to paint a self-portrait is inevitably a fatal act. Such a painting is destined from the start as a deathbed portrait meant for posthumous viewing. Undertaken as a desperate measure to preserve the woman's youthful beauty and unfulfilled desire, the portrait both acknowledges and precipitates her imminent death. The idea that having a likeness painted could be dangerous for a youthful sitter is actually voiced in one sixteenth-century treatise on painting, which warns that "those under thirty ought to forgo having their portraits painted lest their spirit or vigor (*jingshen*) be wrested away."[1] In the symbolic economy of fiction and drama, a portrait imagined as capable of "killing" its female subject could also be pivotal in restoring its subject to life. Indeed, the themes of a woman in a painting coming to life in response to male desire and a man's revival of a dead woman through a sexual liaison with her ghost are closely linked in Chinese literature.

This essay seeks to map how literary representations of death and desire intersected in the sentimental culture of sixteenth- and seventeenth-century China. This is a period that historians in the West now term either "early modern" or "late imperial," depending on whether they wish to draw an analogy to European history or stay within a purely Chinese political framework. The period saw an increasing commercialization and urbanization in China, and an expansion of print culture, especially in the prosperous Jiangnan region of the Yangtze river delta. Scholars have linked this burgeoning print culture with the glorification of sentiment or *qing* at this time.

Verse by women from good families and from the demimonde was increasingly published in individual collections and anthologies, and both poems and paintings by such women are still extant today.[2] The "talented woman," as she

48

was called, aroused intense cultural fascination and ambivalence, particularly if she died young.[3]

My specific aim in this essay is to explore the reciprocity between the literary topos of the female portrait that results in the subject's death and that of a spectral woman—painting or ghost—coming to life. To unravel the complex symbolic and social implications of this theme, I will first consider the art historical genres to which such putative portraits might have belonged—namely, the lowly genre of "beautiful woman" figure painting, and the even lower genre of "effigy portraits," commemorative likenesses of the dead painted by anonymous artisans.

Both portraits and ghosts could be referred to as *ying* or "shadows." In Chinese literature, however, portraits and ghosts are not only linked to an immaterial soul but also to the corporeal materiality of the body. To investigate how the body was conceptualized in the sixteenth and seventeenth century, I will turn to the medical discourse of the period. Medical texts take unfulfilled female desire as a serious factor leading to melancholic congestive disorders and possible death. In late Ming drama, most famously in *The Peony Pavilion* of 1598, I will argue, portraits and ghosts are correspondingly interrelated because both function as exteriorizations of invisible desires concealed within the female body.

In such plays, the portrait of a woman is also affiliated with the body because it is not simply an image but a material object, a hanging scroll. Scenes of the woman painting or inscribing the portrait before her death usually occupy a prominent position in the drama. Such performative scenes reinforce the apprehension of the portrait as posthumously preserving traces of the woman's body in the form of brush strokes. Finally, I will conclude with a brief consideration of the problems of resemblance, copying, and individuation that both beautiful women pictures and ghosts inevitably raise.

I will begin with an essay from 1665 that paradoxically lays claim to the fantasy of an image coming to life by commemorating the "death" of a painting. This obscure autobiographical piece is entitled "Funerary Elegy for the Beauty in the Painting" ("Ji huashang meiren wen"). It was written by Wang Zhuo (1636–after 1705), a minor man of letters with Bohemian leanings from Hangzhou in the Jiangnan region.[4] "Elegy for the Beauty in the Painting" was published in Wang Zhuo's collected works alongside other playful compositions on fanciful, sentimental themes, such as "A Funerary Elegy for Fallen Blossoms" and "A Formal Injunction against Picking Flowers." An undated quatrain entitled "A Dream of the Beauty in the Painting" ("Meng huashang meiren") also appears in the poetry section of Wang Zhuo's collected works. Read within the traditional Chinese convention of treating verse as a nonfictional genre, this quatrain serves as intratextual corroboration of the paint-

Figure 1. An example of "a beautiful woman picture," possibly a self-portrait by Xue Susu, late Ming courtesan.

ing's existence.[5] The poem concludes: "A painting entered my dream; how is it less than real?"[6] As we will see, the elegy pivots on the same willful blurring of illusion and reality. "Elegy for the Beauty in the Painting" opens with a narrative preface:

> In the eighth month of 1651, I came across an old man by the side of the road trying to sell a picture of a beautiful woman. None of the passers-by knew him. I sent my servant boy to purchase the painting for a hundred cash and hung it in my bedchamber. She was simply attired and had an elegant air; her loveliness was bewitching. The only problem was that I didn't know who she was. Since then, fourteen years have passed. One night, a great gust of wind tore the painting down, which fell upon a lighted lamp and started a fire. Greatly alarmed, I rushed to put it out, but my Beauty had already been consumed. How sad![7]

Wang Zhuo then shifts to the flowery euphemisms conventionally used to describe the death of a beautiful woman, comparing the painting's destruction to "a pearl sinking beneath the waves and jade shattering, to powder fading and perfume melting away." This rhetorical turn already implies his interpretation: "Since antiquity 'beautiful girls have suffered misfortune'" [i.e., died prematurely]; this indeed was the only way I could comprehend this event. So I set out an offering of clear wine, along with a few pear blossoms and wrote an elegy for her."

In his account of the painting's purchase, Wang Zhuo notes the anonymity of both the seller and the image, which prevent him from discovering the "true" provenance and identity of the picture. Although the old man is selling the painting as a generic "beautiful woman picture" (meiren tu), Wang Zhuo assumes that the painting must actually be a private portrait of a real woman instead (fig. 1). This scenario is reminiscent of the final act of a thirteenth-century play entitled *Marriage Destiny over Two Lifetimes* (Liangshi yinyuan), in which an old bawd is found on the street hawking the dead heroine's self-portrait as a generic "beautiful woman painting," presumably because this label would attract a wider clientele of buyers. Implicit in Wang Zhuo's account, as in the play, is the casual elision of the commercial traffic in women's bodies and their images.[8] Although our knowledge of painting prices in the seventeenth century is still sketchy, by any account, one hundred cash, the price Wang Zhuo says he paid for the painting, is incredibly low, just as the purchase of a picture from a street peddler would have been the cheapest possible source of a picture.[9]

James Cahill and Ellen Laing have been involved in an important art historical endeavor to reconstruct the iconographic codes of beautiful women pictures in the Ming and Qing period, attempting to distinguish portraits of individual women from generic beauties (Cahill) or mythical goddesses from the languishing ladies of the boudoir (Laing).[10] Although they recognize how easily any representation of a young woman can be absorbed into a homogenized stereotype of ideal beauty, their assumption is that there *were* clear-cut visual categories in the past, which we moderns no longer know how to recognize. Undoubtedly this is true (at least up to a point). However, literary materials from the period (fiction, drama, and essays) are remarkably cavalier and elas-·tic in their labeling of such images; misidentification or reidentification is endemic; and the emphasis is most frequently placed on the freedom of the viewer's imagination to construe the image as he or she pleased.

Wang Zhuo regrets the lack of a specific history or context for the painting, but it is precisely this blank, of course, that allows him to suppress the generic nature of the image and to imagine that the object of his desire is a unique likeness of an actual woman. We have here almost a caricature of what Francette Pacteau has called "that absence of the 'real' woman that is the necessary support of the attribution of Beauty."[11] At the same time, Wang Zhuo betrays almost no interest in describing the pictorial, iconographic, or stylistic qualities of the painting. He is no connoisseur, in part, no doubt, because of the low esteem in which beautiful women pictures were held on the scale of literati artistic values. As the amateur scholar painter scoffs in Wu Bing's *Jealousy-Curing Stew* (*Liaodugeng*), a late Ming romantic comedy written between 1628 and 1644, "Beautiful women are the lowest grade of painting in an artist's repertory."[12] Wang Zhuo's brief characterization of the image as "simply clad with an elegant air" and "lovely and bewitching" is about as detailed as he gets in the whole of this long piece, (and it may be meant more as a statement about his own refined taste than to provide information about what the painting looked like). He makes no attempt to individualize the image in visual terms, to go beyond the label "beautiful woman picture." His sensibility is emphatically literary, not visual, and the point of the piece is his subjective response to the painting as conditioned by his reading of drama and fiction, not the image itself. The very cheapness of the painting's purchase price reinforces the basic point of his essay: not to reveal how he acquired a masterpiece for a song, but how a seemingly worthless painting acquired personal value and meaning in the course of his own life.

Wang Zhuo would have been especially susceptible to the fantasy of possessing ideal beauty in a painting because his acquisition of it most likely preceded any direct erotic experience with women. As he relates in the elegy proper, the painting was his first love:

> I remember that when I first obtained this Beauty, I was only fifteen years old. Morning and night I faced her, regretting the lateness of our meeting. In the moonlight, whenever a cool breeze wafted in, my Beauty would gently stir as though she were about to move, but if I drew near, she would stop. I was always ashamed that

unlike the gentleman who called the lovely Zhenzhen down from the painted screen after forty-nine days, my devotion could never cause my Beauty to step down from the paper. The following year, in 1652, I married Miss Lu, but she died only a few years later, and in 1659 I took Miss Zou as my new wife. My Beauty lived with me without interruption throughout both my marriages. . . .

The adolescent nature of this particular fantasy is beautifully spoofed more than a century later in the famous novel *Dream of the Red Chamber*. The naive young hero of the novel, Bao Yu, "finding himself alone . . . began thinking about a certain painting he remembered having seen in Cousin Zhen's 'smaller study'. It was a very life-like portrait of a beautiful woman. While everyone was celebrating, he reflected, she was sure to have been left on her own and would perhaps be feeling lonely. He would go and have a look at her and cheer her up."[13] When he hears "a gentle moaning" actually coming from the room, he imagines that it must be the beautiful woman in the picture miraculously come to life; it turns out instead to be the sound of his page Tealeaf getting it on with one of the maids, thus acknowledging the inherently sexual nature of this fantasy but enacting it on a much lower social and mimetic scale.[14]

As time passes, the painting in Wang Zhuo's account becomes more and more like an imaginary concubine. In that sense, his elegy bears a resemblance to accounts of imaginary gardens from the same period, in which sites of pleasure too costly for a poor scholar to possess are mapped solely on paper instead.[15] Wang Zhuo playfully attempts to portray the image's unresponsiveness and immobility as virtues: whenever he studied late at night, she was always there for him; she never complained or showed her emotions on her face; and when his friends came over to drink, she never had to retire to the women's quarters. The constant presence of the painting in his life belies the total absence of the woman she represents. Implicitly, her seemingly permanent existence helps compensate for the loss of his first wife and the probable loss of the next, perhaps even for his own mortality:

I once said to my wife Zou: "Your constitution is weak and you're prone to illness: these are not signs of long life. I'm afraid the only one I'll be able to grow old with is this Beauty. But I just don't know what will become of her after my death."

Zou laughed: "Can you really be this much of a fool and care about her so deeply? In that case, wouldn't it be better just to bury her with you, so you could be together?" I laughed back and assented.

By calling her husband a fool (*chi*), Zou is knowingly bestowing praise rather than derision on her husband in the sentimental culture of the seventeenth century. Wang Zhuo's profession of love for a painting, his treatment of fantasy as though it were real, is a textbook case of the "foolishness" that supposedly marks a true man of sentiment in this period and milieu.[16] Throughout the elegy he represents himself acting out the part of the male lead in a romantic comedy like Tang Xianzu's *Peony Pavilion* of 1598 or its many spin-offs, especially Wu Bing's *Lady in the Painting* (*Huazhong ren*) from the 1630s. The literary pose is already so well-worn by 1665 that Wang Zhuo's adoption of it inevitably contains elements of conscious self-parody— but by no means entirely.

At the end of the piece, Wang Zhuo reverts to the mournful tone, formulaic diction, and ritual action appropriate to an elegy (though he still cannot resist the clever double entendre): "Who would have expected you to meet with the disaster of incineration, your fragrant soul to vanish into smoke? . . . Ah, my Beauty, in the end you perished before me. Were you real or a dream? . . . As I pour out this wine drop by drop, my tears fall along with it. The paths of the living and the dead are separate, how truly painful this is. If you have consciousness, my Beauty, please accept this libation."[17]

In the famous Tang story of Zhenzhen, which Wang Zhuo alluded to earlier, it is not only by calling her name that the gentleman brings the woman on the painted screen to life, but by pouring wine on the image, thereby inspiriting her.[18] Now that Wang Zhuo's painting is gone, all he can do is pour out the wine on the ground as a libation, in a ritual act of mourning that finalizes the transformation from image to memory. Only in the destruction of the painting's material form can the analogy to a living woman—with a body subject to mortality—be complete.

More to the point in terms of literary reenactment here, however, is the famous story of Xiaoqing, an ill-fated talented beauty of uncertain ontological status, who was closely associated with the extraordinary reader response to *The Peony Pavilion*. Many versions of her life were written, the earliest being in circulation by at least 1624, and several plays were performed on the subject.[19] On her deathbed, after Xiaoqing has had her likeness painted to her specifications by a master portraitist, she burns some incense, and raising a glass of pear juice as a libation, she addresses the portrait: "Xiaoqing, Xiaoqing, I consecrate my spirit to you." With that she bursts into tears, and dies.[20] You will remember that in the preface to his elegy, Wang Zhuo mentions that he had set out an offering of *pear* blossoms; in the context of his making a libation to the ill-fated portrait of a beautiful woman, the reference is unmistakable; and his staging of the deathbed scene casting himself as the appreciative man of sentiment Xiaoqing lacked during her lifetime would have been transparent to any contemporary reader.

In the Xiaoqing story, as in the others of this type, the urgency to *undertake* the portrait always occurs as a woman lies on her sickbed and contemplates the loss of her beauty. It is often, but not always, combined with the narcissistic motif of her looking at her reflection in the mirror, usually either before or after the likeness is sketched. In a Tang story, which became a popular poetic subject, the courtesan Cui Hui falls ill with grief and resentment after having been abandoned by her lover. She commissions a skilled portraitist to paint her likeness and sends it to her lover along with a letter saying, "Once I no longer measure up to the image on this scroll-painting, I will die for you." Afterwards she goes mad and dies.[21] In the play *Marriage Destiny over Two Lifetimes*, the female lead, who is also a courtesan and is also abandoned by her lover, likewise falls gravely ill. As an innovation, she paints her *self*-portrait, then inscribes it with a lyric of her own composition entitled "Everlasting Longing," and has it sent to her lover. Immediately afterward, she looks in the mirror and discovers that her looks have so deteriorated, she does not in fact resemble the painting; two arias later she dies.[22]

The most famous and by far the most complex realization of the portrait theme is *The Peony Pavilion*, to which I will return later in more detail.[23] For the moment I will simply recapitulate the relevant portion of the plot. The heroine of the play, Du Liniang, is a well-born maiden. Her love sickness is triggered by an erotic and incredibly vivid dream of a lover she has never met. After looking in the mirror during her illness, and realizing that her beauty is diminishing, she paints her self-portrait, inscribes it with a quatrain referring to the dream, then pines away and dies over the course of several scenes. The deathbed portrait became so ubiquitous with the adaptations and imitations of *The Peony Pavilion* and the Xiaoqing spin-offs, that when the female lead in You Tong's 1655 play *Celestial Court Music (Juntian yue)* decides against painting her self-portrait before she dies because her beauty has been too ravaged by illness, we are only too grateful; we can only concur with the commentator on the play who praises the playwright for avoiding such a rampant cliché.[24]

In the cases I have just described, the deathbed portrait of the heroine should be understood as what I will call an "auto-effigy," a posthumous image of the self created for posterity. It is well known that formal portraits of the deceased were used in late imperial mourning rituals, both for public and private remembrance. These portraits were usually specially commissioned posthumous likenesses, but sometimes they had been painted during the subject's lifetime for some other purpose. Such images are often called "ancestor" portraits because of their function in family worship, particularly in a lineage context, but a commemorative portrait need not depict a male or even a member of the previous generation. The evidence suggests that men could seek to have a posthumous likeness painted of their wives, concubines, and even daughters.[25] For this reason I prefer the broader term *commemorative or effigy portrait*.[26]

An effigy portrait, as Richard Vinograd has perceptively commented, "makes up an absence or serves as a stand-in for the deceased but its motives are already conditioned by the death of its subject, since it becomes a portrait of the interest in a memory, a legacy, an ancestor . . . rather than an image of a social person."[27] Ordinarily an effigy portrait aimed to convey the impression of "a veristic rendering" of its subject, to provide "the visual input to the perpetuating function of memory," as the art historian Ladislav Kesner phrases it in a recent article (fig. 2).[28] In the case of a woman's creation of her auto-effigy, however, the point is to preserve a perfect, idealized beauty that no longer completely exists, one that may never have existed in the realm of the "real." In *The Peony Pavilion*, for instance, Du Liniang depicts herself as she looked in her *dream*, not as she looks when she paints the portrait during her illness. In that sense, despite its claim to be understood as an act of profound self-expression, an auto-effigy *is* simply a generic "beautiful woman picture."[29] The reflection in the mirror may be introduced as a counterpoint, to reinforce the subject's actual sickly appearance. The effect is often one of a "double exposure." In the story of the Tang courtesan Cui Hui, there is no mirror but the temporal comparison built into the image works like a delayed or trip "double exposure" shot; in the Xiaoqing story, the portrait is explicitly set up in the reflexive position of a mirror.[30] The idea of a "double exposure" also nicely describes a popular related literary motif, in which a lovesick woman's body—her social body—is immobilized in coma or death, allowing her soul or ghost to leave the body and freely pursue its private, illicit desires. In Wu Weiye's play of 1653, *Spring in Nanjing or the Story of a Pair of Images (Moling chun shuangying ji)*, the female lead's soul is magically wafted away as a reflection in a mirror to encounter the male lead, while her body lies sick and unconscious in bed.[31]

It is worth noting that in the paintings in the National Gallery of Prague on which Kesner based his article, the attempt at "veristic rendering" falls off sharply in the depictions of young wives or concubines flanking the male subject of a commemorative portrait; in these cases the female likenesses are not individualized and have much more in common visually with "beautiful women" pictures" (fig. 3).[32] The ease of slippage between effigy portraits and beautiful women pictures emerges in the late sixteenth-century novel *The Plum in a Golden Vase (Jin Ping Mei)*. In chapter 63, Ximen Qing commissions a posthumous effigy portrait of his beloved wife Li Ping'er for use in her funerary ritual. A draft of the portrait is first circulated among his five other wives for critique to aid the professional portraitist in arriving at an acceptable "likeness." The corrected, finished portrait, which is deemed a success and hailed for "looking as though it were alive," is nonetheless praised a moment later as a "beautiful woman picture."[33]

世祖母周孺人

Figure 2. Anonymous. Effigy portrait of old lady.

Figure 3. Anonymous, late 19th century. Portrait of an official and two women. National Gallery, Prague.

Figure 4. Qiu Ying. "Woman in Spring Longing."

In the case of the auto-effigy, the whole point is to capture sentiment, desire, passion, feeling—each a possible translation of the all-important Chinese term *qing*. After all, *qing* is something invisible and ineffable, private and internal—how can it be seen and felt by outsiders? To borrow a line from a scholar of eighteenth-century England, "it is the body which acts out the powers of sentiment."[34] *Qing* is written on the woman's body in China through illness and death; thus comes the fascination in this period with the sickly beauty type and her untimely demise, a fascination that culminates in the portrayal of the tubercular, poetical heroine Dai Yu in *Dream of the Red Chamber*. (In literature, young men also register *qing* somatically through illness and death, but it is never represented as an erotic spectacle as in the case of young women). One term for Du Liniang's portrait in *The Peony Pavilion* is "spring visage" (*chunrong*), in which spring is short for "spring longing" (*chunsi*) or love sickness. The languishing beauty occupied in "spring longing" familiar from poetry was a popular theme for "beautiful woman pictures."[35] However, as in the case of the woodblock illustrations in editions of fiction and drama, the impression in such pictures is at most one of languor or slight haggardness and far from any actual wasting disease (fig. 4), and there was no visual counterpart in China to the paintings of deathbed scenes of women so popular in nineteenth-century Europe.[36] The double exposure effect of the auto-effigy scene in Chinese fiction and drama has this advantage: it allows the fantasy of ultimate beauty and its devastation through desire to coexist in a single frame.

Because the creation of an auto-effigy appears as a symptom of a fatal case of love sickness, it is worth considering how this disorder was understood in Chinese medical sources. The symbiosis between emotional states and the workings of the body was a basic tenet of Chinese medical thought. *Si*, which I have been translating as "longing," and which refers more broadly to any form of concentrated mental activity, was classified as one of the major emotions, just as the Heart was conceptualized as the seat of consciousness. *The Yellow Emperor's Inner Canon* (*Huangdi neijing*), the theoretical foundation of learned medicine, defines *si* as meaning "the Heart has something stored in it, a point to which consciousness keeps reverting; since the orthopathic *qi* (*zhengqi*) stays put and will not move on, vitality (*qi*) congests."[37] Thus the classification scheme of *The Inner Canon* correlates intense thought with congested *qi*, just as anger causes *qi* to reverse course and rise, or sorrow causes *qi* to waste away. Congestion is a serious disruption in a system where free circulation is taken as key to health, and, left unchecked or untreated, congestion could prove fatal. As early as the Six Dynasties, lovesick girls are described in stories as "dying of congested qi."[38]

One of the most important and broad-based types of congestive disorders was stasis (*yu*), sometimes called static congestion (*yujie*), and often translated

into English as "melancholy" or "depression."[39] Late Ming medical encyclopedias increasingly stress the emotional etiology of stasis, an innovation that
surely reflects the heightened visibility of sentiment as a force in the culture
and society of the period.[40] In her work on medical images of women in the late
imperial period, the historian Charlotte Furth has argued that the dangerous
emotionality conventionally ascribed to women, coupled with the recognition
of their social disempowerment, meant that they were considered particularly
vulnerable to static congestion. Furth describes this as "a kind of melancholy
syndrome of congealed blood associated with spleen system dysfunction. It
was experienced as feelings of oppression and suffocation, pressure or tight-
ness in the chest, languor and loss of appetite, all linked to pent-up resent-
ments and repressed desires."[41]

Both the intensified medical attention to the affective roots of stasis and its
gender-linked nature are apparent in *The Complete Writings of Physician
Zhang (Jingyue quanshu)*, an influential compendium first published in 1624.
The author, Zhang Jiebin, an expert on *The Inner Canon*, explicitly identifies
what he terms a new category of stasis: *qingzhi yu*, stasis related to the passions.[42] Within this new category, stasis from longing, which causes the *qi*-
vitality to congest in the heart and injures the Spleen system, was only likely
to afflict two types of people: maidens and widows on the one hand, whose
sexual desires could not be assuaged, and unsuccessful examination candidates
on the other, whose ambitions were continually frustrated. In the case of a
woman, stasis from longing could be fully cured only by gaining her heart's
desire, but there was hope for a man if he could achieve a state of philosophical resignation.[43] Physician Zhang's pairing of lovesick maidens and aspiring
scholars replicates the typical couple of romantic fiction and drama, such as
The Peony Pavilion. Nonetheless, despite his description of several types of
emotionally based *yu* syndromes and his inclusion of male students among
the types liable to develop stasis from longing, it is clear from the two case histories he appends that unfulfilled female desire epitomizes his view of this
melancholic disorder.

The cases are credited to Zhu Zhenheng (more often known as Zhu
Danxi), the celebrated fourteenth-century physician, but they were widely
quoted in late Ming medical encyclopedias and lead the entry on *yu* in
Classified Cases of Famous Physicians. In the longer case, a betrothed maiden
is unable to eat and takes to her bed after her fiancé, a merchant, postpones
their marriage by staying abroad for two years. Doctor Zhu diagnoses her illness as "the congestion of *qi* due to longing." It is as though her body had
developed an internal obstruction to mirror the unwelcome impediment to
her wedding, as though time could be frozen in the body as stasis. As he
explains his clinical reasoning:

The Spleen system governs longing. Excessive longing will cause *qi* to congest in the Spleen and make someone stop eating. If she grows angry, her *qi* will rise and smash open the congested *qi* in the Spleen. So he had them provoke her. She became furious and burst into tears. About three hours later, he had them comfort her and give her medicine. Then she asked for gruel to eat. Zhu said: "Although the *qi* of longing has now been dispelled, she must rejoice if it is not to re-congest." So they lied and told her that a letter had arrived from her fiancé saying he was about to set off for home any day. Three months later, her fiancé did return after all, and she finally recovered.[44]

The other less detailed case also involves a maiden suffering from fatigue and digestive ailments. After something unspecified "has gone against her wishes," presumably an affair of the heart, she develops static congestion in the Spleen and is unable to eat for half a year. She recovers after simply taking medicine prescribed by the doctor.

The medical possibilities underlying the conventions of the deathbed portrait are exploited in Wu Bing's *Jealousy-Curing Stew*, one of the Xiaoqing plays with a happy ending mentioned earlier. In this southern drama, the portrait painter is conveniently a physician as well. He succeeds in rescuing his female patient from death's door when he fortuitously arrives at the eleventh hour to deliver her finished portrait. The pivotal scene in question is entitled "Restored to Life" ("Hui sheng"); indeed, Xiaoqing has already been mourned as dead for a whole day when the portraitist-physician appears on the scene and detects that she is actually alive (fig. 5).

Wu Bing's innovation of turning the painter into a physician is more than an ingenious solution to the plot enabling him to transform tragedy into comedy. Superimposing the two roles suggests a parallel between them, both practically and symbolically: the portraitist, like a doctor, is an expert able to observe and thus potentially mediate the volatile forces of life and death concealed to the ordinary eye (fig. 6). This ability to detect an invisible interior is all the more important in a medical tradition that did not privilege dissection and anatomy as ways of knowing the body. The doctor in this play, as the body's guardian, is able to use the knowledge gained from painting his subject to override the ordinarily fatal power of the auto-effigy. As he explains: "A doctor's method consists of looking, listening, and questioning. When I painted her portrait the other day, I observed her *qi*-vitality and complexion and listened to the timbre of voice. She didn't resemble someone who would die so precipitously. Most likely her sorrow has congealed and her depression has congested, provoking an attack of phlegm and causing her to fall into a temporary coma."[45] He is led inside to examine the body; upon discerning that the area around the heart is still faintly warm, he administers medicine (a "divine pill"), and she revives. In this dramatic twist, the portrait is ultimately stripped of any residual life-giving or death-bestowing powers. Instead,

Figure 5. "Restored to Life" ("Hui sheng"). Ming woodblock illustration showing the supporting male lead in his capacity of doctor examining Xiaoqing in Wu Bing, *Jealousy-Curing Stew*.

懷念雪裏窨
芭蕉

Figure 6. "Painting the Portrait" ("Hua zhen"). Ming woodblock
illustration showing the supporting male lead sketching Xiaoqing's
likeness in Wu Bing, *Jealousy-Curing Stew.*

agency over life and death is reconfigured as a form of broad knowledge that is transferable between different fields such as painting and medicine. Such knowledge is made the property of a learned third party who serves a crucial deus ex machina function in the plot.[46]

A major theme in the Chinese rhetoric of portrait painting is that the portraitist should aim to capture the true inner spirit of the subject, rather than to depict mere physical likeness. Indeed, "transmitting the spirit" (*chuanshen*) is a common term for portraiture. This theme is fully dramatized in the Xiaoqing story where the portraitist is obliged to paint three different paintings before Xiaoqing is satisfied that he has captured her spirit, not her external likeness, and produced a sufficiently animated portrait of her. Wu Bing's play takes this notion even further. In *Jealousy-Curing Stew*, the portraitist not only succeeds in transmitting the true spirit of his subject, but in his capacity as physician he has literally succeeded in "enlivening" that spirit by preserving his patient from death and resuscitating her.

Wu Bing's rewrite of the Xiaoqing story is unusual in developing the portraitist into a major dramatic role, but it also recognizes that the auto-effigy is primarily a means to externalize the invisible emotional and physical forces at work within the body. Perhaps even more important, the portrait is able to invest the powerful feelings that induced the illness in a transferable, visible, and tangible object—not only in the sense of a visual message that can be decoded by an understanding viewer, but in a more immediate sense, as something that can outlast death and can haunt like a ghost.

In Tang Xianzu's famous preface to *The Peony Pavilion*, the playwright declared: "That which the living cannot die for, or which cannot resurrect the dead, is not love [*qing*] at its most supreme."[47] Like the effigy or the ghost, *qing* manifests itself on the uncanny borders of life and death. These borders are in fact permeable, however, and *qing*'s power may not only rob the living of vitality but also restore it to them. This last point is especially important in *The Peony Pavilion*, where the hero's recovery of the heroine's posthumous portrait, his amorous meeting with her ghost, and his reanimation of her corpse are closely intertwined.

Vinograd has suggested that the effigy function "may lie behind one standard designation of portraiture as *chuanshen*, that which 'transmits the spirit' of the portrayed, with the implication that the portrait is a stand-in or vehicle for harboring the spirit of the subject."[48] In the case of Du Liniang, the heroine of the play, there is certainly the sense when she paints the portrait that she is transferring her spirit and vitality to it, imbuing it with life, in the hope that it will outlast her death and be instrumental in her future revival (fig. 7). As she sings, "That portrait and those brush strokes / which possess my soul / May reach someday someone who understands."[49] In this guise the portrait is associated with her disembodied soul; when she first appears on stage as a ghost, she declares herself magnetically drawn by the painting. When her ghostly tryst with Liu Mengmei is disrupted, she tells him that she will hide beneath the shade cast by the painting—something almost impossible to visualize, and which works mainly to point out the symbolic affinity between her ghost and the painting. The Three Wives' commentary on the play, published in 1694, defines painting as "shadow without form" just as "dream is form without shadow," drawing the parallel that both are "unreal illusions."[50] Indeed as an image, the portrait in the play is conjoined with shadows, dreams, ghosts, mirrors, reflections, and memories—in short, everything that is insubstantial, fleeting, and illusory.

In a brilliant reading of the play, Catherine Swatek has argued that the portrait is not only identified with Du Liniang's spirit, however, but is also treated as an extension of or as a direct substitute for her eroticized body.[51] Here I would like to build upon some of Swatek's insights but push them in a somewhat different direction. After the portrait is done, Du Liniang worries about its fading or being defiled and orders it mounted with care: "From burning of sun and buffeting of breeze, mount and line it well, / For fear that 'finest things are least enduring.'/ My portrait's pretty hues must not be sullied."[52] Before her death she requests that the painting be enclosed within a rosewood box and hidden in the garden near the spot where her body will be buried. Liu Mengmei, the male lead, discovers the box three years later in the ruins of the garden and opens it, anticipating (and mimicking in miniature) his later exhumation of her grave and opening of her coffin. In the vernacular story that most scholars agree served as Tang Xianzu's chief source for *The Peony Pavilion*, Du Liniang's newly finished self-portrait is described as "looking almost as though it were alive;" virtually the identical phrase is used later in the story to describe her newly exhumed corpse.[53]

What makes the self-portrait such an interesting symbol in the play is its protean quality as the woman's double, its ability to signify now her body/corpse, now her spirit/ghost. The point is that the self-portrait is always one or the other though, never both, and thus it always points to something lacking or absent. "The double," Elisabeth Bronfen has recently reminded us, "is by definition . . . a figure for a split or gap, a figure signifying that something that was whole and unique has been split into more than one part."[54] The portrait is ideally suited to represent such a split, because as a painting it is always already a double itself.

We should never forget that the portrait is not simply a painted image, a representation, but a hanging scroll, a material object. In terms of the play, the portrait is not only a literary symbol or plot device woven into the dense poetic arias of the play, but a prop, a physical object present on stage during a

Figure 7. "Sketching the Portrait" ("Xie zhen"). Ming woodblock illustration showing Du Liniang painting her self-portrait in *The Peony Pavilion*.

performance or elaborated in stage directions in the text.[55] The timeless, permanent, inviolate image that uncannily transforms living flesh into inanimate form is a conventional notion in the European artistic tradition, which centered on the easel oil painting or the marble statue.[56] I want to stress the difference with the material form of a hanging scroll made of paper or silk, which must be unrolled and handled in an intimate setting, something that is not inert and frozen, but that can be ruffled by the breeze and actually stir, giving the impression of animation; something that is understood to be perishable and easily damaged; something that can be altered and augmented with poetic inscriptions, colophons, and seals; and something, it was recognized, that survived often only in copies.

Tactile pleasure in the hand scroll is a crucial component of Liu Mengmei's response to the portrait (fig. 8). Scene 26 is entitled "Admiring the Portrait" ("Wanhua"), but the Chinese verb *wan* has the sense not only of appreciating or enjoying something, but handling or fondling or dallying with something. This meaning is underscored by the stage directions. At the beginning of the scene they instruct him "to open the rosewood box and unroll the painting"; in scene 28, when he contemplates the painting again before his first visitation by the heroine's amorous ghost, the stage directions again indicate that he first unrolls the painting. Throughout these two scenes, he repeatedly voices fears about the fragility and vulnerability of the precious scroll even as he projects his own sexual desires onto it. He worries about "soiling its delicate hues" by embracing it, and fears "a lamp spark lighting on the painted scroll." He speaks of "seek[ing] out some eminent painter to make a copy . . . lest the wind tear her portrait." It is significant that he never does actually have such a copy made because to do so would ultimately destroy the claim that the portrait is the actual representation of a unique woman. Any attempt to duplicate a portrait regarded not only as the *image* of a beloved woman but as her *embodiment* must inevitably fail.

Such indeed is the premise of *The Lady in the Painting*, another of Wu Bing's romantic comedies heavily derivative of *The Peony Pavilion*. In this play the male lead paints a picture of an imaginary, ideal woman (fig. 9); the image comes to life in response to his devotion, but she is still mainly confined to the painting, emerging only when they are alone (fig. 10). After the portrait is stolen from him, she disappears altogether. The play actually stages a scene entitled "Painting Anew" (*Zaihua*), which depicts the male lead's fruitless attempt to replicate the portrait. Although he had originally created the painting, his efforts to produce a copy are strangely unsuccessful, and he ends up throwing away his paper and brush in disgust.[57]

The Peony Pavilion is a far more interesting play than *The Lady in the Painting* for many reasons, but in large measure because the conceit of a self-

Figure 8. "Admiring the Portrait" ("Wan zhen"). Ming woodblock
illustration showing Liu Mengmei holding the hanging scroll to
peruse the portrait in *The Peony Pavilion*.

拂鳥綵斗酒
偏豪

Figure 9. "Painting the Sketch" ("Hua lüe"). Ming woodblock illustration showing the male lead painting his imaginary woman in Wu Bing, *The Lady in the Painting*.

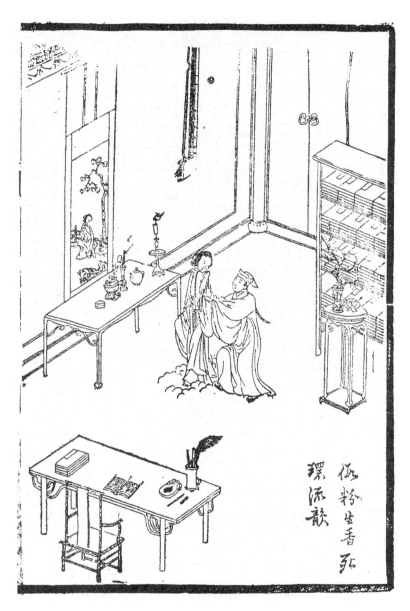

環流散　倚粉生香死

Figure 10. "The Painting Shows Up" ("Hua xian"). Ming woodblock illustration showing the woman in the painting come to life and being embraced by the male lead in *The Lady in the Painting*. The clouds around her feet, used to designate divinities or dream figures, here show that she is the spirit of the painting.

portrait opens up more complex possibilities of female agency and creativity. Du Liniang's self-portrait is double in yet another important respect. The painting is authored by her own hand. It not only preserves from death a *likeness* of her body; it preserves something that originally *came* from her body. The auto-effigy is therefore a physical talisman of the dead, not because it represents the dead but because it was produced by the dead. The somatic origins of the painting are displayed in the traces of the heroine's brush strokes on the hanging scroll, the calligraphic aspect of the self-portrait reinforced by the poem she added above it.

Norman Bryson has observed that the subject of a Chinese painting is not only the picture or image depicted on its surface, but "the work of the brush in 'real time' and as extension of the painter's own body."[58] "The work of production," he argues, "is constantly displayed in the wake of its traces; in this tradition the body of labour is on constant display, just as it is judged in terms which in the West, would only apply to performing art."[59] It says something about Bryson's biases that the contrast he draws centers on the Western nude versus the Chinese landscape; Chinese figure painting or portraiture is omitted entirely from his discussion. This dichotomy is undoubtedly too stark, and Bryson's observation works better for some genres of painting than for others. Still, the performative potential of Chinese painting, at least in the amateur tradition, may suggest why the creation of a portrait, especially an auto-effigy, was such a popular scene in the Chinese theater.

Even when an auto-effigy is not a self-portrait, as in the Xiaoqing story, an inscription in the woman's own hand tends to accompany the painting, to clarify or elaborate the message the portrait is supposed to communicate, of course, but more importantly, to mark it with the woman's own physical signature (her "autograph"). In these cases, inscription and image reinforce one another, indeed may become so interchangeable in function that the image may drop out entirely. I mentioned earlier that in You Tong's *Celestial Court Music*, the play's female lead deliberately decides to forgo painting her self-portrait on her deathbed. Instead she asks her maid to gather up her poems and give them to her betrothed in lieu of a self-portrait when he comes to mourn her after her death: "Take my . . . shattered ink and fragments of writing and give them to him, one by one, so that he may *look* upon these things and think of me. . . ."[60] She says, not read, mind you, but *look upon*.

There is a set phrase in Classical Chinese for posthumous handwriting, "the hand's moisture" (*shouze*), which underscores the intimate connection of writing or brush strokes with the body that produced them. The locus classicus is an injunction from the ancient *Ritual Canon* (*Liji*): "A son may not read his late father's writings because they still bear 'the moisture of his hand'; a man may not drink from his late mother's cup and bowl because they still bear the 'breath of her mouth.'"[61] The phrase, which was applied to women's as well as men's posthumous writings in the seventeenth century, describes the sight of vivid ink traces that still look "fresh and new" even though the author who penned them is dead. The uncanniness of the sensation is closely akin to that aroused by seeing an image, such as an effigy portrait, which "looked as though it were alive."[62]

I do not want to conclude with an assertion of the complete interchangeability between image and writing, however. The fantasy of a posthumous portrait (or any portrait for that matter) coming to life clearly reflects the uncanny assumption that a painted likeness can perfectly duplicate its subject and erase all differences between them. At stake is still a visual likeness to a departed or missing original. In this respect a portrait is very like a ghost.[63] In Chinese tales of the strange, a ghost (often a female one) may indeed be discovered or identified through a perfect resemblance to an effigy portrait; in such cases it is not entirely clear whether it is the ghost or the portrait that is the copy.[64]

In *The Peony Pavilion*, Tang Xianzu subtly interweaves the conventional topoi of a beautiful woman picture coming to life and the revival of a dead woman through a liaison with her ghost. He is careful not to equate these themes perfectly as do revisions of the play or later imitations such as Wu Bing's *Lady in the Painting*.[65] Thus even after Liu Mengmei, the male lead, takes up with the Du Liniang's ghost, he never realizes that she looks like the lady in the painting he is so infatuated with; Du Liniang's ghost actually has to point out the resemblance before he exclaims: "Why it is the very image of you!"[66] Still, the motif of recognizing a ghost by recourse to a posthumous portrait does resurface in *The Peony Pavilion*, in a displaced or unconscious fashion. When Du Liniang's ghost first returns to her burial shrine in scene 27, she is glimpsed by a young novice who excitedly reports having seen some goddess. When asked what she looked like, the novice says, gesturing: "About so tall, so thin, a pretty face, feather hair ornaments, and a gold phoenix hairpin, red skirt and green jacket, jade girdle pendants all atinkle." The immediate response of Sister Stone, the abbess in charge of the shrine, is to pronounce: "This is how Miss Du looked when she was alive. I suspect it must have been a manifestation of her animate soul."[67] On what basis is this likeness being identified? Du Liniang is never described as wearing these particular clothes anywhere in the play. What this sounds like is a generic description of any beautiful woman—or rather any beautiful woman *picture*, because in fact it originally described one. In the vernacular story that the playwright used as his source, these are the exact phrases (minus the qualifications about so tall, so thin, and the redundant pretty face) used to describe the *self-portrait* right after Du Liniang finishes it.[68] In the play this description is used to identify her *ghost* instead, suggesting the essentially reciprocal nature of these two modes of identification or the extent to which the same cognitive operations are involved.

Art historians have all noted the stereotypical nature of beautiful woman pictures in Chinese visual culture. Wu Hung, for example, has pointed out that, in some cases, it is hard even to tell in a given painting or set of pictures whether several women are being depicted in turn or whether one woman is being depicted several times in different poses or costumes.[69] Yao Dajuin has argued that the identity of an individual female portrait in the woodblock illustrations reproduced in Ming editions of plays is established not by "facial distinction," but by clothing, gestures, and setting," which "act as props to inform the viewer of the sitter's social status and personality."[70] By contrast, the fantasy in the literary sources is always of perfect individuation, the rhetoric of an exact resemblance between a female portrait and its subject, and hence the impossibility of ever duplicating the image. As I have suggested, the elasticity of generic labeling—the slippage between beautiful women pictures and individual female portraits—facilitated this fiction. This *slippage* privileged the workings of the imagination and the power of context to allow readers and viewers to blur illusion and reality and construe a female image as they desired.

Notes

1. Yang Shen, *Huapin*, "xiezhao," *Mingren huaxue lunzhu* 1. 12, in *Yishu congbian*, ed. Yang Jialuo (Taipei: Shijie shuju, 1967), first series, vol. 12.

2. See particularly Dorothy Ko, *Teachers of the Inner Chambers* (Stanford, Calif.: Stanford University Press, 1994); Marsha Weidner, *Views from Jade Terrace: Chinese Women Artists, 1300–1912* (New York: Rizzoli, 1989); Ellen Widmer and Kang-i Sun Chang, eds., *Writing Women in Late Imperial China* (Stanford, Calif.: Stanford University Press, 1997). For translations of verse by women, see Kang-i Sun Chang and Haun Saussy, eds. *Women Writers of Traditional China: An Anthology of Poetry and Criticism* (Stanford, Calif.: Stanford University Press, 1999). A huge corpus of published poetry by women is extant; many fewer paintings survive.

3. On the talented woman as a doomed figure in this period because of her talent, see Ellen Widmer, "Xiaoqing's Literary Legacy and the Place of the Woman Writer in Late Imperial China," *Late Imperial China* 13, 1 (June 1992): 111–55; Ko, *Teachers of the Inner Chambers;* and my "Shared Dreams: The Story of the Three Wives' Commentary on *The Peony Pavilion*," *Harvard Journal of Asiatic Studies* 54, 1 (July 1994): 127–79.

4. Wang Zhuo is best known for having coedited with Zhang Chao *The Sandalwood Collectanea (Tanji congshu)*, an influential anthology of seventeenth-century informal writings, and for having compiled *Modern Tales of the World (Jin shishuo)*, a series of anecdotal sketches of himself and his contemporaries.

5. In the predominant *shi* form of verse, the "I" is taken to refer to the historical

poet rather than to a fictional persona, and poems are treated as a species of biographical data.

6. See Wang Zhuo, *Xiaju quanji* (Hishi photocopy of the Qing edition in the Naikaku Bunkô. Oriental Gest Library, Princeton University), pentasyllabic verse section.

7. Wang Zhuo, "Ji huashang meiren," in *Xiaju quanji,* prose (*wen*) section.

8. Charles Stone makes the point that the bawd is selling the posthumous image of the heroine, a courtesan, just as she sold the heroine's services during her lifetime, in his unpublished paper, "Self, Spirit, and Body in Two Chinese Plays." My thanks go to Stone for generously sending me this paper.

9. James Cahill, *The Painter's Practice: How Artists Lived and Worked in Traditional China* (New York: Columbia University Press, 1994), 50–59. A possible subtext may also be discernible: the forced street sale of the painting reflects the straightened circumstances of the seller and could have been a by-product of the turmoil surrounding the Manchu conquest. In 1651, the year Wang Zhuo says he bought the painting, the Jiangnan region was still in upheaval, and Manchu rule was not definitively consolidated until 1662.

10. James Cahill, unpublished lectures on beautiful women pictures first delivered as the Getty Lectures at the University of Southern California, April 1994; see also Cahill, "Where Did the Nymph Hang?" *Kaikodo Journal 7* (1998): 8–15; Ellen Johnston Laing, "Erotic Themes and Romantic Heroines Depicted by Ch'iu Ying," *Archives of Asian Art* 49 (1996): 68–91. I am grateful to Cahill for sharing unpublished work. On the problem of beautiful women painting and the stereotype, see also Wu Hung, "Beyond Stereotypes: The Twelve Beauties in Qing Court Art and the *Dream of the Red Chamber*," in Widmer and Chang, ed., *Writing Women,* 306–65.

11. Francette Pacteau, *The Symptom of Beauty* (Cambridge: Harvard University Press, 1994), 12.

12. Wu Bing, *Jealousy-Curing Stew [Liaodugeng],* in *Nuanhongshi huike Canguangzhai wuzhong,* ed. Wu Mei (1914/15; facsimile reprint, Yangzhou: Jiangsu Guangling guji keyinshe, 1982), scene 21, 2:14b.

13. Cao Xueqin, *Story of the Stone,* trans David Hawkes (Harmondsworth, Eng.: Penguin, 1973), ch. 19, 1: 377.

14. I am grateful to Anthony C. Yu for his elegant exposition of this point in comments on an earlier version of this paper, delivered at the symposium on Chinese Art of the Ming and Qing Dynasties held at the Art Institute of Chicago in 1996.

15. For examples, see Liu Shilong, "Account of the Non-existent Garden" ("Wuyou yuan ji") and Huang Zhouxing, "Account of the Jiangjiu Garden" ("Jiangjiu yuan ji").

16. For a discussion of a similar exchange, but with the parts reversed between husband and wife and dated almost thirty years later, see my "Shared Dreams," 169–70. Wang Zhuo was a close friend of Wu Wushan, the husband involved in the Three Wives' Commentary to *The Peony Pavilion.*

17. Wang Zhuo, *Xiaju quanji* juan 8, pentasyllabic verse section.

18. For the story, see *Taiping guangji,* compiled by Li Fang et al. (Bejing: Zhonghua shuju, 1981), 286.2283. Before Zhenzhen returns to the screen at the end of the story, she vomits the wine back out. For a discussion of this motif's significance in the context of *The Peony Pavilion,* see Catherine Swatek, "Plum and Portrait: Feng Menglong's Revision of *The Peony Pavilion,*" *Asia Major* 3d series 6 #1 (1993): 153–54.

19. On Xiaoqing, see Widmer, "Xiaoqing's Literary Legacy"; and Ko, *Teachers of the Inner Chambers,* 91–112.

20. For this episode, see Widmer's translation, based on the version in Zheng Yuanxuan's *Meiyou ge wenyu* of 1630 in "Xiaoqing's Literary Legacy," 154. The pear juice libation is present from the earliest narrative and dramatic versions of the story onwards.

21. For the complex history of the Tang versions of Cui Hui's story, which survive only in fragments, see Li Jianguo, *Tang Wudai zhiguai chuanqi xulu* (Tianjin: Nankai daxue chubanshe, 1993), 428–31. Yuan Zhen is credited with a ballad and a narrative preface about Cui Hui. For the texts of poems about Cui Hui by Su Shi and the Yuan writer Ya Hu, see *Yuding lidai tihua shilei*, compiled by Wang Yunwu et al. *Siku quanshu zhenben*, sixth series (Taipei: Taiwan Shangwu yinshuguan, 1976), portrait section, 7: 18b–19a.

22. *Liangshi yinyuan* in *Yuanqu xuan*, compiled by Zang Maoxun (Beijing: Zhonghua shuju, 1979), 971–86.

23. For allusions to Cui Hui in the text of *The Peony Pavilion*, see Xu Fuming, *Mudanting ziliao* (Shanghai: Shanghai guji chubanshe, 1986), 38–39.

24. I believe that the commentator was actually the playwright himself. For the arguments, see my "Spirit writing and Performance in the Work of You Tong," *T'oung Pao* 84 (1998), 128, n. 74.

25. For a wife, see Dai Fugu's Song dynasty inscription on a painting of his late wife, included in *Yuding lidai tihua shilei* 7:54.19a; for a concubine, see the episode involving Ximen Qing's funerary portrait of Li Ping'er in chapter 63 of *Jin Ping Mei Lihua* (Taipei reprint of the Japanese facimile of the Wanli edition); for a daughter, see Ye Shaoyuan's occult attempts to procure an effigy portrait several years after the burial of his daughter as recorded in his "Qionghua jing," in *Wumengtangji*, ed. J. Jin (Beijing: Zhonghua shuju, 1998), 735–38.

26. The art historian Jan Stuart restricts the term "ancestral portrait" to a full-length "formal likeness that shows a man or woman posed frontally in an iconic attitude" used for ritual purposes, in "The Face in Life and Death: Ancestor Portraits" (unpublished paper delivered at the conference on Body and Face in Chinese Visual Culture, University of Chicago, April 26, 1998). The portraits I am dealing with in this essay were most likely informal likenesses and thus not ancestral portraits according to Stuart's definition.

27. Richard Vinograd, *Boundaries of the Self: Chinese Portraits 1600–1900* (Cambridge: Cambridge University Press, 1992), 11.

28. Ladislav Kesner, "Memory, Likeness, and Identity in Chinese Ancestor Portraits," *Bulletin of the National Gallery in Prague* 3–4 (1993–94): 6.

29. In this context, the character "zhen" in the term "zhenrong" for "portrait," may mean "true" in the sense of "perfect" or "ideal" rather than in the sense of "real."

30. Another double exposure episode occurs earlier in the Xiaoqing story, when she addresses her reflection in the water.

31. See Wu Weiye, *Wu Meicum quanji*, ed. Li Xueying (Shanghai: Shanghai guji chubanshe, 1990), especially scene 15 "Longing for the Mirror" ("Si jing"), pp. 1275–78, and scene 17 "The Reflection Shows Up" ("Ying xian"), pp. 1281–83. The use of mirror/image/reflection in this play is very complicated; in fact the heroine also first sees the hero as a disembodied reflection but in the bottom of a magic goblet.

32. Jan Stuart rightly challenges the Western cliché that the subjects in Chinese ancestor portraits look identical, but she concedes that young women tend to be the least differentiated: "It is mostly in portraits of young women wearing heavy makeup in which the face becomes a mask just like that of any other young woman" ("The Face in Life and Death").

33. *Jin Ping Mei*, ch. 63, 2a–4a. My thanks go to David Roy for calling my attention to this episode. In *Pictures and Visuality in Early Modern China* (Princeton: Princeton University Press, 1997), 91–93, Craig Clunas finds multiple violations of the ritual protocol concerning effigy portraits in both the production and mourning processes. He therefore interprets the entire episode, particularly the evaluation of the posthumous portrait as a beautiful woman picture in the text, as attempts to satirize and censor the villainous husband who commissioned the portrait and his entire household. However, as Stuart, ("The Face in Life and Death) cautions us, we still lack a sufficiently nuanced geographical and historical understanding of how exactly effigy portraits were produced and utilized. For this reason, and because *Jin Ping Mei* is a novel notoriously open to contradictory interpretation, Clunas's ingenious reading of the effigy portrait episode in the novel must be taken as highly speculative.

34. John Mullan, *Sentiment and Sociability: The Language of Feeling in the Eighteenth Century* (Oxford: Clarendon Press, 1988), 200.

35. Laing, "Erotic Themes and Romantic Heroines."

36. For examples in European painting, see Elisabeth Bronfen, *Over Her Dead Body: Death, Femininity, and the Aesthetic* (New York: Routledge, 1992); and Bram Djikstra, *Idols of Perversity* (New York: Oxford University Press, 1986). Exceptions in China are the extraordinary ritual paintings used in the Land and Water sacrifices ("Shuilu hua"), which may depict a woman dying or lying ill in childbirth. For a wonderful example, see *Baoningsi Mingdai shuiluhua*, compiled by the Shanxi Provincial Museum (Beijing: Wenwu chubanshe, 1995), pl. 175 and pl. 176.

37. *Suwen*, "Jutong lun" in *Huangdi neijing zhangju suoyin*, ed. Guo Aichun et al. (Bejing: Renmin weisheng chubanshe, 1992) 39. 113. I follow many historians of Chinese traditional medicine in capitalizing terms to show that they are not synonymous with their usage in modern biomedicine. Because the term *qi* (basic stuff, vitality, energy) is so fundamental and so multivalent in Chinese thought, it is impossible to fully translate the term. Good accounts of *qi* in medical theory are given in Nathan Sivin, *Traditional Medicine in Contemporary China* (Ann Arbor: Center for Chinese Studies, University of Michigan, 1987), 46–53; and Charlotte Furth, *A Flourishing Yin: Gender in China's Medical History, 970–1665* (Berkeley: University of California Press, 1999). In this passage, *qi* is employed in two different senses. "Orthopathic *qi*," which Sivin defines as "what maintains and renews the measured, orderly changes that comprise the body's normal processes" is understood in relation to "heteropathic *qi*," which he defines as "what causes change that violates this normal order" (*Traditional Medicine*, 49). Unmodified *qi* denotes the primary vital resources of the body here.

38. Gan Bao, *Soushen ji* (Beijing: Zhonghua shu, 1979) 16. 200 #394. For a translation of this story, see Kenneth J. DeWoskin and J. I. Crump, *In Search of the Supernatural* (Stanford, Calif.: Stanford University Press, 1996), 193–94.

39. In *The Inner Canon, yu* is pegged to the seasons and the Five Phases and has a basic meaning of blockage and obstruction. Schemes identifying subtypes of *yu* proliferate in later medical literature, sometimes differentiated according to the visceral system the stasis congests in, sometimes according to what creates or constitutes the stasis, such as blood, phlegm, or food. However, *yu* also has a long history as a broad term for any emotional distress caused by suppressed grief, worry, or desire.

40. For example, Xu Chunfu, *The Complete System of Medicine Past and Present, Gujin yitong daquan* (1556; rpt. Taipei: Xinwen feng Chuban gongsi, 1978), 26.24a (2184), defines *static congestion* as a disorder arising from the repression of emotions; the affective origin of stasis is now said to explain its near ubiquity among patients.

41. Charlotte Furth, "Blood, Body, Gender: Medical Images of the Female

Condition in China, 1600–1850," *Chinese Science* 7 (1986): 60–61.

42. Zhang Jiebin maintains that stasis related to the passions has its own set of symptoms and pulse readings, which must be diagnosed and treated accordingly. Within this category, he further distinguishes three manifestation types, all of which arise from the Heart: stasis from anger, anxiety, and longing.

43. Zhang Jiebin, *Jingyue quanshu* (Shanghai: Shanghai kexue jishu chubanshe, 1984) 19. 357–59.

44. Zhang Jiebin abridges the case; my translation is based on the earlier, more complete version in *Mingyi leian*, compiled by Jiang Guan (Taipei: Honye shuju, 1971), 2. 74–75.

45. *Liaodugeng*, scene 23, 2. 26a.

46. These themes are developed further in my "Ming Case Histories and the Literary Fashioning of Medical Authority: the Writings of Sun Yikui," unpublished paper delivered at the Conference on Cultural Studies of Chinese Science, Medicine, and Technology, University of California, Berkeley, 1998.

47. Translated by Wai-yee Li, *Enchantment and Disenchantment: Love and Illusion in Chinese Literature* (Princeton: Princeton University Press, 1993), 50; original in Tang Xianzu, *Mudanting*, ed. Xu Shuofang and Yang Xiaomei (Beijing: Renmin wenxue chubanshe, 1978), 1.

48. Vinograd, *Boundaries of the Self*, 10–11.

49. Translated by Swatek, "Plum and Portrait," 149, modifying Cyril Birch's translation of *The Peony Pavilion* (Bloomington: Indiana University Press, 1978), 102. Original in *Mudanting*, scene 20, 103.

50. *Wu Wushan sanfu heping Mudanting* (Qing edition in the Tōyō bunka kenkyū jo, Tokyo), scene 26 1: 23a–b.

51. Swatek, "Portrait and Plum," esp. 147–49.

52. Translated by Birch, *The Peony Pavilion*, scene 14, 71–72; original in *Mudanting*, 73.

53. The story is entitled "Du Liniang muse huanhun ji." It was included in *Yanju biji*, a sixteenth-century miscellany published in a number of editions. A convenient source for the story is Xu Fuming, *Mudanting ziliao*, 12–19. For similarities between the wording of the play and the story, see Zheng Peiheng, *Tang Xianzu yu wan Ming wenhua* (Taipei: Yunchen wenhua, 1995), 185–204.

54. Bronfen, *Over Her Dead Body*, 114.

55. For this reason, Swatek, "Portrait and Plum," 146, calls the portrait "a material symbol," a common device in the lengthy plays of the southern drama. Vinograd is also interested in the "ironic" counterpoint between the portrait as a stage prop and its connotations as image and memory trace, in *Boundaries of the Self*, 14.

56. Bronfen, *Over Her Dead Body*, 111.

57. Wu Bing, *Huazhong ren*, scene 18, 2. 1a–2b. In *Nuanhongshi huike Canguangzhai wuzhong*.

58. Norman Bryson, *Vision and Painting: The Logic of the Gaze* (New Haven: Yale University Press, 1983), 89.

59. Bryson, 92.

60. You Tong, *Juntian yue* 1: 8: 24. In *Xitang quanji* (Qing edition in the Regenstein Library, University of Chicago).

61. *Li ji*, "Yuzao," 2: 1484. In *Shisanjing zhushu*, edited by Ruan Yuan (Beijing: Zhonghua shuju, 1980).

62. "Yang Siwen Yanshan feng guren" in Feng Menglong, *Gujin xiaoshuo* (Beijing: Renmin wenxue chubanshe 1981), #24, 366–83. For the earlier sources of this story, see

Tan Zhengbi, *Sanyan erpai ziliao* (Shanghai: Shanghai guji chubanshe, 1980), 140–42.

63. I have been influenced by Marjorie Garber's idea of a ghost as "a copy, somehow both nominally identical to and numinously different from a vanished or unavailable original," in *Shakespeare's Ghost Writers* (New York: Methuen, 1987), 15.

64. The relationship between the effigy portrait and a copy is more complicated, especially in the case of distant ancestors. In "The Face in Life and Death," Jan Stuart argues that ancestral portraits could easily be recopied by later generations because "the image of the ancestor is what needed to be perpetuated, but the painting itself was of little importance." For this reason, ancestral portraits could also be retroactively fabricated when no likeness was available.

65. For an account of how this plot inconsistency was remedied by later adapters of the play such as Feng Menglong, see Swatek, "Portrait and Plum," especially 155–56. The plot of *Lady in the Painting* is rather convoluted; although the male lead paints the picture of an imaginary woman, it turns out that there does exist a real woman who corresponds to the image in the painting. While her body lies immobilized in a coma, her soul is able to emerge from the picture in accordance with the male lead's desires. The woman eventually dies, but her body is eventually revived by the male lead in conjunction with the recovery of her stolen portrait.

66. Translated by Birch, *The Peony Pavilion*, scene 32, 187; original in *Mudanting*, 176.

67. My translation. Compare Birch's translation: "This is the very image of the living Miss Du. It must have been a manifestation of her spirit." (*The Peony Pavilion*, 154); original in *Mudanting*, 149.

68. The repetition of the phrasing is not noted by Zheng Peiheng, *Tang Xianzu yu wan Ming wenhua*, probably because the story and play employ these phrases at different junctures in the plot.

69. Wu Hung, "Beyond Stereotypes," esp. 306–7.

70. Yao Dajuin, "The Pleasures of Reading Drama," in Wang Shifu, *The Moon and the Zither: The Story of the Western Wing*, ed. and trans. Stephen H. West and Wilt L. Idema (Berkeley: University of California Press, 1991), 454.

A Soprano Subjectivity:
Vocality, Power, and the Compositional
Voice of Francesca Caccini

SUZANNE G. CUSICK

Music

This paper[1] arose from an effort to imagine a plausible subjectivity for *sei-cento* singer, teacher, and theatrical composer Francesca Caccini (1587–after 1641), a woman most often remembered today as the first woman to have composed opera.[2] Indeed, she was one of the most prolific and oft-commissioned theatrical composers of her generation, a fact so startling as immediately to raise questions about how she managed it. Part of her success surely resulted from her own talent, industry, and intelligence. Just as surely, part of it resulted from the kinds of enabling circumstances and institutions that we might colloquially dismiss as the influence of "luck." Yet, no combination of talent and enabling circumstances could suffice to have created Francesca Caccini's remarkable career had she not somehow been able to imagine herself able safely to step beyond the musical role for which she had been trained, that of *virtuosa* singer, and into the far more powerful, authorlike role of composer. What could have accounted for her ability to make this imaginative leap? What might have been the sources for her evident agency in crafting her own highly unusual career? I will argue that the the bodily techniques, metaphors, and aesthetics of the particular kind of virtuosic singing to which she was trained in Florence at the turn of the seventeenth century could have combined to create in her a "soprano subjectivity" whence she could easily have believed that the power of musical authorship was as "natural" for her as any man. In order to give that argument context, however, I will first briefly sketch the several "lucky" historical circumstances that enabled Francesca Caccini's surprising, even dazzling career.

First, Francesca Caccini was the daughter of singers whose professional activities centered on the creation and performance of vocal chamber music and music-theatre spectacles for the ruling family of Tuscany, the Medici. Thus, she was raised amid the production system of a then-novel, highly specialized family trade, a trade whose rules of craft and art she might logically be supposed to have internalized as fully as anyone else alive in her time. Indeed, I would argue that Francesca's experience of the family trade—which I want to describe here as "operatic vocality"—was particularly intense, for her father, Giulio Caccini, was the most influential singing teacher and coach of the age. Further, he seems to have been one of the central figures in the creation of the vocal ethos and technique that characterized the first operas. He partly produced—as musical composition and as theatrical event—some of the earliest operatic texts, with his wife and daughters among the performers. Thus, Francesca's childhood was spent amid the forces, the people, and the exchange of ideas that created both the discourse and the production system of early opera. Francesca Caccini was produced as a subject by the same household where these forces, people, and ideas converged to create a new discourse—a web of aesthetics, bodily and intellectual practices, and relationships of power that each opera (or performance of operatic vocality) wove anew into the characterizing genre of the emerging modern age.[3] There is every reason to suppose that at least some parts of her subjectivity would have had a direct, almost homologous relationship to the conventions that characterized the new discourse. Such profound psychological and performative intimacy with opera's norms must surely have made composition in the new genre easy for her.

Second, the circumstances of her parents' relationship to the Medici family made it relatively easy for them to ensure that their talented and well-trained daughters would enjoy careers in Medici service. Upon his accession to the Granducato in 1588, Ferdinand I de' Medici had self-consciously constructed his interlocking service, political, and patronage networks into a single, if complexly managed household that he meant his subjects to understand through the trope of *famiglia*. Capable of connoting at any given moment the duke's extended biological family, his personal household of servants and retainers, and his relationships with his political functionaries and with his subjects in Florence's newly monarchical state, the polyvalent concept of *famiglia* as Ferdinand and his heirs used it included an implied commitment to take care of retainers' children. As the daughter of a man who had helped create opera and operatic vocality as symbolic discourses through which Medici magnificence and the power dynamics of the new state were spectacularly "performed," Francesca was particularly likely to enjoy the favor of her father's patrons. She would be taken care of in some way, whether by a Medici-subsidized dowry or through productive employment for her within the *famiglia*, or both.

Francesca's path to Medici employment was not a completely smooth one. Yet, once she had been assimilated into the *famiglia*, her presence evoked the memory of her father's artistic contribution to the consolidation of Ferdinand's rule. Indeed, Francesca herself cited her father's memory when she wanted to exercise power within the subtle etiquette of the Medici *famiglia,* encouraging her contemporaries to think of her as (in the words of one) "almost the reincarnation of her father," even though they were quite different as persons, as singers, and as composers.[4] By her mid-twenties, in fact, Francesca had replaced her aging father in both his musical and symbolic functions for the Medici—she directed the court's defacto *concerto delle donne,* which he had founded.[5] She was one of the preferred singing teachers for children of the Medici *famiglia;*[6] she routinely coached the treble roles in court-sponsored theatricals;[7] and, almost annually in the 1610s, she produced music for the *famiglia*'s theatrical entertainments, both public and private.[8] Indeed, one might argue that every commission to Francesca evoked and reconfirmed the ideological exchange between the Medici and their household of servants, bureaucrats, and subjects. This exchange had been powerfully crystallized in the relation of Giulio Caccini to his duke, when Caccini created a musical ensemble of his own biological family that served as a sounding metaphor for Ferdinand's polyvalent *famiglia.* Francesca's career, then, may have flourished because to her patrons it was an instrument almost of nostalgia. The act of commissioning Francesca "performed" the past, the most glorious and powerful epoch of Medici pseudo-monarchical history, even as the actual texts she composed for court occasions may have addressed (and symbolically resolved) up-to-the-minute tensions and crises in that monarchy.

Elaborating the several "lucky" circumstances of her life cannot quite explain, however, the necessary fit there must have been between the kind of person Francesca's world formed her to be—a woman *virtuosa* singer—and the kind of person who would be allowed to wield the cultural power of musical "author." We know that in Francesca's time singers could be understood as ideally heroic figures (as in the early operas on Orpheus). Yet, hardly anyone has tried to explain why that might have been so. Few scholars tried seriously to explain the cultural logic by which singers with women's bodies came to be objects of awestruck admiration—divas—in only a generation, after centuries of quite systematic silencing of women's public voices. Without addressing these questions, it has seemed to me, I cannot explain how a woman like Francesca could have acquired the very considerable degree of agency she demonstrated in life and, sometimes, composed into her musical representations of women.

In an effort to account for Francesca's agency, especially as it existed in relation to the emerging cultural construct of the diva that seems to have been an enabling circumstance of her career, I will trace her simultaneous formation as a person in a female body and as a singer. I claim that the subjectivity that was likely to emerge from the entwining discourses of womanhood and singing would have included a comprehensible, if internally contradictory, sense of her self as "naturally" wielding considerable rhetorical and symbolic power. Further, I claim that paradoxically empowering qualities inhered in the combination of bodily techniques and aesthetic principles that constituted the discourse of "new music" or "stile recitativo"—the musical language I called "operatic vocality" earlier, in which operatic characters speak, a vocality that Francesca's father, Giulio Caccini, claimed to have helped invent, and to which he trained her from earliest childhood. This kind of singing, I argue, performed *as* song and *in* song (in the process of singing) some salient aspects of the power dynamics between sovereign and subject that were crucial to consolidating the absolutist rule of Caccini's employers, the Medici in Florence. This "new music" performed a pattern of subjecting power so threatening to its Florentine audiences as to require the most emotionally powerful performances to be ones that would seem to emanate from a female body. Later in the seventeenth century, it became common for the rhetorically and emotionally powerful voice to emerge from a symbolically abject female body, a representation that would have the oddly prurient appeal we still experience, in "high" Eurocentric culture, from the singing female body of the diva. My purpose here is to sketch the outlines of these arguments, moving from some specifics of Francesca's early training as a singer of her father's "new music" to the more general implications of the circumstances that made her a "natural"—a "natural" singer of both subjection and sovereignty in the most intimate circles of the Medici court.

To talk about *voice*, especially in a feminist context, is to enter territory at once theoretically rich, vexingly complex, and, from the point of view of people who sing, oddly disembodied. I will therefore use an alternative word for the matter-of-fact, real-world, fully embodied sounds produced from the throats of human beings—*vocality*. By invoking the word *vocality* here, I mean to mark that section of my argument that focuses on the vocal sounds and techniques that the early *seicento*'s most influential singing teacher—Francesca's father, Giulio—would have taught her to be at the heart of vocal power.[9]

Access to voice, whether it be the physical voice I mean by "vocality" or the metaphorical voice we have come to attribute to authors, is always access to power. For Francesca Caccini her voice must have always seemed quite literally to be an instrument of power. As the child of singers salaried for the performance of vocal chamber music at the Medici court, singers who would never earn enough to set aside a dowry, she would have known from earliest childhood that her ability to find a place in the social order through marriage or convent placement would depend on her voice. It was to be by the work of her voice, entwined with the voices of stepmother, stepbrother, and sister in a family ensemble, that she was expected to earn her own dowry, while contributing to the broadly based musical work for which the Medici clearly meant to pay the Caccini household a family wage.[10]

However, in the household and the wider social world of Francesca's childhood, the equation of vocality with social power far exceeded the bounds of the personal. Descriptions of vocal power abound from the late sixteenth and early seventeenth centuries, power that is sometimes attributed to the sheer sound of voices, and sometimes—more importantly—attributed to the ways those sounding voices negotiated the relationship between the twin discourses a voice can produce—music and language.

At the turn of the seventeenth century, the power of an embodied voice produced by bodily practices was not understood as a matter of a forceful, overwhelming volume of sound. Rather, the vocal power that could "ravish the heart" (as the cliché usually went) was likely to be described as synthesizing qualities of flexibility, sensitivity to verbal and emotional expression, smoothness among registers, spectacularly rapid articulations of sound controlled by tiny unseen muscles in the throat, and, most important of all, breath control.[11] Three of these qualities were especially important to singing the "new music" Francesca's father advocated. Crucial to the emergence of her subjectivity as a singer, they are, as well, central to the vocality through which representations of women would be constructed in opera. These qualities are register, breath control, and so-called throat articulation.[12]

Like all children, the young Francesca grew up singing in a high voice. In terms of the norms of her time, she would have been able as a child to sing all the pitches normally considered part of the soprano range. But because Francesca knew she would always sing in that register as the register commonly assigned to adult women, she would have absorbed into her sense of self an understanding of her voice (source of her social, economic, and familial power) as naturally and inevitably "soprano," probably assimilating as well the common associations writers about singing made with such voices.

According to the Neapolitan physician and amateur singer Giovanni Camillo Maffei,[13] anyone could sing in the soprano range by forcing exhaled air as fast as possible through the larynx. The greater the air speed, the higher the sound. From such an understanding of the physical facts of voice production, Maffei and other early modern theorists of the voice inferred that high voices were produced by an excess of "anima." Maffei further inferred that high singing was particularly appropriate when a speaker wanted "to persuade and move others by his speech."[14] Thus to Maffei the soprano voice was the very sound of eloquence, of rhetorical power. A generation later, Giulio Caccini's mentor Giovanni Bardi (and his mentor Girolamo Mei) would agree that high voices were especially suitable for the expression of *concitato* or excitable affects, and for lamentations.[15] They based their belief on a premise they shared with Maffei, that high voices were the inevitable result of an unusually forceful release of the anima. Their contemporary, music theorist and teacher Gioseffo Zarlino, agreed, likening the soprano part of polyphony to the element of fire: because of the heat generated by fast vibrations the soprano voice was a voice that, like fire, should be considered by composers of polyphony as the part that generated and nourished the whole, providing the greatest satisfaction to the souls of listeners.[16]

Understood as produced by the release of the singer's anima with extraordinary force, compellingly persuasive, as nourishing to a listener's soul as fire, the soprano voice must have been heard by early modern Italians as a voice of nearly irresistible, dominating power. It is little wonder, then, that the word *soprano* could be used as a punning substitute for the word *sovrano* ("sovereign").[17] Yet, the soprano/sovrano voice was not particularly understood as a property of women's voices. Rather, the soprano voice as Maffei, Bardi, and Zarlino described it was understood as simply one of the voices commonly produced by the bodies of adult men using the technique we (and they) call "falsetto." However, for the young Francesca it is likely to have seemed connected to her sense of herself: she would have known early that her entire vocal life would be spent in an affective realm of high energy, high heat, intensely released feeling, and heightened rhetorical power.[18] As it happens, an ideal of "natural" rather than falsetto voices was central to both the aesthetic and the technique of singing that Francesca's father Giulio promoted at the turn of the seventeenth century. Indeed, Giulio Caccini was one of the most forceful opponents of falsetto singing, which he declared antithetical to the goals of his new music on the grounds that it detracted from the expressive power available to a singer with excellent breath control.[19]

Breath control is, of course, central to all singing techniques. It is always a controlling intervention of the conscious mind over one of the body's most crucial, life-sustaining, supposedly involuntary functions. In other words, the breath control required by any singing technique performs the singer's mind as in control of the singer's body. Giulio Caccini's particular ideas about breath control focused on the speed and volume with which a singer released air through the vocal folds, thus controlling to a level of exquisite nuance the louds and softs of singing—what musicians nowadays call dynamics.[20] Good singing—which for Caccini was expressive singing—required a nearly constant ebb and flow of breath to create the sound shapes of impassioned speech. Obviously, a falsettist could not have so flexible an airstream, because the very production of his soprano sound required a steady, high-speed forcing of air through the larynx. Thus, the emotional fluidity and responsiveness performed on (and by) the singer's constantly changing, constantly controlled breath was a performance best done by bodies that produced their voices "naturally." If the general affective world to be invoked was one of high emotional or rhetorical intensity—the soprano's affective world—the "natural" bodies required would have to be those of children, castrati, or women.

These singers—children, castrati, or women—would sing in a way that required almost constant motion of their diaphragms, the muscle that, by changing the relative volume of chest and abdomen in the torso, controls the movement of air into and out of the body. In the terms of sixteenth-century physician Francesco Sansovino, their constant changing of the proportion between chest and abdomen would have changed the proportion, within their bodies, of their "nobile" (rational or human) and "ignobile" (sensual or bestial) parts.[21] Constantly negotiating, then, between the two sides of human nature with an athleticism entirely concealed from a listener's view, the Caccinian singer's breath control produced an audible image of fluid, passionate feeling from her unseen, constantly shifting resolutions of the relationship between reason and sensuality within her body, her constantly shifting rearticulations of intrasubjective order.

Emerging as a seemingly fluid stream of sound from a singer's throat, these constant rearticulations of intrasubjective order between reason and sense were typically articulated again in the throat itself. The third crucial element of Caccini's singing technique was so-called *gorgheggiando* or "singing in the throat," a way of starting and stopping vocal sound by the split-second, infinitesimal opening and closing of the vocal chords as an airstream of whatever speed and pressure came through. Listeners' perceptions that a virtuosic singer exercised exquisite control over the emergence of breath from her body were, then, reinforced by this second level of subtle, last-minute control over the breath's release, articulating the boundary of the body as the resistance of the vocal chords' flesh to the exit of the body's anima.[22] As was the case with the diaphragmatic control that created the new singing's dynamic shading, the physical work required by "singing in the throat" was hidden from view.

The hidden physical prowess she exercised would surely have given Francesca a sense of her own body's power. This power was not intrinsically gendered, yet its implications would have inevitably been filtered through the prism of gender norms. Like any practitioner of an art whose instruments of power are concealed, Francesca probably took pride in her control over effects that could seem mysterious, even magical, to listeners. However, whereas a man in her position might have experienced his hidden artifice as analogous to that of a masterly politician, a woman would be likely, as well, to experience the concealing of her body's artifice and prowess as analogous to that body's modest veiling. Thus the invisibility of her body's prowess might have seemed to her (and to her listeners) like a way of symbolically preserving that all-important sign of female respectability, the appearance of chastity. Yet, her body's prowess, in itself, might also have been perceived as something like sexual agency.

All three qualities that characterized her emerging vocality—a high register, absolute control of the intensity of the breath, and control of the throat's opening—would also have been understood to affect her body's intrinsic heat. As Thomas Laqueur has argued, in pre-Enlightenment Europe a body's heat was understood to determine both its sex and its level of sexual arousal.[23] We have already seen that the soprano voice was associated with fire, and with the generating, productive power of fire's heat, because it was known to be produced by extremely rapid vibrations in the throat. In other words, Francesca's voice poured out from her body as heat, filling her throat with heat. As Bonnie Gordon pointed out in a recent conference paper, ancient medical writers likened a woman's throat to her uterus. Hippocrates, for example, argued that sexual intercourse was likely to lower a woman's voice because her upper throat would "respond in sympathy to the stretching of her lower neck."[24] Even more specifically, Galen likened the passing of air through the throat to the passing of blood through the womb. Neither of these views was, as far as I have been able to discover, challenged by the discoveries of such sixteenth-century physicians as Giovanni Falloppio and Renaldo Columbo.[25] Indeed, Columbo's "discovery" of the clitoris's function in female sexual pleasure only adds to the titillating possibilities of the throat-womb connection, for the clitoris had previously been likened to the uvula on the grounds that both flaps of flesh helped control the heat of the "neck" to which they provided entry. The heat-filled throat of a soprano singer, then, might quite logically have been understood as a space at least metaphorically linked to sexual arousal.

If the heat of her throat was an inevitable, "natural" product of a woman singer's body, the rapid, controlled articulation of the vocal folds with which she sang ornaments and trills surely added to that heat. Indeed, Sansovino argued that the voices most suited to highly flexible, ornamented singing came from the throats of bodies that were "naturally" cold and wet. In a very different part of his text, he points out that the women and "eunuchi" have cool, moist bodies—the bodies most able to tolerate a buildup of heat.[26] Thus, ornamented singing articulated in a soprano's throat added to the danger that the throat was sexually aroused—and that its state of arousal could be controlled by the singer.[27] This danger was presumably not an issue for castrati, but it surely was for sopranos who were women.

One way of controlling the heat in the throat further was to control the breath. In the most common view of early modern medicine, the very purpose of the breath was to control the body's heat: air intake was understood to cool the body, while exhalation released the hot, noxious fumes produced by the heart, the body's furnace.[28] The heat of the body, in turn, was understood as having a causal relationship to both biological sex and sexual desire. Hot bodies were manly ones, and efficient burners of the body's fuel. Cold bodies—bodies Sansovino described as lacking the heat-producing testicles—were inefficient burners of fuel that excreted uncombusted resources through the release of such fluids as menstrual blood. Heated bodies were more likely to experience sexual arousal and, in the right circumstances, to release seed for reproduction orgasmically. Women who sang or danced professionally had been understood since ancient times to experience menstrual dysfunction, because the physical exertion heated their bodies and made them more efficient, lessening their flow.[29] Thus, the power of the new vocality that so controlled the breath's release, and so controlled a woman's heated throat, was inevitably also the power to articulate *as* sound a highly flexible control over both her humoral femaleness and her sexual readiness. Vocality, that is, understood as the embodied practice of singing, would have been comprehensible as implying both a degree of female control over the physical sex of her body (and thus her relationship to the hierarchies of gender) and the kind of power—the terrifying power—we now call female sexual agency. Yet, in the aesthetic regime of the "new music," a singer's personally empowering, intra-subjective performance of the relationship of sense to reason, simultaneous with her performance of the capacity for sexual self-control, was always performed at the service of a poet's words.

The purpose of both the breath control and the throat articulations that were so much easier for a "natural" singer to perform was the faithful rendering in a "singing without song" of what Francesca's father's friends and mentors had consistently referred to as the meaning of the poem.[30] Most often expressed in writing laden with metaphors that evoked such common hierarchical relationships as those of master to servant, father to child, teacher to pupil, mind to body, the governing rule of operatic vocality was the power of the word or idea over music's physical sounds.[31] Put another way, operatic vocality was a regime in which the word was to its musical shape and sounding performance as a master was to his servant, a father to his child, a teacher to his pupil, the mind to the body. A song's words and their musical shapes met first in the imagining mind of a singer, and they then emerged as one from the singer's performing body. Every action of the singer's performing body—the production of vocal sound itself, the subtle shaping of the sound's intensity through the diaphragm's constant motion, the tasteful choice of passagework to be articulated in the throat—was ideally performed in obedience to the power inherent in a song's words. Every gesture was to be a somatically articulated expression of actual words, their meanings, and the affect that surrounded and gave rise to them. Thus every gesture of the singer's body ideally performed obedience to the absolute power of the word. At the turn of the *sei-*

cento these words were almost invariably not those of the singer, for few singers were also poets. The logic of the new music's aesthetic metaphors, then, implied that both the singer and her voice could simultaneously symbolize the intrasubjective power hierarchy that characterized a well-ordered person (reason/sense, mind/body), and the power hierarchy that characterized a well-ordered social unit (father/children, master/servant, teacher/pupil), and the power hierarchy of a well-ordered state. The order was always to be wrought by the virtuosic body's obedience to an external, rational word. For the young Francesca, who was simultaneously pupil, child, and servant until her father's de facto retirement in 1611, the metaphors she performed must have vividly reinforced her experience of subjection within these multiple social hierarchies. Yet, because her performing body could also have been understood to embody (as voice) the well-ordered state, and to produce "naturally" the very voice of eloquence, she could also have experienced herself as able to perform as voice the power of her sovereign.

There is ample reason to suppose that Giulio Caccini's "new music," as a kind of singing, was understood by its aesthetic advocates to have been very much a discourse of power—and not only, not even primarily, the intrasubjective negotiation of power hierarchies that took place within the singer's performing body. Indeed, the single most common trope through which Vincenzo Galilei, Girolamo Mei, Giovanni Bardi, and Caccini himself either praised music or disdained it is a trope of power. Good singing, for all these men, would be like the singing of the "ancients" in its rhetorical and expressive power over those who heard it. Because the aesthetic imperative for rhetorical power automatically valorized the intrinsic qualities of the soprano voice, and because the techniques by which powerful expression was wrought worked better with "natural" soprano voices, the aesthetic of the "new music" automatically increased the cultural usefulness of female and castrato singers. In the view of the close-knit group of Florentines who theorized the new vocality, these singers would do their jobs well if their singing overwhelmed their listeners—pulling them off their affective foundations like so many workers successfully felling a column;[32] focusing their performance of passionate "singing without song" on a single affect so that a listener would be powerless to resist sharing the feeling (Galilei paraphrasing Mei, Bardi); mixing the elements of their art like the chemicals that cause a cannonball to explode in battle, forever changing the landscape around it.[33]

When we try to use their own metaphors to imagine the experience these men wanted a singer to create in her listeners, we begin to realize how closely the intended performance of power between singer and listener might have modeled the flow of power from sovereign to subject. If the singer was herself subject to an absent poet's word, her art was intended to give her the power

utterly to subject listeners who would be powerless before her. Understood by
the cognoscenti to embody and continually rearticulate the very models of
hierarchy on which (according to Aristotle's *Politics,* an amply quoted source
for these writers) the social order of an ideal state depends, the singer's
power—like her sovereign's—was not a power based on force, but on singular
self-discipline, subtlety, flexibility, and hermeneutical skill. Her bodily skills
served as the means by which she interpreted and communicated with overwhelming, *soprano* rhetorical power the ideas she understood to be important
in received texts.

The logic of the new vocality as a discourse of power would allow a singer
whose female body made the performance of symbolically sovereign power
"natural" to conceive herself as "naturally" capable of wielding sovereignlike
power over texts and audiences alike. She might imagine herself as primarily
gifted at the bodily skills required to produce subjecting performances; or she
might imagine herself as primarily gifted at the hermeneutic skills required to
produce such texts. That is, since all the women (and men) trained to produce
the new sovereign vocality were trained to sing, to improvise, and to compose
as part of their daily work, each of them fashioned a career that emphasized
their best skills at the performance of sovereign, subjecting power over their
listeners. Any of the women singers in Francesca's generation might have
seized the opportunity she evidently did—to emphasize in her self-fashioning
the mental skills we today associate with composition over the physical skills
we today associate with divalike performance; to emphasize, that is, her symbolic impersonation of her sovereign rather than her symbolic impersonation
of the process of subjection. Imagining herself as naturally able to embody the
subtle, disciplined, overwhelming rhetorical power of a sovereign, I think,
allowed Francesca Caccini to imagine herself as able to embody, with equal
naturalness, the sovereignlike power of a musical author.

Yet, it was the symbolic impersonation of the experience of subjection that
was to become the cultural work of the seventeenth century's most adored
singers, the women and men who created the subject position we still associate with the figure of the diva. How did spectacularized representations of subjection rather than sovereignty, subjection naturalized onto representations of
female bodies, come to be the norm—instead of a tradition of singing, composing, self-sovereign female bodies? How, that is, could the discourse that
allowed Francesca Caccini to think of herself as able to embody the musical
sovereignty of authorship have produced only one Francesca, and legions of
paradoxically subjecting and subjected divas?

To answer such a question would require more time and space than I have.
Let me, however, sketch the outlines of the answer. From the situation of her
original sovereign listener, the Grand Duke of Tuscany, a singer of the new

"operatic vocality" satisfyingly performs her subjection to multiple social hierarchies, and thus performs the well-ordered state under his command. However, from any other listener's situation—a courtier's or an honored visitor's, for example—the listener, too, is subjected. A listener at the Medici court might well have experienced discomfort at feeling himself or herself subjected and overwhelmed, but might have defended against that feeling by remembering that the subjecting, symbolically sovereign voice was actually produced by the body of a servant. Such a consoling memory would be both reinforced and complicated if the body from which the subjecting voice emerged was represented as that of a woman—particularly because of the way women were understood in relation to prevailing ideas of power and authority. On the one hand, women were naturally subject to men. On the other hand, when women seized power, they wielded it unnaturally, as tyrants—as early modern interpretations of the sorceresses Alcina and Armida suggested.[34]

The paradoxes of power intrinsic to the discourse of the new singing was to be a major theme of opera, which had originally been characterized by almost completely silent women. In the very earliest operas of the seventeenth century, representations of male heroic singers like Orpheus embodied the contradictory impulses toward self-sovereignty and subjection; the conflict was invariably resolved by their pious subordination to the higher authority of the gods. Yet, by 1625, in La Liberazione di Ruggiero dall'isola d'Alcina, Francesca Caccini and her librettists would project the contradictions onto two representations of women's bodies. Both characters were sorceresses, thus both represented women with mysterious, perhaps unnatural relationships to the wielding of power. The plot of La Liberazione turns on their struggle for power over the hapless knight Ruggiero: Alcina's tyrannical spell over the young man is broken by the more powerful magic of Melissa. Melissa's trumphant magic is represented vocally by a low register, the complete absence of throat-articulated ornaments, and an overwhelmingly word-dominated, non-virtuosic, subjected part. Hers is not a soprano/sovrano power, but a power explicitly derived from the institutions she serves, to which she recalls Ruggiero—the institutions of dynastic marriage and manly battlefield adventure. Yet even in defeat it is Alcina who remains in a listener's memory as the more musically interesting and memorable character, both because her vocality incorporates all the vocal symbols of soprano sovereignty, and because she refuses to perform her own subjection.

Exiled rather than contained (or killed) by devices of plot and musical repetition, Alcina differs sharply from most of her exoticized operatic descendants. Increasingly represented during the course of the seventeenth-century as Asian or African queens—Orontea, Astarte, Dido, Semiramide—these figures of female rhetorical prowess were presented to audiences as objects of admiration for their bodily virtuosity. Yet, as Susan McClary has pointed out, their musical utterances were almost always "framed" by arias in repetitive strophic patterns, particularly by the laments they beautifully sang in symbolic struggle against the constraints of an apparently gendered fate.[35] Memorable, beautiful, rhetorically powerful as these standard show-stopping laments in a soprano voice might have been, they helped associate painful gender subordination with voices that seemed to emanate "naturally" from women's bodies. These performances allowed audiences, especially men, simultaneously to identify with, to eroticize, and ultimately to disavow the experience of subjection itself, even as they associated its performed processes with intense aural and emotional pleasure.

The subject position of the diva was only one of several on a continuum of subject positions that could be occupied by practitioners of operatic vocality, whether they were women or men. As we have seen, a singer might equally well imagine herself, in her female body, as singing a kind of symbolic sovereign power. The latter possibility was most evident in opera's first generation, when the reciprocal relations of aesthetic, political, and bodily practices were still part of operatic vocality's common sense. I believe Francesca Caccini took advantage of the latter possibility to create for herself a career that was more composer than diva. Her younger sister Settimia, who engaged in exactly the same practices as Francesca, including what we now call composition, chose to center her career closer to the diva end of the continuum. One consequence of Settimia's choice was that she still sang publicly as an admired diva into her later forties, while Francesca had by then apparently retired wholly into the roles of composer, teacher, and coach.

Francesca's possibility, and her choice to center her career in a way that identifed her voice more with the sovereign than with the subject, did not serve the interests of the modern world's power structure (for it did not, as the diva position did, overdetermine the representation and performance of a subjected subject). I think it worked for her, as a choice within the paradox that was her discursive world, because she worked mainly for two women who served Florence as defacto (and de jure) regents from 1607 to 1628. Over these twenty years, the sovereignty that was musical authorship could serve as an image in microcosm of her patrons' political sovereignty; each kind of sovereignty reinforced the credibility of the other, and of the idea that sovereign power might emanate as naturally from women's bodies as from men's. Florentine disavowal of female political sovereignty after the accession of Grand Duke Ferdinand II (a self-proclaimed misogynist) was swift and thorough—and it required a parallel disavowal of female artistic sovereignty. Very quickly after 1628 the discursive possibility in operatic vocality that had enabled Francesca Caccini to have a composer's voice vanished, forcing the younger women she had trained in both singing and composition (among them her own daughter) to find spaces for power and vocality solely through negotiation with the discourse of the diva.

Notes

1. A version of this essay was presented at a colloquium for the Women's Studies Program at Colby College. I am grateful to Linda Austern, Bridget Kelly Black, Todd Borgerding, Cheshire Calhoun, Sally Sanford, Margaret McFadden, Pamela Thoma, Elizabeth Wood, and the editors of this volume for very helpful comments and criticisms of early drafts.

2. The best general introduction to Caccini's career is the entry in Julie Ann Sadie and Rhian Samuel, eds., *The Norton/Grove Dictionary of Women Composers* (London and New York: Norton, 1994).

3. I am here using the genre designation "opera" rather loosely, meaning to include such theatrical genres as *balli, balletti, tornei, mascherate,* and *favole,* in which dialogues and monologues were entirely sung in the new "stile recitativo." Ellen Rosand's *Opera in Seventeenth Century Venice: the Creation of a Genre* (Berkeley: University of California Press, 1991) argues persuasively that "opera" did not really exist as a recognizable genre until its systematic presentation in the public theatres of Venice after 1637.

4. Lorenzo Parigi, *Il Parigi: dialogo terzo, ove d'alcune cose di medicina si discorre* (Florence: Zanobi Pignoni, 1618), 19: ". . . é rinato il signor Giulio ancor vivendo nella Sig. Francesca sua figliuola. . . ." (Signor Giulio is reborn, even while he is still alive, in his daughter Signora Francesca).

5. "Concerto delle donne" was the generic term for a vocal ensemble featuring women's voices; such ensembles were a fad of North Italian courtly life from about 1580 to about 1630. The most authoritative study of the phenomenon remains Anthony Newcomb's *The Madrigal at Ferrara, 1579–1597,* 2 vols. (Princeton: Princeton University Press, 1979). See also his essay "Courtesans, Muses or Musicians? Professional Women Musicians in Sixteenth-Century Italy" in *Women Making Music: The Western Art Tradition, 1150–1950,* ed. Jane Bowers and Judith Tick, (Urbana: University of Illinois Press, 1986), 90–115. For specific details about the *concerto delle donne* at Florence in the late sixteenth century, see Tim Carter, *Jacopo Peri, 1561–1633, His Life and Works* (New York: Garland, 1989), 23–24. On Giulio Caccini's relationship to the Florentine concerto in its various incarnations, the best published source is the entry on Caccini in Warren Kirkendale, *The Court Musicians in Florence during the Principate of the Medici* (Florence: Leo Olschki, 1993), 119–180. Both the official court diary kept by Cesare Tinghi and various unpublished letters of Giulio Caccini to the Tuscan Grand Duchess Cristina make it clear that in the first decade of the seventeenth century the Caccini family itself performed as a de facto *concerto delle donne.* Described by Tinghi as "le donne di Giulio romano," the Caccini family ensemble broke up in 1611 when Francesca's sister Settimia was abducted by her in-laws and held hostage for nonpayment of her dowry. Gradually, the ensemble's standing gigs in court life were taken by an ensemble Tinghi described with the phrase "la Sig.ra Francesca e le sue fanciulle." Tinghi's manuscript diary is in the Biblioteca nazionale centrale in Florence, Ms Gino Capponi 261, vols. 1 and 2; substantial excerpts of his descriptions

of music and theatre can be found in Angelo Solerti, *Musica, ballo e drammatica alla corte medicea dal 1600 al 1637* (Florence: Bemporad, 1905). As early as 1609, part of Francesca's salary had been paid for teaching young female singers. A letter of hers dated 25 March 1619 vividly describes her work composing new music for these girls, in addition to her teaching and coaching duties. I am grateful to Kelley Harness for drawing this letter to my attention. It is in the Archivio di Stato di Firenze, Mediceo del Principato 1426, fol. 42.

6. Francesca had been assigned teaching duties within the *famiglia* even before she was a full-fledged salaried employee of the court. As a seventeen-year-old in 1605, for example, she was with the Este family in Modena from July to November to teach princess Giulia d'Este singing "in the French style" (ASF, Mediceo del Principato 4860, letter of 25 June 1605 and Mediceo del Principato 5990, letter of 18 November 1605). Payroll records for the Medici court as well as a variety of letters indicate that Francesca taught Emilia de' Grazii, Maria Botti, Caterina di Domenico Avanzilla and Lucretia di Batta, all children of Medici servants who were being trained at court expense; see, for example, ASF, Depositeria generale antico 389, n. 1099. In addition, she was paid by a Medici nephew, Don Virginio Orsini, to teach music to his natural daughter, the nun Maria Vittoria Frescobaldi in the convent of Santa Verdiana. Their letters about Frescobaldi's lessons are in the Archivio storico capitolino in Rome, Fondo Orsini, Prima Serie, vol. 121/1, n. 90, 5 March 1611; vol. 124/2, n. 233, 4 May 1613; vol. 126/1, n. 67, 26 December 1614. Although there is no direct evidence that Francesca taught the royal children, the indirect evidence is highly suggestive. In 1637 Prince Leopold had her harpsichord in his apartments, according to her letter to Buonarroti of 10 July 1637, Casa Buonarroti, A.B. 52, n. 1547. In the 1630s she was listed as a *musica* on the payroll of the adolescent Grand Duchess Vittoria della Rovere, when the girl was known to be studying music (ASF, Depositera Generale Antico 561, opening 36; and Depositeria Generale Antico 1034, n. 182 and 210).

7. Several of Francesca's surviving letters allude to her work as a performance coach. See, for example, her letters of 18 December and 27 December 1614 to Michelangelo Buonarroti, about rehearsals involving both her own pupils and an otherwise unidentified lady-in-waiting called "Sig.ra Giralda"; these letters are in the Casa Buonarroti in Florence, A.B. 44 numbers 441 and 442. Her letter of 25 March 1619 to Andrea Cioli, cited above, describes the work of coaching her pupils for both chamber and church performances (ASF, Mediceo del Principato 1426, fol. 42). Kelley Harness has discovered a remarkably vivid set of letters from the autumn of 1624 that describe rehearsals for the winter 1625 Carnival entertainments at Florence; Francesca's role in these rehearsals is the central point of conflict outlined in the letters by Florence's *corago*, or steward for entertainments, Ferdinando Saracinelli, to Tuscan Regent Archduchess Maria Maddalena. His letters are in ASF, Mediceo del Principato 111, fols. 180–82ᵛ and Mediceo del Principato 1703, (without folio numbers) 18 November to 2 December 1624. All are reprinted with English translations in Kelley Harness, "*Amazzoni di Dio:* Florentine Musical Spectacle Under Maria Maddalena d'Austria and Cristina di Lorena (1620–1630), (Ph.D. diss., University of Illinois, 1996), 374–386. On Francesca's continuing work as a coach in the 1630s, see letters from dowager Grand Duchess Cristina di Lorena's personal secretary Ugo Caciotti to Michelangelo Buonarroti, Casa Buonarroti, A.B. 44, numbers 460–65 (4 to 12 February 1635).

8. The most up-to-date work list is in Julie Anne Sadie and Rhian Samuel, ed., *The Norton/Grove Dictionary of Women Composers* (New York: W. W. Norton, 1995).

9. I was partly moved to adopt this term by the collection of essays edited by Leslie C. Dunn and Nancy A. Jones, *Embodied Voices: Representing Female Vocality in Western Culture* (Cambridge: Cambridge University Press, 1994).

10. I develop this narrative of the Caccini family's economic circumstances, and their relation to Giulio's creation of a family ensemble, in the first chapter of my book on Francesca Caccini, *A Romanesca of One's Own* (Chicago: University of Chicago Press, forthcoming). Bits of the story can be inferred from the entries on various Caccini family members in Warren Kirkendale's encyclopedic *The Court Musicians in Florence during the Principate of the Medici* (Florence: Olschki, 1993). The centrality of the family ensemble to Giulio's ongoing employment is made absolutely clear in a number of his still-unpublished letters to the Medici Grand Duchess Christine de Lorraine; see, for example, ASF, Mediceo del Principato 5992, fol. 359, letter of 5 March 1607.

11. For summaries of recent research on Italian ideas of vocal beauty at the turn of the seventeenth century, see Nella Anfuso, " La vocalità al tempo di Claudio Monteverdi," in " . . . Monteverdi al quale ognuno deve cedere . . ." *Teorie e composizioni musicali, rappresentazioni e spettacoli dal 1550 al 1628: Celebrazioni per il 350o anniversario della morte di Claudio Monteverdi* (Fidenza, 1993), 21–36; Sally Sanford, "Seventeenth- and Eighteenth-Century Vocal Style and Technique" (D.M.A. diss., Stanford University, 1979); Sanford, "A Comparison of French and Italian Singing in the Seventeenth Century," *Journal of Seventeenth-Century Music* 1/1 (1995), http://www.sscm.harvard.edu/jscm; and her essay "Solo singing 1" in *A Performers' Guide to Seventeenth-Century Music*, ed. Stewart A. Carter (New York: Schirmer, 1997); and Julianne Baird, "Beyond the Beautiful Pearl," in *Inside Early Music: Conversations with Performers*, ed. Bernard D. Sherman (Oxford and New York: Oxford University Press, 1997), 225–42.

12. By "register" I mean the part of the pitch spectrum a voice will typically encompass; for example, the "tenor" register typically encompasses pitches from the C below "middle C" to the C above. Any person or instrument capable of producing pitches in that part of the pitch spectrum thus would occupy the tenor register. The voice or instrument might be equally able to produce pitches in other registers; for example, cellos often play in the "tenor" register, although we casually think of them as "bass" instruments because they can produce pitches that are so much lower. (For other musical definitions of the word "register," see Don M. Randel, ed., *The New Harvard Dictionary of Music* (Cambridge: Harvard University Press, 1986).

13. *Delle Lettere del S.r Gio. Camillo Maffei da Solofra. Libri Due. Dove tra gli altri bellissimi pensieri di Filosofia, e di Medicina, v'è un discorsoe della Voce e delo Modo d'apparer di cantar di Garganta, senza maestro, non più veduto, n'istampato. Raccolot per Don Valerio de Paoli da Limosano.* (Naples: Raymundo Amato, 1562). There are three extant copies of this volume: at the Bibliothèque nationale, and the Bibliothèque du Conservatoire in Paris, and the Civio Museo in Bologna. A complete modern edition of the text, including music examples drawn from the Paris copies, was published with a brief introductory essay by Nanie Bridgman, "Giovanni Camillo Maffei et sa letter sur le chant," *Revue de musicologie* 38 (1956): 3–25.

14. Writing about falsetto production of the soprano voice, Maffei says, "E questo modo di fingere la voce fu solo à l'uomo conceduto, massimamente quando egli ragionando desidera persuadere, e movere, et isprimere il voler suo" (And falsetto singing is a gift only of the human being, especially when in speech he desired to persuade, or move, or express his will). Although Maffei seems to mean "male human being" most of the time when he uses the generic "l'uomo," in this particular passage he probably means "human being," as the previous few sentences had discussed the voices of cows. See Bridgman, 17.

15. In his well-known letter to Vincenzo Galilei dated 8 May 1572, I-Rvat, Regina latinus 2021, fols. 16ʳ–16ᵛ, humanist scholar Girolamo Mei wrote of high voices, ". . . e

i troppo acuti sono da animo [16ᵛ] troppo commosso sollevato: e i troppo gravi, da pensieri e abbietto e rimesso. . . ." (The very high are signs of a very excited and uplifted
spirit, and the very low of abject and humble thoughts). A critical edition of the letter
appears in Claude Palisca, *Girolamo Mei (1519–94). Letters on Ancient and Modern
Music to Vincenzo Galilei and Giovanni Bardi* (n.p.: American Institute of Musicology,
1977), 89–122. The translation cited is from Claude Palisca, "The Letter of 8 May 1572
from Girolamo Mei," in *The Florentine Camerata: Documentary Studies and
Translations* (New Haven: Yale University Press, 1989), 58. In his letter to Giulio
Caccini headed "Discorso sopra la musica anticha e'l cantar bene," Giovanni Bardi
wrote: " . . . Hora chi non sa che gl'Hebbri, ei sonnoloneti parlano per lo più in tuono
grave, e tardo, et che gl'huomini di grand'affare in voce mezana, magnifica, et quieta
ragionano, et che quelli che da ira, o, da grand duolo soprapesi sono in voce alta, e conci-
tata favellano. . . . " ("Now who does not know that the inebriated and drowsy speak
mostly in a low and slow tone; that men of big business converse in a median, magnif-
icent, and calm voice; and that those who are burdened by anger or great grief speak in
a high and excited voice?"). Both the Italian text and the English translation are from
Palisca, *Camerata*, 108–9.

16. Gioseffo Zarlino, *Le Istitutione harmoniche* (Venice, 1558), Part III, Cap. 58, p.
281: "nel luogo supremo della cantilena . . . alcuni etiandio la chiamano Soprano, . . . la
parte più acuta d'ogn'altra assimmigliare al Fuoco: ciò feci percioche havendo li Suoni
acuti, che nascono da i movmementi veloci & spessi, tal natura, che per la loro subita, &
veloce percussione si fanno udirere, rappresentandosi all'Udito con prestezza, ven-
gono a ritenere in loro quasi la natura del Fuoco; il quale, non solo è acuto, & raro; ma
etiando veloce, & attivo per se stesso. . . . ritrovaremo che'l Soprano: come quello, che
è più acuto d'ogn'altra parte, & più penetrativo all'Udito, farsi udire anco prima
d'ogn'altra: la onde si come'l Fuoco nutrisce, & è cagione di far produrre ogni cosa nat-
urale, che si trova ad ornamento, et a conservatione del Mondo; cosi il Compositore si
sforzarà di fare, che la parte più acuta del la sua cantilena habbia bello, ornato, et ele-
gante procedere di maniera che nutrisca, & e pasci l'animo di quelli, che ascoltano" (. . .
the highest position of the song . . . being called by some the Soprano . . . the part
higher than every other resembles Fire: this is said to be because high sounds, which
are born of rapid and frequent motion, having the quality of making themselves heard
by rapid vibrations, present themselves to the hearing with such speed that they take
on almost the nature of fire; this part is not only high and rare, but being rapid and
active in itself. . . . we find that the soprano, as the one that is higher than every other
part, and more penetrating to the hearing, makes itself heard first: thus as fire nourishes, and is the producing cause of every natural thing, that adorns and preserves the
world; thus the composer will ensure that the highest part of his song have a beautiful,
decorated, and elegant flow such that it should nourish and refresh the soul of those
who hear it). (Translation mine.)

17. See, for example, Claudio Monteverdi's 1605 dedication of his fifth book of
madrigals to Vincenzo Gonzaga, Duke of Mantua and Monteverdi's employer at the
time. Writing through the expected courtly trope that contrasts the insignificance of a
gift to the magnificence of its recipient, Monteverdi wittily elided that contrast with
several others: the contrast between his gift and his intention, between the lowly and
sovereign in the social world, and between bass and soprano in the musical one, asking
that the duke accept these contrasts as all constituting a kind of harmony: "Sò che alla
grandezza de merti suoi picciol'è il dono; pur non risguardi al dono; ma all'affetto con
che dono, che s'uno è picciolo l'altro è grande, anzi stenda l'orecchio della benignità sua,
che dalla picciolezza dell'uno, et dalla grandezza dell'altro sentirà un'armonia di Basso,

e di Sovrano, che à gara cantano gli honori, et le sue glorie cui l'eternezza bramo. . . ."
(I know that the gift is small compared to the scope of your merit; so do not look at the
gift; but at the feeling of him who gives it, so that if one is small and the other great,
lend your benevolent ear to it, so that from the smallness of the one and the greatness
of the other you will hear a harmony of bass and sovereign [soprano]). For the full text
of Monteverdi's dedication, see Claudio Monteverdi, *Lettere, dediche e prefazioni: edi-
zione critica con note a cura di Domenico de'Paoli* (Rome: de Sanctis, 1973), 391.

18. Even in the absence of cultural imperatives associating the soprano register
inevitably with female bodies, Francesca might have made the association. Because
Giulio Caccini is not known ever to have included male falsettists or castrati in the
ensembles he coached, as a girl Francesca would have experienced the soprano voice as
emerging from the bodies of women—first her *virtuosa* mother Lucia Gagnolanti
before she died in 1593, and then her *virtuosa* stepmother Margherita della Scala, who
had joined the household by 1595. Thus Francesca's identification of herself as a person with a body potentially like her mother's—her sense of herself, in our terms, as a
gendered and sexed being—may well have been bound up with her identification of
herself as a person whose voice naturally occupied a sonic space of emotional intensity
and superior rhetorical power.

19. In the preface to his landmark pedagogical collection of songs in the new style,
Le nuove musiche (Florence, 1602), Caccini wrote thus about falsetto singing and
breath control: " . . . To sing falsetto or at least forced tones, it is necessary to use the
breath in order not to expose them much (since they typically offend the ear). And one
needs breath in order to give greater animation to the increasing and diminishing of
the voice, . . . and to all the other effects we have demonstrated . . . The nobility of good
singing . . . cannot come from falsetto; rather it will arise from a natural voice comfortable on all tones, . . . without relying on the breath for anything other than showing himself to be master of all the best expressive means that are required in this very
noble style of singing. . . ." The translation cited is by Margaret Murata, from *Strunk's
Source Readings in Music History. The Baroque Era. rev. ed.* (New York: Norton, 1998),
108–109. Caccini, preface to *Le nuove musiche,* original Italian, my translation.

20. Sally Sanford, "Comparison," 212.

21. Francesco Sansovino, *L'Edifico del corpo humano nel quale brevemente si
descrivono le qualità del corpo del huomo e le potentie dell'anima* (Venice: Comin da
Trino Monferrato, 1550), vol. 2, fol. 24ʳ, lists as the diaphragm's two functions that "si
divide la parte più nobile di sopra dalla ignobile di sotto" (it separates the more noble
part above from the ignoble below) and that "muove . . . il pulomone accioche egli
attragge e mandi fuor l'aria" (it moves the lungs so that they attract and expel air).

22. From a singer's point of view, this technique *feels* like controlling exactly that—
the vocal folds' resistance in relation to the pressure of exiting air, something that again
requires the flexibility of the airstream only available to "natural" voices.

23. Thomas Laqueur, *Making Sex: Body and Gender from the Greeks to Freud*
(Cambridge: Harvard University Press, 1990).

24. Bonnie Gordon, "'Enemies of Love': Staging Female Excess in Monteverdi's *Il
ballo delle ingrate,*" (paper presented at the 16th International Congress of the
International Musicological Society, London, August 1997), 7.

25. Gabriele Falloppio, *Observationes anatomicae* (Venice: Marcum Antonium
Ulman, 1562); and Reynaldo Columbo, *De re anatomica* (Paris: A. Wechelum, 1572).

26. Sansovino, *L'Edificio . . . ,* vol. 1 (unpaginated), discussing "la voce," claims that
the most flexible voices are produced by humid bodies ("la voce più molle è prodotta
dalla humidità. . . ."). In vol 2. fol. 46ᵛ, in a discussion of white hair and baldness, he

notes that neither women nor castrati go bald, women because their natural humidity keeps their skin moist, and castrati because the absence of testicles keeps them from producing enough heat to dry their skin ("dicemmo . . . che le femine non mai si fan calve, e gli eunuchi; perche quelle come humide danno nutrimento a peli, e questi per mancar di testicoli i quali cagionano in tutte le membre calore.") Women's "natural" humidity, too, resulted from too little heat.

27. It is important to remember Sansovino's point that cold, wet throats produce the most flexible voices.

28. This discussion is based primarily on Laqueur, *Making Sex*, ch. 2.

29. Laqueur, *Making Sex*, 36.

30. See, for example, Caccini's preface to *Le nuove musiche*, as translated in Murata, *Strunk's Source Readings*, 100: " . . . these discerning gentlemen always encouraged me and convinced me with the clearest arguments not to value that kind of music which does not allow the words to be understood well and which spoils the meaning and the poetic meter. . . ."

31. The classic Florentine formulation of this aesthetic can be found in Giovanni Bardi's "Discorso" as translated in Palisca, *Camerata*, 115: " . . . tenendo per costante che così come l'anima del corpo è più nobile, altresì le parole più nobile del contrapunto sono, e come il corpo dall'anima regolato essere debbe, così il contrapunto dalle parole dee prender norma: Hor non vi parebbe egli cosa ridicola s'andando in piazza vedeste'l servo del suo Signore esser eguito, e ad esso commandare: o fanciullo che al Padre, o, pedagogo suo ammaestramento dar volesse?" (. . . just as the soul is nobler than the body, so the text is nobler than the counterpoint, and just as the mind should rule the body, so the counterpoint should receive its rule from the text. Would it not seem to you comical if, while in the square, you saw a servant followed by and commanding his master, or a child giving instruction to his parent or teacher?)

32. Girolamo Mei to Vincenzo Galilei, 8 May 1572, as translated in Palisca, *Camerata*, 61–62.

33. Giovanni Bardi, "Discorso," as translated in Palisca, *Camerata*, 109.

34. For example, see Simone Fornari, *Della espositione sopra l'Orlando furioso* (Florence: n.p., 1549), 2: 34, who sees Alcina as an allegory of ambition and the desire to dominate people and territory.

35. Susan McClary, "Excess and Frame: The Musical Representation of Madwomen," in *Feminine Endings: Gender, Sexuality and Music* (Minneapolis: University of Minnesota Press, 1991), 53–79. See also Wendy B. Heller, "Chastity, Heroism, and Allure: Women in the Opera of Seventeenth-Century Venice" (Ph.D. diss., Brandeis University, 1995). For a very different, transhistorical approach to thinking about the cultural work of divas, see Susan J. Leonardi and Rebecca A. Pope, *The Diva's Mouth: Body, Voice and Prima Donna Politics* (New Brunswick, N.J.: Rutgers University Press, 1996).

Workshop Summaries 1–12: The Body and the Self

Workshop # 1: "Bodies of Light, Bodies of Matter"

Organizers

Louise Schleiner, English, Washington State University; Mary Ellen Lamb, English, Southern Illinois University; Mary Moore, English, Marshall University

Readings

Aristotle, *De Anima*, in *The Basic Works of Aristotle*, ed. Richard McKeon (New York: Random House, 1941); Louise Schleiner, *Tudor and Stuart Women Writers* (Indianapolis and Bloomington: University of Indiana Press, 1996); Philip Sidney, *Sidney's New Arcadia*, ed. Victor Skretknowicz (Oxford: Clarendon Press, 1987); Gaspara Stampa, *Gaspara Stampa, Selected Poems*. ed. and trans. Laura Anna Stortoni and Mary Prentice Lillie (New York: Italica Press, 1994); Gaspara Stampa, *Rime*, ed. Abelkader Salza (Bari: Laterze & Figli, 1913); Lady Mary Wroth, *The Countesse of Mountgomerie's Urania*, ed. Josephine A. Roberts (Binghamton, N.Y.: Medieval and Renaissance Texts & Studies, 1995).

The participants investigated three early modern women authors whose work raises issues about textual and physical bodies. Mary Ellen Lamb's presentation questioned the relationships between linguistic structures and biology in Lady Mary Wroth's use of deliberately long sentences in the two parts of her prose romance, *The Countesse of Mountgomerie's Urania* (1621). Lamb compared Wroth's sentences to similarly lengthy sentences in her uncle's *Countess of Pembroke's Arcadia*, especially focusing on the way both manuscripts end in mid-sentence. In small groups, participants discussed several sample passages, considering the sentences as structures and interpreting differences. Participants decided that Sidney structured his sentences along lines of parallelism, antithesis, and subordination, whereas Wroth built often open-ended sentences, loosely connected by coordinate and participial phrases and replete with ambiguously referenced noun clauses. Sidney's sentences were characterized as displays of logic, and Wroth's as digressive; one participant described Wroth's sentences as leading into and then out of a center, as if weaving and unravelling.

Mary Moore then asked participant groups to consider metaphors about materiality and epistemology in two poems from Gaspara Stampa's 1554 *Rime*. Moore suggested that Stampa's metaphors be considered in light of Aristotelian and Neoplatonic constructions of the female as materiality, rather than soul, and as chaos, rather than form. Agreeing that Stampa alludes to *De Anima* or to metaphors of wax impression derived from it, and noting allusions to Neoplatonic imagery of eyes as stars, the workshop concluded that Stampa is ingeniously complex, and that her complexity and allusion to philosophical contexts helps her female speaker claim intellectual and poetic power.

Louise Schleiner's handouts introduced Elizabeth Weston (1581–1612), an Englishwoman in Prague, herself a crosser of linguistic and national boundaries, whose poetry foregrounds the permeability of mind and body. Schleiner's presentation, cut short due to lengthy discussions on earlier presentations, would have presented Kristevan ideas on abjection and self to facilitate considering Weston's neo-Latin poems. In the "In obitum Nobilis et Generosae Faeminae Dnae. Innae . . . Dni. Edovard Kellei de Imany . . . Viduae" (1609), Weston's sense of Death as a gratuitously malicious alien persona evokes issues of abjection, loss, and the permeability of mind and body. Here, Death takes not the body, but the mind, implying that Death harms the mind more than the body.

For the last segment of the workshop, participants focused on Renaissance parlor games provided by Schleiner. One game in particular, which required a paraphrase of a Latin epigram into an English poem, was especially demanding. Anne Lake Prescott won this translation game. Most participant groups played "Alphabet of Love," which required that two adjectives describing a lover be invented for each letter of the alphabet. The group interpreted the complexity of the games as an index of early modern women's wit and intellectual skill.

Additional Readings

Harsdörffer, Georg Philipp. *Frauenzimmer Gesprächspiele.* Nurnberg, 1641.
Lindheim, Nancy. *The Structures of Sidney's Arcadia.* Toronto: University of Toronto Press, 1982.

McCanles, Michael. "Reading Description in Sidney's New Arcadia: A Differential Analysis." *University of Toronto Quarterly* 33 (1988): 36–52.

Moore, Mary. *Desiring Voices: Women Sonneteers and Petrarchism.* Carbondale: Southern Illinois University Press, in press.

Phillippy, Patricia. "Gaspara Stampa's *Rime:* Replication and Retraction." *Philological Quarterly* 68, no. 1 (1989): 1–24.

Trunz, Erich. *Wissenschaft und Kunst im Kreise Rudolfs II., 1676–1612.* Neumuenster, Germany: Wachholtz, 1992.

Vitello, Justin. "Gaspara Stampa: The Ambiguities of Martyrdom." *MLN* 90 (1975): 58–71.

Winnett, Susan. "Coming Unstrung: Women, Men, Narrative and Principles of Pleasure." *PMLA* 105 (1990): 505–18.

Submitted by: Mary Moore

Workshop # 2: "Conversant Bodies: Salons, Coteries, and Conversation in Seventeenth-Century France and England"

Organizers

Elizabeth C. Goldsmith, French, Boston University; Nathan P. Tinker, English, Fordham University

Readings

Margaret J. M. Ezell, "Reading Pseudonyms in Seventeenth-Century English Coterie Literature," *Essays in Literature* 21 (1994): 14–25; Erica Harth, "The Salon Woman Goes Public . . . or Does She?" in *Going Public: Women and Publishing in Early Modern France,* ed. Elizabeth C. Goldsmith and Dena Goodman (Ithaca: Cornell University Press, 1995), 179–93; Katherine Philips, *Poems* (London, 1667); Madeleine de Scudéry, *Conversations upon Several Subjects* (1683).

In this workshop, participants discussed women's use of social institutions of the salon and the coterie to establish literary, social, or political authority. Primary readings centered on the two most prominent organizers of these circles, Madeleine de Scudéry in France and Katherine Philips in England, while the secondary readings questioned the status of "public" versus "private" writing.

Elizabeth Goldsmith's presentation provided an introduction to Scudéry, her Paris *salon* and the *conversations* she wrote and published, emphasizing Scudéry's connection to the French court and the courtiers who were attracted to her salon. Nathan Tinker spoke about the relationship between coterie activity and the print marketplace, suggesting that salons and coteries provided socially acceptable venues for the introduction of women's literary work into the public sphere.

Because many of the participants were English literature scholars or historians, in the ensuing discussion there was considerable interest in Scudéry and the inner workings of her salon. What were the material ways in which texts were produced within the salon? What role did gender play in the construction and longevity of the circle? Were men invited into the circle and under what circumstances? Since Scudéry often recommended traditionally male genres (such as philosophy or science) as the proscribed arena of conversation, what social, political, or literary boundaries were crossed simply in the choice of topic?

As the discussion moved from Katherine Philips's use of coterie production to crossing class boundaries, participants questioned the nature of her literary relationship with aristocracy. How was the political content of her writing received by the various members of her group? Did Philips's "Society of Friendship" exist in any real sense, or was it a literary trope? These questions led to a more general discussion of women's use of salon and coterie connections in the production and dissemination of their work. One participant suggested that salons and coteries simply reaffirmed patriarchy, relegating women's voices quite literally to the bedroom. Others responded that because women were the organizers and leaders of these circles, salons and coteries allowed women an agency that they did not possess either at court or in society at large.

The circulation of women's writing within coterie and salon circles certainly had a measurable effect in the marketplace. Mary Wroth's *Urania*, Katherine Philips's *Pompey*, Scudéry's *Conversations*, and Jane Barker's works (among many others)—all were engendered within coteries or salons. These considerations led to some final questions about as yet uninvestigated problems: What were the reciprocal influences of French and English circles? What were the specific relationships between coterie culture and print culture? To what extent did all-women circles challenge boundaries of class and gender?

Additional Readings

Goldsmith, Elizabeth C. *Exclusive Conversations: The Art of Interaction in Seventeenth-Century France.* Philadelphia: University of Pennsylvania Press, 1988.

Goldsmith, Elizabeth C., and Dena Goodman, eds. *Going Public: Women and Publishing in Early Modern France.* Ithaca: Cornell University Press, 1995.

Love, Harold. *Scribal Publication in Seventeenth-Century England.* Oxford: Clarendon, 1993.

Submitted by: Nathan P. Tinker

Workshop #3: "Domestic Texts and Objects in Early Modern Europe: Metonyms of the Female Self"

Organizers:

Lisa M. Klein, English, Ohio State University; Sylvia Brown, English, University of Alberta; Mimi Hellman, Art History, Princeton University; Ann Rosalind Jones, Comparative Literature, Smith College

Readings

Margreta de Grazia, Maureen Quilligan, and Peter Stallybrass, "Introduction," *Subject and Object in Renaissance Culture* (Cambridge: Cambridge University Press, 1996); Margaret Ezell, *Writing Women's Literary History* (Baltimore: Johns Hopkins University Press, 1993), 34–35, 54–59; Jennifer Harris, "Hannah Smith's Embroidered Casket," *Antique Collector* (July 1988): 48–55; Jane Hedley, *Power in Verse: Metaphor and Metonymy in the Renaissance Lyric* (University Park: Pennsylvania State University Press, 1988); Mimi Hellman, "Furniture, Sociability, and the Work of Leisure in Eighteenth-Century France," *Eighteenth-Century Studies* (forthcoming); Elizabeth Joceline, *The Mothers Legacie* (British Library, BL Add. Ms 27467); Wendy Wall, *The Imprint of Gender: Authorship and Publication in the English Renaissance* (Ithaca: Cornell University Press, 1993), 282–87.

This workshop explored how domestic objects (including books, needlework, dressing tables, and spinning tools) functioned in the construction of female subjectivity in early modern Europe. How do these objects represent, substitute for, or even speak for early modern women? How is the social construction of femininity and domesticity mediated by material objects?

Lisa Klein opened the workshop by showing and discussing slides of embroidered caskets made in England in the latter half of the seventeenth century. She proposed a close metonymic relation between such boxes, with their decorated exteriors and hidden interiors, and the "private" virtuous, chaste, and enclosed self fashioned by their making. Hellman led us to think about the forms and uses of the dressing table in eighteenth-century France: its metonymic role in the construction of the body and the self (both male and female); its simultaneously private and public uses as both a container for personal possessions and a prop in a social performance. Jones followed by tracing the struggle over the distaff and spindle in visual and written texts from France, Germany, and the Low Countries in the sixteenth century. Jones invited us to consider how women writers, by appropriating the pen, countered the domestic assignments of the distaff and spindle. Brown's presentation on mothers' written legacies to their children enabled us to see the works of Elizabeth Joceline and Elizabeth Richardson in several lights: as metonymic substitutions for the dead or dying mother; as material objects that circulate both within and without the family circle.

In the discussion that followed, we all questioned the facile distinction between "public" and "private" in identity and social practice in early modern Europe. Texts and objects were also problematized; both were subjected to densely symbolic and multivalent readings and descriptive analysis. Several participants speculated about the many possible meanings of the pictures embroidered on caskets and how these might construct female identity. Jones's images of spinners and their tools generated lively discussion of gendered representations of women. One person questioned whether metaphor and metonymy could be separated, and Jones suggested that metaphor may have primacy because it is richer and hence more useful for probing symbolic relationships. Hellman's images of women and men at the toilette provoked discussion of gender and representation, gazing and eroticism, and they reminded us that men's activities, as well as women's, were subject to social control.

Issues regarding methodology, which we had hoped to explore, did not arise. We might ask whether or not the mechanisms for reproducing ideology are different for texts and for material objects. Do we need different theories and methodologies for describing the ideological content of each? How do we bring into view and make sense of anonymous work, such as spinning and embroidery? Where is female subjectivity to be "found," or how is it constructed and reflected by the objects of everyday life?

Additional Readings

Ezell, Margaret. "Elizabeth Delaval's Spiritual Heroine: Thoughts on Redefining Manuscript Texts by Early Modern Women Writers." *English Manuscript Studies 1100–1700* (1992): 216–37.

Fumerton, Patricia. *Cultural Aesthetics: Renaissance Literature and the Practice of Social Ornament.* Chicago: University of Chicago Press, 1991.

Jones, Ann Rosalind. "Dematerializations: Textile and textual properties in Ovid, Sandys, and Spenser." In *Subject and Object in Renaissance Culture*, edited by Margreta de Grazia et al., 189–209. Cambridge: Cambridge University Press, 1996.

Klein, Lisa M. "Your Humble Handmaid: Elizabethan Gifts of Needlework." *Renaissance Quarterly* 50 (1997): 459–93.

Lubar, Steven and W. David Kingery, eds. *History from Things: Essays on Material Culture.* Washington, D.C.: Smithsonian Institution, 1993.

Submitted by: Lisa M. Klein

Workshop #4: "Maternal Bodies in Early Modern Society"

Organizers

Claire Farago, Art History, University of Colorado at Boulder; Naomi J. Miller, English, University of Arizona; Retha Warnicke, History, Arizona State University

Readings

Adrian Wilson, "The Perils of Early Modern Procreation: Childbirth With or Without Fear," *British Journal for Eighteenth-Century Studies* (Spring 1993): 1–19; Elizabeth Clinton, *The Countess of Lincolnes Nurserie* (Oxford, 1622); Londa Schiebinger, "Why Mammals Are Called Mammals: Gender Politics in Eighteenth-Century Natural History," *American Historical Review* 98, no. 2 (April 1993): 382–87.

Maternity was a physical as well as social construct in the early modern period. The physicality of the woman's body, associated with maternal functions and responsibilities that varied in emphasis across classes and cultures, raises questions concerning the womb and breasts as signs signifying "woman." This workshop scrutinized "maternal bodies" in the social history, literature, and art history of England, Germany, Italy, and France. By juxtaposing representations of actual and mythic mothers in different mediums and countries, the workshop enabled participants to attend to some of the cultural undercurrents, encompassing both norms and aberrations, which shaped early modern conceptions of the female body and self. The readings for the workshop indicated some of the ways in which the theoretical boundaries between body and self at times suffered eclipse or even erasure when early modern women were defined primarily in terms of their reproductive functions. At other times, when mothers claimed positions for themselves as generators of their own words and images, issues of authority and authorship collided.

Retha Warnicke considered the nature of the fear of childbirth—whether of pain or of death—and the question of how many mothers died in childbirth in the early modern period. Scholars are beginning to question whether or not the notion that women died in childbirth in huge numbers is correct. In reviewing some of the quantitative studies on childbirth for England and Germany, Warnicke discussed how women viewed their bodies as they prepared for a potentially life-threatening event, without which married women were considered to be biological failures. Warnicke asked the workshop participants to consider how the fear of childbirth—an important social rite of passage, biologically limited to the female sex—might have shaped women's attitudes toward self and identity. Naomi Miller discussed the relevance of nursing practices in early modern England to perceived as well as actual maternal authority. After surveying some of the issues and images associated with breasts and breast milk during the period, Miller focused her presentation on a treatise authored by Elizabeth Clinton, countess of Lincoln, in 1622, which advocated maternal breastfeeding for all women. Challenging the accepted social practice of aristocratic women placing their infants with wet nurses, Clinton urged women to recognize their shared maternal bonds across class lines and claim control over their own bodies despite social prescriptions. Miller juxtaposed this text with some well-known representations of maternal attitudes and behavior by male authors (such as the "nursing rhetoric" of Lady Macbeth). Miller asked workshop participants to examine the physical strategies women devised to advance their own conceptions of mothering roles, as well as the nature of some of the perceived connections between the mother's body and maternal authority. Claire Farago reviewed several categories of images associated with maternity, including some outside the European tradition. Examples encompassed religious images of motherhood; visual evidence of medical practices, ranging from anatomical literature to charms used in curing; portraits of individuals and families; domestic furnishings, including painted scenes of cassoni, birth salvers, and bedroom walls; and antimaternal images, such as depictions of witches and other misogynistic/grotesque representations of women. Farago focused on the visual culture of maternity, queried the relation between societal expectations and visual forms of representation, and asked workshop participants to consider how specific images simultaneously gesture toward and elide discussions of maternity.

The ensuing discussion explored ways in which maternal images were used as propaganda by political and religious leaders, while women themselves worked to reclaim maternal authority. Some women, such as the Countess of Lincoln, could be seen to distinguish themselves from male writers of medical or familial handbooks by choosing not to focus upon the materiality of women's bodies, thus strengthening the authority of women's positions within the household. Several participants, noting the guilt that marked such issues as the use or refusal of wet nurses, considered the ways in which early modern fears surrounding childbirth and nursing are related to current women's issues, including the reliance of working mothers upon other caregivers, and the challenges that confront mothers attempting to balance multiple other roles.

Additional Readings

Crawford, Patricia. "The Construction and Experience of Maternity in Seventeenth-Century England." In *Women as Mothers in Pre-Industrial England*, edited by Valerie Fildes, 3–38. London: Routledge, 1990.

Fildes, Valerie. "Maternal Breastfeeding: The Incidence and Practice of Maternal Breastfeeding, 1500–1800." In *Breasts, Bottles and Babies*, 98–133. Edinburgh: Edinburgh University Press, 1986.

———. "The English Wet Nursing System in the Seventeenth Century." In *Wet Nursing: A History from Antiquity to the Present*, 79–100. Oxford: Basil Blackwell, 1988.

Klapisch-Zuber, Christine. "Holy Dolls: Play and Piety in Florence in the Quattrocento." In *Women, Family, and Ritual in Renaissance Italy*, 310–30. Chicago: University of Chicago Press, 1985.

Miles, Margaret. "The Virgin's One Bare Breast: Nudity, Gender, and Religious Meaning in Tuscan Early Renaissance Culture." In *The Female Body in Western Culture: Contemporary Perspectives*, edited by S. R. Suleiman, 193–208. Cambridge: Harvard University Press, 1986.

Schofield, Roger. "Did the Mothers Really Die? Three Centuries of Maternal Mortality in 'The World We Have Lost.'" In *The World We Have Gained:*

Histories of Population and Social Structure, edited by Lloyd Bonfield, Richard Smith, and Keith Wrightson, 231–60. New York: Basil Blackwell, 1986.

Submitted by: Naomi J. Miller

Workshop #5: "Popular Texts, Historical Evidence, and the Performing Body"

Organizers

Pamela Brown, English, University of Connecticut, Stamford; Melinda Gough, English, Oklahoma State University; Joy Wiltenburg, History, Rowan College of New Jersey; Susan Gushee O'Malley, English, Kingsborough College, City University of New York

Readings

A selection of ballads, including "Have Among you! good Women," in William Chappell and James Ebsworth, eds., *The Roxburghe Ballads* (Hertford: Stephen Austin, 1869–95), 1:1: 435–37; "A Merry Discourse between Joane and the Tinker," *Roxburghe* 1:1: 249–53; "The Patient Husband and the Scoulding Wife," *Roxburghe* 7:1: 182; "The Wanton Wife of Bath" and "Well Met Neighbour" in H. R. Woudhuysen, ed., *The Penguin Book of Renaissance Verse* (London: Penguin, 1993), 127, 158; woodcuts of women balladsellers, hucksters, and alewives from Leslie Shepard, *The Broadside Ballad: A Study in Origins and Meaning* (London: H. Jenkins, 1972) and Peter Clark, *The English Alehouse* (Harlow, England: Longman, 1983); a bibliography.

The workshop explored challenges posed by the female performing body to prevailing scholarly assumptions about the near-invisibility of poorer women in early modern culture. As historians have shown, some nonelite women were visible and active in common spaces of the neighborhood. They took part in selling and singing ballads, playing music and dancing, performing mocking rhymes and jigs, and acting in guild and festive drama. Traces of such performances occur in broadside ballads, pamphlets, jests, plays, and woodcuts. Conveners and participants addressed the status of such material as evidence, examined questions of cost, transmission, mediation, authorship, and literacy, and they questioned whether or not a measure of agency is suggested by some of these texts.

Instead of talking about the performing body, we decided to become players. We performed a scene in costume, set in an alehouse. The script was composed of portions of plays by Margaret Cavendish and Shakespeare, and broadside ballads that were either anonymous or male-authored. After the performance, we distributed a script annotated with our sources. Our scene opened with a segment from Cavendish's *Convent of Pleasure*, in which two poor women meet at an alehouse to commiserate with each other about their husbands, "drunken rogues" who drink all day and then come home only to beat them "black and blew." One complains that her husband spends not only everything he gets, but also what she brings in "through the sweat of [her] brow," depriving her family of food. The two women vow to go to the alehouse and drag their husbands home. They fear being beaten again, however, and soon they are drinking together. A chapwoman-balladseller enters and plies her wares among the audience, singing "Hold Your Hands, Honest Men!" (in which a wife bewails her husband's only flaw: he beats her) and "The Wanton Wife of Bath" (in which Chaucer's Wife, dead and gone to judgment, exposes everyone in heaven as a hypocrite, only to be admitted by Jesus). Lines from *The Winter's Tale* introduce the final song, with the three women joining in on "Well, Met, Neighbor!"—a ballad in which two gossips gripe about the drunken, violent, and lecherous husbands in their neighborhood. Acting out motions of praying, punching, and hanging, the women trade verses and repeat the refrain, "O such a rogue should be hang'd!" They end with a rousing chorus of "Better a shrew than a sheep!"

Joy Wiltenburg opened the discussion, calling the dramatized attempt to connect text to body a valid means of reading and apprehending these texts, and she invited participants to share their own readings. Melinda Gough considered the category of agency. Were women known as critics and judges of this kind of performance, and could their reactions have helped shape plays? If we begin to see women as creative participants in culture, instead of passive absorbers, how would it change the ways we teach and think about popular drama? Susan O'Malley criticized the antiquated yet often-cited *Roxburghe* collection for its antifeminist editorializing, misplacements of woodcuts, and errors in matching ballads to melodies, and she urged feminist scholars to issue new editions. Pam Brown noted that the alehouse setting was a deliberately chosen element of the performance, meant to challenge prevailing judgments (based largely on Peter Burke's *Popular Culture in Early Modern Europe*) about nonelite women's invisibility and exclusion from popular culture. The alehouse was a key site for cultural transmission and performance: matches were made there, ballads were sung and sold, news was traded, and pamphlets were read aloud. Although social historians have claimed that the alehouse was a male milieu, women often owned and managed alehouses, while others worked there or met friends, spouses, and suitors there.

The discussion then turned to questions raised by the male authorship of many ballads, and possible problems involved in recreating a scene of ballad singing and buying. Did women alter and rework ballads, adding and changing lines? Did they act them out with gesture and byplay, as we did in our performance? Were the interests and desires of women more accurately represented in ballads than in elite genres because they were openly targeted as customers? Did this "penny culture" really reach the poorest women? How did it affect the content and reception of native drama and public theater plays? We were not able to answer all these questions, of course, but the workshop suggested that there is a great need for scholars to consider nonelite women as cultural players, and that studying street literature and female performance promises to shed light on ways poorer women may have experienced and produced cultural forms.

Additional Readings

Chartier, Roger. *The Cultural Uses of Print in Early Modern France.* Princeton: Princeton University Press, 1987.

Reay, Barry, ed. *Popular Culture in Seventeenth-Century England.* London: Croom Helm, 1985.

Rollins, Hyder Edward. "The Black-Letter Broadside Ballad." *PMLA* 27 (1919): 258–339.

Stokes, James. "Women and Mimesis in Medieval and Renaissance Somerset (and Beyond)." *Comparative Drama* 27 (1993): 186–96.

Wiltenburg, Joy. *Disorderly Women and Female Power in the Street Literature of Early Modern Germany and England.* Charlottesville and London: University Press of Virginia, 1992.

Wurzbach, Natascha. *The Rise of the English Street Ballad, 1550–1650.* Cambridge: Cambridge University Press, 1990.

Submitted by: Pamela Brown

Workshop #6: "Tudor-Stuart Living: Domestic Style"

Organizers

Lynette McGrath, English and Women's Studies, West Chester University; Lori Newcomb, English, University of Illinois; Allison D. Spreuwenberg-Stewart, Women's Studies, Fashion Institute of Technology

Readings

Janet Arnold, *Queen Elizabeth's Wardrobe Unlock'd* (Leeds, England: Maney Press, 1988), 9, 76, 96, 168; Bartholomew Batty, *The Christian Man's Closet* (London, 1581); 75 ff.; Aphra Behn, *The Unfortunate Happy Lady* (1698), in *An Anthology of Seventeenth-Century Fiction*, ed. Paul Salzman (Oxford: Oxford University Press, 1991), 534; James Boler, *The Needles Excellency* (London, 1634), title page; Pierre Bourdieu, *Distinction: A Social Critique of the Judgement of Taste* (Boston: Beacon Press, 1996), 9–10, 13; Christopher Breward, *The Culture of Fashion: A New History of Fashionable Dress* (Manchester: Manchester University Press, 1995), 54, 61; Ellen Chirelstein, "Lady Elizabeth Pope: The Heraldic Body," in *Renaissance Bodies: The Human Figure in English Culture, 1540–1660*, ed. Nigel Llewllyn and Lucy Gent (London: Reaktion, 1990), 36–59; Anne Clifford, *The Diary of Lady Anne Clifford*, ed. V. Sackville West (London: Heinemann, 1923), entries for April 20, 23, and 24, 1617; Amy Louise Erickson, *Women and Property in Early Modern England* (London: Routledge, 1993), 223; John Evelyn, "Tyrannnus or the Mode: in a Discourse of Sumptuary Lawes," in *The Writings of John Evelyn*, ed. Guy de La Bedoyere (New York: Boyddell, 1995), 164; Kim Hall, "The Gendering of Sugar in the Seventeenth Century," in *Feminist Readings in Early Modern Culture*, ed. Valerie Traub, M. Lindsay Kaplan, and Dympna Callaghan (Cambridge: Cambridge University Press, 1996), 168–90; Anne Laurence, *Women in England, 1500–1760: A Social History* (New York: St. Martin's Press, 1994), 144–47; Stephen Mennell, *All Manners of Food: Eating and Taste in England and France from the Middle Ages to the Present* (Urbana and Chicago: University of Illinois Press, 1996), 67, 82–96; Roy Strong, *The Renaissance Garden in England* (London: Thames and Hudson, 1979), 40, 120; June Taboroff, "'Wife, Unto thy Garden': The First Gardening Books for Women," *Garden History* 11, no. 1 (Spring 1983): 1–5; Christopher Thacker, *The Genius of Gardening: The History of Gardens in Britain and Ireland* (London: Weidenfeld and Nicolson, 1994), 49; Amanda Vickery, "Women and the world of goods: A Lancashire consumer and her possessions, 1751–81," in *Consumption and the World of Goods*, ed. John Brewer and Roy Porter (London: Routledge, 1993), 274–302; Lorna Weatherill, "A Possession of One's Own: Women and Consumer Behavior in England, 1660–1740," *Journal of British Studies* 25(1986): 131–56; Hannah Wolley, *The Accomplisht Ladys Delight* (London, 1685), frontispiece, 103.

The title of this workshop purposely invoked the "domestic sensuousness" of the popular American journal of the late 1990s, *Martha Stewart Living*. To mimic an issue of this currently fashionable magazine, the packet of materials distributed to participants was composed of a collage of references to and about the domestic activities of women in the early modern period, tied with damask-printed ribbon to represent decorative clothing, and accompanied by a packet of seeds to figure the topic of gardens. At the workshop itself, we served sweet "banquetting" foodstuffs: marzipan (marchpane), pretzels (favored in the Low Countries), and walnut-shaped shortbread. Our allusive imitations underlined our interest in the same problematic questions with reference to early modern women as those suggested by the cultural phenomenon that Martha Stewart has become in our own time. To what degree, we wished to ask, were early modern women able to (re)claim their own pleasure and control in areas of domesticity that were at the same time imposed on them by their domestic role? Is there any evidence of the very impulses toward agency, expertise, and bodily enjoyment condemned in early modern warnings against women's consumption?

We looked especially at food and its preparation, garden design and gardening, and the consumption of clothing. Food, clothing, and gardens all seem to us areas that allow the intervention of the aesthetic and the sensuous. We focused on women's desire for, and choices of, aesthetically pleasing material items to furnish their tables, enhance their gardens, and clothe their bodies. These three activities were linked, gendered, and moralized by the myth of the Garden of Eden; the links were reinforced visually by analogies among the realms that preoccupied the period's designs. Multiple slides were used by the presenters to emphasize the visual pleasures related to these areas of domestic production and to tie together the threads of discussion that arose during the presentation.

Lynette McGrath introduced the workshop and showed slides illustrating women's sensuous involvement with food and food production. Lori Newcomb discussed garden design and practice in the period, using her slides to illustrate the precoccupation in both gardens and clothing with making intricate patterns. Allison Spreuwenberg-Stewart discussed and showed slides illustrating women's clothing and its possibilities of comfort at all class levels. Participants in the workshop contributed their own visual images and quotations from early modern texts. In discussions of women's particular comfort, pleasure, and delight, we discovered, issues of sexuality are not far from the surface, but here, too, the interconnections of women's agency with their cultural objectification were debated. Women's pleasures, we acknowledge, are culturally embedded, mediated through, and partially complicit with, the patriarchal, capitalist, and colonialist ideologies that work to mystify the domestic sphere, yet they are not, for that reason, unavailable. To what extent, though, can we claim that early modern women, through domestic consumption, formed their own tastes and generated their own pleasures?

Additional Readings

Beck, Thomasina. *The Embroidered Garden*. London: Angus and Robertson, 1979.
Elliott, Dyan. "Dress as Mediator Between Inner and Outer Self: The Pious Matron of the High and Later Middle Ages." *Mediaeval Studies* 53 (1991): 279–308.
Martha Washington's Booke of Cookery . . . being a Family Manuscript, curiously copied by an unknown Hand . . . in the seventeenth century. Edited by Karen Hess. New York: Columbia University Press, 1995.
Milton, John. *Paradise Lost*. Books IV and V.

Submitted by: Lynn McGrath and Lori Newcomb

Workshop #7: "Two Bodies, One Flesh: Conceiving the Queen's Married Body"

Organizers

Mary Elizabeth Burke, English, University Continuing Education Association; Julia M. Alexandra, Art History, Yale University; Jill Niemczyk Smith, English, Columbia University; Abby Zanger, French and Women's Studies, Harvard University

Readings

Calendar of State Papers Relating to Scotland and Mary, Queen of Scots, 1547–1603, vol. 2, ed. Joseph Bain et al. (Edinburgh: H. M. General Register House, 1898–1969), 128–34, 326–27; A. Francis Steuart, ed., *Memoirs of Sir James Melville of Halhill* (London: George Routledge & Sons, 1929), 78–99; Mary Stuart, *Bittersweet Within My Heart: The Love Poems of Mary, Queen of Scots*, trans. and ed. Robin Bell (San Francisco: Chronicle Books, 1992); Dirck Stoop, *The Infanta Catherine, 1660* (National Portrait Gallery, London), painting; Sir Peter Lely, "Queen Catherine," ed. R. B. Beckett and Lely (London: Routledge & Kegan Paul, 1954); Abby E. Zanger, *Scenes from the Marriage of Louis XIV: Nuptial Fictions and the Making of Absolute Power* (Stanford, Calif.: Stanford University Press, 1997), 1–12.

This workshop examined early modern queenship in relation to the social and political practice of dynastic marriage, which potentially conferred power on queens consort but potentially diminished the power of queens regnant. We focused on how the queen's body reveals conflicts both between national identity and succession represented and enacted on her body and in the identity of the queen herself.

Early modern dynastic marriages, arranged to formalize alliances or ratify treaties, effectively objectified the female body as a negotiable instrument in international diplomacy. However, when a dynastic marriage involved a ruling queen, who participated in negotiating the disposition of her own body, her power as a queen and her desire as a woman complicated the transaction in ways that were manifested by her body. Even queens consort, often sent away from family and nation without their consent, disrupted the objectives of dynastic transactions through their resistance to assimilating to their new nation's identity and to its reproduction through succession. The queen thus embodies assertions of agency and manifestations of resistance even as she bears representations of male power. Considering the queen's body both as symbolic capital and material reality, this workshop investigated the personal and political effects of dynastic marriage for early modern queens.

Jill Niemczyk Smith began the workshop with an examination of representations of Queen Elizabeth's marriageable body. Using the *Memoirs of Sir James Melville* as a starting point, Smith focused on an account of the queen's body during the period of her courtship with Robert Dudley and marriage negotiations with Charles, Archduke of Austria. Elizabeth's body was implicated in marriage negotiations—not as an object to be acquired, nor as an icon to be admired, but as an active player. Mary Elizabeth Burke shifted the discussion north to look at Scottish anxieties over the marriages and widowhood of Mary, Queen of Scots. Throughout Mary's reign, Scots viewed possession of the queen's body as the surest path to power. Participants discussed Scottish anxiety over who controlled Mary's body, its issue, and Mary's responses to her subjects' obsession with her body in her *Sonnets* and in masque performances. Discussion also touched on Mary's use of Galfridian prophecy for political purposes. Abby Zanger led a discussion of the courtships of Louis XIV of France and how they were figured in popular representations of the royal family. Using decorative almanacs with images of Louis, his family, and his potential brides, participants examined the tensions inherent in royal matchmaking. The almanacs reveal an anxiety over possible royal impotence, which the creators attempted to alleviate with reminders of the young king's military victories. Participants also focused on one almanac, which figures France's victory over Flanders as a rape and reclothing of a woman into French garb. Julia Alexander examined portraits of Catherine of Braganza, queen consort to Charles II of England. She demonstrated how these images reflect and embody her liminal status as a barren queen consort. Participants explored the queens' portraits, their props and poses, in the context of topical events, political and personal. They focused on the early portraits that demonstrated her assimilation to "Englishness" (engineered through the pictorial rejection of her native dress), images that stressed her beauty and paintings that reflected her position as a Catholic and a barren queen.

The workshop generated a number of questions. How does the female body constitute or represent female, queenly, religious, and national identities? How do these constitutions and representations figure into early modern notions of marriage and the state? In what ways did the female body enable or limit the exercise of political power? To what extent did royal marriages serve to reinforce the analogy of family and state structures in political and marital ideology?

Additional Readings

Doran, Susan. *Monarchy and Matrimony: The Courtships of Elizabeth I*, 73–98. New York and London: Routledge, 1996.

Johnson, Geraldine. "Pictures Fit for a Queen: Peter Paul Rubens and the Marie de' Medici Cycle." *Art History* 14, no. 2 (June 1991): 192–224.

Woodall, Joanna. "An Exemplary Consort: Antonis Mor's Portrait of Mary Tudor." *Art History* 14, no. 2 (June 1991): 193–224.

Submitted by: Mary Elizabeth Burke

Workshop #8: "Virtuous Bodies: The History of the Hymen"

Organizers

Mary Fissell, History of Science, The Johns Hopkins University; Kathleen Coyne Kelly, English, Northeastern University

Readings

Aristotle's Last Legacy; or his Golden Cabinet of Secrets (London, 1711) 54, 91; *Aristotle's Master-piece: or, the Secrets of Generation* (London, 1694), 87–90; *Aristotle's New Book of Problems* (London, 1725), 53; *Coffee-House Jests*, 4th ed. (London, 1686), 94–5; Helkiah Crooke, *A Description of the Body of Man. Together with the controversies and figures thereto belonging. Collected and translated out of all the best authors of anatomy, especially out of Gaspar Bauhinus and Andreas Laurentius* (London, 1618), 255–56; Nicholas Culpeper, *A Directory for Midwives* (London, 1651), 29; Laurent Joubert, *Popular Errors*, trans. and annot. Gregory David de Richer (Tuscaloosa and London: University of Alabama Press, 1989), 208–22; "The Lass of Lynn's New Joy, for finding a father for her child" (1680–90), *Bagford Ballads*, ed. with intro. by J. W. Ebsworth (London: The Ballad Society, 1876), 466–68; Ambroise Paré, *The workes of that Famous Chirurgion Ambrose Parey, Translated out of Latin and Compared with the French*, trans. Thomas Johnson (London, 1634), 937–38.

In our workshop we examined early modern debates about the hymen and investigated the relationship between representations of the female body and female virtue in order to demonstrate that the hymen *has* a history—a medical history inextricably bound up with a cultural history. We read selected English and French medical and nonmedical texts in order to explore the range of discourses about virginity and its bodily signs, and to question the idea that any easy divisions can be made among popular/learned or medical/nonmedical texts.

The facilitators noted that classical and medieval medical texts did not usually discuss the hymen, but they did include other means and methods for verifying virginity. However, starting in the fifteenth century, authors of learned medical works and popular texts regularly speculated about whether or not the hymen existed, and whether its presence guaranteed virginity. For example, Laurent Joubert attempted to distinguish between those signs of virginity held by foolish laymen (such as the color of a woman's nipple, a measurement of the head, the structure of the end of the nose) and other, more believable signs. He analyzed the signs cited by three different respectable midwives (which included detailed discussions of female genitalia) and concluded that these signs largely agreed, although he continued to be dubious about the absolute nature of all signs of virginity. No test, it seemed, could be foolproof; *Aristotle's New Book of Problems* (1725) even provided a method for making an artificial maidenhead! Early modern jokes and ballads often portray men as victims of women's cleverness in manipulating the signs of virginity, as in the following example:

> A young Fellow told his Wife the first Night he lay with her, "That if she had consented to have lain with him before Marriage, he would never have made her his Wife." "Faith," says she, "I did imagine as much, for I have been cozen'd so Three or Four times before, and I was resolv'd not to be cozen'd so now."
>
> (*Aristotle's Last Legacy*)

In addition to examining these and other texts, the group also discussed how virginity mattered in different ways in different contexts—be those courtrooms, alehouses, or marital beds. We stressed that one of the common features of early modern discourses on virginity, no matter the genre, is the way in which many texts insist that there is no sure physical sign of virginity, and, in denying the reliability of physical signs, reproduce the very anxieties and myths about the body that the texts purport to put to rest.

Our group explored several questions: Why is it that the hymen became a subject for such intense debate in the medical literature in the early modern period? What influence did the practice of dissection and its documentation have on the "discovery" or "construction" of the hymen? What were the specific historical gender relations that produced concerns about women's honesty? What kinds of etymological issues about seeing and knowing link ideas about virginity to larger concerns about the body as an indicator of virtue? We also discussed the advantages and disadvantages of using modern medical terminology and knowledge as a framework for studying past texts and their representations of the body, and the effects of bringing to bear different knowledge-making paradigms—in our case, literary criticism, history, and history of medicine—on medical and nonmedical evidence for constructions of the body.

Additional Readings

Cadden, Joan. *Meanings of Sex Difference in the Middle Ages: Medicine, Science, and Culture*. Cambridge: Cambridge University Press, 1993.

Kelly, Kathleen Coyne, and Marina Leslie, editors. *Menacing Virgins: Representing Virginity in the Middle Ages and the Renaissance*. Preface by Margaret Ferguson. Newark: University of Delaware Press, in press.

Loughlin, Marie H. *Hymeneutics: Interpreting Virginity on the Early Modern Stage*. Lewisburg, Pa.: Bucknell University Press, and London: Associated University Presses, 1997.

Rogers, John. "The Enclosure of Virginity: The Poetics of Sexual Abstinence in the English Revolution." In *Enclosure Acts: Sexuality, Property, and Culture in Early Modern England*, edited by Richard Burt and John Michael Archer, 229–50. Ithaca: Cornell University Press, 1994.

Siraisi, Nancy. *Medieval and Early Renaissance Medicine: An Introduction to Practice and Knowledge*. Chicago and London: University of Chicago Press, 1990.

Submitted by: Mary Fissell and Kathleen Coyne Kelly

Workshop #9: "Vulnerable Bodies"

Organizers

Sylvia Bowerbank, English, McMaster University; Sara Mendelson, History, McMaster University; Mary O'Connor, English, McMaster University

Readings

Selected depositions transcribed from *Office v. Godman et Scoulter*, Diocesan Court Depositions, Oxford Archives. MS Oxf. dioc. papers ca. 26, 1629–34; excerpts from texts by Margaret Cavendish, Duchess of Newcastle, including *A True Relation of My Birth, Breeding, and Life, in Natures Pictures Drawn by Fancies Pencil* (London, 1656) and *Loves Adventures*, in *Playes* (London, 1662); transcripts of Anne Dormer, Letters, Trumbull papers, British Library, Add. MS 72516.

Sara Mendelson opened the workshop by explaining its title, "Vulnerable Bodies." Participants raised some basic historical questions on which our attention centered. First, without wishing to ignore or dismiss the vulnerabilities of sexuality, how could we go beyond the sexualized body to explore other kinds of bodily vulnerability? Second, what strategies of self-care had women evolved to survive a range of physical and emotional vulnerabilities; what narratives and practices permitted coping and healing? Third, to what extent is the vulnerable body transhistorical; how can we historicize it? The organizers considered three women who serve as examples of physical and psychological vulnerabilities: Elizabeth Scoulter, Margaret Cavendish, and Anne Dormer. Sara Mendelson suggested that, in the case of Elizabeth Scoulter's suspected childbirth and infanticide, there was a conflict between the adult female community's role as enforcers of sexual morality and their caring concern for women in childbirth. Female witnesses showed reluctance to persecute Scoulter; their testimony also disclosed signs of the same support network ordinarily invoked for legitimate births, here used to conceal evidence of a single woman's unwanted birth. Sylvia Bowerbank explored Margaret Cavendish's strategies for coping with her self-diagnosed psychological disorder, "melancholia," including Cavendish's concern with food and diet ("a little boiled chicken") as self-medication, and her use of imaginative writing—what she called "paper bodies"—to fabricate a stronger and more invulnerable self. Mary O'Connor described Anne Dormer's struggles to survive her husband's emotional and physical violence, in which she transformed the restrictive "cage" of marriage into a private refuge, sustaining a subversive identity through epistolary female friendship, care of her children, and the use of medicinal diet and drinks such as chocolate.

Two issues were especially prominent in the ensuing discussion: women's use of food and drink in their strategies of self-care, and female vulnerability to male violence, whether physical or psychological. Anne Shaver and other participants noted Cavendish's recurrent concern with food, including the use of food and feasts as metaphors in her poetry and *Sociable Letters*, and the solace Dormer derived from her medicinal chocolate—roles that "comfort foods" like chocolate and chicken soup still have for us today. Traci Abbott, Anne Barstow, and others commented on the seemingly universal (and perhaps transhistorical?) prevalence of women's vulnerability to male violence, both within the context of marriage and outside it. Abbott and other participants spoke of their experiences with current varieties of male violence against women, comparing these to seventeenth-century patterns, and finding that, although some forms appear to differ superficially, little has changed in substance. Participants concluded that the range of women's bodily vulnerabilities, as well as their narratives and practices of coping, can be seen as both historically situated and transhistorical at the same time. We can comprehend seventeenth-century women's narratives of coping with bodily vulnerabilities because, to some extent, we continue to share their experiences.

Additional Readings

Crawford, Patricia. "Sexual Knowledge in Early Modern England." In *Sexual Knowledge, Sexual Science: The History of Attitudes to Sexuality*, edited by R. Porter and M. Teich, 82–106. Cambridge: Cambridge University Press, 1994.

Crawford, Patricia, and Sara Mendelson. "Sexual Identities in Early Modern England: The Marriage of Two Women in 1680." *Gender and History* 7, no. 3 (1995), 361–77.

Gowing, Laura. *Domestic Dangers: Women, Words and Sex in Early Modern London*. Oxford: Oxford University Press, 1996.

Mendelson, Sara. "To Shift for a Cloak: Disorderly Women in the Church Courts." In *Women & History: Voices of Early Modern Women*, edited by Valerie Frith, 3–17. Toronto: Coach House Press, 1995.

Submitted by: Sara Mendelson

Workshop #10: "Witches and Old Women: Interrogating the Paradigm of Beauty"

Organizers

Erika Ohara Bainbridge, Theater History, University of Maryland; Elspeth Whitney, History, University of Nevada, Las Vegas; Diane Wolfthal, Art History, Arizona State University

Readings

On the Art of the No Drama: The Major Treatises of Zeami, trans. J. Thomas Rimer and Masakazu (Princeton: Princeton University Press, 1984), 28–30; Jane Campbell Hutchinson, Albrecht Dürer: a Biography (Princeton: Princeton University Press, 1990), 121–22; Véronique Nahum-Grappe, "The Beautiful Women," in A History of Women in the West, ed. Natalie Zemon Davis and Arlette Farge (Cambridge: Cambridge University Press, 1993), 3: 85–100; Twenty Plays of the No Theatre, ed. Donald Keene (New York: Columbia University Press, 1970), 69–77; Simon Schama, The Embarrassment of Riches (Berkeley: University of California Press, 1988), 430–43; Tableau de l'inconstance des mauvais anges et démons, ed. Nicole Jacques-Chaquin (Paris: Aubier, 1982), 150, 190, 197–98.

The dominant paradigm in early modern Europe holds that goodness is represented as beauty, evil as ugliness. This workshop explored the converse through Japanese drama, witch manuals, and images of old women. The workshop began with short presentations by each of the facilitators. Elspeth Whitney examined the contrasting construction of witches in two influential witch-hunting manuals, the Malleus Maleficarum (1486, Germany) and Pierre de Lancre's Tableau de l'inconstance des mauvais anges et démons (1612, France). The witch in the Malleus is represented as unrecognizable by her physical appearance; she is always powerful, hidden, and dangerous. She may be identified in part by her inability to weep and her capacity to resist and remain silent in the face of male authority. The witch in the Tableau, in contrast, is domesticated, sexualized, and revealed; she collaborates in her own destruction by speaking more freely and shamelessly than the inquisitor would have dared ask. Here female beauty is a sign not of virtue, but of loss of power. Diane Wolfthal explored the dominant association of old women with ugliness and evil in sixteenth-century visual culture by discussing depictions of witches, procuresses, and foolish old women. She also examined two images that constructed them otherwise. Hans Weiditz's illustration for Petrarch's *Book of Chance,* designed in the 1520s, illustrates virtue with an image of an old woman. In Albrecht Dürer's drawing of his elderly mother, dated 1514, her raised eyebrows, prominent vein in the brow, and the focused gaze of her left eye suggest her intelligence and strength of character. Although he painted images of evil old women, such as witches and allegories of vanity, here, with a woman he loved and admired, Dürer was able to step beyond such stereotypes and show an ugly woman as virtuous. Erika Ohara Bainbridge demonstrated that in Japanese Noh drama old women, played by senior male actors, express beauty; in that genre beauty is not associated with sexuality or physical attraction. This aesthetic ideal is in keeping with the special social background of the Muromachi period, when its shogunate tried to revitalize the declining aristocratic culture in order to reinforce its fragile regime. Founder and composer of Noh, Zeami began his career as a Noh actor when he was a youthful lover of the shogun. In order to remain attractive, he redefined beauty in terms of polished skill in an old body rather than an immature acting style in a young body. In addition, Zeami's philosophy that beauty resided in change and surprise reflects Buddhist philosophy, and contrasts with Western Christianity, which valued unchangeable perfection.

In the ensuing discussion, many questions were raised. How are beauty and ugliness defined in early modern culture? In which contexts are older women viewed as ugly? What are the parameters of "old age" and "youth"? In which contexts does early modern culture equate spiritual beauty with physical beauty, and spiritual ugliness with physical ugliness? When is a beautiful body constructed as ugly in spirit? When is an ugly body viewed as beautiful? What ideals or fears does a society reveal by its definitions of beauty and ugliness? Is there a difference, generally speaking, between medieval and early modern conceptions of the older woman? Did early modern society appropriate classical culture because it wanted validation for certain conceptions concerning older women? How does geography affect these constructions (Northern Europe vs. Italy; Europe vs. Asia)? Did early modern culture believe that older women could contribute to society in a positive way? Did it view younger women as dangerous? How did these constructions affect individual women? Were they accepted or subverted? Do they affect us today? Can we retrieve other, more marginalized traditions of centuries past that might offer alternative views of women? How representative are the texts and images we have explored? How fluid was the construction of good as beautiful and evil as ugly? Participants concluded that this was a rich subject for further study.

Additional Readings

Grieco, Sara Matthews. *Ange ou Diablesse. La representation de la femme au XVIe siecle.* Paris: Flammarion, 1991.

Minois, Georges. *History of Old Age: From Antiquity to the Renaissance.* Translated by Sarah Hanbury Tenison. Cambridge: Polity Press, 1989.

Scheidig, Walther. *Die Holzschnitte des Petrarca-Meisters,* 54. Berlin: Henschelverlag, 1955.

Shahar, Shulamith. "The old body in medieval culture." In *Framing Medieval Bodies,* edited by Sarah Key and Miri Rubin, 160–86. Manchester: Manchester University Press, 1994.

Kramer, Heinrich and James Sprenger. *The Malleus Maleficarum.* Translated by Montague Summers. New York: Dover, 1971.

Submitted by: Diane Wolfthal

Workshop #11: "Exposing the Female Body in Seventeenth-Century England"

Organizers

Laura Gowing, History, University of Hertfordshire, UK; Eve Keller, English, Fordham University; Helen Weinstein, History, Cultural History Programmes, BBC, UK

Readings

Examinations of Mrs. Cooper and others, Centre for Kentish Studies, QM/SB/717 (1606); Joshua Kay v. Martha Beevers, Borthwick Institute, CPH 4315 (1692); Examination of Elizabeth Browne, Somerset Record Office, Q/SR 2/12 (1607); George Chaplin v. Ann Pitcher, Somerset Record Office, DD/Cd 102 fo.132v (1688); Examinations of Marie Ryley, Isabel Nicholson, Susanna Vailes, Jane Cowper, Public Record Office, ASSI 45 7/2/117 (1665), 8/1 (1666), 9/1/119 (1668), 13/2/28 (1682); Nicholas Culpeper, *A Directory for Midwives* (London, 1662), 225–26; Petition against Johane Hallett, Somerset Record Office, Q/SR 3/1 (1608); Information of Elizabeth Caterall, Public Record Office, ASSI 45 5/2/38 (1655); Articles against Mary Combe, Somerset Record Office, Q/SR 92/34, 95/2/41 (1655, 1657); *A Merry New Song* (frontispiece)

(London, n.d.); *The Female Tatler,* 14 Dec. 1709, advertisement from "Mrs Frances Pin-gown" (London, 1709); John Dunton, *The Night-Walker,* September 1696, (London, 1696), 1; woodcuts from *The Pepys Ballads,* ed. W. G. Day (Cambridge: Boydell and Brewer, 1987); Aquila Smyth, "Delivery of James Wolveridge, Dr. of Physick, in his Labours on the Labour of Women, etc.," in James Wolveridge, *Speculum Matricis Hybernicum; Or, the Irish Midwives Handmaid* (London, 1670); William Sermon, *The Ladies Companion: or the English Midwife* (London, 1671), 16–20, 34; William Harvey, *On Parturition, in The Works of William Harvey, M.D.,* ed. Thomas Willis (London: Sydenham Society, 1847).

This workshop explored the cultural valences of the female body in early modern England from various disciplinary perspectives, considering the subjectivity of the female body through perceptions and experiences of its parts and attributes and relationships between bodies, their representations, and identities. The texts and images chosen provided a range of representations of female bodies and experiences: quarter sessions and assize records of official and informal examinations of single women for signs of pregnancy, evidence of sexual assault, and legal records of other sorts of bodily exposure; woodcuts presenting women of fashion exposing their breasts, and contemporary commentary on fashion and exposure; midwifery manuals and other texts on reproduction depicting the relationship between fetus and mother in conflicting ways.

These documents, the presenters suggested, revealed a complex set of understandings about the boundaries of the female body. Laura Gowing, discussing legal records, focused on the meanings that breasts and bellies had for working women, particularly single, dependent servants. How far were their bodies open to examination by employers, friends, neighbors, and midwives? What sense did they have of the boundaries around their working, sexual, or reproductive bodies? Helen Weinstein used images and texts from popular print to examine the exposure and eroticizing of breasts in the public world, arguing that the late seventeenth century saw a new focus on the breast as eroticized fashion object—and a new set of tensions about the breast as commodity. Eve Keller, presenting embryological theories and midwifery manuals, examined the ways in which representations of reproduction figured the maternal body and the fetus as subjects and/or commodities, with corresponding implications for gender relations and understandings of female identity.

Discussion focused first on the relationships between the texts and images presented, and the ways in which such images might have been understood by early modern women. Questions of social and economic status, and of rural/urban differences were raised. Did the women represented as exposing their

breasts in contemporary woodcuts have anything in common with those whose
breasts were exposed by midwives to test for recent or current pregnancy? The
exposure of breasts was also considered in the context of punishments such as
carting, for which women were frequently stripped to the waist; and, with reference to the modern context, exposure of the breasts was considered as a subversive act. It was women, participants argued, for whom the place of the breast
in the public realm had the most meaning, and who were expected to read its
signs—as evidence of pregnancy, or as symbol of fashion—most accurately.
Participants then discussed the ways in which early modern women and men
understood the experience of pregnancy. The commodification of the fetus that
was traced in early modern texts on reproduction seemed to have little echo in
popular thought; rather, it exposed a continuing tension in medical understandings, between emphasis on a woman's subjective expression of her experience of
pregnancy and images of the apparently autonomous fetus that could be seen as
erasing that subjectivity. Finally, participants discussed the potential for bridging
the gulf between such disparate sources, in order to reconstruct the impact of
cultural shifts on the experiences and subjectivities of women across England.
Reading printed texts and images against legal records offers one way towards
more complex and inclusive narratives of continuity and change.

Additional Readings

Newman, Karen. *Fetal Positions: Individualism, Science, Visuality.* Stanford,
    Calif.: Stanford University Press, 1996.
Yalom, Marilyn. *A History of the Breast.* New York: HarperCollins, 1997.

    Submitted by: Laura Gowing

Workshop #12: "Women's Bodies in Gendered Spaces"

Organizers

    Sara L. French, Art History, State University of New York at Binghamton;
Sherri Gross, Biology, Syracuse University

Readings

Laurinda Dixon, *Perilous Chastity: Women and Illness in Pre-Enlightenment
Art and Medicine* (Ithaca: Cornell University Press, 1995), 14–15, 38–50,

131–37; Constance Jordan, "The Terms of the Debate," *Renaissance Feminism: Literary Texts and Political Models* (Ithaca: Cornell University Press, 1990) 11–21; John Dod and Robert Cleaver, excerpt from *A Godlie Forme of Householde Government: for the Ordering of Private Families, According to the Direction of Gods Word*, in *Elizabethan Households: An Anthology*, ed. Lena Cowen Orlin (Washington, D.C.: Folger Shakespeare Library, 1995), 90; Jeffrey Singman, "Women's Garments," *Daily Life in Elizabethan England* (Westport, Conn.: Greenwood Press, 1995), 96–99; Mark Wigley, "Untitled: The Housing of Gender," in *Sexuality and Space*, ed. Beatriz Colomina (New York: Princeton Architectural Press, 1992), 332–51.

Introductory presentations focused on two aspects of women's lives in the early modern period: the actual definition of the female body in early modern medical thought, and the way that women's bodies were constrained by both clothing and architectural environments. The organizers came from widely divergent backgrounds in architectural history and biology, but both with a strong interest in women's studies and feminist theory. They were particularly interested in the coincidence of emerging medical theories with issues of appropriate attire, habits, and physical environments.

Sherri Gross outlined both the formal medical view of physicians and the views of the female body among wise women and traditional healers. The classic symptoms of hysteria were presented, followed by a more technical summation of treatments and the inefficacy or dangerous side effects. Descriptions of common women's complaints that resulted in the diagnosis of hysteria in specific cases were given. Gross suggested that ingesting iron filings might have alleviated anemia, but the application of leeches to the cervix in an effort to recall the wandering womb would have had less positive results. Sara French then surveyed the readings that dealt with women's clothing and domestic environments. The molding of the body by the bodice and the caging of the lower body by a farthingale were related to women's economic status. The article by Wigley was cited as an example of how Alberti's architectural treatise reinforced the physical constraints of women's bodies, through the idea that a woman was fit for remaining indoors because her body was soft and weak. By contrast, if a man stayed indoors, rather than going out to work or to participate in politics, then his body would become weak and feminized.

Participants addressed the potential usefulness of prescriptive writings—architectural treatises, sumptuary laws, or conduct books—for the study of the lives of women. Architectural treatises often reflected a wish rather than a reality. Sumptuary laws were designed to control the conduct of the populace, and they reflected the way governing bodies wanted people to dress. Participants noted the divergence between social rules in Italy (Wigley's example) and England or other Northern European countries, where women had more freedom of movement. Questions of class were raised, for class determined the medical care a woman received; aristocratic women had access to the emerging professionals, whereas women of the middle and lower classes relied on traditional medicine. The freedom of movement of queens and noblewomen who controlled property was compared to the constraints on upper-gentry and merchant-class women who had less reason to travel or to transgress prescribed behavior.

Questions remain in the study of early modern women's bodies and the spaces in which they lived and worked. How did women's transgression of prescribed behavior alter their medical treatment or architectural spaces? Where did women find cures, and how did the cures free them or tie them to their prescribed roles? These questions and others can lead to a better understanding of the ways in which women's bodies have been and continue to be shaped by their clothing, their environment, and their medical care.

Additional Readings

King, Margaret L. *Women of the Renaissance.* Chicago: University of Chicago Press, 1991.

Merchant, Carolyn. *The Death of Nature: Women, Ecology and the Scientific Revolution.* 2d ed. San Francisco: Harper San Francisco, 1990.

Newman, Karen. *Fashioning Femininity.* Chicago: University of Chicago Press, 1991.

Siraisi, Nancy G. *Medieval and Early Renaissance Medicine: An Introduction to Knowledge and Practice.* Chicago: University of Chicago Press, 1990.

Submitted by: Sara L. French and Sherri Gross

Part Two
Law and Criminality

Witch Hunting as Woman Hunting:
Persecution by Gender

ANNE LLEWELLYN BARSTOW
History

MOST OF OUR KNOWLEDGE of the persecution of alleged witches comes from court records. Whereas prosecutions for witchcraft varied greatly across Europe, making generalizations difficult, the importance of this material for women's history requires that we must try to set the witch hunts into the larger perspective. Witch hunting reveals a great deal about the gendered nature of law and criminality in early modern Europe. Ultimately, I will argue that changes in law cannot explain the witch hunts, but I will begin by acknowledging that the two topics are bound together.

Those accused of witchcraft are mostly mute in the records; some of them spoke, and eloquently, in the interrogations, but only in reply to the judges' questions, and knowing that they were on trial for their lives.[1] For the historian to place the accused themselves at the center of the action, to allow them to shape their own story, thus proves difficult. Yet, those of us who practice women's history must attempt it, for the European witch hunts are an important chapter in our overall story. We are ill-advised to put women at the margin of this story.

First, I shall ask what this topic tells us about how the legal system and the concept of crime were changing in the Europe of the sixteenth and seventeenth centuries. Then I want to raise an historiographical problem, to investigate how this material challenges historians to struggle with three concepts that often make us uneasy—violence, victimization, and the patterning of oppression. In short, what do you do when your research turns up material you would rather not deal with? Despite continuing work in gender analysis—I think of Gerhild Williams's, Frances Dolan's, and Lyndal Roper's books, among others[2]—a backlash has set in against viewing the witch hunts as women's history, and I want to suggest several ways that we can counter this trend.

For the historian aware of gender, studying the witch hunts focuses us primarily on women, because 80 percent of the accused and 85 percent of those executed were female. The minority, men, were related to women already accused as witches, or criminals whose crimes attracted the additional charge of harmful magic, or persons perceived as capable of witchcraft themselves. The men deserve a study of their own. It is the 85 percent, however, that I discuss in this essay.

Both women and the poor in general began to appear in court more frequently in the sixteenth century. The question for legal history to explore is why, in much of western Europe, common people began using the courts more often to settle their problems.[3] The question for women's history is what this change meant for the status of women.[4] Women were brought into the European judicial system for the first time in a major way in cases of witchcraft and infanticide. They appeared as accused, accusers, or witnesses.[5] In Luxembourg, for example, we see that women were charged primarily for sexual crimes, and they were punished for sexual transgressions more severely than men. Women condemned for doing away with their newborn children were buried alive, whereas the fathers, if known, were either fined or let go free. Charges for sexual crimes and for sorcery often went together; for example, the daughter of a poor worker at Sanweiler was executed for sorcery and for killing her child.[6] We must ask how the notoriety of some women, branded by the courts as servants of the Devil or baby killers, affected how women in general were viewed by themselves and others.

Whereas women used the courts more than has been thought—and used legal process to their advantage[7]—one still must observe that they were not legally on an equal footing with men. As Laura Gowing has noted, most women could neither read nor write; they had less access to money and less experience in using the courts than men; and once they did make it into court, their stories received less credit than men's.[8] Of this last handicap, Susan Amussen has provided us with an apt example:

> When a number of poor women in Suffolk complained about the sexual advances of the churchwarden, the accused man brought in several witnesses who testified that the women involved were "poor needy vile base people of no esteem amongst their neighbors" and "such as he believe for some small reward may be procured to swear falsely." The churchwarden was respected among his neighbors, and given the choice between the testimony of the women and the churchwarden, those of "credit and estimation" in the community chose the churchwarden.[9]

The very language of legal discourse was prejudicial to women: for example, there was no male equivalent for the epithet "whore."[10] Although men could be and were prosecuted for witchcraft, it was women whom the word "witch" conjured up in every one's mind. Witchcraft was perceived as a woman's crime.

We need therefore to proceed very carefully in concluding to what extent women's new presence in court was a help to them. That many of them were there on a charge of using harmful magic can only have damaged the status of all women, connecting them with what was weird, placing them outside what was natural.[11] That many of them also were put to death as enemies of God, in large, instructive public executions, added to the association of all women with deviance and evil.

A second legal change in this period was the way that secular and church courts were becoming more intrusive in people's private lives, the change beginning first within the churches. Let us look at the role that witch trials played in this change. To quote Lenman and Parker, "Sin seems to have been criminalized for the first time during the fifteenth century."[12] Since "sin" often meant "sex," and since "sex" most often meant "females," this new legal trend was ominous for women. Charges of infanticide, adultery, fornication, abortion, bigamy, sodomy, and bestiality rose in the century between 1550 and 1650.[13] Witchcraft was considered to be a sexual crime, so it is not surprising that this is the very period when the witch hunts flourished.[14] Not only inquisitional courts in Spain and Italy, but also church courts throughout western Europe began to investigate and punish sexual matters that had heretofore been tolerated. Witch trials, with their inordinate interest in the accused's sexual relations with the Devil, and their penchant for accusing women already suspect of other sexual crimes, are a prime example of this new trend.

During the sixteenth century, secular courts gradually took over both the methods and the jurisdictions of ecclesiastical courts in some of these sexual matters, especially witchcraft. Without the methodology of inquisitional procedure[15]—especially the use of torture—the major witch hunts could not have taken place. Despite the fact that the charges were theological—serving and worshiping the Devil—and that witchcraft is an invisible crime, which undermines witness's testimony, nevertheless secular judges did not hesitate to try these cases. That juridical caution functioned even in the face of the law's permission to torture and the deep fear of witches was borne out by the fact that the accused survived in about one-half of the cases. Still, death was not the only penalty: a woman might be whipped, fined, or banished. Worse, her reputation as a witch would follow her for the rest of her life.

Secular governments wanted closer control over the population growth, values, and beliefs of their people. This led, for example, to the extraordinary antiabortion edict passed by the French Parliament that every expectant mother must register her pregnancy and have a witness to the birth, or be liable to a murder charge if the child should die. This legal interference in people's intimate affairs struck harder at women than men, for women's lives were more tied to the privacy of families, and women were on average sentenced more harshly than men for the same crimes.[16]

Moreover, witch trials are a prime example of the long-term change in European concepts of justice, from restitutive to punitive practices, from the reconciling intent of community law to the harsher justice of the state.[17] As long as justice was handled locally, people were reluctant prosecutors; before modern times, there was much more crime in Europe than there was prosecution. In early modern Europe, the death penalty was sought only for causes that threatened society—such as heresy, treason, infanticide, sodomy, and murder—and for witchcraft. Of these causes, treason, infanticide, and witchcraft were considered a *crimen exceptum*, a crime so heinous that the very accusation justified a ruthless prosecution.[18] Prior to about 1550, Europeans had settled most of their charges of malevolent magic out of court, by arbitration among neighbors—and there were few witch hunts. Once the tensions were moved into courts of law, the charge altered to Devil worship, and torture allowed to procure confession, then the number of witches multiplied at a frightening rate. These punitive measures, however, did not restore calm or bring reconciliation to the afflicted communities. Instead, witch hunts left wounds that did not heal for generations.

Legal changes did not cause the witch hunts, but the fact that European law was growing more punitive and personally invasive opened up possibilities for prosecuting all kinds of sexually related crimes, including the crime of witchcraft. This supernatural, invisible crime thus played its role in the overall change that was making European law more centralized and powerful.

Now I will turn to the challenge of writing about the violence in this material, and of naming the misogyny that underlay it. I refer not to the violence of criminals but of the criminal justice system, as it developed in the ways described above.

It is difficult for the historian to give gendered violence its due. Let me give an example from my own work. Having written a book, *Witchcraze,* in which I tried to reflect accurately the extent and especially the gendered nature of the violence involved in witch hunting, I then turned to a study of violence against women today. When I gave a report on my new research to a women's studies conference, a member of the audience said, "Do you realize that you spoke entirely in the passive voice?" I was stunned. She was right. I had said, "Women are raped; wives are abused. . . . " I had not named the perpetrators, not mentioned the agents. All these things had "just happened." When we do not name the agent, it begins to sound as if what happened was "natural," that it is the nature of women to be raped, to be abused, to be witches.

I found some consolation in Andrew Delbanco's observation about Americans' inability to name the agent of brutality. He comments that in our time "we cannot readily see the perpetrator . . . cannot see who, or what bears the responsibility" for this most brutal century.[19] He attributes this moral failure to our lack of belief in evil. Although I do believe in evil, yet I, too, was practicing denial; I was running away from acknowledging that some men are abusive to women. Out of loyalty to my sisters I would name their pain, but out of loyalty to men I would not acknowledge that violence against women is institutionalized, and that some men are abusers. By speaking in the passive voice, I was refusing to acknowledge the connection between the agent and the act.

In the witch hunts there is no question that men, as judges, jailors, executioners, and confessors, enacted violence against their mostly female prisoners. The records of what we call the "witchcraft persecutions" indicate not only harsh inquisitorial court procedures but, frequently, jail conditions so severe that being jailed alone caused death from starvation or exposure, or led to suicide. Jail reports for women include sexual harassment and rape.[20] This is what witch hunting was about, but it is at this point that historians begin to look the other way.

A recent example can be found in the work of Robin Briggs. In his long and richly documented study of the social context of European village witchcraft, he makes almost no mention of torture. Yet, near the end he writes, "I do not mean to minimize the unpleasantness of the phenomenon; anyone who has read hundreds of interrogations under torture, as I have, can only feel sickened by the horrors they contain."[21] One must wonder why Briggs chose to leave out *those aspects* of his material. He tells us: he—and many other historians—believe that describing violence sensationalizes the story, overdramatizes history. I have come to the conclusion that leaving out the violence is an act of censorship that distorts history.

Consider, for example, some accounts of torture. Torture—gratuitous, extralegal torture—was used not only to force prisoners to confess or to name names, but even after confession to demonstrate to the public the horrendous nature of their crimes. Being stripped, searched for the Devil's mark, having one's hand cut off, one's bones broken with the strappado or on the rack—all of these savage attacks were imposed on both male and female prisoners. However, torture often had a sexual angle. When performed on women by men, legal torture permitted sadistic experimentation and sexual advances. Executioners were known to search every part of women prisoners' bodies, apply hot wax to their vaginas, brand their breasts with hot irons, even cut off their breasts. In addition, there was psychological sadism. Judges grilled women to tell about their sex lives, especially their intercourse with the Devil, to admit they had given a pubic hair to their satanic lover. These men took advantage of positions of authority to indulge in pornography sessions.[22] It is these acts that reveal witch hunting to be woman hunting.

To leave out these acts is to make the witch hunts gender-neutral. An example of how some historians are trying to defuse the gender issue in witchcraft studies comes from a recent article by J. A. Sharpe on witchcraft and the legal process. Although Sharpe acknowledges that gender is an issue, he asserts that "witchcraft prosecutions cannot be interpreted purely as the oppression of women by a male-dominated legal system."[23] I agree, for, although all the judges and executioners were male, and the majority of accusers were male as well, women also accused and gave evidence against other women.[24] However, notice what can happen when the historian no longer considers this as a persecution by gender. In discussing the search for the Devil's mark as proof of being a witch, Sharpe says, " . . . it gradually became accepted that the mark, with women, most commonly took the form of a teat-like growth in the pudenda, from which it was thought that the witch's familiar sucked blood."[25] At this I become alarmed. *Who* gradually accepted this belief? Because it connects the clitoris with the demonic, I doubt that women were the authors. How did it enter the legal process? Sharpe does not ask. Thus in his account it appears "normal," or at least not worth questioning, that this strange concept gained credence in the courts. It matters to our interpretation of this history, and it certainly mattered to the women being accused, for the very concept of the devil's teat is based on the fact that females provide breast milk. It is an inversion of a natural female function, one turned against women in a lethal context. This belief connected women with witchcraft, assured that witches would be thought of primarily as women.

When we write about the witch hunts without being aware of the misogyny or describing the violence, we trivialize them. We end up with Briggs's conclusion that "the persecution was a relative failure," by which he means that it was smaller than it might have been.[26] Looked at from the point of view of women's history, it seems to me dire that it occurred at all. That Europeans would turn against groups of their own women indicates a level of misogyny that is alarming and demands accounting for.

In writing history, what difference does it make that we look at—indeed, look for—the violence, noting the connection between the agent and the act? In writing about the witch hunts in Europe, I found that it made all the difference. Lawrence Langer's comment about the literature of the Holocaust is apposite: "The mind resists what it . . . wants to disbelieve; and the task of the artist is to find a style and a form to present the atmosphere or landscape of atrocity, to make it compelling, to coax the reader into credulity. . . ."[27] Not only the artist but also the historian must find a style and create a landscape for atrocity, in order to compel the reader into believing what he or she does not want to believe.

Yet, I knew that if I revealed the horrors of witch hunting, I would be accused of voyeurism, of producing pornography, and, worse, of being anti-male. And I have been so accused. There is a belief among some intellectuals that we can keep our hands clean, our writing free of mention of violence and irrationality. The mind resists what it wants to disbelieve. I decided that to ignore the torture and deaths of these women would be to kill them the second time over. I therefore had to construct my study of witch hunting so as to create a landscape of atrocity. Like other historians, I, too, discussed the legal, the theological, the political factors, even adding a chapter on the economic. But these factors do not fully explain why European men would turn on their own women in this brutal way. Any account fails that leaves out the misogyny that fueled the witch hunts. At every opportunity I pointed out what difference it had made to the majority of the victims that they were women, and that their judges were male. With these descriptions I tried to coax the reader to believe that these atrocities, even though they defy reason, did happen.

My problems with naming the perpetrator and describing the violence relate to our larger concern about interpreting women as victims. The writing of women's history has gone through cycles on this issue, and remains, I believe, unsure of itself at present: for our first decade or so, we vigorously named the oppressors, in order to make our case against patriarchal power—only to find that by focusing on the abusers we neglected the abused, whose stories we wanted to tell. We had turned women into passive victims, whereas we needed to make women the chief actors of their histories. By way of correction, for another decade or so we wrote no-fault history, in which we still reported that women suffered from discrimination and abuse, to be sure, but these evils seemed often not to be caused by anyone. They "just happened." True, women became the chief actors of these stories, and they were no longer seen as victims, but important criticisms of patriarchal structures dropped out.

In trying to avoid portraying women as nothing but victims, I began my study of witchcraft looking for independent women, wise women, healers, and folk therapists. The records, however, do not substantiate this positive image. What I found was, for example, women who could not understand the legal charges made against them, women who accused other women (sometimes at their husbands' orders), women in the pay of the courts who searched other women's bodies and certified that they found the Devil's mark. In sum, they were women who were either victims or disloyal to other women, not heroes.

I did find courage of one kind: women who under torture still refused to confess to the lies they were charged with, or to name names. Their integrity deserves to be remembered. However, for the most part none of the women involved were heroes. Women's history is understandably looking for models, not for victims.

Having tried and failed to make the witches into independent women, I finally accepted that there are situations where women are victims, where others have power over them, to make them suffer or to die. One of the terrible ironies of the persecutions was that women were seen as powerful (as having destructive power) and yet often found themselves powerless before the courts. This contradiction requires historians to give a more nuanced reading of this material than we have done. A woman can be courageous, outspoken even, and still be trapped by society's choosing the female gender to be its scapegoat. That is what happened in many communities in sixteenth-century Europe.

This contradiction brings me to the historians' problem of finding patterns of oppression. Nothing brings down criticism on us like the suspicion that we are reading back our views into former times. We are trained rightly to situate our stories in the context of their times but wrongly, I believe, to avoid finding patterns. Imagine, then, my dismay when I recognized much of the background to the witch hunts. I am a medievalist; in teaching women's medieval history I learned to recognize the misogyny in my materials, and it was similar to that underlying the witch hunts—not "the same as" but similar to. Misogyny and patriarchal power change; they too have a history. But the underlying ideas were similar to what Europeans had believed about women throughout the Middle Ages. What changed in the story of the witch hunts was that ancient beliefs about women (that women are inherently weak, evil, and oversexed) and ancient customs of physically abusing women finally ignited into a major persecution by gender. When placed in its proper context as a chapter in women's history, witch hunting has to be seen as woman hunting.

Many critics are concerned lest we read back into the witch hunts our feminist ideas. I am concerned that, although we have documented so well the history of patriarchal power, we may now become afraid to apply this knowledge to our broader reinterpretation of history. If we do apply it, we will find patterns. Lyndal Roper has made a commonsense observation that is helpful here:

> . . . historical interpretation as we undertake it day by day nearly always depends at base on the assumption of a measure of resemblance: how else can we make sense of historical actors? it does not endanger the status of the history to recognize that some of its features are enduring: the importance of fantasy, the centrality of parental figures to psychic life . . .[28]

To Roper's list of enduring features, I would add "patterns of misogyny." By identifying these enduring patterns, we disturb some historians who now question the gender issue in witch hunting, but the patterns are there.

Yet, ultimately we cannot immerse ourselves in times of terror for the sake only of presenting the truth. To remember violence is too painful, too threatening. Either we will find some redeeming quality in this particular history, or we will abandon it. John Berger reminded us that "Memory implies a certain act of redemption. What is remembered has been saved from nothingness."[29] But when what is remembered is evil, only the rendering of justice can make this recognition of past evil redemptive. And that is where past and present meet in this story. There is no redemptive act that can save the witches, but their deaths can illumine the current struggle over violence against women.[30]

I am against forgetting. I am afraid that the scapegoating of women can happen again. I will close with Geoffrey Hartman's words:

> The aim of judgment in historical or literary-critical discourse ... is not that of determining guilt or innocence. It is to change history into memory: to make a case for what should be remembered. This responsibility converts every judgment into a judgment on the person who makes it.[31]

I submit that, ultimately, the witch hunts explain to us something about how men and women related to one another in those centuries. That we do not like what it tells us does not give us the right to censor the violence or ignore the gender message. To do so would render us liable to the judgment that we had distorted the truth.

Notes

1. Lyndal Roper, *Oedipus and the Devil: Witchcraft, Sexuality, and Religion in Early Modern Europe* (London and New York: Routledge, 1994) shows how rich the interrogations can be for women's history.

2. Gerhild Scholz Williams, *Defining Dominion: The Discourses of Magic and Witchcraft in Early Modern France and Germany* (Ann Arbor: University of Michigan Press, 1995); Frances Dolan, *Dangerous Familiars: Representations of Domestic Crime in England, 1550–1700* (Ithaca, NY: Cornell University Press, 1994); Roper, *Oedipus and the Devil*.

3. See, for example, Susan Amussen, *An Ordered Society, Gender and Class in Early Modern England* (Oxford: B. Blackwell, 1988), 31; Cynthia Herrup, *The Common Peace: Participation and the Criminal Law in Seventeenth-Century England* (Cambridge, Cambridge University Press, 1987); Keith Wrightson, "Two Concepts of Order," in *An Ungovernable People: The English and their Law in the Seventeenth and Eighteenth Centuries,* ed. John Brewer and John Styles (New Brunswick, N.J.: Rutgers University Press, 1980); *Crime in England, 1550–1800,* ed. J. S. Cockburn (Princeton, N.J.: Princeton University Press, 1977); Robin Briggs, *Witches and Neighbors: The Social and Cultural Context of European Witchcraft* (New York: Viking, 1996), 340–51 (on the Saarland); Gunther Lottes, "Popular Culture and the Early Modern State in Sixteenth-Century Germany," in *Understanding Popular Culture: Europe from the Middle Ages to the Nineteenth Century,* ed. Steven L. Kaplan (Berlin and New York: Mouton, 1984).

4. See Merry Wiesner's question, " ... the central question for our investigation of the lives of early modern women [may be]: what effects might this have had on women?" In Merry Wiesner, *Women and Gender in Early Modern Europe* (Cambridge: Cambridge University Press, 1993), 235.

5. Christina Larner, *Enemies of God: The Witch Hunt in Scotland* (Baltimore, Md.: Johns Hopkins University Press, 1981), 3–4, 100–102.

6. Marie-Sylvie Dupont-Bouchat, et al., *Prophètes et sorciers dans les Pays-Bas, XVIe–XVIIIe siècle* (Paris: Hachette, 1978), 142–44.

7. Laura Gowing, "Language, Power, and the Law: Women's Slander Litigation in Early Modern London," in *Women, Crime and the Courts in Early Modern England,*" ed. Jennifer Kermode and Garthine Walker (Chapel Hill: University of North Carolina Press, 1994).

8. Jennifer Kermode and Garthine Walker, "Introduction," in *Women, Crime and the Courts.*

9. Amussen, *An Ordered Society,* 152–53.

10. Gowing, "Language, Power, and the Law," 29, 37–38.

11. Frances Dolan discusses how the witch stands outside nature and the law, and thus could be seen as powerful and fearful by English society and its playwrights. See *Dangerous Familiars,* 210–12.

12. Bruce Lenman and Geoffrey Parker, "The State, the Community and the Criminal in Early Modern Europe," in *Crime and the Law: The Social History of Crime in Western Europe since 1500,* ed. V. A. C. Gatrall, et al. (London: Europa Publications, 1980), 37–38.

13. Robert Muchembled, *La Sorcière au Village XVe–XVIIIe siècle* (Paris: Gallimard, 1979); Alfred Soman, "The Parliament of Paris and the Great Witch Hunt (1565–1640)," in *Sixteenth Century Journal* 9, no. 2 (1978); Marie-Sylvie Dupont-Bouchat, et al., *Prophètes et sorciers dans les Pays-Bas.*

14. Anne L. Barstow, *Witchcraze: A New History of the European Witch Hunts* (San Francisco: Pandora, 1994): Luxemburg, 66–7; France, 69–70; Switzerland, 68; and Spain, 92–93. For England, see Marianne Hester, *Lewd Women and Wicked Witches* (London: Routledge, 1992). David Underdown has traced the rise of prosecution of those other unruly women, the scolds, during the same time span. See Underdown, "The Taming of the Scold: The Enforcement of Patriarchal Authority in Early Modern England," in *Order and Disorder in Early Modern England,* ed. Anthony Fletcher and John Stevenson (Cambridge: Cambridge University Press, 1985).

15. Edward Peters, *Inquisition* (New York: Free Press, 1988), ch. 2.

16. Barstow, *Witchcraze,* 25, 40–41.

17. Bruce Lenman and Geoffrey Parker, "The State, the Community and the Criminal Law in Early Modern Europe," in *Crime and the Law.*

18. Christina Larner, "'Crimen Exceptum'? The Crime of Witchcraft in Europe," in *Witchcraft and Religion: The Politics of Popular Belief* (Oxford: Oxford University Press, 1984); Edward Peters, *The Magician, the Witch, and the Law* (Philadelphia: University of Pennsylvania Press, 1978), 152.

19. Andrew Delbanco, *The Death of Satan: How Americans Have Lost the Sense of Evil* (New York: Farrar, Straus, & Giroux, 1995), 7.

20. See Barstow, "Controlling Women's Bodies: Violence and Sadism," in *Witchcraze,* ch. 7.

21. Robin Briggs, *Witches and Neighbors: The Social and Cultural Context of European Witchcraft* (New York: Viking, 1996), 399.

22. Barstow, *Witchcraze,* 131–33.

23. James A. Sharpe, "Women, Witchcraft, and the Legal Process," in *Women, Crime, and the Courts,* 107–8. See also James A. Sharpe, *Instruments of Darkness: Witchcraft in Early Modern England* (Philadelphia: University of Pennsylvania Press, 1997).

24. I know of no European-wide statistical study of accusers. My own partial research indicates that the majority were men, and that some female accusers testified at the behest of their husbands.

25. Sharpe, "Women, witchcraft, and the legal process."

26. Briggs, *Witches and Neighbors*, 400. Whereas it is good to note that about one-half of the accusations that came to trial were dismissed, one must remember that an accusation of witchcraft could not be lived down. So great were the fear and hatred of witches that the accused (and possibly her family as well) would be persecuted for life. Also, punishments less severe than the death penalty were often imposed, such as whipping or banishment.

27. Lawrence Langer, *The Holocaust and the Literary Imagination* (New Haven: Yale University Press, 1975), 22.

28. Roper, *Oedipus and the Devil*, 228.

29. John Berger, *About Looking* (New York: Pantheon Books, 1980).

30. Dominick LaCapra is helpful in dealing with the "historically repressed." See *Representing the Holocaust: History, Theory, Trauma* (Ithaca, Cornell University Press, 1994), especially ch. 6.

31. Geoffrey Hartman, "Judging Paul de Man," in *Minor Prophecies: The Literary Essay in the Culture Wars* (Cambridge, Mass.: Harvard University Press, 1991), 148.

Workshop Summaries 13–21:
Law and Criminality

Workshop #13: "Beyond the Religious Pale: Gender, Marginality, and Persecution"

Organizers

Joan Larsen Klein, English, University of Illinois, Urbana; Anne Lake Prescott, English, Barnard College; Catharine Randall, French, Fordham University; and Betty S. Travitsky, English, CUNY

Readings

Henry Goodcole, *True Declaration of the Manner of Proceeding against Elizabeth Sawyer, late of Edmonton* (London, 1621); Thomas Dekker, *The Witch of Edmonton* (London, 1621); Mme. de Guyon (Jeanne-Marie Bouvier de La Motte), *Le Moyen Court* (Paris, 1685); and William Weston, *The Autobiography of an Elizabethan*, trans. Philip Caraman (London: Longman's, 1955).

The purpose of the workshop was to explore how crossing religious boundaries was read as transgression in England and France and to ask how studying such transgression might take into account how boundaries varied with place (what was illegal in England could be laudable in France) and how the practice and treatment of transgression could be affected by gender. We therefore chose materials that raise questions about perspective as well as gender. We included a presentation on witches, everywhere transgressive, and on Jewish women, who in many places had to conceal transgressive beliefs and practices that more than the adventures of English Jesuits, say, or the prayer meetings of French Huguenots, were focused on the home. Joan Larsen Klein outlined the case of Elizabeth Sawyer, an uneducated and, says some evidence, inarticulate woman executed for witchcraft whose trial and death were soon the subjects of literary attention. Catharine Randall spoke briefly about the aristocratic Jeanne-Marie Bouvier de La Motte (also known as Mme. Guyon), a devotee of quietism accused by Mme.

de Maintenon, mistress of Louis XIV, of teaching heresy to the young. Guyon's *Le moyen court,* said Randall, relates uneasily to the author's mysticism, and even as the author denies being a heretic, she suggests, in ways with which Catholic orthodoxy would be uncomfortable, that God is the work's real author. Betty Travitsky discussed unpublished petitions by two Marrano women: Sara Lopez (wife of Dr. Roderigo Lopez, who was executed in 1594, almost certainly unjustly, for attempting to poison Elizabeth I), and her daughter, Anne Travitsky pointed out that most petitions to retain the property of a traitor were denied, but that in this case the queen agreed to the widow's request and returned all the property except a ring, which for some reason she often wore at her side. Anne Prescott distributed excerpts from the journal of William Weston (translated in 1955 by Philip Caraman), a member of the Jesuit underground in Elizabeth's England, who, despite the help of many Catholic Englishwomen, was caught and jailed. She wondered what difference, such as increased opportunities for spatial mobility within England, his gender made to his activities.

Discussion was lively and included such topics for further thought as gender and enthusiasm in Guyon's work; the portability of margins (Can one take one's marginality with one? Does it become internalized?); the seventeenth-century movement to allow the reentry of Jews and millenialism; how the Protestant projection of monstrosity onto Catholics might connect with gender (are English recusants read as more "female" than Protestants?); the paradox that those outside one's established religious pale might feel exiled at home but accepted abroad (for example, the few English Jews' sense of exile or centeredness might vary depending on whether they were at home or in Amsterdam). Linda Austern speculated about gender, voice, and religious allegiance in Renaissance singing practices. Several participants stressed that "marginalized" groups were not themselves homogeneous, whatever the common experiences within such groups, and that the experiences of men and women would in any case differ.

Submitted by Anne Lake Prescott

Workshop #14: "The Boundaries of Violence: Literary Representations of Sex and Violence in Early Modern England, Spain, and Italy"

Organizers

Deborah Burks, English, Ohio State University (Lima); Emily Detmer, English, Millikin University; and Lisa Vollendorf, Spanish, Wayne State University

Readings

Anonymous, "From a Volunteer at St. Maries to a Friend in London"; "On the Taking [of] St. Maries, a Poem"; and "The Gentleman in London's Answer to his Friend at St. Maries" in *Letters from the Living to the Living*, ed. Malcolm J. Bosse (New York: Garland Publishing, 1973); Pietro Aretino, *Dialogues* (*Capricciosi Ragionamenti* [1536]), trans. Raymond Rosenthal (New York: Marsilio, 1971); María de Zayas y Sotomayor, "Marriage Abroad, Portent of Doom," *The Disenchantments of Love*, trans. H. Patsy Boyer (Binghamton: SUNY Press, 1997); Elaine Scarry, introduction to *The Body in Pain* (Oxford: Oxford University Press, 1985).

We conceived of this workshop as a framework for sorting out the meanings and implications of literary representations of violence in the early modern period. Grouped together, the primary texts—an English ballad, Italian erotic dialogue, and a Spanish novella—provide a rich starting place for considerations of sexual violence because they each deal with violence in unique, yet fundamentally disturbing, ways. In using the term "boundaries of violence" in the session title, we meant to direct our thinking toward the questions of gender, genre, readership, class, nationality, and religion that inform these and other representations of violence in the period.

We opened discussion with a question about the ways in which we read violence and the ways in which male and female authors write about violence. One participant's suggestion that women authors tend to underwrite violent scenes led to a broader consideration of the myriad formulae and *topoi* that inform plot, characterization, and narration. A comparative discussion of Zayas's feminist novellas and the anti-Spanish, anti-Catholic *Letters to the Living* emphasized the importance of taking into account possible readership and the political and didactic purposes of a given text in order to understand the larger context in which violence appears. A difficult question raised by the consideration of gender and genre remains: how can we distinguish between male and female authors' uses of violence when the literature seems bound so strictly to formulas?

Another interesting aspect of the commentary focused on our own interpretations of representational violence. Whereas Aretino's *Dialogues* seems pornographic to the modern reader, participants voiced curiosity about the use of the text in its own time period. Whether read aloud among groups of men or read silently in private, this text clearly was meant to titillate a male reader. Comments on reading and on readership raised the pertinent question of what it means to study—to read, critique, and teach—texts that represent violence against women. We explained that we had decided not to read textual excerpts aloud as a way of avoiding participation in the violence of the texts themselves. Another problematic issue was raised by an historian who said that she was struggling with the use of the term "pornography" to refer to specific sections of a witchcraft treatise she has been studying. A debate ensued about the flexibility (and hence availability) of the term and about the alternative term "erotic text." Some participants suggested—to others' disagreement—that "erotic" was perhaps a better term to use than "pornography." The implicit question here, of course, is that of perspective: who finds violent texts erotic and why?

The workshop provided an opportunity for close comparative readings of works directed at very different readerships in several national contexts. These juxtapositions highlighted the importance of focusing on historical and cultural specificity while simultaneously paying attention to the distancing techniques employed as authors represent violent acts and display the violated body.

Additional Readings

de Lauretis, Teresa. "The Violence of Rhetoric: Considerations on Representation and Gender." In *Technologies of Gender*, 31–49. Bloomington: Indiana University Press, 1987.

Gibson, Suzanne. "On Sex, Horror and Human Rights." *Women: A Cultural Review* 4.3 (1993): 250–60.

Levine, Laura. "Rape, Repetition, and the Politics of Closure in *A Midsummer Night's Dream*." In *Feminist Readings of Early Modern Culture*, edited by Valerie Traub et al., 210–28. Cambridge: Cambridge University Press, 1996.

Scarry, Elaine. *The Body in Pain*. Oxford: Oxford University Press, 1985.

Submitted by: Lisa Vollendorf

Workshop #15: "The Crimes and Punishments of Women"

Organizers

Jane Kromm, Art History and Women's Studies, Purchase College, State University of New York; Guido Ruggiero, History, Pennsylvania State University

Readings

Excerpts, cases brought before the Inquisition, Venice, 1570s–1590s (Archivo di Stato, Venezia, Busta 59,61,64,65,66,68; excerpts, *The Life and Death of Mrs. Mary Frith, commonly called Moll Cutpurse* (1662) (rpt. New York: Garland, 1993); excerpts, Sarah Malcolm, *A True Copy of the Paper, Delivered the Night Before Her Execution* (London: J. Wilford, 1732); engraved portraits of ten criminals, 1650–1750.

This session investigated the ways in which gender informed shifts in the definition and representation of criminal activity through an analysis of British criminal portraits and depositions of women healers brought before the Inquisition in sixteenth-century Venice. The workshop organizers discussed these sources as evidence for two complementary dynamics: a delegitimizing of women's traditional arenas of mastery, and a criminalizing of women's everyday skills and activities. Together, these dynamics created a gendered typology of malfeasance and malefactors.

Guido Ruggiero introduced his archival material in a brief account of the ways in which science in the early modern period needed to break away from a magical and spiritual worldview that permeated everyday culture. Part of that process was predicated on a "delegitimation" of women healers. Labeling them as criminals, frauds, or heretics disempowered these women and moved early science to a "higher" and more aristocratic social level. It served also to disempower and eventually destroy an everyday culture of healing that had been controlled by women. It has proved difficult to recover that culture; however, the crimes of women in the early modern period can provide a rich view of that world. Jane Kromm reviewed the criminal portraits included in the packet sent to participants, emphasizing that the representation of malefactors in British popular prints from 1650 to 1750 was characterized by skillful manipulation of traditional gender stereotypes for sensationalistic and didactic imperatives. Portrait likenesses of scolds, thieves, highwaymen, and murderers employed in varying degrees the gender-weighted imagery of agency and tactical skill, along with or in contrast to conventions for depicting negative capability and evil incarnate. These visual conventions were further affected by claims for authenticity in likeness and by the customary handling of the criminal body after execution. The visual logistics of criminal portrayals gave form to, and were thus distinctive formulations of, culpability and character, and as such, they contribute vital information to our understanding of women's crimes and punishments in the early modern era.

Much of the discussion focused on the use of inquisition records to access popular culture, and on the difficulties inherent in the deposition format. The suppressive elements in inquisition proceedings were noted, as was the recognition that some women were successful manipulators of their inquisitors. The criminal portraits were less familiar to the majority of participants, but there was lively discussion of the logic behind the many disparate renderings of Sarah Malcolm, in which elements of pathos, love magic, and romance became increasingly elaborate. There were also several attempts to understand the consistently effeminate portrayals of the male criminals.

Additional Readings

Dolan, Frances. *Domestic Familiars. Representations of Domestic Crime in England, 1550-1700*. Ithaca: Cornell University Press, 1994.
Pointon, Marcia. *Hanging the Head: Portraiture and Social Formation in Eighteenth-Century England*. New Haven: Yale University Press, 1993.
Rawlings, Philip. *Drunks, Whores, and Idle Apprentices. Criminal Biography in the Eighteenth Century*. New York: Routledge, 1992.
Straub, Kristina. "Heteroanxiety and the Case of Elizabeth Canning." *Eighteenth-Century Studies* 30, 3 (Spring 1997): 296–304.

Submitted by: Jane Kromm

Workshop #16: "Curly, Curvy Language: Male Representations of Feminine Copia"

Organizers

Mary Bly, English, Washington University, St. Louis; Anne Cotterill, English, Rutgers University; Diane Senior, Italian, University of Vermont

Readings

Dante's *Inferno*, V (New York: Oxford University Press, 1939); Milton's *Paradise Lost*, Book X (New York: Norton, 1992); Shakespeare's *Hamlet*, Act IV (New York: Norton, 1975).

This workshop sought to explore the tensions in male-authored works between the narrator-hero and a female figure who is portrayed as dangerously copious and whose language and, in some cases, appearance, is mystify-ingly digressive. The organizers chose three canonical texts of the Late Middle Ages and Renaissance from Italy and England with the hope of finding dis-tinctions that would aid in the interpretation of male-authored female speech.

Diane Senior discussed Francesca in *Inferno* V of Dante's *Divina Commedia*, questioning whether her adulterous behavior and subsequent defense of such behavior were the products of her being a poor reader. Was Dante saying that the passive, literalist tendencies of women readers caused her fatal misreading of *Lancelot?* Senior denied such claims and pointed out that Francesca's speech showed considerable sophistication and that the failures in her mental process, which landed her in hell, were no more pronounced than those of her male coun-terparts. Francesca was, nonetheless, dangerous because she manipulated her audience's affective response through seductive language and rhetoric. Senior concluded that Francesca erred not because of an overly literal interpretation of what she read, but because of her use of the figurative. Through the character of Francesca, Dante compared traditionally feminine allures with the abuses of what he considered a faulty interpretive mode common to a male writing com-munity, carrying out a complicated gender reversal that warrants further ques-tioning. Mary Bly examined the example of Ophelia's winding, fluid, flowery language in Shakespeare's *Hamlet*. In the early acts, Ophelia appeared threaten-ing to Hamlet both as her father's pawn and as a distracting sexual presence. Bly questioned why in Act IV Ophelia broke her silence with an appearance and rhetoric that exposed the inadequacy of her characterization as the straight line. Bly concluded by drawing parallels between Ophelia's words and those of Queen Elizabeth. Was it possible that historic female figure's strategic digressions and manipulative and hidden rhetoric served as a model for women's speech in Shakespeare? Anne Cotterill addressed how Milton's Eve appeared to Adam as disturbingly overelaborate, "too much of ornament," in *Paradise Lost*. For all her visible ornament, Cotterill acknowledged, Eve evolved through dreams and silences. Cotterill argued that Eve exposed the ambiguity of divine abundance: that is, the first mother who reforms the anachronistic, rigid law and sounds of God the Father by internalizing and containing the pressures of physical and aural profusion in this poem. Cotterill considered how Eve's healing speech in Book Ten erupted like a spring from one of the underground rivers in Eden and turned Adam from an angry father to a forgiving son. How did Eve's startling parturition of an original voice anticipate the virgin birth of Milton's quiet hero, "the great Son," and mark the digressive progress and accomplishment of an epic that held all in suspense, even death, until the hidden moment was ripe?

Discussion focused on issues of women's speech in these texts and how they raised similar questions for other texts, such as *Othello, Canterbury Tales*, and lesser-known historical texts. Many participants were engaged by the idea that male authors would portray women as literalists and truth-tellers as a way of cutting through male rhetoric. In Dante, for example, Francesca's words acknowledge and transcend the revelation that she and Paolo loved in accordance to or because of a book, the medieval romance of Lancelot. Francesca's account of their passion, of the kiss that ends their lives, in effect, closes the mouth of book speech and reveals the contrast between "real" and "literary" passion or between what could be described as "feminine" and "male" rhetorical formulas. Further dialogue also associated female literality with anatomy, the womb, and the biology of reproduction. The effortlessness of female interiority and creativity was seen to contrast with the effortful, book-trained verbal productions of men. For example, Ophelia's literal flowers disprove all the male flowers of rhetoric she reproduces in garbled form. Finally, Satan's words to Eve presented questions for yet another avenue of future exploration concerning how male speech invades and colonizes the female body's interior spaces. Such an avenue of study is equally valid for Satan and Eve, Hamlet's relationship to Ophelia, Paola and Francesca's seduction by the words of a book, and many other male-authored texts.

Additional Readings

Finucci, Valeria, and Regina Schwartz, editors. *Desire in the Renaissance: Psychoanalysis and Literature.* Princeton: Princeton University Press, 1994.

Parker, Patricia. *Literary Fat Ladies: Rhetoric, Gender, Property.* New York: Methuen, 1987.

Solterer, Helen. *The Master and Minerva: Disputing Women in French Medieval Culture.* Berkeley: University of California Press, 1995.

Walker, Julia M. *Medusa's Mirrors: Spencer, Shakespeare, Milton, and the Metamorphosis of the Female Self.* Newark and London: Associated University Presses, 1998.

Submitted by: Diane Senior

Workshop #17: "The Elizabeth Canning Case: Truth and Myth-Making"

Organizers

Amy Masciola, History, University of Maryland at College Park; Dana Rabin, History, University of Michigan; Jennifer Thorn, English, Duke University

Readings

"The trial of Elizabeth Canning," May 1754, *Old Bailey Proceedings*, 157–73. One item in one of the following categories: 1. PAMPHLET LITERATURE: Henry Fielding, "A Clear State of the Case of Elizabeth Canning" (London, March 1753), in Malvin Zirker, ed., *An Enquiry into the Causes of the Late Increase of Robbers and Related Writings* (Middletown, Conn.: Wesleyan University Press, 1988), 283–313 (especially pp. 286–95 and 307–12); and Allan Ramsay, "A letter to the right honourable the Earl of—" (London, June 1753; reprint, "On Elizabeth Canning" in *The Investigator* London, 1762), 16–39. 2. POPULAR ACCOUNTS: "Elizabeth Canning, Drawn from the Life" (London, Aug. 1754); "The Devil Outdone" (1753/54?); and "The Truth's Found Out at Last" (April 1753).

Our intention in organizing "The Elizabeth Canning Case: Truth and Myth-Making" was to stimulate discussion of a particular historical event and the nature of evidence. We chose as a case study the disappearance of and subsequent trials surrounding Elizabeth Canning. In our exploration of the meanings of representations of Canning and her accused kidnapper, Mary Squires, we considered both popular and official documents, as well as works of art. Canning's disappearance in 1753, Squires's trial, and Canning's own trial in 1754 for perjury generated dozens of pamphlets, broadsides, ballads, and legal and medical accounts. We asked participants to read a variety of sources revealing a contemporary debate between those who saw Canning as the young, simple, virgin and those who saw a promiscuous infanticide who was willing to sacrifice Squires's life to protect her own reputation.

After introductions of all the participants, the workshop began with Amy Masciola's suggestion that Canning embodied the "dangerous domestic servant" in the middle of the eighteenth century, when the influx of young single women into the capital became a source of tension between both men and women and middle- and working-class people. Dana Rabin questioned the conventional approach historians have taken to infanticide as a woman's crime. She pointed to evidence suggesting that Canning was aided and abetted in her crimes (infanticide or abortion) by a "mystery man." Rabin and other participants expressed a desire to "solve the mystery," and tension between those who wanted to theorize about what might have happened to Canning and those who wanted to focus on what the representations of her meant led to a lively discussion. Jennifer Thorn asked questions about the nature of agency and how texts reveal and construct individual agency. She also saw the figures in the case as representative of larger cultural forces.

Workshop participants included literary scholars and historians. One in particular, historian Carole Levin, had been drawn to the case by reading Josephine Tey's mystery novel, *The Franchise Affair*, which is based on the Canning case. Levin uses the Canning case in her teaching, and the group discussed the potential problems and benefits of using notorious criminal cases in teaching history or literature. How can a discussion of the indeterminacy of historical knowledge help students think about texts and their importance? Other participants pointed to more psychoanalytic interpretations of Canning's story, suggesting that the reason for her not eating or experiencing any bodily functions during those four weeks was her suppressed knowledge about her own body.

Inevitably, the discussion raised more questions than it answered. It succeeded in generating a dialogue between scholars from different disciplines on a range of topics, from pedagogy to the nature of historical evidence. At the end of the workshop, we examined several illustrations of Canning and the gypsy. The group analyzed the symbols and references in each picture, and agreed that future work on Canning will need to focus much more attention on the visual representations.

Additional Readings

McCue, Lillian Bueno. "Elizabeth Canning in Print." *University of Colorado Studies,* series B 2, no. 4 (Oct. 1945): 223.

Moore, Judith. *The Appearance of Truth: The Story of Elizabeth Canning and Eighteenth-Century Narrative.* Newark: University of Delaware Press; London and Cranbury, N.J.: Associated University Presses, 1994.

Straub, Kristina. "Heteroanxiety and the Case of Elizabeth Canning." *Eighteenth-Century Studies* 30, no. 3 (Summer 1997): 296–304.

Treherne, John. *The Canning Enigma.* N.p: Cape, 1989.

Wilner, Arlene. "The Mythology of History, the Truth of Fiction: Henry Fielding and the Cases of Bosavern Penlez and Elizabeth Canning." *The Journal of Narrative Technique* 21, no. 2 (Spring 1991): 185–201.

Submitted by: Amy Masciola

Workshop #18: "Exploring Boundaries between Law and Practice"

Organizers

Ann Crabb, History, James Madison University; Barbara Ann McCahill, History, Bradford College

Readings

Photocopies of laws in effect in Henry VIII's England on treason, wife beating, and the feme couvert, and cases from court records and letters shedding light on these subjects; laws on women and property from fifteenth century Florence and evidence from Florentine wills and letters about women's inheritance of patrimonial and dotal property and control over what they inherited.

The workshop organizers, in their separate researches on women in sixteenth-century England and fifteenth-century Florence, each noticed that practice often varied from formal law in cases involving women. Wills, letters, and other contemporary sources juxtaposed with relevant laws provided a fruitful subject for group discussion. Barbara Ann McCahill described evidence that wives of noblemen who had been found guilty of treason in Henry VIII's England often, contrary to the law of confiscation, preserved their husband's wealth and property; that although law allowed husbands to physically punish wives, noblemen accused of doing so expressed shame and denial; and that, although under common law wives as "femes couverts" were ineligible to make wills, nearly a fourth of the noblewomen in her sample did so. For Florence, Ann Crabb reported that women could have an informal role in politics not recognized by law; that women had more autonomy acting in legal matters than the law allowed; and that women's position in inheritance was much better in wills than the laws of intestate inheritance decreed. On the other hand, her evidence about dowries shows that practice could sometimes conform to the law, which protected dotal property from creditors, and sometimes be worse than the law, which required heirs to return a widow's dowry to her promptly.

The discussion of issues raised by the presentations centered on three main topics. The participants discussed the importance of establishing what normal practice was, in order to provide standards to evaluate the degree to which law and practice diverged, because practice may coincide with law, may be better than law, or may be worse than law. Second, participants were interested in the intermediate position of wills between law and practice. Wills indicate practice in the sense of intention, and that in itself has significance in evaluating the position of women in the family. However, wills do not indicate how property transfers work out. Were wills with female principal heirs more likely to be contested by relatives than those with male heirs? Did female heirs have enough control over their property before widowhood to make possession significant? What percentage of men and women wrote wills, what percentage died intestate, and what were the implications for female inheritance? What was the influence of social class on the writing of wills and on the choice of heirs? In England, how many women outside the nobility with living husbands left wills? The third topic that held the group's attention was the relationship between inherited property and dowries and other matrimonial settlements in law and practice. What share of family property did women get, compared to their brothers, when inheritance and matrimonial settlements were combined? What impact did the legal protections granted matrimonial settlements have on women and their families, and how did this affect family strategies?

Participants left the workshop saying that they could talk about these issues for hours, but that the best plan was to do further research into them and to continue the discussion another time with more evidence.

Additional Readings

Bridenthal, Renate, Claudia Koonz, and Susan Studard, editors. *Becoming Visible: Women in European History*, 226–230. 2d ed. Boston: Hougton Mifflin, 1987.

Erickson, Amy Louise. *Women and Property in Early Modern England*. New York: Routledge, 1993.

Ruggiero, Guido. *The Boundaries of Eros: Sex, Crime and Sexuality in Renaissance Venice*. New York: Oxford University Press, 1985.

Submitted by: Ann Crabb

Workshop # 19: "Tongues, Swords, Needles, and Pens: Engendering Tongues in Popular Culture and in the Courts"

Organizers

Laura Deal, History, University of Colorado; Ina Habermann, English, University of Munich; Erna Kelly, English, University of Wisconsin, Eau Claire

Readings

"The Discontented Married Men: Or A merry new Song . . . Of a Scold that could not keep her lips together" and "Keep a Good Tongue in Your Head," *The Roxburghe Ballads* (Hertford, Eng.: Stephen Austin, 1877; rpt., New York: AMS, 1966); *The Witches of Northamptonshire* (London, 1612); Defamation Cases from the Consistory Court of the Diocese of Chester; *Swetnam, The Woman-hater*, ed. Coryl Crandall (Purdue, Ind.: Purdue University Studies, 1969); *Lingua* (London, 1607); Thomas Overbury, "A Wife" in *Overburian Characters*, ed. W. J. Paylor (Oxford: Basil Blackwell, 1936); Thomas Jordan, "A Virtuous Wife" in *Pictures of Passions, Fancies, and Affections . . . in a Variety of Characters* (London, n.d.); Richard Braithwait, *The English Gentlewoman* (1631; rpt. Amsterdam: De Capo, 1970); Daniel Tuvil, *Assylum Veneris.* (London, 1616); Joseph Swetnam, *The Arraignment of Lewd, Idle, Froward, and Unconstant Women and Ester Sowernam, Ester Hath Hanged Haman: or, An Answere to . . . The Arraignment of Women*, in *The Whole Duty of a Woman*, ed. Angeline Goreau (New York: Doubleday, 1985); Margaret Cavendish, *Poems and Fancies* (1653; rpt., Menston, Yorkshire, Eng.: Scolar Press, 1972); "The Prologue," in *The Complete Works of Anne Bradstreet*, ed. Joseph McElrath Jr. and Allan Robb (Boston: Twayne, 1981).

Workshop participants read excerpts of trial transcripts, plays, ballads, pamphlets, conduct books, and Theophrastan characters concerning women's speech. Laura Deal's opening remarks (read by Susan Amussen in her absence) pointed out that women's speech was characterized by its power to create or destroy neighbors' reputations informally through gossip and formally through court testimony. Both Deal and Ina Habermann pointed out that men drew up the rules for, presided over, and transcribed trials, thus to a degree controlling women's speech in the courts. Habermann noted further that the plays *Lingua* and *Swetnam, the Woman-hater*, which both include trial scenes, judge speech along gender lines. When women speak, they fight with their tongues and thus are guilty of social disruption; however, when men contend, their tongues are not only acquitted of social disruption but are awarded such epithets as "reasonable," "authoritative," and even "eloquent." Erna Kelly's introduction focused on popular images ancillary to the gendered tongue: for men not only the sword but also the pen, both agents of power, and for women, needles instead of pens, needlework being associated with painting, the silent sister of poetry. Kelly concluded by showing slides of English and Continental emblems of tongues and related images. All three organizers emphasized the conflation of female speech with sexual promiscuity.

Among topics discussed were the continuation of communal shaming rituals, which left women a nonmale dominated arena for protecting their reputations, and the authorization of women's speech in certain situations. For example, midwives were authorized to force names of fathers out of women in labor, and in some communities a woman had the right to yell outside the door of a woman who had taken her husband. Another point raised was the predominance of defamation cases initiated by men rather than by women in some regions of England. Several participants questioned whether an emblem of a tongue with wings was ungendered: they saw it as serpentine, leading some to align it with female monsters of antiquity and others to align it with maleness, given its phallic resemblance and the Renaissance shift to depicting serpents at times as male. Participants likewise noted that needlework might be silent when viewed as a product but not when viewed as a process: women were sometimes read to as they embroidered and at other times, no doubt, conversed as they worked.

The discussion led the group to observe the importance of placing evidence from popular literature and the courts within the context of social practices and regional variations of those practices. Finally, the group raised the following questions for consideration in future research. To what extent did prescriptions of silence really silence women? What kind of authority did women have despite the courts' authority? Was women's authority only informal and thus marginalized? Why do we so often choose to read the attacks against women's speech instead of the defenses?

Additional Readings

Gowing, Laura. *Domestic Dangers: Women, Words, and Sex in Early Modern London.* Oxford: Clarendon, 1996.

Ingram, Martin. *Church Courts, Sex and Marriage in England, 1570–1640.* Cambridge: Cambridge University Press, 1987.

Purkiss, Diane. "Material Girls: The Seventeenth-Century Woman Debate." In *Women, Texts and Histories, 1575–1760,* edited by Clare Brant and Diane Purkiss, 69–101. London: Routledge, 1992.

Wiltenberg, Joy. *Disorderly Women and Female Power in the Street Literature of Early Modern England and Germany.* Charlottesville: University Press of Virginia, 1992.

Woodbridge, Linda. *Women and the English Renaissance.* Champaign-Urbana: University of Illinois, 1984.

Submitted by: Erna Kelly

Workshop #20: "Unlawful Knowledge: Female Textuality on Trial in Early Modern Europe"

Organizers

Marina Leslie, English, Northeastern University; Geraldine Munoz Wagner, English, Brown University; Naomi Yavneh, Renaissance Studies, University of South Florida

Readings

Giovanni Boccaccio, *Concerning Famous Women,* trans. with intro. and notes by Guido A. Guarino (New Brunswick, N.J.: Rutgers University Press, 1964), ch. 99, "Pope Joan," 231–33; Elizabeth Cellier, *Malice Defeated: Or a Brief Relation of the Accusation and Deliverance of Elizabeth Cellier, Wherein her Proceedings both before and during her Confinement, are particularly Related, and the Mystery of the Meal-Tub fuly discovered: Together with an Abstract of her Arraignment and Trial, written by her self, for the satisfaction of all Lovers of Undisguised Truth* (London, 1680), title page and preface; Thomas Collins, *The Tryal and Sentence of Elizabeth Cellier: for Writing, Printing, and Publishing, a Scandalous Libel, called Malice Defeated, & c. At the sessions in the Old Bailey, held Saturday the 11th and Monday the 13th of September 1680,* (London, 1680), title page and description of Elizabeth Cellier's sentence for libel; Mary Carleton, *The Case of Madam Mary Carleton, Lately Stiled The German Princess, Truely Stated: With an Historical Relation of her Birth, Education, and Fortunes; in an appeal to His Illustrious Highness Prince Rupert. By the Said Mary Carleton,* (London, 1673), title page, frontispiece, 86–92, and 112–15.

Our workshop explored the legal sanctions employed against early modern women who exceeded normative boundaries determining the realm of authorized female knowledge. In addressing the issue of how law served patriarchy in its construction and policing of the borders between appropriate roles for early modern men and women, we focused primarily on one legendary woman (Pope Joan) and two historical women (Elizabeth Cellier and Mary Carleton) who resisted such containment and transgressed gender boundaries in ways deemed legally actionable.

We began with a brief introduction and explication of one of the "transgressive women" who were the subjects of the three primary texts circulated in advance. Naomi Yavneh presented a number of fifteenth- and sixteenth-century images of Pope Joan, the legendary ninth-century transvestite scholar whose public childbirth (in the midst of a papal procession!) is represented as a revelation of her monstrous nature: as learned woman, as cross dresser, as female prelate, as pregnant pope. Both Elizabeth Cellier and Mary Carleton were considered through their self-inscriptive defenses and the corollary legal attacks against these attempts at textual self-definition. Marina Leslie explained that, as a practicing midwife and outspoken advocate of the female craft of midwifery as well as a practicing Catholic, Cellier found herself the focus of multiple suspicions. As Leslie underscored, although Cellier was unjustly implicated in the Popish and Meal Tub Plots, she was able to vindicate herself in writing from charges of treason only to be condemned for libel. Geraldine Munoz Wagner considered how Mary (Moders) Carleton, accused of committing bigamy by disappearing into the false impersonation of a German princess, so successfully performed this identity in print and on trial that she won acquittal and notoriety. She subsequently continued to reinvent herself, exploiting the marriage market for financial gain and sexual adventure until her execution a decade later for petty thievery.

Each of the three women considered possessed what was viewed as a very dangerous knowledge of the cultural construction of gender norms; they demonstrated this knowledge through their ability to impersonate, manipulate, and subvert these norms. The discussion focused on the criminal and canon laws that were brought to bear on these women and helped to bring into relief the resulting legal reformation and deposition of the unruly female subject. Pope Joan is condemned, rendered monstrous and unnatural by the very female nature she would disguise; Carleton and Cellier are accused under assumptions of female craftiness that link feminine expertise with treacherous overreaching. We also explored issues raised by our topic regarding the intrinsic interdisciplinarity of the subject of female criminality as the intersection of a variety of legal, theological, medical, literary, and other discourses governing female sexuality and textuality. In our discussion, the participants considered the cultural and historical differences between early Renaissance Italy and Restoration England, and ecclesiastical and secular laws. Yet, despite these disparities, the three women demonstrate the way legal hegemonies shaped women's roles and even the representation of their bodies, by controlling their access to textuality and the public sphere.

Additional Readings

Dolan, Frances. "Reading, Writing and Other Crimes." In *Feminist Readings of Early Modern Culture: Emerging Subjects,* edited by Valerie Traub, M. Lindsay Kaplan, and Dympna Callaghan, 142–67. Cambridge: Cambridge University Press, 1996.

D'Onofrio, Cesare. *La papessa Giovanna: Roma e papato tra storia e leggenda.* Rome: Editrice, 1979.

George, Margaret. "Elizabeth Cellier, Misfit." In *Women in the First Capitalist Society,* 112–33. Champaign-Urbana: University of Illinois Press, 1988.

Jordan, Constance. "Boccaccio's In-famous Women: Gender and Civic Virtue in the *De mulieribus claris.*" In *Ambiguous Realities: Women in the Middle Ages and Renaissance,* edited by Carole Levin and Jeanie Watson, 25–47. Detroit, Mich.: Wayne State University Press, 1987.

Marland, Hilary, editor. *The Art of Midwifery: Early Modern Midwives in Europe.* New York and London: Routledge, 1993.

Submitted by: Naomi Yavneh

Workshop #21: "Women, Magic, Religion and Ritual: Women as Defenders of Faith and Community"

Organizers

Stephanie S. Dickey, Art History, Indiana University-Purdue University, Indianapolis; Allyson Poska, History, Mary Washington College

Readings

Elizabeth Honig, "In Memory: Lady Dacre and Pairing by Hans Eworth," *Renaissance Bodies: The Human Figure in English Culture c. 1540–1660,* ed. L.

Gent and N. Llewellyn (London: Reaktion Books, 1990), 61–85; Guido Ruggiero, "The Women Priests of Latisana: Apollonia Madizza and the Ties That Bind," *Binding Passions: Tales of Magic, Marriage and Power at the End of the Renaissance* (New York and Oxford: Oxford University Press, 1993), 130–74 (abridged); Sharon T. Strocchia, "Funerals and the Politics of Gender in Early Renaissance Florence," *Refiguring Woman. Perspectives on Gender and the Italian Renaissance*, ed. M. Migiel and J. Schiesari (Ithaca and London: Cornell University Press, 1991), 155–68.

This workshop explored women's roles in early modern communal and religious ritual. Aspects initially proposed for discussion included rituals surrounding life events, such as birth, marriage, and death (e.g., the expression of grief in mourning); women's participation in mainstream and radical religion; and their roles in folk culture and custom. We hoped that the discussion might illuminate ways in which patriarchal systems failed to recognize, feared, challenged, or deliberately subverted traditional female authority, as well as circumstances in which female authority prevailed. Readings included Elizabeth Honig's article on Hans Eworth's portrait of Lady Dacre, considering the iconography and conventions of widowhood in sixteenth-century England; Guido Ruggiero's essay exploring the friction between Roman Catholic orthodoxy and women's authority as healers and matchmakers in Italy; and Sharon Strocchia's examination of the relationship of Florentine funeral ritual to circumstances of status, age, and gender.

Stephanie Dickey presented a brief survey of women's social and religious roles in seventeenth-century Holland as codified in visual imagery, especially portraits and genre paintings. She illustrated aspects of women's participation in Dutch Protestant culture and considered some of the methodological problems posed by visual evidence, which, while offering insights into daily experience, is also responsive to pictorial, rhetorical, and iconographic conventions and traditions. Allyson Poska summarized her recent research on the impact of Roman Catholicism on early modern peasant women in the Spanish province of Galicia. Her findings show that Roman Catholic priests did little to encourage women's faith, even discouraging it by such practices as barring small children from services, thus effectively preventing many women from attending mass.

The discussion focused especially on women's religious roles. Differences between Protestant and Catholic culture were brought out, as, for instance, visual evidence suggesting that women and children were welcome in Dutch Protestant churches, in contrast to their marginalization in Galicia. A discussion of the role of the pastor's wife emerged from Dickey's analysis of Rembrandt's *Portrait of the Mennonite Minister Cornelis Claesz Anslo with his Wife Aeltje Gerritsdr Schouten* (1641, Berlin), in which husband and wife play complementary roles in Mennonite devotion, and Poska's discussion of the important community services performed by concubines of Galician priests until forbidden by Catholic authority. Important avenues for future inquiry include the intersection of class and gender in the construction of women's social roles and the widespread evidence for frictions between organized religion and folk culture, where the eventual dominance of church authority may have curtailed or diminished women's traditional authority. As Poska pointed out, evidence for women's power often surfaces only when that power is taken away.

Additional Readings

Dickey, Stephanie S. "'Met een wenende ziel . . . Doch droge oogen' [With dry eyes and a weeping soul]: Women Holding Handkerchiefs in Seventeenth-Century Dutch Portraits." *Nederlands Kunsthistorisch Jaarboek* 46 (1995): 333–67.
Poska, Allyson, "When Love Goes Wrong: Getting Out of Marriage in Seventeenth-Century Spain." *Journal of Social History* 29 (1996): 871–82.

Submitted by: Stephanie Dickey

Part Three
Travel and Settlement

Navigating the Waves (of Devotion): Toward a Gendered Analysis of Early Modern Catholicism

JODI BILINKOFF
History

I BEGIN WITH A TEXT.[1] It is the life of a holy person written by a priest. The clerical author describes in detail the extreme asceticism and bodily pain experienced by the servant of God in imitation of Christ's sufferings: eating only one meal a day, patiently undergoing illnesses, rigorously mortifying the flesh. This servant was literate, but not versed in Latin or formal theological studies. Nevertheless, God directly infused this holy exemplar with knowledge, especially of scripture. Thus, although some came to question the servant's orthodoxy, after rigorous tests, prelates and men of learning were all left amazed, even edified. "Compared to [this servant of God]," a respected Jesuit exclaimed, "I haven't even started my spiritual ABCs!" Indeed, far from heretical arrogance, the servant displayed admirable discretion, modesty, and deference to members of the clergy. The biographer proclaimed that never before had been seen a person so "fond of solitude, so focused on interior things and quiet, so poor and humble." The holy person's continuous and efficacious prayers attracted many suppliants seeking counsel and consolation. After an exemplary death, attended by a most sweet odor, miracles of healing were worked through the servant's intercession.

Given the virtues stressed here, a modern reader might well expect this to be one of the many stories of saintly women produced in late medieval Europe. However, this is the life of a holy lay *man*, Gregorio López, who was born in Madrid in 1542 and died in New Spain (modern central Mexico) in 1596.[2] His popular biography, composed by the parish priest Francisco Losa and published in Mexico City in 1613, underwent many subsequent editions and translations into English, French, Italian, and Portuguese throughout the seventeenth and eighteenth centuries.[3]

Naturally, I could play this little game only in English; if I had been citing the original Spanish, López's sex would have been immediately apparent from the gender endings of nouns and adjectives. Encountering the text in this rather artificial way, however—gender-neutral and as a mere collection of *topoi*—raises a number of intriguing questions. Could not this have been the hagiographical account of a holy woman—a nun perhaps—from fourteenth-century Italy? What, if anything, distinguishes it as a text about a male, lay subject, from Spain or Spanish America and from the early modern period? Can works such as Losa's *Life* of Gregorio López help to identify the contours of religious sentiment during something often called the "Counter Reformation?"[4]

In what follows I attempt to cross or even blur several conceptual boundaries, of chronology, geography, gender, and genre, in my first tentative travels toward a Brave New World, a gendered analysis of Catholic culture, in both hemispheres during the period roughly between 1450 and 1750. As is by now apparent, I am the frequently perplexed, if determined Navigator alluded to in the title of this essay.

Despite the theoretical work that questions some aspects of periodization, I think most academics in their work, and certainly in their teaching, still make rather uncritical use of a traditional periodization that posits an entity called "the Middle Ages" that ended sometime between 1400 and 1500. I know I do. Yet, it is fascinating and instructive to look more closely and see precisely which features of European culture are consistently associated with a pre-1500 medieval past and which with a later Renaissance or early modern period.[5] Here matters of religion (read "Catholicism") loom large. If you mention that you are studying any of the following aspects of religious history, you will certainly be presumed to be a medievalist: nuns, mysticism, hagiography, reports of miracles—perhaps anything Spanish. Hagiography offers a particularly interesting example of such chronological pigeonholing, because it is so commonly assumed to be a purely "medieval" genre. In fact, in terms of sheer numbers of texts produced, the age of printing should be considered the "Golden Age" of hagiography.[6] In any case, Cornell Unversity Press always lists my book *The Avila of Saint Teresa* under Medieval Studies in its catalogue of Medieval and Renaissance Studies, despite its subtitle "Religious Reform in a Sixteenth-Century City." Would such treatment happen if the book treated, say, the wool trade in Avila or an English city in the same period? I doubt it. We need to recognize the northern European, Protestant bias inherent in what Judith Bennett, in a somewhat different context, has called "The Great Divide" of 1500.[7] In this prevailing cultural construct, the watershed represented by 1500, or more precisely, by 1517, truly is a "great" divide, in both senses of the word.

In women's history we have also become comfortable with a notion of a charismatic style of spirituality construed not only as female, but also as medieval. Features of this spirituality include the mystical reception of visions and infused wisdom, and a social role as healer, advisor, and prophet. Recent research has focused on the physical, bodily manifestations of penitential asceticism and voluntary suffering: fasting, self-inflicted mortifications, the experience of illness, demonic attacks, or an intense eucharistic piety. Frequently holy women sustained intimate relationships with priestly confessors or confidants, who then either ordered them to write or dictate some sort of spiritual memoir and/or composed their biographies after their deaths, the vehicles through which both contemporaries and scholars came to know of their existence. Perhaps no one has explored this whole realm of religious expression and experience more insightfully than Caroline Walker Bynum. Her extraordinarily influential study *Holy Feast and Holy Fast* ends around 1400, after which time, she explains, women's spiritual friendships and networks "attenuated," collective biographies of women by women "disappeared," "fewer holy women wrote," and things generally wound down.[8]

However, I will now return to Losa's *Life* of Gregorio López. Here we have a text that not only complicates ideas about gender and religious roles, but also calls into question this chronological divide. Well past 1500 we find nearly all the manifestations of the supposedly "medieval" spirituality enumerated above. I cite two more examples from precisely this later period, the age of printing, when hundreds of such texts were produced. The French Jesuit Paul Ragueneau published the *Life* of Catherine de Saint Augustin, mystic and hospital sister in New France (Québec) in 1671, three years after her death. Just before her own death in 1742, Francisca Josefa de la Concepción, known as Madre Castillo,—a renowned if controversial nun and visionary in New Granada (modern Colombia)—wrote her spiritual autobiography.[9] More than 300 years have now passed since Jean Gerson's works on the discernment of spirits and some 200 years since the Council of Trent, both presumed to have been effective in shutting down charismatic female spirituality and its expression. However, one should also note the provenance of these texts, their authors, and subjects: Spain and Spanish America, France and French Canada.

By now it should be clear that we need to reexamine our assumptions about not only chronology but also geography, in the cultural sense of the term. I am suggesting that after 1500 many aspects of Catholic belief and discourse concerning charismatic holy persons were not so much replaced or repressed as displaced. As Elizabeth Petroff has noted, the medieval women's religious movements and their attendant texts had definite geographical "epicenters" concentrated in the Low Countries, Rhineland Germany, and northern and central Italy.[10] Naturally, in those regions that became Protestant, these female spiritual styles, and traditional Catholicism in general, eventually faded away, or at least took on different forms (perhaps only to resurface in Pietism).

Nevertheless, by stopping their studies in 1400, Bynum and others missed a rather surprising and significant development: the emergence of what has come to be called "Spanish mysticism." It is important to recognize that this religious and literary phenomenon is not a "medieval" one if we use that conventional 1500 divide. The tradition of the ecstatic female mystic or prophetess, so well known in Liège or Umbria by 1300, did not develop on the Iberian peninsula until well into the fifteenth century. Ironically, Spain, which has acquired a reputation as a timeless "land of mystics," had only one well-known Christian mystic of either sex during the Middle Ages, the Mallorcan Ramón Llull (ca. 1232–1316). We have no record of women visionaries or devotional writers from the interior heartland of Castile until the mid-fifteenth century; from Portugal and Catalonia, not until the very end of the century.[11] The pervasive confusion among scholars may stem from a retroactive reading of Spain's militant brand of religiosity in the later sixteenth and seventeenth centuries back into an earlier period. In any case, the "takeoff" period for Spain as a producer of mystics and their texts is the second half of the sixteenth century. This trend, quickly transplanted to Spain's New World colonies, continued unabated throughout the seventeenth and eighteenth centuries, during which time, to rephrase but also reverse Bynum, women's spiritual friendships and networks, collective biographies of women by women and writings by holy women fairly proliferated.[12]

By the early seventeenth century the shock waves created by this new, Iberian "epicenter" were being felt across the Pyrenees in France. The "Devout Movement" and flourishing of French religious literature, due in such large part to the activities and creativities of women, has at last begun to receive systematic, including feminist treatment. In the French case, as in the Spanish, institutions, values and traditions of discourse were soon exported across the Atlantic and persisted into the eighteenth century.[13]

I would like to return to two of the texts mentioned above, Francisco Losa's Life of Gregorio López (1613) and Paul Ragueneau's Life of Catherine de Saint Augustin (1671), in order to investigate further the implications of this profound geographical shift in the history of Catholic charismatic spirituality. To what extent are these distinctively "colonial" texts? Losa and López were both born in Spain; Ragueneau and Catherine both natives of France. The texts share an emphasis on their subjects' interior spiritual lives. Neither clerical author commented much on the fact that these servants of God happened to be living in areas never before settled by Europeans and still in the early stages of christianizing the Native American inhabitants. As Natalie Davis notes, the young Catherine de Saint Augustin seemed to have directed her "religious energies"—fervent prayers, care of the sick and wounded, ecstatic conversations with the Virgin Mary—toward her fellow French settlers in Québec, not toward the Hurons in their midst. Likewise Losa, constructing as exemplary the life of Gregorio López for an intended Spanish audience, made only a few references to "indios." In fact, whereas he mentioned López's prayers for the conversion of "Jews" and "heretics," there are no references to "pagans" or "idololaters" as one might expect in this New World setting.[14]

Yet, one notices a difference of context if not essentially of content. For example, like so many *mulieres sanctae* before her, Catherine de Saint Augustin developed a close bond with a particular spiritual director. While still living in France, the nun began an intense correspondance with the Jesuit Jean de Brébeuf, a renowned missionary in New France. Several years before her own arrival in Québec, Brébeuf was killed by hostile Iroquois. Catherine was certain, however, that he continued to communicate with her mystically, advising and comforting her from beyond the grave. Ragueneau told the story of the pious Catherine but also devoted a good deal of space to the life and gruesome death of his fellow Jesuit. He stressed Catherine's special relationship with Brébeuf, whom God gave to her as "a director chosen from Paradise." Hearing the news of his violent death in 1649, Catherine immediately begins to pray to him as a martyr. In 1666 she is rewarded with a vision of the priest "all brilliant with light, wearing a glittering crown of glory . . . ," and she speaks with him through the Virgin's intercession. For the next two years, until her own death at the age of thirty-six, Catherine had periodic encounters with Brébeuf and came to regard him as her celestial protector.[15] All this takes on added significance when one realizes that Catherine's biographer, Paul Ragueneau, also wrote many of the accounts of priests martyred in New France intended for their processes of beatification and canonization. (This group of martyrs was finally beatified in 1925, canonized in 1930, and declared patron saints of Canada in 1940.)[16] Ragueneau's *Life* of Catherine seems to have figured as part of a larger effort to promote Jesuit missionary activity in Canada in general and to support Brébeuf's cause in particular.[17] The use of a woman visionary to underscore the saintliness of her male spiritual director was, of course, a classic motif by this time, but Ragueneau's text must be situated within this vast new missionary enterprise, as well as continuing polemics against Huguenot "heretics" back home, who would deny completely the cult of the saints.

In Francisco Losa's *Life* of Gregorio López, a colonial discourse utilizing both gender and racial hierarchies makes a subtle, but unmistakable appearance. Losa, celebrating his subject as New Spain's first hermit, used many elements of early Christian narratives of solitude and prayer in "the desert." Yet, here Chichimeca Indians substitute for the ferocious animals of more ancient wildernesses.[18] His depiction of them as brutes who nonetheless refrained from harming the wandering penitent served to signal both their distinction from and potential to become Christians. Losa also offered the following anecdote as proof of López's saintliness. Several days before his death "una india" came to visit the recluse. She spoke in her own language, which Losa understood but not López. The holy man asked the priest to translate "in case she has some advice for me." Losa marveled at the Spanish hermit's great humility, that "he thought himself of less worth than an Indian woman and that she could [possibly] enlighten him."[19] In the final analysis, the mere presence of traditional figures such as Catherine de Saint Augustin and Gregorio López on American soil helped Europeans to accept these strange lands as "New France" and "New Spain," and to expand the boundaries of a resilient Catholic culture.

I have been focusing on hagiographical texts, not only because they were so plentiful in the early modern period but also because I believe that they came to play a pivotal role in perpetuating certain religious styles and values. They also make fascinating reading. These accounts often reveal as much or more about their authors and their agendas than about the persons who are their ostensible subjects. Upon close inspection, imagined boundaries between genres—hagiography-history, biography-autobiography—become blurred; distinctions between author and subject, fuzzy. The two texts under discussion display many of these complexities and ambiguities. Paul Ragueneau included excerpts from Catherine de Saint Augustin's own journal and letters in his biography, and the text consequently moves between third and first person voice.[20] Francisco Losa often inserted himself into the narrative of Gregorio López's life; the priest actually resided at a hermitage with the holy man for some seven years.[21]

Looking at these texts with an eye toward the processes involved in constructing and publicizing certain lives as exemplary leads to a number of questions. I raise one here somewhat whimsically: Did women have a Counter Reformation?[22] To put it another way, how did women experience the Tridentine era? For many scholars the answer is a gloomy one. Gabriella Zarri, in her seminal essay "Le sante vive," saw the Council of Trent as the decisive end of an era for female religious, particularly in Italy. After a "fleeting season" in the early years of the sixteenth century, when women had been allowed to "play a distinctive role in the political, literary and religious arenas," she explains, Trent's "doctrinal imperatives plunged them back into silence and stillness."[23]

This scholarly narrative, depicting a total lockup of women's bodies and creativities in the post-Tridentine period, is as compelling for its poignancy as it is attractive for its sense of closure. It remains, however, unsatisfactory in many respects. We have the apparent paradox that by the 1620s and 1630s active orders for women were being founded, especially in France. By the end of the seventeenth century, women were so numerous as nurses, teachers, and catechists that, as Patricia Ranft has recently suggested, "Counter-Reformation society would have found it nearly impossible to fulfill its active apostolate without them."[24]

Thus, I am trying to map out an analysis that accounts for the complexity and diversity of the messages presented to women and men in early modern Catholic Europe, one that engages the simultaneous suppression *and* promotion of women as charismatic religious figures. In order to examine these mixed messages, I will return to the popular hagiographical texts and the alliances between certain clergymen and certain women responsible for their production.

Paul Ragueneau, for one, displayed a keen awareness of the misogyny of his times and the skepticism, if not outright hostility, of many of his fellow clerics toward women who claimed mystical gifts. He acknowledged women's vivid imaginations and vulnerability to demonic deception. However, in establishing the credentials of his spiritual daughter, Catherine de Saint Augustin, the Jesuit launched a passionate defense of holy women in general. He excoriated those men who refused to believe any reports of the supernatural, reminding his readers of how the Apostles at first dismissed Mary Magdalene and the other women who brought news of the Resurrection. "God," he continued, "bestows his grace on whomever he wishes and whenever he wishes, and if at times he rewards more women than men it is often [due to] a lack of humility in us. . . ." That is why the Lord granted visions and other favors to women such as saints Gertrude, Brigit, Mechtild, Catherine of Siena, Genoa, and Bologna, and "in our own times" to Saint Teresa "and a great many others of the same sex. . . ."[25] Thus did Ragueneau situate Catherine within an illustrious female genealogy. He insisted, moreover, that reading her life "will be very useful for the spiritual direction of those souls whom God leads down extraordinary paths," expressing confidence that there would indeed be more such souls in the future.[26] I propose that texts such as Ragueneau's were written with precisely this goal in mind, as recruitment tools designed to provide models for and perpetuate a tradition that, after all, validated both holy women and the priests who had the grace and wisdom to discern "extraordinary souls."[27]

Even when the exemplary figure was male, as in the case of Gregorio López, his biographer Francisco Losa, as we have seen, stressed qualities often associated with women (or priests): humility, silence, and submission to clerical authority. Describing the hermit's total lack of worldly ambition, Losa noted how this was usually a passion among "the Sons of Adam," further differentiating López from ordinary laymen.[28] Antonio Rubial, in discussing Losa's hagiographical treatment, points out that López's "detachment from material goods made him a model of poverty, a very needed virtue in a land that produced gold, silver, and greed."[29] This dichotomy, "poverty-greed," could very well be gendered female-male. I speculate that for a priest like Losa distinctions between persons based upon status—that is, clerical as opposed to lay—were as important or even more important than distinctions based upon sex. Perhaps for him all laypeople fell into the same conceptual category of spiritual dependency upon the clergy, and were therefore all appropriately gendered as "female."

I compare Losa's text with one of the few other contemporary hagiographies of laymen, that of Portuguese-born saint John of God (ca. 1495–1550). Here, too, the priestly biographer emphasized the holy man's docility, his illnesses, his deference to clergymen. Interestingly, both texts derive from frontier societies, New Spain and Granada, where clerics struggled mightily to Christianize, civilize (and feminize?) unruly populations of native peoples and single male Spanish immigrants.[30]

Thus a "Counter-Reformation Church" supposedly bent on snuffing out all vestiges of female charismatic spirituality did an excellent job of perpetuating it. At the same time that many clerics were subjecting religious women to increased suspicion and surveillance, other, differently disposed, clerics were busily promoting women as exemplars, and constructing saintly religious behavior for both women and men as "female." Clearly we need to move away from assumptions about an undifferentiated and monolithic "Church." As I begin my investigative travels, I will search for approaches that take seriously the lives, self-understandings, agendas, and conflicts among individual men who decided to become priests, monks, or friars, and examine their interactions with women—and other men—within specific local contexts. I hope to explore and contextualize the abundant autobiographical and hagiographical literature from the early modern period, concentrating on Spain and Spanish America, but also looking at texts from Italy, Portugal, France, and French Canada. I will need to attend carefully to issues of gender, in all their complexity and in combination with other factors such as chronology, geographical origin, clerical versus lay status, and generational difference. At stake here are some rather crucial issues: the politics and uses of exemplarity, and the role of religion in the construction of identities. Far from petering out after 1400, the history of Catholic charismatic spirituality takes on new meanings and new urgencies in the age of printing, of Protestantism, and of the settlement and "spiritual conquest" of the New World. If and when this sensibility begins to die out has less to do, I suspect, with legislative fiat than with the emergence of a scientific and industrial culture that comes to see religion in general as too "irrational," too "superstitious," and dare I say, too "feminine" to fit any longer its explanatory needs. By navigating the fascinating, if complex intersections of religion and gender in the early modern period, I may just arrive at a somewhat unexpected destination: our own times.

Notes

1. I am grateful to the organizers of the conference "Attending to Early Modern Women: Crossing Boundaries" for inviting me to present this paper as a plenary talk. I would also like to thank the following colleagues for reading and commenting on earlier versions: Allan Greer, Christopher Hodgkins, Ronald Morgan, Antonio Rubial García, Carole Slade, Elisabeth Sommer, Marjorie Woods, and members of the North Carolina Research Group on Medieval and Early Modern Women.

2. Francisco Losa, *La Vida que Hizo el Siervo de Dios Gregorio Lopez, en algunos lugares de esta Nueva España . . .* (Mexico: Juan Ruyz, 1613). Biblioteca Nacional, Madrid R/7897. 21ʳ⁻ᵛ: "Por cierto, Señor, que en comparacion de este hombre, yo no he començado el ABC espiritual," 81ᵛ: "un hombre solitario, tan interior y callado, tan pobre y humilde . . ." On the question of López's orthodoxy, see Alain Milhou, "Gregorio López, el Iluminismo, y la Nueva Jerusalén Americana," in *Actas del IX Congreso Internacional de Historia de América,* vol. 3 (Seville: Universidad de Sevilla, 1990), 55–83.

3. Losa's text went through at least eight editions in Spanish, three each in English and French, and one each in Italian and Portuguese between 1615 and 1841. For the colonial context see Antonio Rubial Garcia, "Espejo de virtudes, sabrosa narración, emulación patriótica: La literatura hagiográfica sobre los venerables no canonizados de la Nueva España," in *La Literatura Novohispana: Revisión crítica y propuestas metodológicas,* ed. José Pascual Buxó and Arnulfo Herrera (Mexico: Universidad Nacional Autónoma de Mexico, 1994), 89–110, "Tebaidas en el Paraíso: Los ermitaños de la Nueva España," *Historia Mexicana* 44 (1995):355–83. Also see Rubial, *La santidad controvertida: Hagiografía y conciencia criolla alrededor de los venerables no canonizados de Nueva España* (Mexico City: Fondo de Cultura Económica, 1999).

4. For a penetrating analysis of the origin, utility, and pitfalls of the use of the term "Counter Reformation," see John W. O'Malley, *Trent and All That: Renaming Catholicism in the Early Modern Era* (Cambridge, Harvard University Press, 2000). I am indebted to Father O'Malley for sharing his work with me before publication.

5. Only recently have periodization and other historiographical problems in the study of premodern Spain been systematically examined. For an essay that touches on the ways that North American scholars have constructed certain aspects of Spain's history as "medieval" or "modern," see Richard L. Kagan, "Prescott's Paradigm: American Historical Scholarship and the Decline of Spain," *American Historical Review* 101(1996):423–46. I am grateful to Alison Weber and Paul Freedman for discussing with me these and many other topics.

6. The impressive "Reportorio" included in *Donna, Disciplina, Creanza Cristiana dal XV al XVII Secolo: Studi e Testi a Stampa,* ed. Gabriella Zarri (Rome: Edizioni di Storia e Letteratura, 1996) documents the numerous lives of exemplary women published between 1450 and 1700 in Italy alone. As Thomas J. Heffernan points out, the genre of hagiography has one of the longest continuous histories, "beginning with St. Luke's rendering of St. Stephen's martyrdom in Acts and having no de facto end . . ."; *Sacred Biography: Saints and Their Biographers in the Middle Ages* (New York: Oxford University Press, 1988), 15–18, 38–61.

7. Judith M. Bennett, "Medieval Women, Modern Women: Across the Great Divide," in *Culture and History 1350–1600: Essays on English Communities, Identities and Writing,* ed. David Aers (London: Harvester Wheatsheaf, 1992), 147–75.

8. Caroline W. Bynum, *Holy Feast and Holy Fast: The Religious Significance of Food to Medieval Women* (Berkeley: University of California Press, 1987), 22–23.

9. Paul Ragueneau, *La Vie de la Mere Catherine de Saint Augustin, Religieuse Hospitaliere de la Misericorde de Quebec en la Nouvelle France* (Paris: Florentin Lambert, 1671). Houghton Library, Harvard University *FC6.R1286.671v. This text was also translated into Italian in the mid-eighteenth century. Madre Castillo's *Vida* was first published in 1817. I have used the modern edition prepared by Dario Achury Valenzuela, *Obras Completas de la Madre Francisca Josefa de la Concepción de Castillo* vol.I (Bogotá: Banco de la República, 1968). See also Kathryn J. McKnight, *The Mystic of Tunja: The Writings of Madre Castillo, 1671–1742* (Amherst: University of Massachusetts Press, 1997).

10. Elizabeth A. Petroff, *Body and Soul: Essays on Medieval Women and Mysticism* (New York: Oxford University Press, 1994). The term is also used by Patricia Ranft, *Women and the Religious Life in Premodern Europe* (New York: St. Martin's Press, 1996), for example, 113.

11. Ronald E. Surtz, *Writing Women in Late Medieval and Early Modern Spain: The Mothers of Saint Teresa of Avila* (Philadelphia: University of Pennsylvania Press, 1995); Jodi Bilinkoff, "Establishing Authority: A Peasant Visionary and Her Audience in Early Sixteenth Century Spain," *Studia Mystica* 18(1997):36–59. My thanks go to Maria de Lurdes Correia Fernandes for discussing with me the Portuguese situation.

12. The literature on this topic is extensive and growing. To mention only a few general works: José L. Sánchez Lora, *Mujeres, conventos y formas de la religiosidad barroca* (Madrid: FUE, 1988); Electa Arenal and Stacey Schlau, *Untold Sisters: Hispanic Nuns in Their Own Words* (Albuquerque: University of New Mexico Press, 1989); Angela Muñoz Fernández, *Beatas y santas neocastellanas: ambivalencias de la religión y políticas correctoras del poder, ss.XIV–XVI* (Madrid: Comunidad de Madrid, 1994); Isabelle Poutrin, *Le voile et la plume: Autobiographie et sainteté féminine dans l'Espagne moderne* (Madrid: Casa de Velázquez, 1995); and Kristine Ibsen, *Women's Spiritual Autobiography in Colonial Spanish America* (Gainsville: University Press of Florida, 1999). There are numerous studies of individual figures and religious communities.

13. Elizabeth Rapley, *The Dévotes: Women and Church in Seventeenth-Century France* (Montreal: McGill-Queen's University Press, 1990); Leslie Choquette, "'Ces Amazones du Grand Dieu': Women and Mission in Seventeenth-Century Canada," *French Historical Studies* 17(1992): 627–55; Wendy M. Wright, "The Visitation of Holy Mary: The First Years (1610–1618)," in *Religious Orders of the Catholic Reformation,* ed. Richard L. DeMolen (New York: Fordham University Press, 1994), 217–50; Anya Mali, *Mystic in the New World: Marie de l'Incarnation (1599–1672)* (Leiden: Brill, 1966); Linda Lierheimer, "Preaching or Teaching? Defining the Ursuline Mission in Seventeenth-Century France," in *Women Preachers and Prophets through Two Millenia of Christianity,* ed. Beverly Mayne Kienzle and Pamela J. Walker (Berkeley: University of California Press, 1998), 212–26; Marie-Florine Bruneau, *Women Mystics Confront the Modern World: Marie de l'Incarnation (1599–1672) and Madame Guyon (1648–1717)* (Albany: State University of New York Press, 1998); and Susan E. Dinan, "Confraternities as a Venue for Female Activism during the Counter Reformation," in *Confraternities and Catholic Reform in Italy, France, and Spain,* eds. John Patrick Donnelly and Michael W. Maher (Kirksville, Mo.: Sixteenth Century Journal Publishers, 1999), 191–214.

14. Natalie Zemon Davis, *Women on the Margins: Three Seventeenth-Century Lives* (Cambridge: Harvard University Press, 1995), 121–22. For Losa's brief references to Native Americans in the *Life* of Gregorio López: 4^r-8^v, 17^v, 48^{r-v}, 90^r, 124^r. Milhou: 74–77. See also Kenneth R. Mills, *Idolatry and its Enemies: Colonial Andean Religion and Extirpation, 1640–1750* (Princeton: Princeton University Press, 1997).

15. Ragueneau, 179–182: "Dieu luy donne un Directeur choisi dans le Paradis: sçavoir, le Pere Iean de Brebeuf. . . ." Catherine recorded in a journal entry of 25 September, 1662 "apres la communion, je pensay avoir veu devant moy le R.P. de Brebeuf tout brillant de lumière, portant une couronne éclatante de gloire . . ."; for other postmortem encounters, see also pp. 187, 191. These, too, were associated with the eucharist. For more on relations between spiritual directors and female penitents, including connections with eucharistic devotion, see Jodi Bilinkoff, "Confessors, Penitents, and the Construction of Identities in Early Modern Avila," in *Culture and Identity in Early Modern Europe (1500–1800): Essays in Honor of Natalie Zemon Davis*, ed. Barbara B. Diefendorf and Carla Hesse (Ann Arbor: University of Michigan Press, 1993), 83–100. See also Patricia Ranft, "A Key to Counter Reformation Women's Activism: The Confessor-Spiritual Director," *Journal of Feminist Studies in Religion* 10(1994): 7–26.

16. "Paul Ragueneau," in Carlos Sommervogel, *Bibliothèque de la Compagnie de Jésus* (Brussels and Paris, 1893) vol. 6, cols. 1390–1392. Ragueneau himself became the subject of a biography written at the end of the seventeenth century by the younger Jesuit Jacques Bigot (d. 1711). I have used the modern critical edition, with extensive introductory material by Guy Laflèche, *La vie du Père Paul Ragueneau de Jacques Bigot* (Montreal: VLB, 1979).

17. Allan Greer, "Colonial Saints: Gender, Race, and Hagiography in New France," *William and Mary Quarterly*, 3rd series, 57 (2000): 323–48.

18. Losa, 4^r-8^v. Milhou also makes this observation, 75, as does Rubial, "Tebaidas," 366.

19. Losa, 90^r: "Tres o quatro días antes de su muerte, entró a veerle una india de este pueblo. Y como yo estubiesse hablando en su lengua, porque él no la entendía, me dixo: 'Advierta V.M. a lo que dice, que por ventura me quiere avisar alguna cosa.' Donde noté yo su mucha humildad; pues se tenía por de menos méritos que una india, pensando que ella le podía dar luz de lo que a lo último de la vida le convenía." Milhou discusses this passage (77) and notes that this is the only time in Losa's text that "un indio individualizado" appears. His comment, however, obscures the fact that this was an Indian *woman*.

20. For example, Ragueneau, 17, 22, 56, 182, and 185–87. See quotation in note 15 for an example of these shifting voices and points of view. For more on "co-authored" life-writing and the processes of negotiation involved, see Jodi Bilinkoff, "The Many 'Lives' of Pedro de Ribadeneyra," *Renaissance Quarterly* 52 (1999):180–96.

21. See, for example, Losa, prologue, 71^v–72^v, and 107^v. The quotation in note 2 is a good illustration of how the text is "about" both López and Losa. For a closer examination of the ways in which Losa interweaves the narrative of his own life with that of López, see Jodi Bilinkoff, "Francisco Losa and Gregorio López: Spiritual Friendship and Identity Formation on the New Spain Frontier," paper delivered at conference "Colonial Saints: Hagiography and the Cult of the Saints in the Americas, 1500–1800," University of Toronto, 12–13 May 2000.

22. This is, of course, my tribute to Joan Kelly's celebrated essay, "Did Women Have a Renaissance?", first published in *Becoming Visible: Women in European History*, ed. Renate Bridenthal and Claudia Koonz (Boston: Houghton Miflin, 1977), 137–64, and frequently reprinted.

23. Gabriella Zarri, "Living Saints: A Typology of Female Sanctity in the Early Sixteenth Century," in *Women and Religion in Medieval and Renaissance Italy*, ed. Daniel Bornstein and Roberto Rusconi (Chicago: University of Chicago Press, 1996), 253–54, essay originally published in Italian in 1980.

24. Ranft, "Key," 7.

25. Ragueneau, 10–15: "Dieu fait des graces à qui il veut, & quand il veut, & si quelquefors il se fait voir aux femmes plûtot qu'aux hommes, c'est souvent un manquement d'humilité en nous . . . & en nos derniers siècles a Sainte Therese & a quantité d'autres de même sexe. . . . "

26. Ragueneau, 1–2: "Quelques personnes de pieté & de merite en ayons au communication, ont jugé qu'elle seroit tres-utile pour la direction particulière des ames que Dieu conduit par des voyes extraordinaires. . . . "

27. Ragueneau's systematic efforts to collect data on Catherine de Saint Augustin, both before and after her death (conferring with former confessors, interviewing fellow nuns and family members, reading her letters, etc.), are quite evident thoughout the text, especially pp. 203, 364–365, 375. This is also true of Losa with regard to López, especially fols. 3^v, 4^r, 8^v–9^r, 19^v, 30^r.

28. Losa, 89^v: "Pasión suele ser de los Hijos de Adam, el deseo de ser tenidos por mas excellentes, y aventajadas que sus proximos. De esto estaba tan desnudo Gregorio que siempre se tuvo por menos que los demas . . . " I realize that the phrase "Hijos de Adam" could conceivably be translated as "Children of Adam," but I am virtually certain that Losa was referring to men only. I base this in part on the usage of his near-contemporary Teresa of Avila. In *The Way of Perfection* (3:7), Teresa appealed to a God who was a just judge "and not like those of the world. Since the world's judges are sons of Adam and all of them male, there is no virtue in women that they do not hold suspect . . . " ["y no como los jueces del mundo, que como son hijos de Adán, y en fin, todos varones, no hay virtud de mujer que not tengan por sospechosa . . ."]; *Collected Works of St. Teresa of Avila*, trans. Kieran Kavanaugh and Otilio Rodríguez (Washington, D.C.: Institute of Carmelite Studies, 1976–1985), vol. 2. The translator of the 1638 English edition of Losa's text rendered the passage this way: "The sons of Adam, have for the most part ingrafted in them a desire to be esteemed more excellent then their neighbors. Gregory was so free from this that he allwaies preferred others before himself . . ." (207). I have used the fascimile edition published by Scolar Press in 1969, vol. 3 of the series "English Recusant Literature, 1558–1640."

29. "Espejo," 101: "El desapego a los bienes materiales la hacía espejo de pobreza, una virtud muy necesaria en una tierra que producía oro, plata y avaricia."

30. I have looked at a Portuguese version of *Vida de S. Ioam de Deos Portuguez* attributed (I believe incorrectly) to the Spanish Jesuit Pedro de Ribadeneyra (Lisbon: Domingos Carneyro, 1691), Houghton Library, Harvard University *SC5.R5207.Ej691v. See also David W. Coleman, "Creating Christian Granada: Religion and Community on the Old-World Frontier" (Ph.D. diss., University of Illinois, Urbana-Champaign, 1996), especially ch. 4.

Sor Juana's Arch: Public Spectacle, Private Battle

ELECTA ARENAL
Spanish and Women's Studies

> . . . este tan glorioso asalto.
> . . . .
> tus pensamientos Gigantes
> no aspiran menos, que al Cielo.
> [. . . this, so glorious an assault
> . . . .
> your Giant thoughts
> aspire to nothing less than the Heavens.]*

THE TRIUMPHAL ARCH TITLED *Allegorical Neptune, ocean of colors, political simulacrum . . .,*[1] was a public literary-artistic construction and spectacle, which took place in Mexico City on 30 November, 1680. The full textual program for the spectacle—plan, libretto, and explanation, about fifty pages long—was published nine years later, in Spain, as the final piece in the first book of its author Sor Juana Inés de la Cruz (fig. 1).[2] On the day of the spectacle, however, the arch, built and painted following Sor Juana's detailed specifications, transformed one of the lateral portals of the Cathedral of Mexico. The arch served as the elegant, silent set design for an allegorical enactment of the transfer of political power to a new viceroy of Spain in the northern territories of the so-called New World.[3] The eight-part poem she wrote to be performed in front of it entertained the assembled throng. In his biography of Sor Juana, Octavio Paz calls *Allegorical Neptune* "a hieroglyph . . . an emblem, an enigma."[4]

Indeed, it is difficult to decipher the multiple and ingenious meanings of this Baroque *fiesta* (festival).[5] Among other things, it is a feminist political treatise. Sor Juana Inés de la Cruz's keen intelligence and her consummate ability to elaborate texts, employing a wide variety of discursive modalities, allowed her to revise discourse itself in order to give women full voice. For that purpose she created variations on old cosmographies. The need to do so was both political and personal. This essay explores the connections between both words and images, and among several of the fourteen paintings inserted on the

173

Figure 1. Sor Juana Inés de la Cruz. Engraved frontispiece from the first edition of her second book, *Segundo volumende las obras* (Sevilla, 1692).

arch. Therein lie keys to some of the enigmas of *Allegorical Neptune*. The purpose of the essay is to present some initial decodings of the complex interweave of myth, metaphor, and allegory that comprises the arch.

I want to argue something that has not been pointed out before with regard to this work: that the secret of the arch, its principal subtext, is the conflict of its author, Sor Juana Inés de la Cruz, with her confessor, Antonio Núñez de Miranda. A Jesuit, and one of the most influential men in the church hierarchy, Núñez wrote tracts, supervised convents, and was confessor to the capital city's leading citizens. Sor Juana, who had become a nun in the Order of St. Jerome, in part under Núñez de Miranda's tutelage, was already widely celebrated for her learned intelligence and her poetic genius.[6] According to a letter Sor Juana would write just two years after completing the text for the great public state event, she had long been silent regarding her difficulties with him.[7] In the letter, Sor Juana censures Núñez's open criticism of her labors as a writer, and she defends her acceptance of the commission to invent the arch:

> . . . the Arch for the Church. This is my unpardonable offense, which was preceded by my having been asked three or four times and my having as many refused, until two lay magistrates came who before calling upon me called first upon the Mother Prioress and then upon me, and commanded in the name of His Excellency the Archbishop that I do it because the full chapter had so voted and His Excellency approved.

> Now it would be my wish that Y[our] R[everence], with all the clarity of your judgment, put yourself in my place and consider what you would have replied in this situation. Would you answer that you could not? That would have been a lie. That you did not wish to? That would have been disobedience. That you did not know how? They did not ask more than I knew. That the vote was badly taken? That would have been impudent audacity, vile and gross ingratitude to those who honored me by believing that an ignorant woman knew how to do what such brilliant minds solicited. So I had no choice but to obey.

> These are my published writings that have so scandalized the world, and so edified the good. . . .[8]

After providing cultural and historical contexts, I shall return to this letter, in which Sor Juana severs the spiritual tie to her confessor and, with startling sarcasm, parades before him the arch's success.

The ancient Roman tradition of constructing arches, elaborately decorated with mythological themes, was revived during the Renaissance. In Mexico, in the century and a half before Sor Juana's arch was built, triumphal arches and the accompanying ceremonies regularly substantiated both the real and the symbolic aspects of the arrival of new governors, representatives of the

Spanish monarchy, and of the papacy. Beginning in 1528, two temporary
arches were customarily built for these occasions in the capital of the viceroyalty, which extended from what is today California, Texas, and Florida in the
United States, to Guatemala in Central America.[9] One freestanding arch was
erected in the Plaza de Santo Domingo, site of the Holy Office. A second, a few
blocks away, was placed on the western facade and portal of the cathedral. The
long procession first stopped at the Plaza de Santo Domingo for the enactment
of the secular part of the rite, the official delivery of the keys of the viceroyalty to its new viceroy. Headed by the new governors and their Spanish
entourage and followed by the *criollo* (descendants of Spaniards born in New
Spain), *mestizo,* Indian, and African populations of the city, the procession
then walked a few blocks further, pausing at the large central Plaza or Zocalo
for the second ceremony. Finally, hundreds of citizens entered the cathedral to
sing the *Te Deum* and to watch the new viceroy swear fealty to and defense of
the Holy Mother Catholic Church.

The Mexico City arches built in 1680 (and later dismantled) welcomed two
distinguished representatives of high Spanish nobility: Tomás de la Cerda,
Marquis de la Laguna, Count of Paredes, a descendent of Alfons X, the Wise;
and his wife, María Luisa Manrique de Lara y Gonzaga, Marquise de la
Laguna, Countess de Paredes, related on her maternal side to great writers
such as Jorge Manrique, the Marquis de Santillana, and Gómez Manrique.

The authors of the two arches were the two most prominent intellectuals
and cultivators of letters in New Spain, Don Carlos Sigüenza y Góngora, and
Sor Juana Inés de la Cruz. Sigüenza authored and designed the freestanding
arch at the Plaza de Santo Domingo, and Sor Juana the one superimposed on
the lateral portal of the great Cathedral of Mexico, where the final acts of
investiture were celebrated. Both writers were looked upon with suspicion by
some of the highest church and state authorities. For that reason, as well as for
their notable intellectual talents, critics have speculated, the interim viceroy
and archbishop, Payo de Rivera had sought the commission for these particular writers. The text by Sigüenza y Góngora has received more critical attention than the one by Sor Juana has. Hers has not yet been seen in all its radical dimensions.

In this essay I will argue that when verbal and iconographic interpretation
is based on a close reading of the *Allegorical Neptune,* it seems clear that Sor
Juana's program for the arch is far from traditional or orthodox as has been
claimed; it is, rather, as novel and radical as Sigüenza y Góngora's.[10] Both of
them follow the counsel he proffers in the epigraph to the text for his arch:
"Those who take up foreign subject matter should consider what is closer to
home (what is their own)." Both writers situate "Imperial Mexico" in a tradition of creative, peace-loving virtues.[11] The two highly cultured *criollos* follow

European models that reject the heroism of the militarily aggressive—Herculean—prince in favor of the Neptunian defender of abiding peace.[12]

Brief Description and Comparison of the Two Arches

Many comparative studies remain to be made of the two triumphal arches, especially of their emblematic and enigmatic dimensions. Several scholars have already contributed to illuminating the relationship between the two friends and intellectual rivals, the viewpoints they express, their importance for the political culture of the epoch, and for the formulation of criollo-Mexican identity.[13]

In the light of new research, revisions will be made in what is commonly said regarding the content and character of the arches and the differences between them. If Sigüenza y Góngora revises historiography in order to establish a genealogy that links Spanish and Aztec royalty, Sor Juana revises discourse itself in order to make room for the half of humanity that was disembodied and deprived of a full voice. Subtly and humorously, she creates a new genesis by altering inherited cosmographic and cosmological concepts, by distorting artistic renditions of mythological figures, and by subversively encoding her true theme.

During Sor Juana's lifetime (1648/51–1695), there was hardly a soul in New Spain who did not know what a triumphal arch was. Whenever a new archbishop or viceroy docked at Veracruz—with or without a vicereine—several arches were built on the way to Mexico City, as well as two in that capital itself. An ephemeral art form, the arch was like an adaptable or reusable stage set. When the festivities were over, it would be taken down and often stored by the artists/craftworkers responsible for its execution; they would merely replace the canvases and panels with the words and images invented by the author of the new allegory when the next commission came along. Nearly the entire population participated in the theatrical spectacle of formal acknowledgment and bestowal of power. In an article titled "Minerva Receives Viceroy Count Alba de Liste," María Concepción García Saíz describes the long poetic performance presented in front of an earlier arch, designed and written by Alfonso Alavés Pinedo and built in 1650, in which an actress, declaring "I am Mexico," is transformed from a Mexican Indian woman into the goddess Minerva. The personified transformation, explaining the symbolism of the arch, "transmit[s] a clear message to the new viceroy: the government of Mexico holds such importance, that its proper accomplishment will bring immortality to the one who successfully undertakes the task."[14]

Indeed, at the particular historical moment, on the day of welcoming ceremonies, what was most significant were the arches, and the theatrical, poetic

Figure 2. Anonymous painting. Early eighteenth century. Triumphal arch erected in the city of Puebla (Mexico) for the entry of a new viceroy.

performances that took place in front of people's eyes. Sor Juana's arch of 1680 was an impressive architectural structure, five stories high, with canvases or panels on the upper part and "hieroglyphs" on the columnar bases, each panel with two texts—a motto and a poem inscribed above or within and below the paintings themselves. Although there is more ample documentation on triumphal arches and the festivities surrounding them in Europe, all we have to testify visually about what these ceremonies and their ephemeral sets looked like in New Spain are one painting, a painted screen, and several engravings (fig. 2).[15] What do remain are Sor Juana's texts with dedications, scholarly chronicles of the ideographic and iconographic programs, the physical description of the arch, and elaborate explanations of the images, of the words that framed them—the Latin mottos above, the epigrams or other verse forms below. Generally, the long performance poem recited during the event was placed at the end of the texts prepared for the occasion. The whole text was dedicated to those honored by the arch.

The arch described in *Neptuno Alegórico [Allegorical Neptune, Ocean of colors, political simulacrum]*, although made with architectural relief, had a single facade. It held eight canvases on top and six "hieroglyphs" on the bases. Following emblem books, a fundamental model for triumphal arches, each of the fourteen paintings was tripartite: it had a Latin motto ("the soul"), a pictorial image ("the body"), and a *subscriptio* in verse epigram, sonnet, *octava* or *redondilla*. The entire text for *Allegorical Neptune* was, as mentioned, included nine years later in Sor Juana's first book, *Inundación castalida [Castalian Flood]*, published in 1689.[16]

Don Carlos Sigüenza y Góngora's freestanding triumphal arch, *Theatro de Virtudes Políticas . . . [Theatre of Political Virtues]* erected on the Plaza de Santo Domingo, had four sides and three arches. The hieroglyphs on the four pedestals were subcontracted by Don Carlos to another writer. (Could it be an indication that these bases were considered of minor importance in comparison to the upper part of the arches and were a safe place for Sor Juana's allegorical ironies?) Each facade had a central panel: on the north, a portrait of the new viceregal couple; on the south, the insignias and emblems of the two antecedent princes. Other panels represented Huitzilopochtli and eleven Aztec kings taken from Aztec pictorial codices that Sigüenza y Góngora had in his possession.

Don Carlos Sigüenza y Góngora himself may possibly be held responsible for one of the often repeated comments regarding Sor Juana. When he stated that "it has been customary for [Spanish] American intellectuals or wits [*ingenios*] to beautify the majority of triumphal [arches] with the lies of mythological fables,"[17] critics have thought that he was alluding principally to Sor Juana, and that her representations were indeed traditional. For example, in an otherwise excellent study of the "emblematic structuring of several panels" of the *Theatre of Political Virtues,* Helga von Kügelgen defines the program of Sor Juana's arch as "very traditional."[18] Georgina Sabat de Rivers, in her valuable essay on Sor Juana's arch, also claims that "Sor Juana preferred to follow traditional orthodoxy and chose the mythological figure of Neptune."[19] Sigüenza sets up a silent dialogue with Sor Juana in Prelude III—and especially in Prelude II—of the text for his arch. I find in the conversation a mix of contention, playful argument, the complicity of fellow artists, paternalism, and praise. Because his patriarchal judgments continue to influence interpretations of Sor Juana's arch, it is imperative that we reassess her work with attention to gender.

We are still learning to read with sensitivity toward gender as reflected in grammar and lexicon, modes of inclusion, invisibility and asymmetry. Gender-conscious readings allow for awareness of Sor Juana's combatively comic and serious treatment of the ample and profound theme of language and image. My readings focus, then, on Sor Juana's treatment of questions of gender, sexual and grammatical; literary form; the theme of women, real and fabled; and the relationship between men and women, human and divine.[20]

The female figure is, of course, not absent from Baroque representations; rather it lacks subjectivity and "interpretive power."[21] Don Carlos Sigüenza y Góngora, for instance, includes in his arch various female figures: Ruth, Rachel, Judith, Venus, "Their Excellencies the [Viceregal] Consort," "Their Excellencies the Princes [the Viceroy and Vicereine]," the Vicereine Doña María Luisa, and the Graces.[22] Additionally, the Aztec emperors are each accompanied by Virtues.[23] Sigüenza y Góngora places, next to the parade of indigenous emperors, characters drawn from the very same fabulous symbolism of classical Europe used by other writers and which he claims he has rejected in other passages of his text. He justifies contradictions; Sor Juana problematizes them.

Several variations introduced by Sor Juana stand out, as does her inversion of conventional emblematic schemes, when we observe her treatment of the Virtues, of hands, and of Mexico City. In Don Carlos Sigüenza y Góngora's Arch of the Plaza Santo Domingo, the Virtues, perhaps full-figured, accompany the Aztec kings, full-figured; the most important one in his arch is Prudence. In Sor Juana's Arch of the Cathedral, the Virtues are synthesized— commuted, she would say—in a necklace worn by Neptune. Virtue is at once multiple and one, composing divinity, which is Wisdom, and composed by her; Wisdom is the most important virtue. In the image (*empresa*) of the lower part of *Allegorical Neptune,* which I cite in the epigraph and which I will come back to, "Hands grabbing at the sky are painted."[24] They represent taking risks, daring to reach the heights of knowledge. This particular representation seems original. My search of numerous collections of emblematic images has failed to reveal that particular conjunction of hands and heavens (although there are hundreds of hands and skies in all sorts of positions and gestures).

Don Carlos Sigüenza y Góngora represents the city of Mexico with a traditional image: an "*Indian woman* wearing a native dress and a crown of towers [*corona murada*] reclining against a *nopal* [a cactus plant]. . . ."[25] Sor Juana employs a classical tale of two women to represent Mexico. Asteria, a poet transformed into a bird and then into an island, provides a "refuge and haven" for Latona—mother of the sun and moon—who is painted at the painful moment of giving birth—another image I have failed as yet to find.[26] Sor Juana employs Latona on Asteria's island to represent the city in the third of the eight large canvases. In the eighth and last she creates a *mise en abyme* by having the unfinished Cathedral itself painted on her Cathedral portal arch, representing (1) herself, (2) a task to be accomplished by the new governor, and (3) the ecclesiastical authority of the city, patron of the entire spectacle.

The view of nation and power that informs the discourse and program of Sigüenza's arch is an entirely traditional gesture. It refers to a royal Aztec genealogy in which women are totally absent, except as silent, symbolic figures of the Virtues the imperial heroes are said to embody, or as decorative Indian maidens. Sor Juana's text and the various images she asks the artists to paint indicate that she, like Sigüenza, derives her "mirror" from literary, pictorial, hieroglyphic, and emblematic sources for viceroys of a kingdom that integrates pre-Columbian, New Spanish, and universal visions.[27] Sor Juana, however, put forth a conception of creation and culture in which knowledge flows from a female principle; in which both sexes appear at each worldly level as dynamic and reasonable subjects; in which matrimony becomes patrimony and metaphors of giving birth and of maternal and paternal nurturance supplant those of bloody battles and of exclusively masculine genealogies.

Don Carlos finds a male-headed origin in Vergil: "Everything begins with Jupiter."[28] Sor Juana finds, in Lucan, a genealogy of female leadership: "In our Roman temples we welcome your Isis."[29] In Sigüenza the Neptunian lineage presented is one that changes the maritime god into a biblical figure, a precursor of the Aztec kings. In Sor Juana there is a similar lineage, but it finds its source in Isis, the mother of Neptune.[30] Sigüenza reaffirms the Catholic faith, inserting the pre-Cortesian world into a Hispanic-Catholic providentialism. Sor Juana explores, questions, and redefines the discourses of faith. She identifies with and speaks through Isis, she of "various names" who "said of herself . . . I was engendered by custom, I was born of memory: Sophia I am called by the Greeks, and Wisdom by you" (fig. 3).[31] Sor Juana's curiosity regarding nature and science, her embrace of the immensity of knowledge, placed her in the intellectual sphere of Athanasius Kircher. Indeed, what is claimed in a

Figure 3. Isis. Engraving in Athanasius Kircher, *Oedipus Aegypatiacus* vol. 1 (Rome, 1652–54), p. 189.

recent study of his work may well be said about Sor Juana: like Kircher, she "embodied multiple truths, possessing a series of identities that traverse a vast chronological expanse between the beginning of civilization and the events of [her] own times."[32]

Sor Juana added *matristics*—to use a term coined by the Norwegian theologian Kari Elisabeth Børresen[33]—to the patristics of the Jesuitical culture of her surroundings.[34] *Allegorical Neptune* amply illustrates Sor Juana's all-embracing vision, catholic, and antithetical to the pervasive androcentrism of her time.[35] Like women such as Julian of Norwich and Hildegard von Bingen, Sor Juana proposed an *imago dei* that transcends categories such as masculine or feminine; at times she also imagined the need for an ungendered abstraction, for an extension of the incorporeal asexuality of the soul. Sor Juana's representation of Neptune stretches the limits of the imagination beyond male and female, beyond gender, beyond mortality, and beyond even conventional Renaissance iconography using pagan deities. Sor Juana questioned and researched the construction of knowledge, which she knew to be gendered, and suggested alternatives for the ideas and conditions imposed on women (conditions imposed by women themselves at times, as we see in her letter to her confessor, Núñez de Miranda, as Amanda Powell and I discussed in our introduction to *The Answer*).[36]

The androcentric system of sexual asymmetry was a subject discussed from century to century by many thinkers, women and men, whose works Sor Juana read. The study of her texts and of her intertextual strategies reveals a reader who, given a central position because of her intelligence and knowledge, yet marginalized because of her status as an autodidact and a woman, navigates with perpectives quite different from those of her male contemporaries. I will trace some of these perspectives in several upper "canvases" and lower "hieroglyphs" at the bottom of the arch, with their respective mottos and epigrams. To keep in mind Sor Juana's reasoned and clarifying sensibility regarding the historiographic, grammatical, rhetorical and aesthetic complexities of gender is to garner a richer, multifaceted reading of her triumphal arch.[37]

The text of *Allegorical Neptune* abounds with allusions to the political and social problems of New Spain, which only those implicated and their ruling circles would understand. Among them, as we have seen, was her own personal problem. The *Neptune* text can be read as a prelude to Sor Juana's letter to her confessor, cited at the beginning of this essay.[38] In the letter, she insists that what finally provoked her to cease confessing with Núñez de Miranda and to express anger and dismay directly in writing was his repeating in public that her behavior constituted a scandal for the viceroyalty, and that, if he had known she would follow her natural bent toward learning and letters, he would have had her married. The sentence full of sarcasm in which she refers to having "scandalized the world" and "edified the good" plays with one of the very objectives of the arch: a defense of creative freedom. Her tone reveals not only the tensions between Sor Juana and Núñez de Miranda, but also the tactics with which she had learned to subvert the discourse of power.[39]

Allegorical Neptune is designed as not only a personal, but also as a collective response: the text refers often to "everyone" and "all." It requests that Neptune be painted surrounded by all of his divine and semidivine seafaring companions. It mentions the many wise and rebellious men and women, and gods and goddesses who are worshiped for nothing more than for their knowledge and wisdom.

Emblems and Verbal Metaphors

In many passages of *The Answer*, Sor Juana defends wisdom and learning for women against the pervasive climate of antihumanist misogyny. In his sermons, rules for nuns, prologues to biographies and other writings, and in his role as an officer of the Inquisition, Núñez represented the Tridentine position regarding monastic women. Sor Juana had come in for harsh and biting words from his tongue—but she would not bow. Rejection of all anti-intellectual stances continued to guide her work: one earned sanctity only on the road away from ignorance, she suggested to her confessor, and in *The Answer/La Respuesta* that envy was one of the motives of those who would silence her. *Allegorical Neptune* became a pointed, if semioblique, vehicle for opposition to the policies restricting women's access to knowledge.

Let us turn for a moment to one of the most complex and disguised of these expressions of disagreement and protest, one of the most enigmatic and emblematic. Very much in character, its seriousness is based on a play of words: trident/tridentine. The motto and the words of the the plot for the "first base on the left side"[40] seem at first reading simply lavish praise for the new prince. Yet, the explanation in Sor Juana's text describes ancient maritime customs, the sea, "greater than all the earth," the scientific studies about which Pliny wrote, and a passage from Ovid's *Metamorphoses* on the transforming powers of the waters. It is the longest verse citation in the entire work. It is not inscribed on the arch itself, but is rather part of the exegesis. Glaucus (a god related to silence) narrates how he is purified and made divine by Oceanus and Thetis, who recite "nine times a poem of enchantment in my favor," and how in thought he receives "a different body." In her citation of Ovid's *Metamorphoses*, she chooses the passage in which Glaucus describes his metamorphosis from a mortal being into a divine one.[41] In this passage, Glaucus, after being transformed, is cleansed by the power of the sea.

Neither the explanations of the image that I have just summarized nor the emblem or "hieroglyph" seem innocent: "in it was painted a world surrounded by a sea, and a trident the size of the diameter of the entire globe, dividing it. . . ."[42] I associate this with the trident that appears in a citation from Vergil in the description of the third canvas, "The savage trident and the mastery of the sea,"[43] one of utmost significance for the parallel drawn between Mexico and Sor Juana, as we shall see.

The "hieroglyph" on the panel suggests the Tridentine Convention by which the ordering of life on earth was fixed militarily, civically, and legislatively (the three branches of power). This might explain the absence of any image like it among the hundreds of emblems I have reviewed. Precedents do exist for a negative representation of the globe, or its mistreatment at the hands of authorities. Emblem 87 in the Solórzano Collection shows "two personages with crowns that drive their swords into a small globe."[44] Sor Juana's globe is immobilized by the three-pronged—tridentine—fork, but the sea flows freely, brimming with variegated life, according to the explanation and citations. This globe is surrounded by the *"laguna mar"* [sea lake], a watery play on the new viceroy's name, the Marquis de la Laguna (Neptune). *Mar* [sea] also refers to the Virgin Mary and to her patroness, Mar-ía Luisa (Amphitrite, Neptune's initially reluctant consort).

On the most obvious level, again, the emblem is laudatory. The prince's praises do not fit on the earth alone; they must encompass the sea. Yet, there is something more. The trident has been identified by Sor Juana, in earlier passages of the *Neptune*, in several ways: as the triple power of Neptune—the mythological three-headed Cerberus;[45] the tripartite thunderbolt, the triple power of Jupiter (the pursuer of Asteria in the third canvas); and as a scepter capable of being transformed into a symbol of peace. Sor Juana expresses the wish to the viceroy that his scepter-trident become a laurel-trident.[46] The scepter as representative of aggressive force is rejected, and the hieroglyph of which I speak seems to refer to this meaning as well.

The triumphal arch is a hymn to wisdom; it develops one of Sor Juana's fundamental ideas: that adored beings have always been sages—thus the "assault of the heavens" by the Giants, who are but gigantic thoughts. Sor Juana opens the subject of the godliness of human intelligence. Pliny, she tells us, claims that "Discoverers are held to be gods." She demonstrates that beliefs about creation depend on discursive and metaphorical projections of Indian and Catholic beliefs; that feminine and masculine gender are in great part fluid and figurative. She also writes that on a real, corporeal level the female is as important as the male:

> . . . nothing is more a child of man than his thoughts . . . through their means of absolute generation: for in the corporeal means, a father is only halfway so, precisely sharing with the mother half the making [properties/property] of the offspring; which is not the case with concepts issuing from the soul. . . .[47]

The words quoted from Pliny come near the end of the text for the arch, when Sor Juana explains the story of the hieroglyph for the second right hand base,[48] and they are charged with innuendo. Read in relation to other parts of the arch, as if they were part of a set, a piece in a puzzle, they allow us to decipher even more clearly the principal subtext of the entire work. Specifically, they strengthen the hypothesis that *Allegorical Neptune* is, among many other things, an urgent answer to the tridentine prohibition of women's access to learning. As opposed to the "holy ignorance" the Council of Trent recommended for women, Sor Juana espouses a path of "holy knowledge" and fertile imagination.

Neptune appears in the upper part of the third canvas, stabilizing the unstable "island" with his trident, protecting it from the agitated waters that represent the metaphorical instability of the state, the very real instability of Mexico City, which suffers floods and earthquakes, and the insecure situation of thinkers, and poets, herself included. Sor Juana had been requested to solicit the new viceroy's attention to the city's severe drainage and other problems with water and plumbing systems. In the erudite mythological text that includes the description of what was to be painted on the third canvas, Sor Juana narrates the story of the island of Delos.[49] She gives us the various scholarly opinions regarding origins and outcomes. She tells of "chaste Asteria, daughter of Ceo, and granddaughter of Titan, although according to some his daughter, and sister of Latona." In attempting to escape the deceitful and feather-adorned lover Jove, Latona "fell into the sea, and as if virtue were a fault, was condemned to perpetual motion." Stillness is conceded to her by Jupiter, according to some, but according to Macrobius "Apollo and Diana, grateful for the beneficence (favor) shown to their mother, Latona, or to aggrandize her as their homeland, made her stable [*consistente*]." However, Lucian attributes the deed to Neptune, who was moved by compassion for the tribulations of Latona. Citing Vergil and Homer, Sor Juana recounts the story of this mother who "gave the world, and even more the Heavens, those luminous sources of light, Phoebus and Diana." That is why, in her words, "The panel is adorned with valiant and attractive landscapes, leafy [*copados*] trees, and intricate rock formations; the brush expressed with brilliant [*gallarda*] exactness the affliction of Latona [who has been refused a place at which to give birth] and the beauty of the two tender young lights, Phoebus and Diana."[50]

The third canvas is also emblematic in its use of color and object: gold for Phoebus, the Sun, day; silver for Diana, the Moon, night; a variation on the emblem by Alciatus, mentioned later in her text and quite well-known at the time.[51] It is also spectacular: "It represented the entire attractive [*vistoso*] appearance of our Imperial Mexico." In this painting Sor Juana tells of the birth and situation of Delos, an image of Mexico City, which the viceroy

(Neptune) comes to stabilize. The trident is also represented as an emblem of stability in the following quotation: "serving as a nail [*clavo*] to the voluble fortune [of Latona], to give stable haven to her anguished beauty, to those two luminous lamps, Apollo and Diana, as Homer said." The painting and its explication also announce, emblematically and enigmatically, Núñez's attempt to deny her a place in which to give birth to her suns and moons, her poetic creations, the offspring of her imagination. When she sent the Bishop of Puebla her writing on Vieyra's sermon some years later, Sor Juana would also use a metaphor of parturition: she was sending it as a fetus, like the newborn of a she-bear. Metaphors of birth are numerous in Sor Juana's work. There are several in the text of the arch itself.[52]

Sor Juana used sources in a distinct and brilliant manner, a manner appropriate to the freedom of her temperament and talent, while drawing from the same books and engravings that inspired all educated people of her time.[53] The introductory prose text for the triumphal arch has an epistolary element; it is supposed that the viceroy and vicereine and their circle would read it, almost like a letter addressed to them by the Metropolitan Cathedral Council of Mexico and by the author herself. It is framed by a reference to the Egyptians, to the hermetic philosophy that attracted cultural elites of the period, who believed, Beuchot says, that "its origins go back to a somewhat imaginary ancient Egypt, in its equivalent of the god Theut or Thot, inventor of writing."[54] Sor Juana explains, in contrast, that the "inventor of letters" is Isis, whom she presents not only as a divinity but also as Poet[55] and in many other guises, because she is the "elderly [*añosa*] mother of the gods."[56] The Mexican nun did not call upon the law of the Father alone but rather that of Mother or of Mother and Father. When she appeals to abstractions, she projects mythological explanations of culture that posit female origins for existing genealogies.

As a poet and intellectual who had to carefully tend her place as Tenth Muse (*décima musa*), of exceptionality—wings for her talent on one hand, a limiting cage on the other—Sor Juana learned to be an advocate for others. She spoke for the subalterns of her country—for herself and for women and men whose right to request and use speech was ambiguous if not illicit—by lacing the discourse of power with the finest irony. For this reason it matters that we attend to her ubiquitous wordplay, to linguistic surprises and deeply formed subtleties. At times they are found where least expected. Actually, Sor Juana prepares us from the beginning for what is to come. She says, for example, that the Egyptians adored their "deities" by means of hieroglyphs and "a variety of forms." Lacking gods of visible form, they invented symbolic modes of representing them. They represented God with a circle, symbol of the infinite.

She seeks to take advantage of the possibility of using feminine or abstract nouns whenever she can. Every time she mentions God in the masculine [Dios], she refers three times to deity in the feminine [Deidad, Deidades].[57] Such usage was common in the period; she merely exaggerates it wherever possible. These linguistic and conceptual maneuvers are attempts to open times/tenses and sites/spaces to virtues and values often categorically excluded from art and thought.

The metaphor of engendering/generating and maternity—both corporeal and incorporeal—winds thematically through the arch's text and images. Because wisdom itself was conceived in Isis, "Neptune her son . . . had no less an obligation: for to be born of knowledgeable parents gives one not so much merit as an obligation to follow suit; so as not to degenerate, nor belie the mysterious dogmas of the platonists."[58] Later on in the text Neptune appears as a father, but not until he has been brought up and educated by his mother: "And its being accepted that maternal habits are normative and exemplary, not only tender childhood but robust youth compose their own by imitating them. . . ."[59]

Neptune was such a good student of his mother—Isis—that he became a propagator of her values: "Wisdom so pleased Neptune, that even his lowliest servants . . . were educated, wise, more due to Neptune's vigilance, which kept them exercised, than because of their own hard work."[60] The eleven initial pages devoted to proving the unique importance of Wisdom as an "attribute" upon which all the remaining virtues depend are fundamental also to the presentation of a framework that, while following them closely, breaks with traditional frameworks regarding the education and triumph of the Christian prince. Here, and in other passages of the text and even in several iconographic elements, Sor Juana speaks obliquely not only to the viceregal couple but also to the entire wing of the power structure, which, like Núñez de Miranda, defended what might be called intellectual mercantilism—that is, the economic system of domination and control in the Spanish colonies paralleled by the Counter-Reformation ideological strictures of the Council of Trent.

I have become convinced that Sor Juana selects cannily from among hundreds and hundreds of mythological and biblical narratives and decides to utilize those most appropriate to her political-didactic program. She chooses 220 citations in Latin with the intention of demonstrating not only her peerless virtuosity but also the creative possibilities of verbal and visual discourse. They also show how established custom, imposed and held in place by the ruling class, makes all but official truths invisible.

In such a way she gives a lesson in freedom of thought, in such a way she continues to amaze people with the breadth of her knowledge, and in such a way she undermines the aggressive rhetoric of persuasion. Predominant among recurrent themes in her selection of myths and classical citations are those that take up questions of the position of women, and those that reverse commonly held beliefs or interfere with the conventional sense of things.[61]

Sigüenza y Góngora announces in the title of his Prelude II that he is seeking "a more plausible idea" for love of the homeland than the one given by fables (myths). Sor Juana intertwines myth and reality in an unusual manner, weaving a novel cultural tapestry that problematizes power and knowledge, genealogy (lineage/heritage), the relationships between men and women, matrimony, birthings, illegitimacy, and legitimacy. She also seeks a more plausible idea than that given by the realities and some of the myths current in her milieu. Her love cannot be for the homeland or nation that excludes her; she invents, to counter the *patria* (fatherland/hisland), a sort of *matria* (motherland/herland); (she creates a new *ma/pa*—a play on map [*mapa*] in Spanish). What was plausible for Sor Juana has barely begun to be appreciated in the twentieth century.

I want to thank my research assistant, Román Santillán, for his patient and painstaking searches; poet Beatrix Gates, and Renaissance scholar Elizabeth Pallitto, for their expert and efficient editorial help; and the editors, Jane Donawerth, professor of English and affiliate in Women's Studies, and Adele Seeff, director of the Center for Renaissance and Baroque Studies at the University of Maryland, for their careful readings and insightful comments.

*Sor Juana, *Obras Completas*, vols. 1–3, ed. Alfonso Méndez Plancarte; vol. 4 ed. Alberto G. Salceda (México: Fondo de Cultura Económica, 1951–57), 396.

Notes

1. Other editions of Sor Juana's works cited in this essay are *The Answer/La Respuesta* (including a Selection of Poems), trans. and ed. Electa Arenal and Amanda Powell (New York: Feminist Press at the City University of New York, 1994); and Sor Juana Inés de la Cruz, *Inundación castálida*, ed. and annotated by Georgina Sabat de Rivers (Madrid: Editorial Castalia, 1983). "*Neptuno alegórico, océano de colores, simulacro político* . . . " is the title of the work referred to in this article by its shortened version, *Allegorical Neptune*. All translations from *Allegorical Neptune* are from a translation in progress by David Randall with Electa Arenal.

2. The original edition was entitled *Inundación castálida de la única poetisa, musa décima, soror Juana Inés de la Cruz* (Madrid: Juan García Infanzón, 1689–90). For a concise introduction to Sor Juana's life and works, see my entry "Cruz, Sor Juana Inés de la" in *Encyclopedia of Mexico: History, Society and Culture*, ed. Michael S. Werner (Chicago and London: Fitzroy Dearborn Publishers, 1997), 379–82.

3. These territories, present-day Mexico and parts of Central America, were then called New Spain.

4. Octavio Paz, *Sor Juana, or, The Traps of Faith*, trans. Margaret Sayers Peden (Cambridge, Mass.: Harvard University Press, 1988), 178; Spanish edition: *Sor Juana*

Inés de la Cruz, o, Las trampas de la fé (México: Fondo de Cultura Económica, 1983), 240.

5. This essay is part of a larger research plan that has already entailed the building of a conceptual maquette of what the arch may have looked like. It is part of a project for an amply illustrated and annotated book that will gather appropriate contextualizing materials and scholarly opinions, and facilitate further study as well as make the text accessible to a nonspecialized reading public.

6. Whereas Saint Jerome was a prominent source of misogynistic argument, he also emphasized the virtues of studious women and criticized the "commonplace censorship" of women's letters. The clarification of Jerome's position is a theme in her letter to her confessor. See the introduction to *The Answer/La Respuesta*, 36.

7. There is but one extant letter from what was said to be a voluminous correspondence.

8. Paz, *Sor Juana*, 496–97.

9. Carlos de Sigüenza y Góngora, *Obras históricas*, ed. with a prologue by José Rojas Garcidueñas, 3rd ed. (México: Editorial Porrúa, 1983), 236.

10. Despite strong disagreement with some aspects of Octavio Paz's biography of Sor Juana, I have been encouraged in undertaking the task of decoding the arch's enigmas by his calling attention to their presence and complexity.

11. Rejection of military force in favor of peaceful tactics is also a theme in Sor Juana's other writings. In the *Loa for the Divine Narcissus*, for example, the female figure of Religion conquers the male figure of Zeal, dressed as a soldier. The argument is that Religion will succeed where Zeal has not, because the natives, intrinsically spiritual, are already practitioners of a religious rite that has to do with purification and sacrifice. Religion's lines are as follows:

Put up your sword.
Forebear, Zeal, do not attack,
it is my nature to forgive,
I do not want their immolation,
but conversion, let them live.

Quoted from *Loa for the Divine Narcissus*, trans. Lee A. Daniel (Fredricton, New Brunswick: York Press, 1994).

12. Carlos de Sigüenza y Góngora, *Obras históricas*, ed. with a prologue by José Rojas Garcidueñas, 3rd ed. (México: Editorial Porrúa, 1983), 232.

13. See the following articles and books: Antonio Alatorre, "Para leer la *Fama y obras pósthumas* de Sor Juana Inés de la Cruz," *Nueva Revista de Filología Hispánica* 29 (1980), "La *Carta* de Sor Juana al P. Núñez (1682)," *Nueva Revista de Filología Hispánica* 35 (1987); José Pascual Buxó, "El resplandor intelectual de las imágenes: jeroglífica y emblemática," in *Juegos de ingenio y agudeza: La pintura emblemática de la Nueva España*, Jaime Cuadriello, curator, exhibition catalog, Museo Nacional de Arte, November 1994–February 1995 (México: Universidad del Claustro de Sor Juana, Instituto de Investigaciones de la Cultura, 1995); Fernando Checa, "Arquitectura efímera e imagen del poder," in *Sor Juana y su mundo*, ed. Sara Poot Herrera (México: Universidad del Claustro de Sor Juana, Instituto de Investigaciones de la Cultura, 1995), 251–305; Kari Elisabeth Børresen, "Discours sûr Dieu: patristique et matristique," *Augustinus* 38 (1993): 121–35, and "Matristics: Ancient and Medieval Church Mothers," in *Theologie zwischen Zeiten und Kontinenten*, ed. Theodor Schneider and Helen Schüngel-Straumann (Freiburg: (i.Br.): 1993) 64–83; Mauricio Beuchot, "Sor Juana y el hermetismo de Kircher," in *Los Empeños: Ensayos en homenaje a Sor Juana Inés de la Cruz* (México: UMAM, 1995), 1–9; José Pascual Buxó, "El arte de la memoria

en el *Primero sueño. Introducción al estudio de un poema enigmático,"* in *Sor Juana y su mundo. Una mirada actual,* ed. Sara Poot Herrera (México: Universidad del Claustro de Sor Juana, Instituto de Investigaciones de la Cultura, 1995), 307–50; Vincenzo Cartari, *Le imagini con la spositione de i dei gli antichi* (Venezia, 1556); *The Ceremonial Entry of Ernst, Archduke of Austria, into Antwerp, June 14, 1594,* text by Johannes Bochius, engravings by Peter van der Borcht, after designs by Marten de Vos [1595], with an introduction by Hans Mielke (rpt. New York: Benjamin Blom, 1970); Jaime Cuadriello, "Los jeroglíficos de la Nueva España," in *Juegos de ingenio,* 84–113; Fernando Checa, "Arquitectura efímera e imagen del poder," in *Sor Juana y su mundo,* 251–305; Paula Findlen, *Possessing Nature: Museums, Collecting, and Scientific Culture in Early Modern Italy* (Berkeley: University of California Press, 1994); Jean Franco, *Plotting Women: Gender and Representation in Mexico* (New York: Columbia University Press, 1989); María Concepción García Sáiz, "Minerva recibe al virrey Conde Alba de Liste," in *Juegos de ingenio,* 162–68; Yves Giraud, ed., *L'Emblème a la Renaissance: Actes de la journeie d'études du 10 mai 1980,* Société Française des Seizièmistes (Paris: Société d'Edition d'Enseignement Supérieur, 1982); Margo Glantz, "La casa del respeto y la casa del placer," in *Sor Juana Inés de la Cruz y el pensamiento novohispano: Memoria del coloquio internacional* (México: Instituto Mexiquense de Cultura, 1995), 121–39; González de Zarate, *Emblemas regio-políticos de Juan de Solórzano* [1653], with a foreword by Santiago Sebastián (rpt. Madrid: Ediciones Tuero, 1987); Arthur Henkel and Albrecht Schone, *Emblemata: Handbuch zur Sinnbildkunst* (Stuttgart: J. B. Metzlersche Verlagsbuchhandlung, 1976); Horapollo, *Hieroglyphica* (Naples, 1551); Athanassi Kircheri [Kircher], *Prodomus Coptus Aegyptiacus* (Rome, 1656); Helga von Kügelgen, "Carlos de Sigüenza y Góngora, su *Theatro de Virtudes Políticas que Constituyen un Príncipe* y la estructuración emblemática de unos tableros en el Arco de Triunfo," in *Juegos de ingenio,* 151–60; and "The Way to Mexican Identity: Two Triumphal Arches of the Seventeenth Century," in *World Art: Themes of Unity in Diversity. Acts of the XXVIth International Congress of the History of Art,* vol. 3, ed. Irving Lavin (University Park and London: Pennsylvania State University Press, 1989), 709–16; Francisco de la Maza, *El guadalupanismo mexicano* (México: Fondo de la Cultura Económica, 1953); Mabel Moraña, "Sor Juana Inés de la Cruz: letra, lengua, poder," in *Sor Juana Inés de la Cruz y el pensamiento novohispano,* 271–83; Octavio Paz, *Sor Juana Inés de la Cruz;* Sara Poot Herrera, ed., *Sor Juana y su mundo;* Cesar Ripa, *Iconologia* (Rome, 1603), and *Iconologie ou Explication nouvelle de plusieurs images* (Paris, 1644); Georgina Sabat de Rivers, "El Neptuno de Sor Juana: fiesta barroca y programa político," in *Estudios de literatura hispanoamericana: Sor Juana Inés de la Cruz y otros poetas barrocos de la colonia* (Barcelona: PPU, 1992), 241–56; Carlos de Sigüenza y Góngora, *Obras históricas,* ed. with a prologue by José Rojas Garcidueñas, 3rd ed. (México: Editorial Porrúa, 1983); and *Theatro de virtudes politicas,* in *Obras históricas,* 225–361; Marie Tanner, *The Last Descendent of Aeneas: The Habsburgs and the Mythic Image of the Emperor* (New Haven and London: Yale University Press, 1993); Manuel Toussaint, *Homenaje del Instituto de Investigaciones Estéticas a Sor Juana Inés de la Cruz en el tercer centenario de su nacimiento* (México, 1952), and *Iglesias de México: La Catedral de México,* vol. 2, fotografías by Kahlo (1924; rpt., Banco de México, 1979); Tovar de Teresa, *Bibliografía Novohispana de Arte: Part 1, Impresos mexicano relativos al arte de los siglos XVI y XVII,* Introduction by José Pascual Buxó (México: Fondo de Cultura Económica, 1988); Elías Trabulse, *El enigma de Serafina de Cristo: Acerca de un manuscrito inédito de Sor Juana Inés de la Cruz (1691)* (México: Instituto Mexiquense de Cultura, 1995); Joannis Pierii Valeriani, *Hieroglyphica, Seu De Sacris, Aegyptiorum Aliarumque Gentium Literis Commentarii* (n.p., 1586).

14. García Saíz, María Concepción, "Minerva recibe al virrey Conde Alba de Liste," in the exhibition catalog, *Juegos de ingenio*, 162–63.

15. For documentation on European spectacle and festival, see Roy Strong, "The Medieval Inheritance," in *Art and Power: Renaissance Festivals 1450–1650* (Berkeley: University of California Press, 1984), 3–19; Barbara Wisch and Susan Scott Munshower, eds., *"All the world's a stage . . .": Art and Pageantry in the Renaissance and Baroque*, 2 vols., (University Park: Pennsylvania State University Press, 1990), 1: xv–xx; for paintings and engravings on Sor Juana's arch, see Cuadriello, *Juegos de Ingenio*, 132–35, 235.

16. Sigüenza y Góngora's text has 358 citations in Latin and two in Greek; Sor Juana's 220 in Latin and one in Italian. In both cases such formal and stylistic attributes were considered indications of erudition and the most up-to-date fashion or "modernity."

17. Sigüenza y Góngora, *Obras históricas*, 238.

18. Helga von Kügelgen, "Carlos de Sigüenza y Góngora, su *Teatro de Virtudes Políticas que Constituyen un Principe y la estructuración emblemática de unos tableros en el Arco de Triunfo*," in *Juegos de ingenio*, 158.

19. Georgina Sabat de Rivers, "El Neptuno de Sor Juana: fiesta barroca" in *Estudios de literatura hispanoamericana*, 241–56, 246.

20. See the section entitled "A Different Worldview, A Different Law: A Woman-Centered Vision," in *The Answer/La Respuesta*, edited by Arenal and Powell, 31–37.

21. For a definition of the term "interpretive power," see introduction, Jean Franco, *Plotting Women*.

22. Sigüenza y Góngora, *Obras históricas*: Ruth (235), Rachel (266), Judith (355), Venus and "Their Excellencies the [Viceregal] Consort" and "Their Excellencies the Princes [the Viceroy and Vicereine]" (274–75, 277), the Vicereine Doña María Luisa (277), and the Graces (277).

23. (Underscoring is his.) Acamapichtli with Hope and Fame; Hitzilíhuitl with Meekness and Clemency; Izcoóhuatl with Prudence; Moctezuma Ilhuicamina "sending arrows that symbolize Piety;" Azayácatl crowned by Fortitude; Tizoc, Peace painted in the figure of Concord—carrying branches of palm olive and laurel—facing Discord who carries military instruments; Moctezuma Xocoyotzin, Liberality and Magnificence, painted as a lion spewing pearls, silver, and gold from its mouth. See Tovar de Teresa, *Bibliografía Novohispana de Arte*, vol. 1, *Impresos mexicanos*, 262.

24. Sor Juana, *Obras Completas*, 396.

25. Sor Juana, *Obras Completas*, 274.

26. (Underscoring is his.) The many important symbolic values of this particular representation will be explained in the section "Emblems and Metaphors."

27. Von Kügelgen, 151–52.

28. Sigüenza y Góngora, *Obras históricas*, 290.

29. Sor Juana, *Inundación castálida*, 348.

30. Sor Juana, *Obras Completas*, 606.

31. Sor Juana, *Inundación castálida*, 349.

32. Findlen, 116, 343.

33. "Discours sûr Dieu: patristique et matristique," *Augustinus* 38 (1993): 121–35; "Matristics: Ancient and Medieval Church Mothers," in *Theologie zwischen Zeiten und Kontinenten*, ed. Theodor Schneider and Helen Schüngel-Straumann (Freiburg: I. Br.,1993), 64–83. See also "Recent and Present Research on Women in the Christian Tradition," paper, International Patristics Conference, Oxford, 1995, 1, 2, 7–8: "Among the humanistic disciplines, present Gender Studies in Religion are at the scholarly forefront by applying human, that is male or female *genderedness* as a main analyti-

cal category. . . . In historical perspective, the patristic innovation is followed by the matristic achievement of Northern European church Mothers, mainly between the twelfth and fifteenth centuries. . . . Gender Studies of the Christian tradition display varied female dismantling of male-constructed barriers. The obstacles raised by theological anthropology . . . were surmounted by many women, as we see in their history, writings, and hagiographical accounts."

34. Electa Arenal, "Sor Juana Inés de la Cruz: Reclaiming the Mother Tongue," in *Letras femeninas* 11:1–2 (primavera-otoño 1985), 63–75 [in English].

35. In the article cited above (note 7), Børresen writes, "the terms *androcentrisme/androcentrique* . . . describe the axiomatic gender hierarchy. . . . Firmly established in international scholarship lacking in the normative dictionaries."

36. See the section entitled "The Issues at Stake."

37. For a historical contextualization, identification of sources, and a panoramic view of Sor Juana's text, see Georgina Sabat de Rivers's essay, "El *Neptuno* de Sor Juana: Fiesta barroca y programa político," in *Estudios de literatura hispanoamericana*, 241–56.

38. See the introduction to *The Answer*, especially the subsection entitled "Letter to Her Confessor" in the section "The Issues at Stake," 25–30.

39. These tactics are studied well by Mabel Moraña.

40. Sor Juana, *Inundación castálida*, 315–16.

41. In the *Neptuno alegórico*, Sor Juana cites Ovid's *Metamorphoses* 13. xxx as follows:

"And it [the sea], was held by them in such great reverence, that not only did they believe it could cleanse one from sin, but also that it communicated a certain type of divinity; thus Glaucus purified his human aspect:

Di[i] maris exceptum socio dignatur honore,
utque mihi, quaecunque feram mortalia demant,
Oceanum, Tethymque rogant. Ego lustror ab illis
et purgante [befas] novies mihi carmine dicto,
pectora fluminibus iubeor supponere centum.
Nec mora, diversis lapsi de partibus amnes;
totaque vertuntur supra caput aequora nostrum.
Quae postquam redeunt, alium me corpore toto,
ac fueram nuper, nec eundem mente recepi.
Hactenus acta tibi possum memoranda referre
hactenus et nemini, nec mens mea caetera sensit.
[The gods of the sea receive me, deem me worthy
of friendly honors, call on Oceanus
and Tethys that they might remove from me
whatever mortal nature I might bear. I am cleansed
by them—and, with a song that purges me of sin
sung over me nine times, I am commanded
to place my breast beneath a hundred streams—
that flow without delay from every side
and a whole sea is rolled above my head.
I find—once mind and body have returned—
that I am wholly otherwise in body
from what I was, and not the same in mind.
I can report to you my recollections
up to this point—up to this point remember,

but there is nothing else my mind perceives.]

Alluding, then to the greatness of the sea . . . [the panel is a painting of] a world encircled by the sea, and divided by his trident [Neptune's/the new viceroy's], which formed the diameter of the whole globe. . . ."

From a translation in progress of the *Neptuno* by David Randall.

42. Sor Juana, *Obras completas*, 397.

43. Vergil, *Aeneid* I.138–39.

44. González de Zarate, *Emblemas regio-políticos de Juan de Solórzano*, 214.

45. Sor Juana, *Obras completas*, 608.

46. Sor Juana, *Obras completas*, 372.

47. Sor Juana, *Obras completas*, 395–96.

48. Sor Juana, *Inundación castálida*, 314.

49. Delos represents Mexico City, at the time an "island" within a land mass, full of canals.

50. Isidore, *Etymologies*, XIV; Ovid, *Metamorphoses*, VI, 185.

51. [Alciatus] Andrea Alciato, *Emblematum* (Padua, 1613).

52. Sor Juana, *Obras completas*, 379, 384.

53. There are parallels with Goya insofar as Sor Juana was also an artistic servant to the court and church with a critical eye that led her to unmask injustices, corruption, and stupidity, and that for a time at least (only in part because of the lack of understanding) tolerated and even appreciated her genius.

54. Mauricio Beuchot, "Sor Juana y el hermetismo de Kircher," in *Los Empeños*, 1.

55. Sor Juana, *Obras completas*, 362.

56. Sor Juana, *Inundación castálida*, 364.

57. Sor Juana, *Inundación castálida*, 268.

58. Sor Juana, *Obras Completas*, 362.

59. Sor Juana, *Inundación castálida*, 276.

60. Sor Juana, *Inundación castálida*, 279.

61. Of St. Paul's injunction for silence among women, Sor Juana writes, "I would like these interpreters and expounders of St. Paul to explain to me how they understand the passage, 'Let women keep silence in churches.' For they must understand it either materially, to mean the pulpit and the lecture hall, or formally, to mean the community of all believers, which is to say the Church. If they understand it in the first sense (which is to my way of thinking its true sense, for we can see that indeed it is not permitted by the Church for women to read publicly or to preach) why then do they rebuke those women who study in private? And if they understand it in the second sense and wish to extend the Apostle's prohibition to all instances without exception so that not even in private may women write or study, then how is it that we see the Church has allowed a Gertrude, a Teresa, a Brigid, the nun of Agreda, and many other women to write?" from *The Answer*, 91.

Workshop Summaries 22–28: Travel and Settlement

Workshop #22: "Culture Crossings: Self-Determination through Assimilation"

Organizers

Cherron A. Barnwell, English, Howard University; Lynda B. Salamon, English, The Essex Campus of the Community College of Baltimore County

Readings

Moira Ferguson, ed., *The Hart Sisters: Early African Caribbean Writers, Evangelicals, and Radicals* (Lincoln: University of Nebraska, 1993); James E. Seaver, *A Narrative of the Life of Mrs. Mary Jemison*, ed. June Namias (Norman: University of Oklahoma Press, 1992).

This workshop was designed to explore the ways in which two very different groups of eighteenth-century women found liberation through assimilation into alien cultures. In North America, colonial women captured by Native Americans were forced to accommodate in order to survive; paradoxically, they often found that crossing cultural boundaries opened new social and economic roles and freed them to forge new identities. These women came to criticize white society, some explicitly in their narratives, and others, perhaps more eloquently, in their refusal to return to white society even when "rescued." In the Caribbean, the Hart sisters adopted the discourse of Methodism to liberate themselves from their subjugated position and to reconstruct African-Caribbean womanhood. In doing so, they built the first Antiguan Methodist congregation and defined and empowered themselves as piously dignified free women.

In their opening presentations, the workshop facilitators provided historical context for the preassigned readings and then elaborated on the materials already distributed. Lynda Salamon supplemented the Mary Jemison readings with summaries of the captivities of Mary Rowlandson, Hannah Dustan, and Elizabeth Hanson. She suggested that the expanded gender roles and increased freedoms associated with Native American life partially explain why nearly one-third of the female captives resisted being returned to their former communities. Cherron Barnwell contrasted the forced physical "travel" of the colonial captives with the travel between cultural and religious abstractions accomplished by the Hart sisters.

These presentations led to spirited and productive discussion, in which participants eagerly shared their own experiences with teaching captivity narratives and contributed references to articles for future research. The attendees were particularly interested in the Hart sisters; few of them were familiar with these figures. The discussion dealt with specific ways in which the sisters were able to use language to carve for themselves a space in which they could exercise self-determination. Cherron underscored the contemporary relevance of the workshop by distributing an article, "The Affinities Between Feminists and Evangelical Women," which appeared in *The Chronicle of Higher Education* of October 17, 1997. The author, R. Marie Griffith, identified several surprising similarities between members of NOW and wives of men associated with the Promise Keepers and concluded by encouraging researchers to seek common ground among women, instead of pitting groups against one another, in order to understand more fully the ways in which individuals form unique identities.

Additional Readings

Castiglia, Christopher. *Bound and Determined: Captivity, Culture-Crossing, and White Womanhood from Mary Rowlandson to Patty Hearst.* Chicago: University of Chicago Press, 1996.

Ferguson, Moira. *Colonialism and Gender Relations from Mary Wollstonecraft to Jamaica Kincaid.* New York: Columbia University Press, 1993.

Gilroy, Paul. *The Black Atlantic: Modernity and Double Consciousness.* Cambridge, Mass.: Harvard University Press, 1993.

Namias, June. *White Captives: Gender and Ethnicity on the American Frontier.* Chapel Hill: University of North Carolina Press, 1993.

Vaughan, Alden T., and Edward W. Clark, eds. *Puritans among the Indians.* Cambridge, Mass.: Belknap Press, 1981.

Submitted by: Lynda B. Salamon

Workshop # 23: "Fantasy and Fiction Writing: The Imaginings of Three Early Modern Women"

Organizers

Hilda Smith, History, University of Cincinnati; Susan Staves, English, Brandeis University; Melinda Zook, History, Purdue University

Readings

Excerpts from Aphra Behn's *The Widow Ranter*, ed. Janet Todd (London & New York: Penguin Classics, 1992), Acts I & II, 253–85; excerpts from Margaret Cavendish's *The Blazing World and Other Writings*, ed. Kate Lilley (London: Penguin, 1994), 124–59, 188–96; excerpts from Elizabeth Griffith's translation of *The Shipwreck and Adventures of Monsieur Pierre Viaud* (London, 1771), x–xii, 155–57, 163–77, 182–87, 212–19.

The intention for this workshop was to explore the worlds imagined in the writings of three extraordinary early modern women: Margaret Cavendish, Duchess of Newcastle, Aphra Behn, and Elizabeth Griffith. In *The Blazing World*, Margaret Cavendish constructed an imaginary world where she could express a uniquely woman-ruled intellectual and political vision. In her play, *The Widow Ranter*, set in America, Aphra Behn created a new world wherein class and gender distinctions were fluid and ambiguous. Elizabeth Griffith's translation of *The Shipwreck and Adventures of Monsieur Pierre Viaud*, a French travelogue detailing the misfortunes of a shipwrecked party on the Florida coast, examines how European norms and morals were subverted when transported to a hostile land void of civilization. Through these imagined places—whether Cavendish's own fantasized utopian universe or Behn's unruly Virginia colony or Griffith's wilderness—each woman was able to explore and critique the values of her contemporary society. Despite the diverse genres, each writer sought to transport and test the standards of her world through these imagined realms. Whereas Cavendish's utopia raises issues of gender and class, Behn's play and Griffith's translation address not only these issues but also race.

Hilda Smith centered her discussion on the novelty of many of Cavendish's ideas, particularly her political ideas, which Smith believes scholars have hitherto misrepresented. Smith argued that Cavendish's royalism was not, as is often posited, simply a by-product of the Newcastle circle, but unique to

Cavendish herself; indeed, unique to all royalist theory. Melinda Zook presented *The Widow Ranter* as Behn's attempt at the end of her life to explore an alternative society free of rigid structures. Zook believes that the play represents a departure from many of the political, gender, and class tropes and stereotypes that characterized Behn's earlier plays. Susan Staves noted that Griffith's translation seems to both condone and condemn the very un-European behavior of the Europeans described in Viaud's narrative of their life-and-death adventure. Two instances of transgression of Western morality stand out in the narrative: the cannibalism by Viaud and Madame La Coutre of the African slave, and Madame La Coutre's "unnatural" (and hence unwomanly) strength and courage, which enables her to abandon her dying son and consume the African in order to save herself.

Much of the discourse revolved around the nature of Behn's and Cavendish's political royalism. Participants wondered how anyone could doubt the royalism of either writer. Smith responded by remarking that Cavendish's royalism—too often portrayed as derivative—was essentially different from the aristocratic ethos of her contemporaries. Zook added that royalism was an understudied strain of political thought, noting that there were many strains of Tory thought during Behn's time.

The workshop left several questions unanswered. Among the most important: How much were Behn's play and Griffith's translation influenced by nationalistic empire building? Were these patriotic texts or subversive ones? Further, what links can be drawn between these women writers and political theorists such as Locke and Hobbes?

Additional Readings

Todd, Janet. *The Secret Life of Aphra Behn.* Ch. 29. London: Andre Deutsch, 1996.

Smith, Hilda. "'A General War Amongst the Men but None amongst Women . . .' : Political Differences between Margaret and William Cavendish." In *Politics and the Political Imagination in Later Stuart Britain,* edited by Howard Nenner, 143–60. Rochester, N.Y.: Rochester University Press, 1997.

Zook, Melinda. "Contextualizing Aphra Behn: Play, Politics & Party, 1678–1689." In *Women Writers and the Early Modern British Political Tradition,* edited by Hilda Smith, 75–93. Cambridge: Cambridge University Press, 1998.

Submitted by Melinda Zook, Department of History, Purdue University

Workshop # 24: "Home (and) Away from Home: Men, Women, and Travel, 1500–1800"

Organizers

Elizabeth Bohls, English, University of Illinois; Ann Christensen, English, University of Houston; Barbara Sebek, English, Colorado State University

Readings

Elizabeth Bohls, *Women Travel Writers and the Language of Aesthetics, 1716–1818* (Cambridge: Cambridge University Press, 1995), 27–38; James Clifford, "Traveling Cultures" in *Cultural Studies*, ed. Lawrence Grossberg, Cary Nelson, and Paula Treichler (New York: Routledge, 1992), 105–8; handout of excerpts from Bernal Diaz, *The Conquest of New Spain* (Baltimore: Penguin, 1963); Tzvetan Todorov, *The Conquest of America* (New York: Harper and Row, 1984); *Platter's Travels in England* (London, 1599); Lisa Jardine, *Worldly Goods: A New History of the Renaissance* (New York: Nan Talese, 1996); Henry Peacham, "Of Travaile," in *The Compleat Gentleman* (London, 1622); Merry Wiesner, *Working Women in Renaissance Germany* (New Brunswick, N.J.: Rutgers University Press, 1986); excerpts from Mary Wortley Montagu's letters.

Beginning with the premise that home is not a counterpoint to travel, but rather that which creates the conditions for travel, this workshop juxtaposed home and away-from-home, "domestic" and "foreign." We conceptualized travel as a gendered practice that includes movement or exchange between houses, neighborhoods, towns, nations, continents, or cultures. These categories ensured that considering global travel would not entail leaving women behind. After reading the pre-workshop packet, participants had many questions: What counts as a "travel narrative"? How do we define travel? How do men and women use space differently? Can we separate travel for instrumental reasons from travel as pleasure? When travel is a metaphor—as in the case of a missionary's inner spiritual journey or a fictional character's unfolding subjectivity—where does it fall within our categories?

Before breaking into subgroups on the topics of religion, cross-cultural contact, and commerce, the entire group began by trying to theorize travel. The potential problem with using travel as a "catchall" category prompted us to consider whether or not movement alone constitutes "travel." In order to attend to differences of region, culture, class, and epistemology, one participant argued that we should attend to what was *experienced as* travel. Another cited a male traveler who described himself as "out of my knowledge" while on the road. What do we make of aristocratic households that moved from one estate to another, thus never really leaving "home" behind? What of seasonal mobility? Raising examples such as slaves, the Marian exiles, and Equiano—who traveled as a free black man—we asked how forcible removal, exile, or banishment fit the category of travel. Uncomfortable with the potential exclusivity of restricting the topic to those who intended to travel, one participant suggested that we should always consider "chosen travel" in relation to forced travel.

Many participants agreed that travel necessarily entails discomfort and danger, so we particularized the different forms that danger and discomfort might take. We questioned whether safety and comfort were automatically associated with home. What of the case of troubled homes? Some posited an alternative view of travel as the disruption of *others'* homes—bringing disease, war, or economic upheaval. Royal progresses were a form of travel, for example, that disrupted the homes a monarch visited. Considering the ways that travelers disrupted others' homes prompted us to consider the traveler as curiosity, the object of the gaze and interest of those whom they visited. Other specific examples included Gluckel of Hameln, a European Jew encountering the danger of traveling in different countries; Quaker women who traveled as missionaries; and gentry women in seventeenth- and eighteenth-century China who accompanied their husbands when they moved to fulfill official duties. These questions and examples were then taken up in more detail in small group discussions.

Additional Readings

Fuller, Mary. *Voyages in Print: English Travel to America, 1576–1624.* Cambridge: Cambridge University Press, 1995.

Gluckel of Hameln. *The Memoirs of Gluckel of Hameln.* New York: Schocken Books, 1977.

Naquin, Susan, and Chun-fang Yu, editors. *Pilgrims and Sacred Sites in China.* Berkeley: University of California Press, 1992.

A Short Relation of Some of the Cruel Sufferings of Katharine Evans & Sarah Cheevers. London, 1662.

Vos, Alvin, ed. *Place and Displacement in the Renaissance.* Binghamton, N.Y.: Medieval and Renaissance Texts and Studies, 1995.

Submitted by: Barbara Sebek

Workshop #25: "Moving Bodies, Moving Souls: Religious and Secular Women and Travel in the Early Modern World"

Organizers

Jennifer Selwyn, History, University of New Hampshire; Amanda Angel, History, University of California, Davis

Readings

Amanda Angel, "Crossings," in "Spanish Women in the New World: The Transmission of a Model Polity in New Spain, 1521–1570" (Ph.D. diss., University of California, Davis, 1997); Mary Ward, "Plan of the Third Institute," in *The Heart and Mind of Mary Ward* (Wheathampstead, Hertfordshire, Eng.: Anthony Clark, 1985), 111–24.

This workshop examined the tension between the desires of individual women to travel and to define their rightful place in the world and the often conflicting desires of religious and secular institutions, or male family members. Jennifer Selwyn considered the strong motivations for women inspired by the atmosphere of spiritual renewal of the Catholic reform movements in the sixteenth and seventeenth centuries to move beyond the conventional, gendered constraints on the apostolic vocation. Mary Ward (1585–1645), an English nun, exemplifies the efforts of religious women to negotiate a more active role for themselves in the Catholic Reformation. Beginning in 1611, Ward developed an "Institute" for the founding of a female missionary order, heavily modeled on the Jesuits' own "Institute," which could theoretically send women across the globe. Although rejected by both the Papacy and the Jesuits, Ward's "Third Plan of the Institute" illustrates women's efforts to expand the range of roles available to them Amanda Angel's examination of the Spanish Crown's concerted efforts to convince women to migrate to the Americas casts a wholly different light on the meaning of "women's place." Angel explored issues and conflicts involving honor and sexuality that developed as women traveled to the New World. She analyzed letters concerning the safety of women traveling and the perceived perils that they faced. Her research reveals that Spanish women had the legal right to refuse to go to New Spain. She notes concerns about single women emigrating to the New World and the not uncommon practice of women cross-dressing on board ship.

This workshop inspired a lively discussion. Responding to Ward's "Third Plan," participants wondered how Ward actually conducted her long-distance travel to Rome to present her document to the pope, the political context in which to understand her brief imprisonment in a Munich papal prison, why the Jesuit missionary model proved so attractive to many religious and lay female reformers, and the possible impact of Ignatius Loyola's *Spiritual Exercises* on inspiring active female spirituality in the period. Participants discussed the demographic profile of women going to the New World during the sixteenth century, the effects of immigration on women who stayed behind in Spain, the extent to which the Crown assisted women in conducting the voyage to the Americas, and the frequency of crimes committed against women on board ship.

Additional Readings

Gonzalbo, Pilar. *Las mujeres en la Nueva Espana: Educacion e vida cotidiana.* Mexico D.F.: El Colegio de Mexico, 1987.

Liebowitz, Ruth. "Virgins in the Service of Christ: The Dispute over an Active Apostolate for Women During the Counter-Reformation." In *Women of Spirit: Female Leadership in the Jewish and Christian Traditions,* edited by Rosemary Ruether and Eleanor McLaughlin, 131–52. New York: Simon and Schuster, 1979.

Peters, Henriette. *Mary Ward: A World in Contemplation.* Leominster, United Kingdom: Gracewing, 1994.

Wright, Mary. *Mary Ward's Institute: The Struggle for Identity.* Sydney, Australia: Crossing Press, 1997.

Submitted by: Jennifer Selwyn

Workshop #26: "Unsettling Discoveries: Material Bodies, Female Figures, and the Exchange of Land, Power, and Language"

Organizers

Angelica Duran, English, Stanford University; Martha Rojas, English, Stanford University

Readings

Sandra Messinger Cypess, *La Malinche in Mexican Literature: From History to Myth* (Austin: University of Texas Press, 1992); Bernal Diaz del Castillo, *The Conquest of New Spain*, ed. (J. M. Cohen. Harmondsworth, Eng.: Penguin, 1963); Stephen Greenblatt, "The Go-Between," in *Marvelous Possessions: The Wonder of the New World* (Chicago: University of Chicago Press, 1991) pp. 119–51; Allison Heisch, "Queen Elizabeth I and the Persistence of Patriarchy" *Feminist Review* 4 (1980), 45–56. Francisco Lopez de Gomara, *Cortez: The Life of the Conqueror by His Secretary*, ed. L. B. Simpson (Berkeley: University of California Press, 1964); Roy C. Strong, *Portraits of Queen Elizabeth I* (Oxford: Clarendon Press, 1963); Roy C. Strong, *Gloriana: The Portraits of Queen Elizabeth I* (German Democratic Republic: Thames and Hudson, 1987); Frances Teague, "Queen of England: Elizabeth I," in *Women Writers of the Renaissance and Reformation*, ed K. M. Wilson (Athens: University of Georgia Press, 1989); Elizabeth Tudor, "Latin Oration at Cambridge University" (1564) and "On Marriage and Succession" (1566), in *The Public Speaking of Queen Elizabeth I*, ed. G. P. Rice, Jr. (New York: Columbia University Press, 1951); Elizabeth Tudor, "Written on the Wall at Woodstock," in *The Poems of Queen Elizabeth I*, ed. L. Bradner (Providence: Brown University Press, 1964); Elizabeth Tudor, "All human kind on heart" and "Ah, silly pug, wert thou so sore afraid," in *The New Oxford Book of Sixteenth Century Verse*, ed. E. Jones (Oxford: Oxford University Press, 1991) 184, 185.

Concentrating on Elizabeth I, Queen of England, and Malintzin/Dona Marina (translator and mistress of Hernan Cortés), we proposed a discussion of their foundational roles in the early modern discourses of conquest, colonialism, imperialism, and female subjectivity and objectification. Martha Rojas provided some context for the "production" of La Malinche/Dona Marina/Malintzin. Her history is recorded in the words of contemporary and "educated" males: Hernan Cortés, Francisco Lopez de Gomara, the Florentine Codex, Fray Bernadino de Sahaghun, Bernal Diaz, and the Lienzo de Tlaxcala. Rojas focused on the conditions that prepared Malintzin for her eventual role as translator and cultural mediator. She noted Cortés's silence on the subject of Marina relative to the agency granted her by other sixteenth-century texts. The discussion turned to the challenges of recovering this woman's history given the limits of the archive, the inadequate understanding of the pre- and post-encounter indigenous cultures of Mesoamerica, and the ideological weight of Mexican and Chicano/a national and cultural myths that designate La Malinche alternatively as traitor to and mother of race and nation.

Angelica Duran took up the difficulty of adequately understanding Queen Elizabeth I through her vast but mostly male constructions. She focused on the distinct uses of maps and poetry by the queen, especially the active role she took in the production of Christopher Saxton's cartographic formulas to represent power. What rhetorical and visual modes did women use, and what sorts of modes were used about them? Many suggestive comments were made as to the multiple sexual and gender roles that can be represented by land, especially in the Dutch engraving, *Queen Elizabeth I as Europa* (Ashmolean Museum, Sutherland Collection, C. II-91). Here the queen is superimposed on a strategic map of Europe—her right arm is made up of Italy, her left arm of England and Scotland, and her feet are planted in Poland. To her left, the Spanish Armada is defeated, and to her right a triple-headed pope rides away in a boat rowed by clergy and escorted by a fleet of ships, all of which are numbered and allude to papal allies.

The questions raised in the discussion reflected the possible connections between these two figures. How can we avoid the stereotypes of masculine conquest and enterprise and female victimization posed by Dona Maria? How can we evaluate the representations of feminine enterprise, power, and prestige surrounding Elizabeth as a female ruler? One way of addressing these questions would be to contrast the representations of sexuality of the figures. The de-sexualized representation of Marina/Malintzin by the Spanish narratives and Aztec and Tlaxcalan pictographs, which document the role of mediator, translator, and diplomat, contrast with the nationalist nineteenth-century representations of La Malinche as La Chingada, the treacherous woman who serves as a despised emblem for the conquered, a symbol for the rape of indigenous peoples and cultures by European conquerors and contemporary Chicana feminist reappropriations of her as mother of the cosmic race. Queen Elizabeth's representations have likewise run the gamut from repressed virgin to self-assigned political prostitute. Multiple visual and textual constructions pose vexed problems to historians as they attempt to design and assign power and weakness in the politics of conquest, resurgence, and translation.

Additional Readings

Barker, Felix, and Peter Jackson, eds. *The History of London Maps*. London: Barrie & Jenkins, 1990.

Block, R. Howard. *Medieval Misogyny and the Invention of Western Romantic Love*. Chicago: University of Chicago Press, 1991.

Harvey, P. D. A. *Maps in Tudor England*. London: The Public Record Office and The British Library, 1993.

Marshal, Rosiland K. *Elizabeth I.* London: HMSO and The National Portrait Gallery, 1991.

Stallybrass, Peter. "Patriarchal Territories: The Body Enclosed." In *Rewriting the Renaissance: The Discourse of Sexual Difference in Early Modern Europe.* Edited by Margaret W. Ferguson, Maureen Quilligan, and Nancy J. Vickers, 123–42. Chicago: University of Chicago Press, 1987.

Submitted by: Angelica Duran

Workshop #27: "Women's Spaces"

Organizers

Nicola Courtright, Art History, Amherst College; Sheila ffolliott, Art History and Women's Studies, George Mason University; Linda Austern, Music, Purdue University

Readings

Julia [M.] Cartwright [Ady], *Isabella d'Este* (London: J. Murray, 1903), 1: 88–89, 318–19, 324–5, 329, 331–32, 343; Sheila ffolliott, "Exemplarity and Gender: Three Lives of Queen Catherine de Medici," in *The Rhetorics of Life— Writing in Early Modern Europe,* ed. T. F. Mayer and D.R. Woolf (Ann Arbor: University of Michigan Press, 1995), 321–40; Catherine Wilkinson Zerner, "Women's Quarters in Spanish Royal Palaces," in *Architecture et Vie Sociale (Actes du colloque tenu à Tours . . . 1988),* ed. Jean Guillaume (Paris: Picard, 1994), 127–36; Craig A. Monson, "Lucrezia Vizzana's Musical Apprenticeship," in *Disembodied Voices: Music and Culture in an Early Modern Italian Convent* (Berkeley and Los Angeles: University of California Press, 1995), 48–55; *Diary of Lady Margaret Hoby, 1599–1605,* ed. Dorothy M. Meads (Boston: Houghton Mifflin, 1930), 99.

The goal of this workshop was to investigate how women used or created their spaces, and how they invested these spaces with meaning. The materials, including letters from a female patron concerning the art she commissioned for a space in her palace, ground plans and an inventory of domiciles, travel itineraries between residences, and contemporary descriptions of domestic musical performance, were intended to serve as an introduction to different aspects of women's spaces.

Nicola Courtright compared painting programs for the domiciles of an aristocrat in Renaissance Italy, Isabella d'Este, and a queen of Italian origin in early seventeenth-century France, Marie de' Medici. She suggested that these unusual women claimed a degree of political power not only through the iconography of the art they commissioned, but also through the control they exerted over the artists' actual creations, so that their demonstration of *ingegno* in art (invention) served as proof of their intelligence and consequent ability to rule as men did. Sheila ffolliott, by examining inventories and itineraries of an earlier Italian-born French regent, Catherine de' Medici, concluded that a significant feature of Catherine's regency, despite her substantial building program, was traveling from domicile to domicile with possessions; indeed, that she probably spent more time in her litters than in her palaces and châteaux. ffolliott noted that all royal women were, by definition, travelers— foreigners to the courts they came to inhabit—and reclaimed their own family identities only in widowhood. She suggested that travel from place to place had a political function; it was a way of making and maintaining peace within the kingdom. Demonstrating how music creates its own space with a variety of musical examples, Linda Austern discussed distinctions between music and the other arts. She showed that music belonged to a variety of classes; that music was perceived as literally invading the body; that women who were invisible in society were not necessarily inaudible; and that music was a way of experiencing transgressions that other arts did not permit.

Participants initially debated the issue of whether the intentions of women who commissioned paintings or performed music might overcome the interpretation embedded in the work by a male artist or composer. Participants then focused on the question of how space was used differently for women than for men and how women sometimes appropriated spaces meant for men. Queens sometimes gave a different character to spaces they took from men—i.e., through their paintings that emphasized "feminine" abilities, such as the establishment of peace and concord. Interest was expressed in the domestic arrangements and travels of other classes, such as the women who accompanied aristocrats. Did upper-middle-class women travel as well? Questions were raised about how music, itself an excellent medium for travel between cultures and genders, could be a tool for understanding class distinctions as well. Some participants pointed out that because aristocratic women and queens were in a special category distinct from most women, one could not generalize about women's spaces from these extraordinary examples. It was suggested that visual art, like music, might be a vehicle for presenting contested ideas.

Additional Readings

Dunn, Leslie, and Nancy Jones, eds. *Embodied Voices.* Cambridge and New York: Cambridge University Press, 1994.

ffolliott, Sheila. "Catherine de Medici as Artemisia: Figuring the Powerful Widow." In *Rewriting the Renaissance,* ed. Margaret W. Ferguson et al., 227–41. Chicago: University of Chicago Press, 1986.

Verheyen, Egon. *The Paintings in the Studiolo of Isabella d'Este at Mantua.* New York: College Art Association, 1971.

Submitted by Nicola Courtright

Workshop #28: "Courtly Women Blazing Interior Worlds"

Organizers

Margaret Oakes, English, Furman University; Caroline Bicks, English, Stanford University; Ruth Capasso, French, Kent State University, Stark Campus

Readings

Margaret Cavendish, Duchess of Newcastle, *The Description of a New World, Called the Blazing World,* in *The Blazing World & Other Writings,* ed. Kate Lilley (London: Penguin, 1994), 177–195; Aemilia Lanyer, "The Description of Cooke-ham," in *The Poems of Aemilia Lanyer: Salve Deus Rex Judaeorum,* ed. Susanne Woods (New York: Oxford University Press, 1993) 130–38; Madeleine de Scudéry, "The Land of the New Sauromates," in *Artamenes, or the Grand Cyrus,* vol. 10, trans. F. G. (London: Moseley and Dring, 1653–1655).

This workshop was intended to explore fictional spaces created by women who were constrained by their societies in various ways from exploring and controlling exterior spaces. Margaret Oakes opened with a discussion of the ambivalences that Aemilia Lanyer expresses towards men in her poem, "The Description of Cooke-ham," which describes the female world of the Countess of Cumberland's estate where men are either completely absent (and not missed) or are equal partners with women in religious and charitable endeavors.

She noted that male-female relationships opened up the male world for Margaret Cavendish. Lanyer moved with some degree of ease through the male-created systems in which she participated and adjusted them to her own needs as a poet when necessary. However, the patronage system, which controlled Lanyer's life as a poet, did negatively affect female-female relationships. Caroline Bicks assessed the questions of female creation: what does it mean that Cavendish creates her whole world in her head and does not show it to the world; that her handwriting is (intentionally?) illegible? Unlike Lanyer, Cavendish seems to undercut the importance of female friendship. The participants pointed out the importance of women writing themselves into history, as Cavendish shows with the proclamation of herself as "Margaret the First." This kind of self-promotion does seem to negate the importance of female cooperation and companionship in favor of competition and individual achievement. The work of Madeleine de Scudéry was addressed by Ruth Capasso in terms of the concept of preciosity and how its value system shaped Scudéry's view of her utopia. The isolated land (it is set in the middle of a large, empty plain) can be a symbol of the space of anonymity that Scudéry chose, perhaps to protect her individual freedom, and even an image of the celibacy that *précieuse* women wanted in order to maintain control over their own bodies.

The workshop participants were an extremely well-informed group of scholars from varied backgrounds—from high school and college educators to museum and library personnel—with diverse opinions about these women and their works. Many were new to Scudéry, and they were interested in the isolation of the world that she creates as a way of physically escaping the unsatisfactory "real" world, and a way of gaining artistic freedom for women. The severe restrictions in this society were discussed as a way of avoiding the warfare of the outside world, and of personalizing this world. Participants questioned the frequent characterization of Cavendish as "crazy Margaret," and they had a spirited discussion about the true importance of her work. The group benefited from the presence of Gweno Williams, who praised the depth and intelligence of Cavendish's work and predicted their increasing importance.

Submitted by: Margaret Oakes

Part Four
Keynote Address

Armchair Travel

KAREN NEWMAN
Comparative Literature

Early in her study of seventeenth-century Parisian culture entitled *Cartesian Women*, Erica Harth delimits the gendered boundaries within which women of that period and place lived:

> The demands of feminine modesty and the inaccessibility of the educational apparatus . . . formal schooling, voyages, materials, and equipment—kept even the most educated women well within the limits of orthodoxy.[1]

By my own spatial vocabulary—delimits, boundaries, place—I mean to emphasize the spatial aspect of this exclusion: women were proscribed from the space of the school and the academies in which the new science so crucial to the Enlightenment was being constituted. A great deal of recent feminist work has been concerned, of course, with both school and academy, and there is interesting work to be done certainly on women's exclusion from materials and equipment. In this essay I will explore women's exclusion not from institutions of learning, but from travel, from the voyages that, in the course of the seventeenth century, became a crucial form of knowledge identified increasingly with the newly developing empiricism. This claim requires, of course, important qualification: medieval and early modern Europe was inhabited primarily by, in the great French historian Jacques Le Goff's expression, sedentary beings, "des êtres sédentaires." Few medieval and Renaissance men or women traveled at all. The travel of which I write in this essay was not only proscribed to women, but materially to all but a few men as well. Nomadic travel from one palace or house to another characterized the habits of both the French and English aristocracies of the early modern period; young boys and girls often traveled to live in other households as part of their upbringing; demographic records show that all sorts of persons, both men and women, traveled to urban centers in search of work or preferment; and pilgrims, religious minorities, explorers, and mercantile adventurers traveled the globe. But the inter- and extra-continental travel associated with education of which I write here was ordinarily the privilege of a male elite.

Though much recent work in early modern studies has been interested in travel, it has primarily been concerned with the so-called age of discovery and with colonial expansion.[2] In the seventeenth century, however, Europeans traveled in increasing numbers not only to colonize the so-called New World and bring back to Europe its commodities—gold, tobacco, sugar, hardwoods— but to accumulate cultural capital in what are already the early stages of the Grand Tour. Jonathan Dewald describes the appeal and significance of travel for the French elite: young nobles traveled because contemporaries believed separation from home to be an important element in education. Such ideas touched all social classes.[3] Travel offered not only knowledge of newly discovered or visited lands and cities, peoples and things; travel became an important epistemological model for knowing. Here is Descartes in the *Discourse on Method* (1637):

> as soon as I was old enough to escape the authority of my teachers, I gave up letters entirely and resolved not to pursue any study except that which I might find in myself, or rather, in the great book of the world. I spent the rest of my youth traveling, seeing courts and armies, frequenting persons of varied types and conditions, gathering varied experiences, proving myself in the encounters that fortune dealt me, and everywhere reflecting on whatever came my way so that I was able to take some profit from it. It seemed to me that I would be able to meet much more of truth through the judgments each person exercises in his own affairs, the consequences of which punish him soon after he has judged wrongly, than through those made by a scholar in his study (translation mine).[4]

What interests me here again is the spatial dimension of knowledge: travel and what it teaches as opposed to what goes on in the *cabinet* or private study. *Method*, after all, derives from the Greek word *hodos*, meaning route, road, or way. Descartes goes on, famously, to abandon travel as well as letters and to call for the study of self: "after I had spent some years studying thus in the book of the world and applying myself to acquiring some experience, I resolved also to study myself, and to use all my mental powers to choose the ways/roads I ought to pursue/follow," (translation mine).[5] Significantly, however, that self-study, which is the only form of knowledge worth pursuing, the only knowledge that can lead to truth, is enabled through travel that has delivered the speaker, little by little, from the errors that beset reason. Not only does Descartes not forsake travel in this passage—one day "I resolved also"— "aussi"—"to study myself," he says, but he can only describe self-study as travel: "I resolved to use all my mental powers to choose the paths/roads I ought to follow." As many commentators have noted, metaphors of the road or route abound in the *Discours de la Méthode* and elsewhere in Descartes.[6] Nor does the philosopher forsake the language of travel after his famed retreat, when he formulates the *cogito* in his *Meditations*.

Like the French, the English also recognized the educational importance of travel. Much maligned by the sixteenth-century humanists, in the course of the seventeenth-century travel's usefulness comes to be widely acknowledged. In his study of English travelers abroad, John Stoye illustrates how "travel by young men on the continent came to be accepted as an essential part of their education."[7] Here is Samuel Purchas's uneasy defense of travel from *Hakluytus Posthumus, or Purchas his Pilgrimes* (1625):

> As for Gentlemen, Travell is accounted an excellent Ornament to them; and there-fore many of them comming to their Lands sooner than to their Wits, adventure themselves to see the Fashions of other Countries, where their soules and bodies find temptations to a twofold Whoredom, whence they see the World as *Adam* had *knowledge of good and evill*, with the losse or lessening of their estate in this *English* (and perhaps also in the heavenly) Paradise, and bring home a few smatter-ing termes, flattering garbes, Apish crings, foppish fancies, foolish guises and dis-guises, the vanities of Neighbour Nations . . . without furthering of their knowledge of God, the World, or themselves. I speake not against Travell, so usefull to usefull men, I honour the industrious of the liberall and ingenuous in arts, bloud, educa-tion: and to prevent exorbitancies of the other, which cannot travell farre, or are in danger to travell from God and themselves, at no great charge I offer a World of Travellers to their domesticke entertainment.[8]

Purchas's address to his reader looks backward to the sixteenth-century fear of foreign travel as perilous to body and soul. He rehearses the antiquated and gendered English paranoia about travel and its temptations found in the early humanists, including Roger Ascham, who, it will be remembered, bemoaned the Circean dangers Italy posed young Englishmen. It is a prejudice still repeated in Stoye's *English Travellers Abroad, 1604–1667: Their Influence on English Society and Politics*, which, though published in 1952, remains the only full-length study of seventeenth-century English travel in Europe. There Stoye laments the "wasting away of life in pleasant places on the continent, supported on rentals from English property," that he claims has been "com-mon throughout a long period of English history."[9] In the passage cited from Purchas, who was himself a clergyman, he represents travel as a gendered alle-gory of the fall. Travel offers knowledge of good and evil, its pursuit whore-dom, and its costs, like fashion with which it is linked, the alienation of prop-erty: "the losse or lessening of their estate in this *English* Paradise." Purchas's dual message presents travel on the one hand as original sin and dangerous temptation, on the other as ornament, fashion, vanity, but both are linked to femininity. We should appreciate the irony of that onus because women were in fact long proscribed from the educative and epistemologically enabling travel commended by thinkers, writers, diplomats, military men, here even by the Protestant clergy.

Yet, finally Purchas's attack on travel is, of course, a canny argument on behalf of travel *writing,* which eschews travel's pitfalls: expense and temptation to sin. As he puts it, "at no great charge I offer a World of Travellers to their domesticke entertainment." Purchas's pronoun *their* refers to the beginning of this passage: travel is accounted an excellent ornament of Gentlemen; he looks forward to the Grand Tour when travel was not only the prerogative, but also the prerequisite, of a gentleman's education. It also reminds us once again that women, with certain important exceptions, and those classes of men excluded from gentlemenly pursuits, were by and large excluded from the cultural capital travel proffered.[10]

The new spatial practices associated with travel were recorded in numerous new representational forms, including not only travel accounts, but also the survey, the guidebook, and books and pamphlets on the art or practice of travel. By the mid-seventeenth century, English apologies for travel no longer enumerate its dangers, but instead extol its educational uses and advantages. As the English traveler James Howell declares in his popular *Instructions for Forreine travell* (1642), "*Peregrination . . . may be not improperly called a moving Academy, or the true Peripatetique Schoole.*"[11] Howell alludes, of course, to Aristotle's school named for the walk in the Lyceum where that philosopher taught. Like Descartes, Howell defends travel as philosophical learning and argues for its educative and epistemological value.

As does virtually every travel writer of the seventeenth century, Howell claims to write from "experience," the *locus classicus* of travel writing. He emphasizes the importance of the traveler's movement through space as eyewitness, what might be termed a kind of scopic *cogito:*

> to run over and traverse the world by *Hearesay,* and traditionall relation, with other mens eyes, and so take all things upon courtesie, is but a confused and imperfect kind of speculation, which leaveth but weake and distrustfull notions behind it; in regard the *Eare* is not so authentique a witnesse as the *Eye;* because the *Eye,* by which as through a cleare christall Casement, wee discerne the various works of *Art* and *Nature,* and in one instant comprehend halfe the whole Universe. . . . (12)

Howell's praise of the eye and the eyewitness dramatizes the importance of a scopic drive in producing the effects of a hegemonic subjectivity that depends on presence. As Howell memorably puts it, speaking of Alexander the Great, "he had surveyed more Land with his Eye, than other Kings could comprehend with their thoughts"(13). That subjectivity, organized around the seeing eye, interestingly and paradoxically, produces the "I" of writing. Howell's writing project disrupts the very hegemony of the eye he praises because his own eyewitness account can only be recorded in a book. Both Descartes in the *Discours* and Howell here resort, after all, to what both claim as a discredited writing, to what Howell terms and denigrates as "auricular"(13) knowledge, a locution that reminds us that early modern readers frequently read aloud. Subjectivity then is produced *not* by moving through space—through the city, through Europe, through the so-called New World—but by the "I" that recounts those peripatetic journeys. In both Descartes and Howell, space is negated in the very act of inscribing it, in writing that offers mastery not in presence, but *in absentia*. When Descartes writes of travel and the experience it provides, of course, his is an epistemological project, a metaphysics that exceeds the naive empiricism advertised by Howell and Purchas. They merely offer "travel" on the cheap to those aspiring or simply curious men, and of course women, who perhaps cannot afford to travel, but can manage the price of a book.

It is in that space—the space of the book, the space of writing and reading—that I would like to locate the seventeenth-century romance novel, which notoriously fictional travels the world over, through territories of emotion and relationship as well as exotic spaces and places, mapping fictional travel of the educative sort, travel as a source of social knowledge from which women were largely excluded, but to which they traveled in the course of the century as avid writers and readers. I wish to argue that the romance novel, the mobile genre *par excellence,* figures in interesting ways both the exclusions and possibilities confronted by women in response to the new importance of travel as cultural capital in seventeenth-century Europe, and allowed them the possibility of travel in one of the few venues permitted them—as writers and readers.

Commentators have long opposed the romance novel and travel writing; they often quote a letter dated 1663 by the minor poet and academician Jean Chapelain in which he observes that French reading habits were changing: "voyages," he opines, "are in vogue both at court and in town," while novels have fallen out of favor.[12] However, even in the course of asserting the fall of the novel—and it is worth remembering here that in both the French and English traditions, we are still someways away from what modern critics have been willing to call a novel at all—Chapelain indicates its extraordinary popularity: travel writing, he asserts, is "an entertainment much wiser and more useful than that offered by these agreeable pleasantries that have so enchanted all the idlers, male and female, all about us, and from which our Italian, German, and Dutch neighbors have imbibed poison to their disadvantage and our shame" (trans. mine).[13] Chapelain rehearses the charge of frivolity, already familiar in the seventeenth century, against the romance novel and opposes it to the utility of travel writing, but he nonetheless admits the genre's extraordinary popularity.

Though Chapelain omits the English from those poisoned by the French novel, we know that the English were avid readers of the genre from d'Urfé's *l'Astrée* to Wroth's *Urania* to Madeleine de Scudéry's romance novels. Though the evidence of women's reading is at present scant and anecdotal, the references to Scudéry's *Artamène ou le Grand Cyrus*, perhaps best known through Molière's satiric portrayal of it as the favored reading matter of his provincial aspiring *précieuses*, are particularly interesting. Dorothy Osborne's letters, for example, reveal that she was particularly fond of French romances; during her three-year courtship with William Temple, which was opposed by both their families, Osborne sends him *Artamène* volume by volume in the early 1650s and, as Jacqueline Pearson has pointed out, "uses the situations of that novel to address their own situation and problems."[14] *Artamène* appeared in the midst of the French civil uprising known as the Fronde, between 1649 and 1653, the final volume appearing only in September of that year, which means that, despite the upheavals in Paris, extraordinarily, Scudéry's popular novel managed to reach its audience abroad immediately. Pepys, whose diary occasionally records conjugal reading, reports his wife reading *Artamène* sometime before his own scurrilous, one-handed perusal of the pornographic French novel *L'école des filles*. Scudéry's novels, which remain today unavailable in any modern edition in French or English, were translated immediately after they appeared in Paris into Spanish, Italian, German, English, and even Arabic. Aphra Behn's earliest endeavor with her pen, *The Young King*, was virtually a translation of the well-known author of romances La Calprenède, and she put her own hand to romance in her popular, if notorious, *Love Letters between a Nobleman and his Sister*.

As a major commentator on the seventeenth-century French novel observes, it is the genre at once most despised by critics but, despite occasional complaints about its length, mostly from critics rather than readers, most adored by the public.[15] That public, constituted and expanded by a burgeoning urban print culture, awaited the publication of a new volume with such anticipation that readers were willing to pay exorbitant prices for single sheets before an entire print run was completed and bound.[16] In France we know that booksellers charged more for the romances than for other kinds of books, two, even three times as much as for books materially comparable.[17] We have evidence that individual volumes of Scudéry's ten-tome *Clélie* were divided into even smaller sections and sold separately to inflate profits; even the typography of Scudéry's novels witnesses the profit to be made from romance fiction: large type ensured multiple volumes for an avid market.

The opposition of *utile et dulce* alleged by Chapelain in distinguishing between travel writing and the novel is only one of many charges leveled against the romance novel. These texts were also criticized for *invraisemblance* and for what in French is termed *dépaysement*—for producing in their readers a sense of rootlessness or displacement, we might say; these romances are said to lack specificities of place and therefore to displace their readers in both time and space. Scudéry's three multivolumed novels published between 1640 and 1660, *Ibrahim*, *Artamène ou le Grand Cyrus*, and *Clélie*, are set respectively in the Mediterranean from Monaco and Genoa to Constantinople, in Persia, and in the ancient Roman world. Long maligned for roving flagrantly through space, Scudéry's novels have been shown by recent commentators to demonstrate scholarly care and precision in their presentation of ancient history and place.[18] She never mistakes the situation of countries or cities, rivers or seas. There is no seacoast in Bohemia here. The novels have been remembered primarily as *romans à clé* of the Fronde years, so the critique of placelessness is in part no doubt a response to the displacement of contemporary personnages and events back in time and into other, often exotic places.[19] Yet, the countless critical objections to the seventeenth-century romance novel are also due to their insistent idealism so contrary to the dominant realism on which arguments about the rise of "the" novel are founded.[20] Settings in and travel to exotic locales were both an appropriation of the experience of travel on the part of those denied its cultural and epistemological capital and an important marketing strategy aimed at metropolitan readers avid for such exotic curiosities.[21]

Scudéry's characters recognize and assert the power of travel. In the first volume of *Artamène*, the hero of the title, sounding very much like Descartes, declares: "I want to educate myself by traveling, I want to prove myself through whatever befalls me, I want to know myself" (translation mine).[22] The romance novel was, in Purchas's phrase, *domestic* entertainment, but like the travel writing he hawks, it was also a mode of travel for its sedentary readers, so often, we should remember, said to be women; it offered them access to the new ways of knowing from which they were so frequently materially excluded. The characters of these novels are constantly on the move, not only through space, but through feeling and desire, mapped famously as travel through space, as an emotional and emotive geography with its own rivers, seas, cities, and towns, its *terra incognita*, in the repeatedly reprinted, widely imitated, often ridiculed but rarely seriously considered, *Carte de Tendre* (fig. 1).[23]

Scudéry's allegorical map seems to have come about as a *jeu d'esprit* amidst the *galante* conversation and collaborative cultural production of her famous Saturdays, the name given to her regular gatherings of an urban elite we have since termed the salon.[24] After having circulated apparently for some time among her circle in manuscript, it appears in print in the first volume of *Clélie*. The map displaces courtship from the temporal world of the sonneteer to the spatial world of the geographer; its presumed travelers are positioned on a promontory above Tender, a privileged position of territorial power and appro-

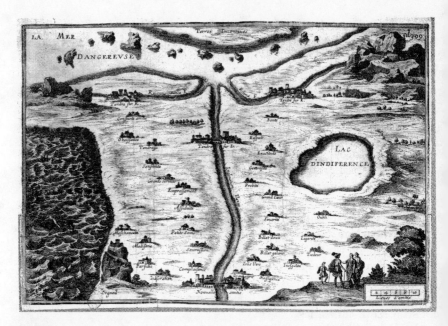

Figure 1. La Carte de Tendre, *Clélie, histoire romaine* (1654). Reproduced by courtesy of the Bibliothèque nationale de France, Paris.

priation.[25] In the novel, *amitié* is a problem of traversing space. At the moment when the map is introduced, it is in response to the plea "tell me *where* I am."[26] The development of feeling and emotion is presented not as a development in time, but in spatial terms: as cities and towns along the rivers of Inclination, Esteem, and Gratitude or Recognition. Diectics—the linguistic forms that anchor the speaker or character in space and time—situate Scudéry's characters, but instead of the temporal diectic markers characteristic of the sonnet, Scudéry uses spatial diectics (where, here, there, far) and the language of movement through space (which way, place, lead, go, voyage, route). Herminius engages himself to undertake a voyage through Tendre—"I would rather have made that voyage than to have seen the entire globe."[27] Scudéry uses terms employed by geographers: beyond tender *amitié*—a state stronger than friendship, but not yet dangerous desire—lie the *terres inconnues*, the unknown lands. The *Carte de Tendre* inspired countless knock-offs, libertine versions, and parodies; it was written of in poems, pamphlets, and letters, reproduced in books and pamphlets, on fans, boxes, and fire screens. The *Carte* with its obstacles and barriers, rivers and mountains, stops and layovers, models the narrative strategies of romance itself with its set pieces, so-called detours and digressions that thwart linear progress.[28]

Travel writing or writing of travel, whether in the romance, travelers' accounts, defenses and arts of travel, or in Descartes's *Discours*, as I have argued, paradoxically depends on the homebody—that is, the reader with access to the book market. In short, in the seventeenth century before the development of lending libraries and organized serial publication, travel writing depends on a metropolitan consumer/reader in search of "domestique entertainment."[29] Such writing, particularly the seventeenth-century novel, appealed primarily to a metropolitan audience in London and Paris and served as its armchair recreation.

In closing I want to turn briefly to the issue of disciplinary boundary crossing, the theme of the 1997 "Attending to Early Modern Women" conference, by way of a piece of historical evidence, a fact, in fact. Since Molière's send-up of provincial would-be salonnières in *Les précieuses ridicules*, literary historians have been fascinated by the seventeenth-century salon culture of men and women engaged in learned and witty conversation. Our evidence has been chiefly "cultural"—that is, reference and allusion in various literary sources. Historians have often been skeptical about such claims, but recently Annick Pardailhé-Galabrun in her fascinating study of things, *La naissance de l'intime*, has gathered with painstaking exactitude from Parisian testamentary inventories evidence that documents the enormous appeal of what we anachronistically call salon culture across status lines. What she finds is an extraordinary plethora of chairs encumbering seventeenth-century Parisian interiors. Listen to the names of only a few: *chaises à bras, tabourets, escabeaux, vertugadins, caquetoires, fauteuils, sièges.* "Chairs are omnipresent and encroaching" ["Les chaises sont omniprésentes et envahissent"], she declares, on average twelve chairs per household, always many more than there were occupants.[30] This evidence of an excess of chairs is presented in a section of her book devoted to sociability, but Pardailhé-Galabrun never interprets this evidence; she hazards no inferences or conclusions, no judgments or interpretations, nor does she cite any of the varied literary evidence that corroborates salon culture. She has done the archival work that documents this excess of chairs, but she eschews the work of interpreting the facts she has amassed.

Carolyn Lougée argued over twenty years ago that the salons were first and foremost arenas of sociability, which, though they promoted social mobility, actively discouraged women's learning and intellectual exchange. Women's roles were severely constrained, and *savante* was a term of derision assiduously eschewed by salonnières.[31] Scudéry certainly takes pains to distance herself from both the term and the role, most emphatically in the final volume of

Artamène, Bk. X, in the so-called "Histoire de Sapho," in which Scudéry's namesake Sapho is distinguished from her ludicrous *savante* double Damophile.[32] The appeal of salon culture extended from the highest aristocratic circles to the *noblesse de robe* and down the social hierarchy. In a popular pamphlet from mid-century, *Le caquet de l'acouchée* (1652), which might be roughly translated *The New Mother's Chat Room* by borrowing from contemporary cybertalk, the ailing speaker seeks medical advice and is told to make her way "à la ruelle." *Ruelle* was the name given to the space of conversation, the alcove or area between bed or couch and wall where one of the earliest salonnières, Madame de Rambouillet, is said to have received her intimates. "That will rejuvenate you and return you to perfect health" ["Cela vous fera rajeunir e remettre en vostre pristine santé"], she is told. The speaker eventually makes her way to the home of a friend recently delivered where she encounters a host of other women, rich and poor, single and married, young and old, who "started to chat or talk" ["commencerent à caqueter"].[33] The widely reprinted pamphlet is a generic amalgam, related on the one hand to the old popular form "when gossips get together." On the other hand, it is a satiric send-up of plebian aspiring salonnières.

Though the work of reconstructing salon culture in seventeenth-century London has only begun, there are tantalizing pieces of evidence from across the channel: the matchless Orinda and her circle; Behn's coterie named in her poem "Our Cabal" with its pastoral pseudonyms after the style of Scudéry; and finally Hortense Mancini, Duchess of Mazarin, who fled husband and uncle in France to arrive in London in what seems, according to both the novel and contemporary accounts, the safest way for a woman to travel, dressed as a man. There she set up what Charles Tinker dubbed "a genuine French salon."[34]

Literary evidence, of course, poses difficulties for the historian, but inventories and accounts are hardly free from the conventions, generic constraints, rhetorical organization, even exceptionalism of literary materials. As a literary historian I also dig in the archives, tracking down the uncanonized, sometimes ephemeral writings of the early modern period, but the secondhand fact from outside the domain of the literary, the fact of an excess of chairs, is keenly interesting to my work as an interpreter of texts. We are all, after all, historians and literary critics alike, dealing with the secondhand, with what the French term *brocante*, or in the argot of a passing moment in literary history, the "always already." What did the denizens of seventeenth-century Paris do in all those chairs? From the limit cases of seigneur de la Grange with his 173 "sièges" [seats] in a household of ten to a certain widow Ollivier whose one room in the rue d'Anjou where she lived alone contained ten chairs and five armchairs,[35] seventeenth-century Paris was apparently a city of conversation, of the salon culture in which, as literary historians have long supposed, women and men conversed, performed, collaborated and read aloud, made reputations and lost them, won preferment and failed to advance, and engaged in what I have called armchair travel.

After volume 5 of Scudéry's *Artamène, ou le grand Cyrus,* heroic deeds and action give way to the depiction of contemporary life and persons, to characters from Scudéry's famed *samedis. Clélie,* said to have been the bestselling book of the seventeenth century, is made up primarily of conversations. When the vogue for romance faded later in the century, Scudéry published several volumes of "conversations," some taken from the earlier novels, some supposedly reconstructed from her *samedis. Conversation,* as Elizabeth Goldsmith points out at the outset of her book on salon culture entitled *Exclusive Conversations,* comes from the Latin "to frequent, or live with"—that is, etymologically the word is imbued with *place.*[36] In the world outlined by Erica Harth with which I began, in which women are excluded from places of institutionalized learning and from educative travel, conversation and the novel, so often read aloud in the salon, come to have enormous educative and even epistemological status. In conversation, the salonnières could travel to disallowed places, could speculate in the optative on all kinds of *terrae incognitae*—on the limits and disadvantages of marriage, on pleasure and desire, on higher mathematics and the movement of the planets. They could traverse the epistemological routes and byways Descartes urges on his readers, a way that led to the *cogito* and to the subject of modernity, not overland or by sea, but in the urban spaces of early modern Paris.

Notes

1. Erica Harth, *Cartesian Women, Versions and Subversions of Rational Discourse in the Old Regime* (Ithaca: Cornell University Press, 1992), 62. On women and exclusion from travel in England, see John Stoye, *English Travellers Abroad, 1604–1667: Their Influence on English Society and Politics* (London: Jonathan Cape, 1952; rev. ed., New Haven: Yale University Press, 1989), 38.

2. See, among many recent publications, Mary B. Campbell, *The Witness and the Other World: Exotic European Travel Writing, 400–1600* (Ithaca: Cornell University Press, 1988); Stephen Greenblatt, *Marvelous Possessions: The Wonders of the New World* (Chicago: University of Chicago Press, 1991), and the recent collection he edited, *New World Encounters* (Berkeley: University of California Press, 1993); Anthony Pagden, *European Encounters with the New World* (New Haven: Yale University Press, 1993). Recently scholars have begun to consider European travelers to those many geographic locales known as the "East" or the "Orient." On the popularity of the so-called Orient in seventeenth-century France, see, for example, Barthélemy d'Herbelot's compendium entitled *Bibliothèque orientale,* a best-seller at its publication in 1697, which went through a number of editions and inspired numerous imitations.

3. Jonathan Dewald, *Aristocratic Experience and the Origins of Modern Culture, France, 1570–1715* (Berkeley: University of California Press, 1993), 87. See also E. S.

Bates, *Touring in 1600, A Study of Travel as a Means of Education* (Boston: Houghton Mifflin, 1911).

4. "Sitôt que l'âge me permit de sortir de la sujétion de mes précepteurs, je quittai entièrement l'étude des lettres; et me résolvant de ne chercher plus d'autre science que celle qui pourrait trouver en moi-même, ou bien dans le grand livre du monde, j'employai le reste de ma jeunesse à voyager, à voir des cours et des armées, à fréquenter des gens de diverses humeurs et conditions, à recueillir diverses expériences, à m'éprouver moi-même dans les rencontres que la fortune me proposait, et partout à faire telle réflexion sur les choses qui se présentaient que j'en puisse tirer quelque profit. Car il me semblait que je pourrais rencontrer beaucoup plus de vérité dans les raisonnements que chacun fait touchant les affaires qui lui importent, et dont l'événement le doit punir bientôt après s'il a mal jugé, que dans ceux que fait un homme de lettres dans son cabine," in Descartes, *Discours de la méthode* (Paris: Classiques Hachette, 1997), 17. All references are to this edition.

5. "Après que j'eus employé quelques années à étudier ainsi dans le livre du monde, et à tâcher d'acquérir quelque expérience, je pris un jour résolution d'étudier aussi en moi-même, et d'employer toutes les forces de mon esprit à choisir les chemins que je devais suivre"(18).

6. See Nathan Edelman, "The Mixed Metaphor in Descartes," *The Eye of the Beholder*, ed. Jules Brody (Baltimore: Johns Hopkins University Press, 1974), 107–20; Sylvie Romanowski, *L'illusion chez Descartes* (Paris: Klincksieck, 1974); Jean-Luc Nancy, *Ego Sum* (Paris: Flammarion, 1979); G. V. Van den Abbeele, "Cartesian Coordinates: Metaphor, Topography and Presupposition in Descartes," *Voyages. Papers on French Seventeenth-century Literature, Biblio* 17 (1984): 3–14; and Normand Doiron, "L'art de voyager. Pour une définition du récit de voyage à l'Epoque classique," *Poétique* 73 (1988): 83–108. On travel and the *theatrum mundi* topos in Descartes, see Harth, 74.

7. Stoye, *English Travellers* (1989), 38.

8. Purchas, [par] 5.

9. Stoye, *English Travellers* (1952), 40.

10. Exceptions include such women as Margaret Cavendish, exiled with the royalist court in France; Hortense Mancini, the so-called vagabond duchess; Queen Christina of Sweden; and Aphra Behn, among others. However, such exceptions do not refute the broader claim about women's exclusion from the model of educative travel. See Stoye (1989), 11.

11. James Howell, *Instructions for Forreine Travell,* ed. Edward Arber for the English Reprint series (London: 1869).

12. "Les voyages sont venus en crédit . . . dans la Cour et dans la Ville," quoted in Doiron, 84, cited above and by J. Chupeau in his useful essay, "Les récits de voyages aux lisières du roman," *Revue d'histoire littéraire de la France* (1977): 539.

13. Travel writing is "un divertissement bien plus sage et plus utile que celui des agréables bagatelles qui ont enchanté tous les fainéants et toutes les fainéantes de deça, dont nous voisins italiens, allemands, hollandais ont sucé le venin à leur dommage et à notre honte" (Chupeau, 539).

14. Jacqueline Pearson, "Women reading, reading women," in *Women and Literature in Britain, 1500–1700,* ed. Helen Wilcox (Cambridge: Cambridge University Press, 1996), 80–99. On women readers and sixteenth-century romance, see Caroline Lucas, *Writing for Women: The Example of Woman as Reader in Elizabethan Romance* (Milton Keynes, England: Open University Press, 1989).

15. Maurice Lever, *Le roman français au xviie siècle* (Paris: Presses Universitaires, 1981), 11.

16. On the constitution of a reading public, see for England Jonathan Barry's "Literacy and Literature in Popular Culture: Reading and Writing in Historical Perspective," in *Popular Culture in England, c. 1500–1850*, ed. Timothy Harris (New York: Saint Martin's Press, 1995). The best overview for France remains Roger Chartier's essay in *Histoire de la vie privée*, eds. Philippe Ariés and Georges Duby and Henri-Jean Martin, *Livre, Pouvoir et Société à Paris au XVIIe* (Genève: Droz, 1969).

17. See Maurice Lever who gathers the evidence, particularly from Martin, cited above.

18. See especially René Godenne, *Les romans de Mademoiselle de Scudéry* (Genève: Droz, 1983), 134, and Joan DeJean, "No Man's Land: The Novel's First Geography," *Yale French Studies* 73 (1987): 175–89.

19. The great promoter of Scudéry as the author of *romans à clé* is Victor Cousin, who claimed to have discovered a key, now lost, in the Bibliothèque de l'Arsenal, which matched *Artamène's* major characters with well-known persons and events of the Fronde period. See his *La Société française au XVIIe siècle d'après Le grand Cyrus* (Paris: Didier, 1873).

20. On idealism, realism, and the feminine, see Naomi Schor, *George Sand & Idealism* (New York: Columbia University Press, 1993); on Scudéry and idealized spaces, see Elizabeth Goldsmith, *Exclusive Conversations: The Art of Interaction in Seventeenth-Century France* (Philadelphia: University of Pennsylvania Press, 1988).

21. On Aphra Behn and exotica, see Margaret W. Ferguson, "Feathers and Flies: Aphra Behn and the Seventeenth-Century Trade in Exotica," in *Subject and Object in Renaissance Culture*, eds. Maureen Quilligan, Margreta de Grazia, and Peter Stallybrass (Cambridge, 1996), especially p. 255; see also Julia Douthwaite, *Exotic Women: Literary Heroines and Cultural Strategies in Ancien Régime France* (Philadelphia: University of Pennsylvania Press, 1992).

22. "Je veux m'instruire par les voyages, je veux m'éprouver dans les occasions, je veux me connaître moi-même. . . . " from Madeleine de Scudéry, *Artamène ou le Grand Cyrus* (Paris, 1649–1653, Genève: Slatkine Reprints, 1972), 1:52.

23. Critics ridiculed the *Carte* even before its publication, as Scudéry's defensive claims about it reveal in vol. I of *Clélie*. On its reception, see Claude Filteau, "Le pays de Tendre: l'enjeu d'une carte," *Littérature* 36 (1979): 37–60. On the *Carte* generally, see Jean-Michel Pelous, *Amour précieux, amour galant (1654–1675)* (Paris: Klincksieck, 1980).

24. On Scudéry's novels and collaboration in the salon, see Joan DeJean, *Tender Geographies: Women and the Origins of the Novel in France* (New York: Columbia University Press, 1991).

25. On the *Carte* and territorial and military power, see Alain-Marie Bassy, "Supplement au Voyage de Tendre," *Bulletin du Bibliophile* (1982), 13–33.

26. "Dittes moy *où* j'en suis," Madeleine de Scudéry, *Clélie, Histoire romaine* (Paris, 1654–60, rpt. Genève: Droz, 1973), 1: 391.

27. "J'aimerois mieux l'avoir fait que d'avoir veû toute la Terre," *Clélie*, 395.

28. See Bassy, cited above.

29. On the salon's relation to a newly developing public interested in literature and letters, see Alain Viala, *Naissance de l'écrivain* (Paris: Editions de Minuit, 1985).

30. Annik Pardailhé-Galabrun, *La naissance de l'intime: 3000 foyers parisiens XVIIe–XVIIIe siècles* (Paris: Presses Universitaires de France, 1988), 304.

31. Carolyn C. Lougée, *Le Paradis des femmes* (Princeton: Princeton University Press, 1976); for a more nuanced perspective on the salon, see Harth, cited above, and particularly her discussion of Habermas and the salon's relation to a developing public sphere.

32. See Joan DeJean's excellent article on Scudéry and the "Histoire de Sapho," "Amazones et Femmes de lettres: Pouvoirs politiques et littéraires à l'âge classique," in *Femmes et pouvoirs sous l'ancien régime,* eds. Danielle Haase-Dubosc and Eliane Viennot (Paris: Rivages, 1991), 153–74, as well as her *Tender Geographies* cited above.

33. Le caquet de l'acouchée (Paris, 1652), p. 5.

34. Charles Tinker, *The Salon and English Letters: Chapters on the Interrelations of Literature and Society in the Age of Johnson* (New York: Macmillan, 1915), 96.

35. Pardailhé–Galabrun, 309.

36. Goldsmith, cited above, 2.

Part Five
Pedagogy

Whose Voice Is It Anyway? Teaching Early Women Writers

BARBARA F. MCMANUS
Classics

An incident that occurred in Great Britain in 1988 highlights the significance of my title. Virago Press and the Women's Press had both accepted for publication short stories by a new writer named Rahila Khan, a woman from India who dramatized the lives of young Asian women in contemporary Britain. However, when Khan's agent arranged television and newspaper interviews for the author, it quickly became apparent that Rahila Khan was a middle-class white minister, a male with the ironically appropriate "real name" of Toby Forward. The media uproar that followed this incident came to be known as "The Vicar and Virago Affair." In the *London Review of Books*, Reverend Forward defended himself in the following way: "I was . . . accused of pretending to occupy a position I didn't hold, to speak with a voice that wasn't mine. I had thought that was the purpose of art."[1]

Whose voice is it anyway? What difference does it make who wrote a text? My title (modeled on Brian Clark's play *Whose Life Is It Anyway?*) poses challenging questions for those who would teach about texts, particularly when the choice of texts is apparently grounded in concepts of authorial voice, as for example in my subtitle, "Teaching Early Women Writers." Issues of authenticity of voice are exacerbated when we teach about texts that were produced in periods when there were no journalists or television cameras to unmask a vicar in virago's clothing.

Since my readers may represent many different disciplines and different types of institutions, this essay will concentrate on theory and methodology rather than specific assignments. Though I will draw my examples from the subjects I know best, women writers from classical antiquity and Renaissance England, these methods can be adapted and applied in diverse teaching situations. While I will not pretend to offer definitive answers to the questions posed above, I will suggest some strategies to help students grapple with them in all their complexity and perhaps in the process develop a stronger sense of their own voices and how to use them.

One important consideration that is often overlooked in discussions of ped-agogy has to do with the theoretical framework that underlies the structure of a particular course, specifically, its title and organizing principle. Do we ground the course structure in authorial voices that are classed, or raced, or gendered in specific ways—as in "Working-Class Writers," "African-American Writers," "Women Writers," or even all of the above? Or, do we seek to include such authorial voices in courses that are organized around periods or genres, courses that have traditionally included only upper-class white male authors who have been presented simply as *writers?* The first option is fre-quently invoked and has many advantages, enabling an in-depth focus on pre-viously neglected texts, a range of comparative studies, and considerations of influence and changes over time. However, this strategy also has many pitfalls, including the danger of essentializing the very categories we are seeking to problematize, of removing the texts from their conditions of production, and of trivializing them. For example, I have heard students claim that a course dedicated to women writers is not a "real" literature course, and some depart-ments will list such courses only as electives. The second option, including pre-viously marginalized texts in traditionally structured courses, means fewer of these texts, less in-depth study, and a real potential for comparative devalua-tion. This strategy, however, is less likely than the first to essentialize author-ial voices, presents a better approximation of the situations in which the texts were produced, and can disrupt the concept of the unmarked "writer" and make it possible to show how class, race, and gender shape *all* authorial voices. These are difficult choices to make, and many of us do not have the luxury of choosing because we must teach within prescribed curricular structures. My own preference is for the second option because I think that it offers the teacher more flexibility and ultimately more transgressive possibilities. Yet, no matter how our courses are organized, we should at least be cognizant of the disadvantages of either type of organizing principle and seek to minimize its negative effects.

I will devote the rest of this essay to theoretical frameworks and methods that can be used with any structure or topic that draws heavily on primary texts, whether literary or nonliterary. Why should we be concerned with the-ory? I share bell hooks's conviction that feminist theory can be a "liberatory practice."[2] Theory can help us turn experience into knowledge; once under-stood, theory can provide a kind of third eye, enabling us to see the interpre-tive scaffolding that supports even the most apparently straightforward and "natural" of facts and values.[3] However, most undergraduates are not ready for theory straight up, in the abstract, and it is our challenge as teachers to pres-ent theoretical principles through concrete applications. For example, any type of course dealing with primary texts can begin by problematizing the concept of authorial voice: whose voice is it anyway? Instead of assigning readings from Michel Foucault, Roland Barthes, or even Laurie Finke, I suggest that we use that radical new technology—the blackboard[4]—and ask students to list all the possible varieties of authorial voices from the perspective of gender that they can imagine. Then we can ask students to describe which published attributions are possible with each of these voices and what effect the various combinations would have.

Here is my list, but in class it would be more effective to elicit this from students, with examples.

Published Attribution
- Anonymous
- Obvious pseudonyms (male, female)
- Purportedly real names (male, female)

Authorial Voice or Standpoint
- Ungendered/gender-neutral voices
  - Obtrusive or Unobtrusive
  - Universalized or Located/Situated
- Gendered voices
  - Overtly claimed masculine or feminine standpoint
  - Implied masculine or feminine standpoint
  - Transparently counterfeit masculine or feminine standpoint

Let me illustrate this exercise with some brief examples, on the understanding that it can be implemented with any type of primary texts.

By "published attribution," I mean the name under which the text was put in circulation, whether or not this involved the medium of print. The first, anonymous, is easy, referring to works published without an authorial name, as for example the play *Swetnam, the Woman-hater*. Then there are obvious pseudonyms, such as Thomas Tel-troth for the male and Mary Tattle-well for the female. Finally, works can be published under purportedly real names, such as Joseph Swetnam for the male and Rachel Speght for the female.[5]

"Authorial voice or standpoint" is more difficult to describe and interacts in interesting ways with published attribution. Ungendered/gender-neutral voices tend to occur in third-person narratives, though they may occasionally appear in first-person narration. Homer provides a good example of an ungendered voice that is unobtrusive and universalized, whereas Vergil's narrating voice, though ungendered, is occasionally obtrusive and is located both temporally and historically in Augustan Rome. Ungendered voices can be anonymously attributed, or they can carry a male pseudonym or name, but cultural gender constructions ensure that the minute a female name or pseudonym is attached to a work, the authorial voice is automatically perceived as gendered. In Western culture, only male voices can be viewed as ungendered or gender neutral.

During the Renaissance, the only texts that successfully coupled a female attribution with an ungendered voice were women's translations of works by men, though in the fourth century of the Common Era, a Roman woman named Faltonia Betitia Proba managed to circumvent this problem in an ingenious way by writing a cento, a patchwork that takes lines and phrases from another poet out of context and pieces them together to tell a new story. Proba weaves together lines and half-lines from Vergil to tell the biblical story of the creation and redemption. She is borrowing Vergil's ungendered voice but, unlike a translation, she is also composing something new. In her preface, she emphatically associates her female name with this act of writing. Invoking God as her muse, she says, "Unlock the innermost regions of my heart, / so that I, Proba the seer, may tell of everything that is hidden" (lines 11–12).[6]

Let us look now at the category of gendered voices. These frequently appear in first-person narratives, though third-person narratives may employ an implied masculine or feminine standpoint. By "overtly claimed masculine or feminine standpoint," I mean that an author explicitly proclaims that he is speaking as a man on behalf of men, or she is speaking as a woman on behalf of women. This type of authorial voice precludes attribution under a name belonging to the opposite sex but does not preclude anonymity. For example, the anonymous author of *The Schole house of women* clearly speaks from an overtly masculine standpoint. Jane Anger provides a good illustration of an overtly feminine authorial voice (in this case attributed rather than anonymous). She writes *Jane Anger her Protection for Women* as a woman speaking to, for, and about other women, and she constantly underlines this standpoint by using phrases like "we women" and "our sex."[7]

An implied masculine or feminine standpoint is more subtle, presenting a gendered perspective without explicitly claiming to do so. Both masculine and feminine standpoints are likely to be published under gendered names or pseudonyms, though a masculine standpoint can be conveyed anonymously because that is already the "default option" in Western culture. Sappho provides a good example of an implied feminine standpoint. At least in the tattered remains of her work that survive, Sappho does not speak in the "we women" mode or explicitly speak for women as a sex, although her poetic voice, a strong personal "I," is grounded in women's experience and feminine subjectivity. An example of an implied masculine standpoint can be found in the Roman poet Catullus, and it is interesting to analyze how the meaning of one of Sappho's love poems (fragment 31) is affected when published under the name of a male poet

(Catullus 51 is a Latin rendering of Sappho's poem with an additional stanza in which Catullus emphatically addresses himself by name).[8]

Finally, a "transparently counterfeit masculine or feminine standpoint" occurs when an allegedly feminine authorial voice is published under a male name, or vice versa. For example, Sir Thomas Elyot speaks through the persona of Zenobia in his dialogue *The Defence of Good Women,* and Edward Gosynhill writes much of *Mulierû Pean* in the voice of Venus (though he sometimes slips up on the pronouns). The Roman poet Propertius wrote an entire elegy (4.11) in the voice of a contemporary historical woman named Cornelia.[9] Cultural constructions, especially in earlier periods, supported such ventriloquism in the case of men, and audiences were accustomed to dramas in which male authors spoke through female characters who were played by male actors. However, this kind of authorial voice was much more difficult for women to assume, and I was hard put to come up with an example from early literature. I finally settled on a Hellenistic Greek epigram, a brief first-person epitaph for Rhinthon, a writer of Sicilian farces, since the speaking voice in the poem is male but the published attribution is female, the poet Nossis (*Anth. Pal.* 7.414).[10]

By the time this exercise is over, students may be less inclined to focus on questions of sincerity and authenticity and more ready to grasp the theoretical concept of authorial subject positions that are constructed by discourse. In order to clarify these concepts in my courses, I rely on example and analogy instead of abstract theorizing. To explain discourse as a connected and coherent mode of speaking that has its own codes and conventions, vocabulary, syntax, and allowable subject positions from which to speak, I find it useful to draw on the example of academic discourse, which is something all my students understand because they are striving to learn it. Also, none of them considers academic discourse "natural," so we do not have to worry about essentialism. I like to define the concept of subject position as "a platform from which to speak." Academia offers subject positions such as scholar, researcher, teacher, student, and administrator (and this last one—administrator—is actually a modern invention, showing how discursive subject positions can be changed and new ones added). Since platforms are obviously and quite literally "built," the analogy helps to emphasize the constructed nature of subject positions, and one can ask students to name literal platforms that they know—like those in a courtroom, for example—and explain how each platform permits only certain kinds of speech and speakers.

However, the analogy of platforms also permits us to envision possibilities for the expression of experience and individuality within these constructed subject positions. In the words of Marilyn Williamson, "the construction of subjectivity is . . . produced not only by external social patterns and discourses but through the individual's interaction with such discourses and cultural practices. Such thinking does not compel a choice between the extremes of the essentialist feminine subject and the genderless subject produced by discourse."[11] This abstract theoretical concept becomes meaningful to students when they are asked to deconstruct concrete examples from public life. I have found the example of the courtroom useful here as well, particularly a media event such as the O. J. Simpson trial. With only a little prompting, students can readily analyze how each of the opposing attorneys in that case, Marcia Clark and Johnnie Cochran, performed issues of class, race, and gender quite differently, though both spoke from a traditional legal platform.

Returning to the question of authorial voice, Laurie Finke poses several important questions that the concept of subject positions helps us to ask:

> If as feminists we ask, to paraphrase Foucault (1979, 160), Who really spoke? Is it really she and not someone else? With what authenticity and originality? And what part of her deepest self did she express in her discourse? then we are perpetuating essentialist notions of the subject, of masculinity and femininity, and of the text as a closed hermeneutical totality. If instead we ask, again paraphrasing Foucault, What are the modes of existence of this discourse? Where has it been used, how can it circulate, and who can appropriate it for herself? What are the places in it where there is room for possible subjects? Who can assume these various subject-functions? then we open up our criticism to a more dialogic conception of subjectivity and gender relations, as well as to the historical and political struggles through which they are constituted and resisted.[12]

Or, as Sheila Fisher and Janet Halley put it, "what are the relationships of historical women to the forms of power mediated by writing?"[13]

I would like to suggest that we get students involved with these questions by giving them concrete tasks, tasks that can be most effectively carried out in small groups, preferably involving both men and women. First ask the students to describe all the authorial subject positions they find in a set of texts on a particular theme or in a particular genre. Then ask them to deconstruct these subject positions to reveal how they are created by the *intersection* of authorial attribution and authorial voice or standpoint. Using the Renaissance pamphlet wars on the nature of woman as our example, we can see that defense treatises were published anonymously, under both male and female names, and under male and female pseudonyms. Their authorial voices were usually gendered, employing either an overtly claimed masculine or feminine standpoint, or a transparently counterfeit feminine standpoint. Pamphlets attacking women, however, offered much more limited possibilities; none were published under female names or pseudonyms or employed voices gendered as feminine (except for a few, brief instances of transparently counterfeit feminine voices). Given the nature of the subject matter, most authorial voices in these pamphlet wars were gendered, though Cornelius Agrippa did employ an ungendered voice in his defense treatise,[14] just as the earlier philosopher Aristotle had used an ungendered, universalized voice when allegedly proving that women were by nature inferior to men. It is very instructive to compare the different subject positions created by these various intersections. How does an overtly masculine defender differ from an overtly feminine one? In either defense or attack treatises, what is the effect of an ungendered versus a gendered masculine authorial voice? Does it make any difference if a defense treatise is published under a feminine name or a feminine pseudonym?

Analyzing the intersection of subject position and voice can also lead to discussion of the cultural gender constructions in effect when the texts were produced. Love poetry is particularly useful for this purpose, since so many societies surround the expression of erotic passion with powerful gender expectations and constraints. Until recently in Western literature, love poetry was dominated by the masculine perspective, by the voice of the male poet as desiring subject, with the female relegated to the role of desired object. The voice of the love poet interacted with the dominant culture in varying ways—sometimes integrated, sometimes subversive, but predominantly *male*. In antiquity, a few female poets were able to adapt amatory conventions to a female subject position: most notably Sappho, but also the poet Sulpicia from Augustan Rome, who successfully employed the subject position and poetic conventions of desiring elegiac lover as she wrote of her sexual passion for a man ("Cerinthus") who was not presented as her husband.[15] There is evidence that Sappho's culture supported both poetic and erotic expression by women; this was less true of Sulpicia's society, but aristocratic poetic circles in Augustan Rome did offer some opportunities for feminine voices. In early modern England, however, the public expression of erotic passion or indeed any kind of secular publication by women came into conflict with stringent standards of female respectability. One exercise that will help students grapple with these issues would be to examine examples of amatory conventions and subject positions in the work of typical male poets in late sixteenth- and early seventeenth-century England. Then students can be asked to analyze how female writers like Lady Mary Wroth, Katherine Philips, and Aphra Behn adapted these conventions and subject positions for a feminine voice, paying attention to effects of class as well as gender and surveying the reception of their work by the dominant culture.

As students examine how traditional subject positions are changed when coupled with an untraditional authorial voice, ask them to analyze how authors negotiate the ensuing tensions and conflicts with varying degrees of success. For example, Rachel Speght, apparently unaware that Jane Anger had published a defense treatise some thirty years earlier, stresses the novelty of her treatise *A Mouzell for Melastomus*. She adopts a subject position constructed for a masculine voice (that of the chivalrous champion of women), which had been used by earlier defense writers like Edward More, and we can observe her trying out various types of authorial voice.[16] In her dedicatory epistle, which is addressed to all women, she employs an overtly feminine standpoint, writing in the first person, referring to herself as a woman, and using the phrase "our sex" several times. In the treatise itself, however, she attempts a distanced, gender-neutral authorial voice, referring to women throughout in the third person. Furthermore, she appends to her treatise three pseudonymous poems that use authoritative (and somewhat patronizing) masculine voices to justify her writing, though it is at least possible that she composed these poems herself. With all these shifts and hesitancies of voice, it is little wonder that she later referred to this treatise as "my abortive" and found that readers were questioning her authorship of the pamphlet:

> I know these populous times afford plenty of froward Writers and critical Readers. Myself hath made up the number of the one, too many by one; and, having been touched with the censures of the other by occasion of my *muzzling Melastomus*, I am now (as by a strong motive) induced for my right's sake to produce and divulge this offspring of my endeavor, to prove them further futurely who have formerly deprived me of my due, imposing my abortive upon the father of me, but not of it. Their variety of verdicts have verified the adage *quot homines, tot sententiae* and made my experience confirm that apothegm which doth affirm Censure to be inevitable to a public act.[17]

Yet, this complaint of hers also reveals how seriously early women writers took the question "Whose voice is it?" and how different the situation was for early modern male writers. It is hard to imagine a male author of the time stating that *his* experience proves that blame will inevitably follow a public act like writing, and it is impossible to imagine him proclaiming that readers had been attributing his writing to his mother!

In a related exercise, you can ask students to envision other possible authorial subject positions within the discourse they are studying and to imagine how they would rewrite individual pieces from a different subject position. This exercise can be particularly effective if the men are asked to rewrite in a feminine voice and the women in a masculine one.

A key goal of any of these exercises is to enable students to come to their own understanding of the *difference* it makes when the authorizing voice of a text is feminine, a difference that has both literary and extraliterary consequences. One frequently used technique for demonstrating the literary consequences of this difference is to juxtapose works on similar topics by men and women writers working in the same genre and period. Let us consider an illustration using archaic Greek poetry. In one of her longer extant lyrics (fragment 16), Sappho exemplifies the power of "whatever one loves" by presenting Helen as a desiring subject rather than a desired, feared, or loathed object. Though Helen herself was the most beautiful woman, says Sappho, she chose to leave husband, home, and child for the sake of what was most beautiful to her, her lover, Paris. This story reminds Sappho of her own desire for the absent Anaktoria, for Sappho says that she would rather see Anaktoria's "lovely walk and the bright sparkle of her face" than the most splendid array of chariots and infantry. The Trojan War is not mentioned in Sappho's poem but is present as a subtext in the prominent military imagery through which the war comes to seem the result of men's choices and love for military glory rather than the result of *Helen's* action. However, when Sappho's contemporary Alcaeus, a male lyric poet who was also from Lesbos, wrote about Helen (fragment 283) the effect was quite different. When Alcaeus thinks of Helen's leaving husband and child, *he* is reminded of all the "lively-eyed" men lying slaughtered on the Trojan plains and the chariots befouled with dust—all, he says, "because of that woman."[18]

Authorial voice affects not only the content of a work but also its readers. One important effect that texts written with a feminine authorial voice can have upon other women as both writers and readers is what we usually term "the role-model effect." Sappho was particularly important as precedent and model for later woman poets because she not only wrote but was *heard;* she was acknowledged as a master poet over many centuries. Just as Sappho provided a significant precedent for early modern poets like Katherine Philips and Aphra Behn, so they served as precedents for the women poets who followed them. Time after time women writers testify to the power they draw from female predecessors. Aphra Behn, for example, invokes the precedent of female poets as well as the solidarity of shared feminine experience when she cleverly claims her right to the poetic crown of laurel leaves by addressing another female, the nymph Daphne, who was turned into a laurel tree to escape rape by Apollo:

I, by a *double* right, thy bounties claim,
Both from my sex, and in Apollo's name.
Let me with Sappho and Orinda be,
Oh ever sacred nymph, adorned by thee.
And give my verses immortality.[19]

There is, as bell hooks points out, a "passion of experience" that marginalized voices can bring to literature, a contribution of tremendous value for those who share that experience and also for those who do not, whose eyes need to be opened to other possibilities and alternative meanings.[20] Yet, that passion of experience is not communicated to us as lived but rather as *spoken*, as mediated and shaped by highly constructed discursive platforms. Hence it is important to consider subject positions and questions of voice along with the passion that comes from experience.

The suggestions I have made in this essay offer a few ways to begin the process of considering these issues, but it is crucial that we do this without pre-empting students' own voices. As teachers, we are not transmitters of the content of knowledge, but rather leaders and guides in an interactive process of discovery, a process whereby we together construct knowledge. I once heard a wonderful reply to the old saw "You can lead a horse to water, but you can't make him drink." "Yes, but I can make sure that he's damn thirsty!" Good pedagogy is the process of creating that thirst in our students, of engaging their own "passion of experience" in the process of knowledge construction. Each of you will have your own methods of doing this, but I want to conclude by sharing with you two methods that I have found particularly helpful.

The first involves providing students with what one might call opportunities for "publication." I have found that students put more time, effort, and care into projects that will be disseminated to a wider audience than simply their teacher, and that the resulting process and product are more satisfying and productive for all concerned. In practice, this means designing assignments that call for many different types of expression—not simply tests and term papers, but also group projects, enactments, various types of productions. Here the new Internet technologies can be helpful, because they make it possible to undertake and publish in cyberspace many kinds of activities that would be too complex and costly to implement in real life, including editing a text and simulating a play production.[21] In fact, the process of working on such projects may itself lead students to grapple with the questions I have been discussing, since the disembodied nature of electronic communication prompts reflection on issues of voice, gender, identity, and location.

The second method I use to get students invested in the process of learning is to share with them my own experiences as a learner and researcher, showing how my thoughts and approaches to texts have changed as I engaged with feminist theory. For example, when I was writing *Half Humankind*, I was preoccupied with the questions Laurie Finke, already quoted, urges us *not* to pose: "Who really spoke? Is it really she and not someone else?"[22] Thus I was unsettled by the suggestion that some of the defense pamphlets published under female names might have been written by men, for this seemed to challenge and undermine the significance of their female attribution. However, when I recently wrote an article that took me back to those pamphlets (but with much more feminist theory under my belt), I started to ask Finke's second set of questions. At that point, I realized that the key issue was how these early writings by and about women show a new and distinctly feminine subject position in the discourse of the defense treatise as it was in the process of being constructed. So if John Taylor actually used that feminine subject position to write *The womens sharpe revenge*, as Simon Shepherd claims, this simply testifies to the fact that it was strong and attractive enough by 1640 to tempt a male author to try it out. I now view this as a valorization of the subject position of female defender rather than as "a two-fold silencing of women."[23] Because there does not seem to be any evidence that readers of the time attributed the pamphlet to Taylor, if he did write the work it was the masculine authorial voice that was effectively silenced.

I have also used my own experience to illustrate for students the difficulty of finding a "voice of one's own" in academic discourse. When I wrote a feminist analysis of Vergil's *Aeneid* for my recent book *Classics and Feminism*, I went back and looked at the dissertation I had written on the epic more than twenty years ago. As I reread, I was surprised by how totally oblivious I had been to the major role that gender plays in the *Aeneid*, and I was quite dismayed to realize that I had written the following sentence with no perceptible sense of its phallic significance: "If a man does not actively thrust himself into the future, the inexorable movement of life toward death will pull him into the past, and he will leave no lasting imprint upon time."[24] As I tell my students now, I was the perfect example of a person who had not found her own voice within the subject position of scholar; I was unreflectively allowing the prevailing academic discourse to dictate my words. By showing them how differently I read a text now, I can vividly demonstrate how feminist theory has helped me to forge a voice that is not only scholarly, but also infused with my own passion of experience.

Ultimately, all these pedagogical strategies are designed to help students come to recognize that questions of voice are extremely complex but also extremely—and personally—important. Struggling to answer the question "Whose voice is it anyway?" with regard to texts written by others may prompt students to examine their own voices and standpoints with more critical and discerning eyes.

Notes

1. Quoted in Dympna Callaghan, "The Vicar and Virago: Feminism and the Problem of Identity," in *Who Can Speak? Authority and Critical Identity*, ed. Judith Roof and Robyn Wiegman (Urbana: University of Illinois Press, 1995), 196.
2. bell hooks, *Teaching to Transgress: Education as the Practice of Freedom* (New York: Routledge, 1994), 59–75.

3. I like to think of this third eye as analogous to the special vision that Venus gives her son Aeneas during his last night at Troy, enabling him to see the mighty forces at work beneath surface appearances, the divinities who are uprooting the city: "Look! For I will tear away from your eyes all the mist that now veils them in moist darkness and dulls your mortal vision." *Aeneid* 2.604–606, my translation.

4. "Remarkable new technology is introduced into the school system and experts predict education will be revolutionized. . . . The technology will, as never before, allow the widespread dissemination of new concepts and ideas that stimulate young minds and free the teacher for more creative pursuits. . . . Yet the magic fails to materialize, and within a few years articles appear in the popular press asserting that the failure, obviously, arises from teachers not being skilled enough in the new technology," in Peter H. Lewis, "New Technology Getting Mixed Grades in School," *New York Times*, 1840. This article was describing the blackboard!

5. *Swetnam, the Woman-hater, Arraigned by Women. A new Comedie, Acted at the Red Bull by the late Queenes Servants* (London, 1620); see Coryl Crandall, ed., *Swetnam the Woman-Hater: The Controversy and the Play* (West Lafayette, Ind.: Purdue University Studies, 1969). The first edition of *The Araignment of Lewde, idle, froward, and unconstant women: Or the vanitie of them, choose you whether* (London, 1615) was published under the pseudonym of Thomas Tel-Troth, though the name Joseph Swetnam was attached to all subsequent editions. Mary Tattle-well and Joane Hit-him-home were the pseudonymous authors of *The womens sharpe revenge: Or an answer to Sir Seldome Sober that writ those railing Pamphelets called the Juniper and Crabtree Lectures* (London, 1640). Rachel Speght authored the defense treatise *A Mouzell for Melastomus* (London, 1617) and the religious work *Mortalities Memorandum* (London, 1621).

6. For a translation of the entire preface and a discussion of Proba, see Jane McIntosh Snyder, *The Woman and the Lyre: Women Writers in Classical Greece and Rome* (Carbondale: Southern Illinois University Press, 1989), 136–39.

7. *Here begynneth a lytle boke named the Schole house of women: wherin every man may rede a goodly prayse of the condicyons of women* (London, 1541?); despite its title, this work was a thoroughgoing attack on women. The full title of Jane Anger's defense treatise was *Jane Anger her Protection for Women. To defend them against the Scandalous Reportes of a late Surfeiting Lover, and all other Venerians that complaine so to be overcloyed with womens kindnesse* (London, 1589).

8. For a translation and discussion of all the fragments of Sappho, see Snyder, *The Woman and the Lyre*, 1–37. The Loeb Classical Library provides a convenient edition of the poems of Catullus, including Latin text and facing translations by Francis Warre Cornish (though the translations are dated): *Catullus, Tibullus, and Pervigilium Veneris*, 2nd ed., rev. G. P. Goold (Cambridge: Harvard University Press, 1988).

9. Sir Thomas Elyot, *The Defence of Good Women* (London, 1545); Edward Gosynhill, *The prayse of all women, called Mulierû Pean. Very fruytfull and delectable unto all the reders* (London, 1542?). The Loeb Classical Library edition of Propertius includes both Latin texts and English translations: *Propertius, Elegies*, ed. and trans. G. P. Goold (Cambridge: Harvard University Press, 1990).

10. For a translation of this four-line epitaph and a general discussion of the work of Nossis, see Snyder, *The Woman and the Lyre*, 77–86.

11. Marilyn L. Williamson, *Raising Their Voices: British Women Writers, 1650–1750* (Detroit, Mich.: Wayne State University Press, 1990), 10.

12. Laurie A. Finke, *Feminist Theory, Women's Writing* (Ithaca: Cornell University Press, 1992), 107.

13. The full quotation is instructive for the issue we are considering: "The problems confronting the effort to locate historical women in the periods we are studying place special pressures on what Elaine Showalter has called 'gynocritics'—on the criticism of the literary activity of women themselves. The critical desire to seek in early texts by women the harbingers of 'the woman's voice' presupposes an essential female self, and reintroduces into feminist discourse that repressive identity which has been so evident in the masculinist literary canon and criticism. But even more obviously here than in work on the male literary tradition, the problem of real women's subjective experiences of selfhood is the decentered pole around which our thinking should rotate elliptically. Without denying the importance of Showalter's central question—'What is *the difference* of women's writing?'—we must acknowledge that earlier writings by women demand that we pose a prior question: what are the relationships of historical women to the forms of power mediated by writing?" Sheila Fisher and Janet E. Halley, eds., *Seeking the Woman in Late Medieval and Renaissance Writings* (Knoxville: University of Tennessee Press, 1989), 10.

14. Heinrich Cornelius Agrippa von Nettesheim, *De nobilitate et praecellentia fœminei sexus* (1529); for an analysis of the "deliberately ambiguous tone" of this treatise, see Barbara Newman, "Renaissance Feminism and Esoteric Theology: The Case of Cornelius Agrippa," *Viator: Medieval and Renaissance Studies* 24 (1993): 337–56.

15. For a translation of the six extant elegies generally accepted as Sulpicia's and a general discussion of her work, see Snyder, *The Woman and the Lyre*, 128–36.

16. Rachel Speght, *A Mouzell for Melastomus, The Cynicall Bayter of, and foule mouthed Barker against Evahs Sex: or an Apologeticall Answere to that Irreligious and Illiterate Pamphlet made by Jo. Sw. and by him Intituled, The Arraignment of Women* (London, 1617); Edward More, *A Lytle and Bryefe treatyse, called the defence of women, and especially of Englyshe women, made agaynst the Schole howse of women* (London, 1560). Speght's hesitancies of voice can be effectively contrasted with the more assured subject positions adopted by Munda and Sowernam, both of whom write from a strong, overtly feminine standpoint: Constantia Munda, *The Worming of a mad Dogge: or, A Soppe for Cerberus the Jaylor of Hell. No Confutation but a sharpe Redargution of the bayter of Women* (London, 1617); Ester Sowernam, *Ester hath hang'd Haman: or An Answere To a lewd Pamphlet, entituled, The Arraignment of Women. With the arraignment of lewd, idle, froward, and unconstant men, and Husbands* (London, 1617).

17. Rachel Speght, "Epistle Dedicatorie," *Mortalities Memorandum, with a Dreame Prefixed* (London, 1621). For ease of reading, I have modernized the spelling and punctuation.

18. See Snyder, *The Woman and the Lyre*, 1–37. Diane Rayor provides translations of all the major poems and fragments of the male and female archaic lyric poets, including these poems of Sappho and Alcaeus, in *Sappho's Lyre: Archaic Lyric and Women Poets of Ancient Greece* (Berkeley: University of California Press, 1991), 55 and 88.

19. These lines are quoted by Dorothy Mermin, "Women Becoming Poets: Katherine Philips, Aphra Behn, Anne Finch," *ELH* 57, no. 2 (1990): 350; Behn included them with her translation of Cowley's *Sex Libri Plantorum*. Orinda is a poetic name for Katherine Philips.

20. "Now I am troubled by the term 'authority of experience,' acutely aware of the way it is used to silence and exclude. Yet I want to have a phrase that affirms the specialness of those ways of knowing rooted in experience. I know that experience can be a way to know and can inform how we know what we know. Though opposed to any

essentialist practice that constructs identity in a monolithic, exclusionary way, I do not want to relinquish the power of experience as a standpoint on which to base analysis or formulate theory. For example, I am disturbed when all courses on black history or literature at some colleges and universities are taught solely by white people, not because I think that they cannot know these realities but that they know them differently. . . . Although I learned a great deal from this white woman professor [who taught African-American critical thought], I sincerely believe I would have learned even more from a progressive black professor, because this individual would have brought to the class that unique mixture of experiential and analytical ways of knowing—that is, a privileged standpoint. It cannot be acquired through books or even distanced observation and study of a particular reality. To me this privileged standpoint does not emerge from the 'authority of experience' but rather from the passion of experience, the passion of remembrance." bell hooks, *Teaching to Transgress*, 90.

21. See the following demonstration Web pages created for the 1997 workshop on "Integrating the WWW into the Women's Studies Curriculum," organized by Susan Jenson, Karen Nelson, and Michele Osherow: Textual Editing and Interpretation Exercise <http://www.wam.umd.edu/~klnelson/knlssn.html> and Dramatic Production Exercise <http://www.wam.umd.edu/~klnelson/molssn.html#>. These pages were still on-line in August 1998.

22. Katherine Usher Henderson and Barbara F. McManus, *Half Humankind: Contexts and Texts of the Controversy about Women in England, 1540–1640* (Urbana: University of Illinois Press, 1985); see especially the section on "Female Authorship," 20–24.

23. Simon Shepherd, ed., *The Women's Sharp Revenge: Five Women's Pamphlets from the Renaissance* (New York: St. Martin's Press, 1985), 23. My new article is "Eve's Dowry: Genesis and the Pamphlet Controversy about Women," in *Women, Writing, and the Reproduction of Culture in Tudor and Stuart Britain*, ed. Mary E. Burke et al. (Syracuse, N.Y.: Syracuse University Press, 2000), 193–206.

24. Barbara F. McManus, "*Inreparabile tempus:*" *A Study of Time in Virgil's Aeneid* (Ph.D. diss., Harvard University, 1976), 97. I present my current reading of the epic in "Transgendered Moments: Revisiting Vergil's *Aeneid*," in *Classics and Feminism: Gendering the Classics*, (New York: Twayne Publishers, 1997), 91–118.

"If we can't know what 'really' happened, why should we study the past?"

FRANCES E. DOLAN
English

My title is a question an exasperated student once asked me in response to my attempt to answer one of *her* questions as carefully as I could—that is, to offer an answer that reflected how mediated and provisional historical knowledge is. Hers is the kind of question that I provoke more often as I myself learn more. As you all know, the more you learn the harder it can be to offer canned mini-lectures. Indeed, it is quite unnerving to begin questioning your own formulations even as you replay them—unnerving not only for the teacher, but for the student who is not sure how to evaluate narrative interruptions, and pauses for reflection. Should you record them in your notes or not? I think that these disruptions should go in students' notebooks, since they are where the intellectual action is. However, I do not always succeed in convincing my students of this. I have chosen to begin with this student question because it marks a shift for me from trying to transmit information, which, of course, I still do, to getting students to think about the kinds of questions they ask, and why they ask them, the ways that the question determines the answer, the range of materials one might consider, and the skills one might hone, in order to shape, rather than uncover, an answer.

When I teach *Hamlet*, I often ask students whether Hamlet uses the play-within-the-play to discover a truth, or to make one? If he does create or expose some kind of truth, what truth is it? I also ask how characters in *Hamlet* more generally create knowledge: How do they know and prove? On what grounds are they certain that they know? Increasingly, those questions seem useful to me in classes other than those about *Hamlet*. How do we define, gain, and ratify knowledge?

My students are deeply invested in assessment, as I imagine most students are. This naturally complicates any attempt to qualify what constitutes knowledge. "OK," they say, "there are many narratives of the past: which one will be on the test?" For students in the United States, uncertainty about proof is not

as much "postmodern" as it is "post-Rodney King" and "post-O.J." These
recent, highly visible and controversial trials led many students to believe that
even videotapes and DNA are not outside of or beyond interpretation. As a consequence, they are prepared to believe that physical evidence is no more stable
or incontrovertible than any other kind of evidence; they can question the
boundary between fact and fiction, hard evidence and representation. Yet, at the
same time, they want to believe in certainty more than ever. Other people's
knowledge is situated; theirs is not. Furthermore, when they turn to the study
of the past, they often assume that indisputable proof is recoverable, that different bodies of evidence will corroborate rather than contradict one another,
and, indeed, that only certainty can justify our forays into the past. Hence the
question of my title: "If we can't know what 'really' happened, why should we
study the past?" There's got to be a bedrock and some certainty somewhere:
why can't it be in the past? The dead should be easier to catch and anatomize.

This expectation fuels, I think, the continuous fantasies in films and television about paleontology, archeology, and forensics. In these fantasies, the truth
is not "out there," as *The X-Files* elusively promises, but rather "down there"
or "back there." All we need to do is dig it out, and reassemble the fragments
into meaningful patterns. At that point, of course, we get into trouble, because
there isn't only one way that the pieces will "fit," but many.

I have only gradually become more self-conscious about my role as an
expert in the classroom. First I had to gain some knowledge that I could actually presume to convey, then I had to gain enough confidence in that knowledge and in my own role as teacher to begin to wonder what exactly it is that
I am teaching, what the "new knowledge" is that I create as a scholar and how
it is important. In my first years as a full-time teacher, I taught a humanities
core course at the University of Chicago. Teaching texts such as Kant's
Foundations of a Metaphysics of Morals and Aristotle's *Ethics* to very bright
students, I learned two things: 1) a reckless willingness to wade right in and
teach anything; and 2) how to read closely. If anything will compel you to pull
as much out of the text before you as possible, whatever your discipline, it is
the certainty that only your skill as an explicator distinguishes you from your
students. There was no time to swat up in the library; it was just me and the
big books. I was constantly aware that I had no cushion of knowledge, that I
was singing the top and bottom notes of my range, which my voice teacher
had always sternly advised against doing in public. Yet, for all the terrors of
this introduction to teaching, it required me to act as discussion leader rather
than expert witness, a role that was congenial to my sense of the democratic—
and feminist—classroom.

As soon as I began teaching in an English department, I encountered the
opportunity to teach texts about which I knew more: for instance, one of many

Shakespeare plays I'd read, some of the many representations of domestic crime on which I was then working. This was an immediate relief because it made me feel like less of a tightrope walker; the very expertise that was giving me the materials and the confidence with which to conceive a first book also began to spread out under me like a net. At its best, expertise fosters rather than stifles spontaneity. It has made it possible for me to go with students where their curiosity leads them, rather than guide them back to the one little track I've prepared; it makes it possible to introduce expertise as a response to questions as they arise; it has made me more rather than less interested in what the untutored question can reveal, in what students have to say and to teach. On the other hand, my growing confidence seems to invite questions to which neither I nor anyone else could possibly know *the* answer. What did "the Renaissance" think about: women, wife beating, blackness, Jews, homosexuals, oral sex—you name it.

I do not want to suggest—to you, or to my students—that these are somehow "bad" or "stupid" questions. Indeed, they are difficult to answer because they prompt me to talk about the most interesting issues and debates in our field—the ways in which the early modern period I study now, is not the Renaissance I was taught. My problem with these questions is that they hold up a distorting mirror to historical knowledge, and they beckon me into the role of the stage pedant: "In the Renaissance, as we know. . . ." I've tried lots of approaches to responding. First, I tried to answer the question without qualification. However, these assured and tidy answers increasingly began to collapse into self-parody.

For some time, I have been trying to show students how one goes about making an answer to a question. My answers are becoming narratives of a process, rather than articulations of a conclusion. I strive to locate my answers to students' questions as hypotheses based on certain kinds of evidence: if you look at these materials, you might think this, but if you look over here it will look like that. This requires not just conveying to them a body of knowledge, but sharing with them the evidence, and the methods, by which that body of knowledge is constantly being reconstituted. It also requires mapping out the ways that evidence both opens up and limits interpretive possibilities. I have also pointed out that most people in the class would not feel comfortable filling in the blanks in the following statement: "The attitude of Americans in the twentieth century toward x is y." Why then should sixteenth- and seventeenth-century England be any more consensual? Why would we even need or want "the early modern world picture"? The answer to that question is easy. When you stick to hegemony, it is easier to prepare for the final.

Most recently, I have been trying to help students think about not only the process by which one crafts a provisional answer, but also the importance of how one frames the question in the first place. Why do students want to know the particular things that they want to know about early modern England? How would certainty be helpful? What value might the messy answers I am more comfortable with have? Or my current favorite: why do you ask?

Coping with these issues in the classroom is especially challenging at a time when how we handle evidence is one of the most pressing but least theorized methodological problems facing scholars of the early modern period. I would like to survey a number of scholars' statements about evidence, paying close attention, on the one hand, to the value attributed to legal documents, often considered the repositories of the "real," and, on the other hand, to prescriptive literature, which, as we constantly remind one another, does not describe "what really happened." How do different scholars explain what constitutes proof for them? Interestingly, the approaches to evidence do not divide neatly along disciplinary lines.

Nervous efforts are sometimes made to insist on the difference between representation and reality, literature, and history. For instance, Sharon Achinstein advises that "The truths of works of art are not historical truths, but they are truths nonetheless." This raises the question of just what kind of truths they are. Achinstein elsewhere claims that "literary sources are always a shaky ground on which to build history." But are they any more shaky than anything else? I cite Achinstein here simply because she works at the inter-section of the disciplines of literature and history, and is thus in a position to articulate a trepidation about the interdisciplinary enterprise and its use of evidence that many of us share. Some want to ally such anxieties by redraw-ing distinctions between literature and history. Identifying participants in this conference by discipline might be seen as one such move. In practice such a distinction has grown very uncertain. For many scholars eager to find solid ground, the grail of historical truth is often the court record. I implicate myself fully in the desire to view "the law" as synonymous with "the real." However, although I have resorted to court records for more reliable or more direct access to "what really happened," like many others I increasingly view court records as themselves representations, shaped by venue, occasion, and conven-tion, rather than as standards against which to check the accuracy of other kinds of sources.

Published accounts of trials can stand as one example of how indistin-guishable are "documents" and "representations." Multiple narratives survive for the most notorious crimes and trials, each inflected by its author, its authorization, its intended audience, its timing. We do not, however, have "transcripts"—that is, official, exhaustive manuscript accounts that purport to record verbatim what happened in the courtroom. As a consequence, the full drama played out therein is usually lost to us. Furthermore, for some trials the fullest accounts of witnesses' testimony are those published in pamphlet form. If they existed, transcripts would not necessarily offer the historian any greater certainty. Yet their absence reminds us that we have no recourse outside of representation.[2]

To make this point in the classroom, all one needs to do is ask, for instance, without requiring a show of hands, how many students have been molested or assaulted at a fraternity party or on a date? How many have reported that incident? How accurate, then, are rates of "sexual assault" on this campus? At Miami, we have a new sexual harrassment policy that allows the accused to appeal nine times and the accuser twice. Anyone who looks at the chart describing the process can see that the judgment reached by its end indicates many things but *not* how often sexual harrassment occurs on campus. Making the connection to students' own experiences in defining and reporting transgressions helps to clarify: to talk about evidence in these terms is not to say that sexual assault and sexual harrassment never occur on campus, but rather that who defines these transgressions and how, and what mechanisms are available to prosecute them, affect what incidents "go on the record." So perhaps what we can learn is not how often did it happen *then* versus how often does it happen *now,* but what is the history of the processes by which women's voices are authorized and recorded and acted on? What kinds of stories can women tell that will be found credible? How has that changed? How can we change it?

Furthermore, I hope that such discussions prompt students to consider what value there might be in going on the record. At Miami, a student group painted red hearts on the campus at the sites of assaults on women; the hearts are now fading, and some students are agitating to repaint them. What will be lost if weather and footsteps wear these memorials away? The controversy surrounding this matter foregrounds what is at issue in the desire to mark a particular history in space, to force it into visibility, to press charges.

At the same time that historians of women are demonstrating just how valuable legal documents can be, they are also urging that we consider carefully what these documents prove. For Natalie Davis in her pioneering work, what it meant to argue that she had found fictions in the archives was that she had found evidence that "authors shape the events of a crime into a story" and that in this very shaping they created testimony that would strike their readers as "true"—true because it was recognizable and conventional. The law directed certain narratives— "include this but not that, emphasize this and suppress that"; a context of storytelling and listening influenced speakers' sense of what made for a good story.[3] A speaker's status and circumstances, audience, and venue would all inform the story he or she would tell. Because evidence suggests that witches and vagrants self-consciously crafted their tes-

timony, and that servants angled their testimony to exonerate or incriminate
an employer, it is ill advised to assume that such shaping is too "sophisticated"
for some speakers.[4]

The line between shaping and lying was a difficult one to draw then; it continues to be a conundrum now. Our research puts us in the oddly uncomfortable position of legal personnel; like them, we assess these narratives, looking
for just the right balance of the conventional and the particular/peculiar.
However, the "heads-up" effect of the odd detail is worth questioning. If listeners then would find most plausible a story that was most conventional, can
we simply just reverse that process, finding most plausible those stories that
are least conventional? We must also scrutinize the significance of our own
belief. What does it mean, for instance, when, in response to a man's statement, Miranda Chaytor says: "I believe him"?[5] Where does this certainty
come from? What is it based on? How is it produced? What role should it play
in our assessments of evidence?

Lynda Boose, who reads court depositions with great care and insight, also
questions the "authority of the document," and dwells on the complex
processes by which some charges rather than others were prosecuted, and by
which court records were composed. When we lack a context (of rates of conviction in similar cases, for instance), she points out that "the masculine bias
that indisputably pervaded the culture makes . . . any . . . document that only
mirrors and reaffirms that bias unreliable as evidence of anything except the
privilege it most likely reflects."[6] In her wonderful book on women and property, Amy Erickson insists that historians cannot make generalizations about
women's history unless they "ask the women themselves." Yet, she also concedes that even in the probate documents she interprets so effectively
"women's voices are muted not because they did not speak at the time, but
because the probate court in which those documents were created was oper-
ated entirely by men."[7] So even here, we are not exactly getting unmediated
access to "the women themselves"; we are not hearing their authentic voices
or learning what really happened, although we may be getting as close as possible. I find it useful to teach, for instance, a play and a ballad attributed to
men, a deposition attributed to a woman, a woman's printed scaffold speech,
and a letter or diary entry signed by a woman all in the same unit in order to
facilitate discussion of the processes by which women's voices were invented,
recorded, or performed in a variety of genres on a variety of occasions, for
widely different purposes and audiences. In *all* of these forms, gender and
authorship are in question.

Because conduct books and sermons work so well in the classroom, I continually struggle to distinguish prescription from practice for students, but I
am trying to do so in more supple (if more confusing) ways. Here, too, I rely

on inviting students to think about their experience as participants in and readers of contemporary culture. For instance, how many people really live by *The Rules?*[8] Does that popular book describe how women and men actually relate? Or does it demonstrate something else? Might age, ethnicity, race, class, or region inflect heterosexual courtship in ways for which the book does not account? Reading studies of early modern women and gender will constantly remind you that prescription and practice diverge. Happily, these statements, which authors often use to reprimand how other people use evidence or to qualify their own use of evidence, are changing and becoming less confidently admonitory and altogether more muddy and confusing. For instance, although Amy Erickson demonstrates the richness of probate records, she frequently refers to a pervasive misogyny for which those records cannot fully account. If, as Erickson argues, "cultural misogyny" does not have its basis in the economic, then how else shall we understand it? Where else should we look, since what people felt, thought, and feared must then be as relevant as what they did, or had, or bequeathed? If daughters and sons have equal economic value to fathers, as Erickson demonstrates, then why have daughters "lower ideological value"? Throughout her exploration of how women outwitted or mitigated coverture, Erickson stresses how big a difference an "undercurrent of restraint" on women's behavior still made.[9] Legal fictions, prescriptions, and representations shape lived life, even if they do not always describe or reflect it.

In her recent book on women, words, and sex in early modern London, Laura Gowing, who depends largely on ecclesiastical court records, moves rapidly beyond the caveat that prescription does not equal practice to a messier formulation of that relationship. Gowing reminds her readers that "the ideal that literature propagated remained fundamentally inapplicable to the real household"; and that "the family itself was infinitely more complex than its literary model, and its relationships more awkward." Why should scholars or students care about this prescription that is divorced from practice? Gowing's work is a model, I think, of how to think about that. As she suggests: "One starting-point might be to enquire how members of real households interpreted such ideology, and to what particular uses they put it: not how far household practice and gender order reflected ideology, but in what ways individuals sought to use such prescriptions. The records of marriage disputes suggest violent husbands used the rhetoric of household order to discipline their wives; the language of insult played on the specific rules of feminine behaviour to describe and defame women as whores."[10] Whereas Gowing acknowledges "real households," she quickly shifts her attentions to some of those documents through which we have access to them— "records of marriage disputes" and of insults, records that register their indebtedness to popular literature. Furthermore, she stresses that what happened in real households, to the extent that we can imagine it, may well have been informed by, as it must also have fed into, prescriptive and imaginative texts. Although real households and discourses are not the same thing, neither are they neatly separable. For me, Gowing's work is most interesting, and most helpful in the classroom, when the oppositions—between the real and records, between records and stories—do not hold.

In the introduction to his massive new book on gender, sex, and subordination in early modern England, Anthony Fletcher somewhat sheepishly explains his reliance on ballads and drama, "neither of which is the usual stock in trade of the early modern social historian." Although Fletcher seems to feel a bit guilty, he is obviously not doing anything unusual; most social historians have had some recourse to such sources, for ornament and illustration, if not for evidence. For Fletcher, ballads and plays are valuable because they tell us what "absorbed people" and what people were willing to pay to hear about. Fletcher argues that, because plays "derive as much from a 'social milieu' as from an authorial point of view" they "can thus properly be used as historical evidence, not of realities but of the imaginative and ideological constructions of the period, of its mentality."[11] Thus, for Fletcher, a movement away from "the author," with a presumably ideosyncratic, if locatable, point of view, raises the value of plays and ballads as evidence. Whereas Fletcher keeps "reality" distinct from "the imaginative and ideological," he also, in his very method, concedes that he cannot quite reach "reality" except through "constructions"; he further concedes that "mentality" is a part of one's experience.

Recent scholarship on difference, fear, and hatred has emphasized how the imaginative overlaps with or constitutes the real. In *Shakespeare and the Jews*, for instance, James Shapiro points out that the formation of English national identity "depended on fears and projections that are more often revealed in works of art and literature than in the archival records that historians have long relied on."[12] In *Things of Darkness*, Kim Hall demonstrates that a concern with racial difference pervades early modern English culture, inflecting language and standards of beauty, so that only a resolute refusal to attend to race could miss it.[13] Rather than argue for a considerable Jewish or African presence in early modern England, these two books instead demonstrate how groups such as Jews and Africans were perceived to pose a threat disproportionate to their actual numbers or resources. Both Shapiro and Hall shift the question—not how many Jews or Blacks were there in England, but how and why did Englishness get defined against or in contrast to these kinds of difference (among others)? Why did the English need narratives of exclusion and expulsion by which to define themselves? As this work helps to make clear, perceptions and representations participate in cultural process whether or not they are "accurate." After all, fears and hatreds are always "real," whether or not the perceived threat can be proved to exist.[14] In the library and in the classroom, I keep returning to how early modern English culture located threat because, for me, these are compelling questions.

I do not assume, however, that they are necessarily my students' questions. This semester, I am experimenting with having students who do independent research on certain topics—like gender and sexuality, race and religion—bring their research into the class in the form of questions, rather than presentations of evidence and argument from what they have read. These are not questions to be addressed to me, but to their peers. For instance, if you read Mario DiGangi's essay on "queering the Shakespearean family," then what might you want to question or challenge or reconsider in some of our class discussions about households and families?[15] What haven't we been thinking about? What assumptions have limited our discussion? If you read Kim Hall's book, then how might you wish to extend and deepen our understanding of how race matters in, say, Othello?

I am especially interested in dislodging my students' dependence on one of two narratives regarding women's history: regress or progress, failure or success. These narratives bring with them attendant assumptions that we study the past because, if we do not know it, we are doomed to repeat it, or because it is a relief to know that the situation used to be worse, or we need to be reminded that we have not come far enough. This is not a very helpful way to think about women's history; furthermore, the linear narrative of change or no-change, forward or backward, can be used only if one holds gender separate from other categories, such as class, race, religion, and sexuality. What is the alternative? Less sweeping and more qualified. If one looks at Protestant aristocratic women, one will see this, but if one looks at Catholic servants one will see something else.

I understand why my students crave a big narrative in which to arrange all of their fun facts and details. However, if I do not challenge those narratives, then students just store any new information they gather in their unquestioned mental filing systems. If I can handicap their reliance on the most simple of narratives, that may be more important than conveying lots of information. Consequently, some of the scholarship that has impressed me the most lately—the scholarship I have mentioned today—is that which has not only provided me with information I did not know, but has also made me look in new directions, challenge some of my own assumptions, and rethink categories.

What is my answer to my student's question? It is provisional and personal. Today, I would say that I study the past for many reasons.

1. It is interesting; the fact that it is messy and confusing only makes it more interesting. Because I feel that one of the things I do as a teacher is model

affect and engagement, my own interest in the early modern period is an important part of what I bring into the classroom.

2. It is a collaboration. I do not want to have the last word; I want to be in a conversation. Given the financial constraints limiting publishing and hiring, I think that it is a gift to see new faces and hear new voices and purchase new books at a conference like this one. Furthermore, if the focus is on questions, then everyone in the class has something to add.

3. It is a process. Mary Beth Rose, one of my teachers and mentors, once said to me of research and writing, "it's the process that attaches you to life." I do not want to give my students the results of my own inquiry; I want to engage them in that animating process, and I want to attach them to life.

4. Life is chaos. Why should my class be tidy and reassuring?

5. If the past is not a stable object of study, but instead constantly shifting and reconfiguring itself in response to our interrogations, then anyone can have a Renaissance. I want my students to know that what the early modern period looks like has changed in large part because the demographics of who studies it have changed. If you want a different Renaissance, roll up your sleeves and start asking your own questions.

6. Students sign up for Shakespeare who would never sign up for "race, gender, class, and sexuality in early British literature."

7. I may not know what "really" happened, but I am learning a great deal about patterns of representation and interpretation, social and narrative structures, that still mold my own culture. The better I understand them, the more effectively I can disrupt them—and help my students to do so.

Notes

1. Sharon Achinstein, "Introduction," *Women's Studies* 24, no. 1–2 (1994): 1–13, especially 4; and "Women on Top in the Pamphlet Literature of the English Revolution," *Women's Studies* 24, no.1–2 (1994), 131–63, especially 156.

2. I draw here on arguments about evidence made in my *Whores of Babylon: Catholicism, Gender, and Seventeenth-Century Print Culture* (Ithaca: Cornell University Press, 1999), 1–4. For helpful reflections on the relationships among different kinds of evidence, see Lena Orlin's essay, "Women on the Threshold," *Shakespeare Studies* 25 (1997): 50–58.

3. Natalie Zemon Davis, *Fiction in the Archives: Pardon Tales and Their Tellers in Sixteenth Century France* (Stanford, Calif.: Stanford University Press, 1987), 2.

4. Jodi Mikalachki, "Women's Networks and the Female Vagrant: A Hard Case," in *Maids and Mistresses, Cousins and Queens: Women's Alliances in Early Modern England*, ed. Susan Frye and Karen Robertson (New York: Oxford University Press, 1999), 52–69; Garthine Walker "Rereading Rape and Sexual Violence in Early Modern England," *Gender & History* 10, no.1 (1998): 1–25.

5. Miranda Chaytor, "Husband(ry): Narratives of Rape in the Seventeenth

Century," *Gender & History* 7, no. 3 (1995): 378–407, especially 399.

6. Lynda Boose, "The Priest, the Slanderer, the Historian and the Feminist," *ELR* 25, no. 3 (1995): 320–40, especially 329.

7. Amy Louise Erickson, *Women and Property in Early Modern England* (London and New York: Routledge, 1995), 19, 223.

8. Ellen Fein and Sherrie Schneider, *The Rules: Time Tested Secrets for Capturing the Heart of Mr. Right* (New York: Warner Books, 1996).

9. Erickson, 97, 128.

10. Laura Gowing, *Domestic Dangers: Women, Words, and Sex in Early Modern London* (Oxford: Clarendon, 1996), 26, 27.

11. Anthony Fletcher, *Gender, Sex, and Subordination in England, 1500–1800* (New Haven and London: Yale University Press, 1995), xix, xx. Similarly, Boose defends the value of fictional stories as a place where "the culture's own, self-producing narratives and the mechanisms that construct them" are especially accessible (330).

12. James Shapiro, *Shakespeare and the Jews* (New York: Columbia University Press, 1996), 212.

13. Kim F. Hall, *Things of Darkness: Economics of Race and Gender in Early Modern England* (Ithaca: Cornell University Press, 1995).

14. See my *Whores of Babylon,* 4 and throughout.

15. Mario DiGangi, "Queering the Shakespearean Family," *Shakespeare Quarterly* 47, no. 3 (1996): 269–90.

Directly from the Sources: Teaching Early Modern Women's History without the Narrative

MARTHA HOWELL
History

It has, of course, long been traditional pedagogical practice to teach history courses "directly from the sources." In proposing that we do just that, I am not, however, recommending a continuation of traditional methods. I am not, for example, suggesting that we teach undergraduates how to do primary research—how to construct research hypotheses or how to locate and evaluate evidence. That I have long been doing. Nor am I recommending that we add more primary sources or a wider range of secondary readings to our syllabi. Like many of my colleagues, I have typically designed syllabi in this way. In all my undergraduate classes, we have watched films and looked at pictures almost as much as we have read texts. We have used all kinds of written sources—diaries, letters, law codes, tax lists, inquisition records, poems, contracts, wills, theological tracts, pamphlets, diplomatic correspondence, minutes of council meetings, legislation, and novels, to name just a few. The secondary literature I have chosen for my students has been as eclectic; we have regularly read sociologists, political theorists, anthropologists, literary critics, and economists as well as historians.

So I am not urging more of the same. Instead, I am suggesting that we use primary and secondary courses in new ways. Specifically, I am proposing that we pose for students, or enable them to pose for themselves, questions about how we construct knowledge about the past. Although, as I will argue, this approach has particular relevance in teaching women's history, it has relevance elsewhere as well, everywhere, in fact, that teachers wish to make critical readers of their students and make the process of doing history—rather than reading history—more visible.

Let me pause briefly to consider the differences between this approach and the way I taught women's history fifteen, ten, or even five years ago. Then, I did what historians traditionally do in the classroom. I tried to describe and account for change over time. I talked about cause and effect, about chronology and agency, about power, about the intentions and the interests of the actors in the historical drama I was relating. In short, I constructed narratives—stories with plots, with beginnings, middles, and ends, even with good guys and bad guys. I used sources—primary and secondary—simply to help tell that story.

Although I have argued elsewhere—and would argue today—that these tasks lie at the heart of the historical enterprise, I would also argue, along with some of my colleagues in history (and along with many of our critics outside the discipline) that historians have sometimes been naive about the kinds of assumptions we are making when we take on these matters.[1] What is important here, however, is not what our critics think; it is what our students think. They, by and large, are certain that the traditional ways of doing things are the appropriate ways. They expect us to deal with matters of cause and effect, intentionality, chronology, and agency. They expect plots. I would even go so far as to say that every single one of my undergraduate students in women's history courses both at Rutgers University, where I used to teach, and at Columbia University, where I now teach, came to my courses with expectations of this kind.

Some wanted simple facts. "How many women in sixteenth-century France could read?" they hoped to discover. "How often was the typical woman pregnant?" "How many children did she have?" "Could women own property in their own name? If so, what did they do with it?"

To be sure, most also wanted more than raw facts. They wanted what they often called "context"—usually as background for their studies in literature, or religion, or art history. "What was the 'real' early modern family like?" some art history students would ask. By this, they generally meant, "what meaning am I to ascribe to the family portraits of the period? Were the moral tales visible in these paintings actually lived?" Perhaps they had in mind the portraits depicting a kind, aging patriarch standing; sweet-faced, adoring wife sitting; and smiling children encircled in loving arms. A student of literature—perhaps of the Renaissance lyric—might want to know more about the sexual practices of the day so that she could make sense of the erotic poetry that circulated in aristocratic circles of Elizabethan England, as though I had a way of finding out whether everybody did all those things in bed with everybody with the abandon that these literary artifacts implied. A student of religion wanted me to tell her about the "effects" of the Reformation on women. "Did women 'benefit' from the closing of the monasteries?" "Did the abolition of the priesthood allow women to claim spiritual leadership?" If so, my students demanded to know, was this "good" for women?

Others wanted something slightly different, something I would describe as relief from the indeterminacy, the limbo, in which poststructuralist scholarship and much feminist theory left them. They wanted some benchmarks for evaluating women's status, for measuring oppression, for relativizing male dominance. They wanted to know about a past when things were clearly different—clearly better, clearly worse—for women—and why.

Thus, students coming to my women's history courses wanted to study a world that was knowable, and they thought that historians could provide them with that knowledge. They believed that we had privileged access to the facts, and they wanted us to construct a story based on those facts. So, I complied with my student's expectations—expectations, after all, that lay at the epistemological heart of the discipline in which I had been trained. I designed courses with a narrative in mind, a story about how things changed for women from about 1300 to 1700. I explained how transformations in the economy and demography, in social organizations, in political structures, in cultural forms and practices, and in religion combined to create new definitions of womanhood, new opportunities for women, new dangers, new forms of oppression, and new mechanisms for resistance. I took pains to explain that during these centuries key elements of today's western gender system took root. I talked, for example, about the rise of the nuclear family, of affectionate or romantic marriages, about new conceptions of male and female sexuality and desire, about the reform of education during the Renaissance and the exclusion of women from new kinds of learning, about the division of the economy into market and nonmarket sectors, and about the sexual redivision of labor that accompanied this change. Then I looked for readings and sources that helped me tell that story or helped flesh out that outline. I used primary sources such as legal codes, legislation, financial records, letters, or chronicles, along with secondary sources that elaborated a portion of the narrative, analyzed the institutions in which it was located, or examined the discourses that expressed its ideology.

This does not mean that I forced my evidence or that I did not allow my students into historiographical debates. I tried very hard to show them how it was that we knew what we thought we knew, to expose them to the uncertainties in our narratives, to show them the places where we were only guessing. I had them read, for example, both Ariès and Pollock on childhood (the first of whom argued that parents did not "invest" in children in the medieval and early modern centuries, whereas the second contended that they did).[2] Thus, my students learned not only that there was a debate about the quality of parental affection in premodern Europe, but also that there was good evidence for both interpretations. My students were not spoon-fed a seamless narrative; they were made to see that evaluating the evidence we had about the past was no easy task.

I had them consider, as well, interpretive differences that derived as much from the position of the inquirer, from the kind of question asked, as from the evidence assembled. I had them look, for example, both at interpretations of the medieval and early modern household like Alan MacFarlane's, which emphasized the mutuality, cooperation, and affection between husband and wife, and at investigations like Miranda Chaytor's, which exposed the tensions and instabilities of the early modern household.[3] I made them look both at Puritan households and Counter-Reformation female monasteries before I allowed them to draw conclusions about the "benefits" of the Reformation for women. I urged them to deconstruct the category of woman (although I did not yet use that phrase), insisting that they ask "which women" or what is "woman."[4] For example, I asked them to consider who "benefited" when motherhood was elevated to a moral ideal or what "woman" was being imagined when a sexual double standard was the norm.

So I did invite challenges. I did try to draw students into the process of historical interpretation, and to introduce them to sources. Yet, I did so, in effect, by presenting sources either to illustrate (and thus to confirm) the narrative or, in contrast, to call it into question.

I have come to think that there are at least two reasons to stop teaching that way. First, it does not accord with what more and more of us are doing as historians. In the last ten or fifteen years, historians, along with most humanists and social scientists, have been right in the center of academic debates about disciplinary methods, and as feminists we have been right in the middle of the middle. Although not all of us—certainly not all historians—have come out in the same place, all of us have had to take ever more seriously the questions posed by what is loosely called "poststructuralist" theory about reading strategies, about sources, about evidence, and about knowledge. This is not the place for a discussion of historiography in the postmodern age, and at this stage in the development of historiography after the so-called "linguistic turn," it is probably unnecessary.[5] The issues at the heart of this debate are, moreover, not entirely new, for in some ways questions like this have long been before historians, although somewhat less urgently and always in different form. Here I simply want to point out that we are more aware than ever about the difficulties inherent in our presumptions, about our access to knowledge about the past, more aware of how we construct meaning by insisting on the relevance of chronology, more aware of how fragile our category of agency really is, and more aware of how we collapse interest, intentionality, and outcome when we try to talk about cause and effect. I want to propose, first of all, that we try to bring students along with us. Whether we have figured all this out satisfactorily or not, I think that we owe it to them to share with them our thoughts, our uncertainties, and our strategies for coping.

Second, our traditional method of teaching history can frustrate and disempower students by denying them the tools to respond critically to what they read or are told. Although the old method does more or less live up to students' expectations about what history does, it allows them little or no entry into the process of doing history. We see this most clearly when in the course of our lectures or seminars we disrupt our narratives and present students with a historical debate about an issue. We might, for example, stop, as I often used to stop, to look at something like MacFarlane's argument about the nature of marriage in early modern England, which I just mentioned. His claim, that marriages were affectionate because households were nuclear and property was shared, is very different from Miranda Chaytor's argument about the fragility and the permeability of the nuclear household and the tensions that constantly threatened its unity. How do we get students to evaluate this debate? Typically, we look first at the argument each scholar makes, and we evaluate whether the evidence each adduces adequately supports the argument. Then we look at the evidence itself. Is it representative, persuasively read, and fairly drawn?

Although these are certainly good questions—good, solid, *historians'* questions—they are not questions the typical undergraduate is equipped to answer. How is she or he to know whether MacFarlane has selected the right letters and diaries and laws and wills to make his case? How is the student to judge whether Chaytor's demographic evidence is representative? By and large, undergraduates simply cannot know enough to make competent judgments about these matters. So, in order to get them started, we wind up telling them. For some students, this method works. Some learn enough in the process to want to go on and find out more, to engage in historical research themselves, to acquire a taste for rummaging around in archives. However, most simply take our word for it, passively concluding that making historical judgments is for specialists, not for them. Their job, they reason, is to accept our judgments and rehearse our debates. So this method very often—too often in my experience—reinforces the bad intellectual habits we are trying to break. Worse still, this method does not dislodge students' reverence for facts—or their belief that we are the keepers, and the authenticators of facts.

I will return to these issues, but first let me turn to the kind of course plan that I think helps remedy these faults, the kind of course I have found myself developing in the last few years. Rather than grounding my course in a narrative, in a story about women, as I once did, I now try to present a series of problems, or topics, if you will. Of course, it is not new to teach a history course through topics. Yet, what is new for me is that I do not embed the topics in a larger story about linear change. Instead, I tell my students that historians are largely agreed that gender definitions and meanings were in motion—and were highly charged, contentious issues—during the early modern period. I tell them that we are going to focus on some fixed number of issues or arenas in which change was most marked, or most fraught. I then try to explore with students the way various kinds of sources construct these topics.

Depending on the course—its level, the time I have to cover the material, the size of the class—I pick three to ten such issues or arenas and collect secondary and primary sources that bear on the chosen topic. For example, I might look at the household, the family, and marriage—the demography of the family or household, the functions of these social units, and their internal dynamics. I might look at property—its meaning, its uses, and its ownership. I might look at sexuality and the body or at faith and doctrine and religious practice. I might look at criminality and witches and heresy.

I do, admittedly, place these topics against a narrative, but it is a very schematic one. In lectures I talk about and in seminars I ask students to talk about, for example, the commercialization of European society and the concomitant erosion of manorialism; about the collapse of feudalism and the rise of territorial sovereignties and national states; about the implosion of Latin Christianity; or about the expansion of Europe. In short, I outline the standard narrative about the period.

However, the principal work of the course is to discuss and write about the sources I give them that bear on the topics I have chosen. Here I try to juxtapose secondary and primary sources of different kinds. I ask my students to read, for example, different kinds of sources treating the same event; or to consider different kinds of sources that treat different matters but that converge on a single issue. I do not ask the students to decide which interpretation is better or which primary source is "truer" or "more reliable" but to think about how any of these sources—primary or secondary—works: what truth it establishes, and on what terms.

Let me be more concrete, with three different kinds of examples. First, I have, for example, used the film and Natalie Davis's book *The Return of Martin Guerre* not just to tell the story—although the wonderful story is, of course, the hook—but to ask the students to consider how differently the film and Davis's book tell the story.[6] In some classes—advanced seminars to be sure—I have also given the students some of the primary evidence on which Davis and the film are based. In one course I even had a student return to the original French texts and to the exchange between Davis and one of her critics published in the pages of the *American Historical Review*.[7] My point in juxtaposing these sources, even the film and the book, is not, however, to point out the flaws of the film as history or to ask the students to make a judgment about whether Davis's interpretation was persuasive. My intention is to get them to think about the larger interpretative framework on which she depended—one based on a certain understanding of French society, of religion, and of gender. My hope is to compel them to examine the structure of her narrative, its mix of storytelling and analysis of voices, and then to contrast it both with the interpretative framework that informed the film, one that made love the dynamic, and with the film's narrative structure.

This material is surely familiar to readers, and many may have used it the way I described. What I want to emphasize here is not the novelty of my choices but that I once used this material in a slightly different way. Once I used it just to get the story told—to put the issues of households and marriage and property in rural society, of religion and conjugal love and gender relations, before my students. Of course, if I showed the film alongside the book, I had to ask questions about interpretation and evidence, for the book tells a different story than the film. Yet, in doing so I tended to ask about the failures of one or the other medium to interpret evidence "correctly." I did not concentrate so much on the way the respective stories are constructed, on how each uses facts, highlighting some and suppressing others, reading evidence one way in one case, another way in another, omitting evidence in one case, and including it in another. I did not ask, as I now ask, how another lens might change the way the story was told. I did not ask the students to think, as I now do, about whether Davis's book could have made a movie.

To turn to a second example, my course might also include a section on consumption, commercial wealth, and gender in the Renaissance. Here I would use a variety of sources: I might study paintings that not only display a costume of the age, but that also elaborate the object itself (jewels and clothing, for example); I might show a Dutch still life and read a scholarly article locating these paintings in a cultural history of the luxurious or commercial object; I might put sumptuary legislation before the students, choosing some legislation that took men's dress as the problem, as well as other examples that focused on women; I might read a series of wills or marriage contracts that assigned property to men and women in different ways; I might read Chaucer's "Shipman's Tale" in which a woman's lust for or need for finery sets in motion a tale of moral and social upheaval. I might read moralists on usury, a merchant's account book, and a series of town ordinances regulating markets. I might study tax records to track the role of trade in generating revenues for central governments.

Next I might ask the students to do two things. First, I would propose that they think about how any of these individual sources talks about property and how each genders it. Then, second, I would charge students to contrast a group of sources with each other according to the way each treats these matters. I might very well *not*, however, ask my students to come up with a story about the relationship between property and gender meanings in this age. Instead, I might well ask them simply to focus on the stories each of these sources tells.

Let me give one last example, of a still different kind of exercise. I might ask students to read sources that tell incommensurate stories, stories about love for example. I might read a fabliau that elaborates and concentrates on the tension between men and women—"The Lady who was Castrated" is one of my favorites. I might read that tale along with a traditional medieval romance, or a Puritan sermon on marriage, or a colloquy from Erasmas, or Luther on marriage, or a conduct book from the period. I might read a marriage contract, or read an article about marriage rituals. Perhaps, then, I might ask students to consider how conjugal love is imagined in each of these narratives and how it is or is not achieved, what threatens it, and what furthers it.

My principal objective in proceeding this way is to allow students to think about how historical narratives are constructed. I want them to emerge from these exercises not only with a fuller understanding of the varieties of family forms, of the complexity of early modern markets, and of the difficulties of romantic love in this age. I want them to understand that what we can know about these social forms and cultural practices comes to us through sources that *construct* the meanings of these institutions, practices, and mentalities. I want my students, thus, to appreciate that we must study these sources as historical products themselves if we are to understand their strategies of representation. Finally, I want my students to sense that the early modern people who lived in these villages and towns, who made these marriages, who bought these goods, or who spoke these words of love were dependent upon the same constructions as are we, their historians. Thus, we learn that whatever narrative we construct is in fact a construction out of narratives. None of the students exposed to this kind of material can escape recognizing that this "evidence"—whether primary or secondary—is not the same thing as "data," as unmediated, unprocessed "fact." They also cannot escape thinking about genre—about the way that the formal structure of a source produces meaning. I do not try to make the students into literary critics—I am not one. Yet, I want them to consider, for example, the rhetorical strategies and formal structure in both medieval romance and legislation, and to contrast them. I want them to ponder the kinds of characters each of these sources construct, the kinds of dynamics they allow.

Before concluding with an accounting of the pluses and minuses of this *kind* of teaching, let me hasten to add several important comments or qualifications. Obviously, I am not trying to reproduce the process of doing historical research. In fact, my course breaks at least three rules of historical research. First, I have defined the topics—quite narrowly—for my students. I have already decided what is important to study about early modern women, and I have framed questions. Second, I have chosen their sources, and I have done so strategically—to expose certain questions of fact, of interpretation, and of methodology. So I have not let the sources determine the categories of inquiry; thus I have prohibited that productive dialectic between sources and questions that motivate good historical research. Third, and finally, I have juxtaposed sources arbitrarily, with little of the attention to social location I would demand of myself or of my fellow professionals. I draw from sixteenth-century Puritans and fifteenth-century Franciscans indiscriminately, from Bruges and London and Florence, as though they were interchangeable.

So this is not an exercise in how to do history. It is an introduction to how historians create meaning. It is an intellectual exercise in creating meaning and, I hope, a better way of teaching beginning students about early modern women.

Let me summarize the advantages. The principal advantage, at least for me, is that it gives students some tools for thinking about historical interpretation. It locates historical debates in matters of interpretation based on what sources we have and how we read them, and less on disputes about "facts" or about the "biases" of the historian. Thus, it allows students a way out of the dead end into which they are usually led when we introduce historical debates into our narratives. No longer are students asked to judge which interpretation is better, which begins with the "right" assumptions about gender or class or some other category, or which is closer to the evidence. This method avoids these traps by implicitly acknowledging that students do not know enough about the evidence on which a typical historical monograph is built, its provenance or its representativeness, to make a judgment about these matters. Yet, they can read intelligently what is put before them, and they can offer their own interpretations. In this way, they can join us, their teachers, in extracting meaning from sources.

A related advantage is that it puts the students in charge of their own learning. It is they who create meanings in the classroom, out of the material they have been given. Students get involved in their material, they do not forget it, and they become sophisticated in thinking about the complexity of historical change and of historical interpretation. Thus, this method can help achieve what we all dream of accomplishing, what seems to me a principal object of feminist pedagogy—making students responsible for their own learning.

Admittedly, there are some disadvantages in teaching this way. First, the technique gives up the psychic satisfaction of narrative—the beginning, middle, and end, the closure—and it gives up the control of the material a narrative provides both students and teachers. To be sure, we avoid the problem of having to choose among the competing narratives offered up by historians. However, we lose any sure sense of exactly what happened, to whom, and why. This has been the one consistent complaint I get from students. It takes many forms: "I could never decide whether things got better or worse for women," some students lament. Others complain that "I didn't know whether conjugal love actually existed, could ever exist." Still others miss the facts, often with horrifying results: "I could never keep straight whether King Henry VIII was before or after the commercial revolution."(!)

A related risk is that students produce bizarrely naive interpretations. Some of my students have thought that sixteenth-century London was fourteenth-century Florence or that either was fifteenth-century Bruges. Their mistake is, of course, the result of my teaching; because I skipped from one to another city in studying conjugal affection or parenting or sexuality, they have been unable to recognize the differences among the cities. They cannot remember whether St. Francis or Luther came first because I taught faith and doctrine and religious practice as a topic, not as a history of the Reformation. This is a real problem, and one I have never satisfactorily solved, and probably cannot solve unless the undergraduate curriculum at colleges like Columbia (or Rutgers, and most others) is significantly reformed. Only if students are led though a more rigorously hierarchical program of historical studies, in which my course came after students had already studied premodern Europe, could we hope to eliminate these problems. That reform is not going to happen very soon (and I for one would not want to pay the price that would be exacted if it did), so I have learned to be consoled by remembering that similar confusions arose even when I taught my courses more conventionally. Then, too, students sometimes thought that Luther preceded and somehow prepared the way for St. Francis or that the Tudor monarchs made the wool trade possible. In those days, however, I was truly devastated by such confusion, for then my course had been designed precisely to achieve a certain sophistication about these matters of chronology. Today, I am looking principally for another kind of sophistication.

On balance, then, I am pleased to be teaching this kind of course. Let me reiterate that although it represents a fairly subtle shift in course content, it has quite different objectives from the courses I once taught. It seeks to expose the problems of interpretation I once sought to suppress, and it exposes as well how indeterminate, how historically constructed this thing called "gender" is. It brings students into the arena of history writing, at least in a limited way, and engages them in debates about historical knowledge that are now current in our discipline. It puts the classroom and learning more powerfully in students' hands—and it makes teaching more fun.

Notes

1. See my "A Feminist Historian Looks at the New Historicism: What's So Historical About It?" *Women's Studies* 19 (Spring 1991): 139–47; and for a discussion of how we might preserve this approach while, simultaneously, distancing it, my *The*

Marriage Exchange: Property, Social Place and Gender in Cities of the Low Countries, 1300–1550 (Chicago: University of Chicago Press, 1998), especially "Introduction." For a general introduction to and survey of the crisis in history associated with the so-called linguistic turn (along with an extensive bibliography), see Keith Jenkins, ed., *The Postmodern History Reader* (New York and London: Routledge, 1997).

2. See Philippe Ariès, *Centuries of Childhood* (New York: Vintage, 1962); and Linda A. Pollock, *Forgotten Children: Parent-Child Relations from 1500 to 1900* (Cambridge: Cambridge University Press, 1983).

3. See Alan MacFarlane, *Marriage and Love in England: Modes of Reproduction, 1380–1840* (Oxford and New York: Blackwell, 1986); and Miranda Chaytor, "Household and Kinship: Ryton in the late 16th and early 17th centuries," *History Workshop* 10 (Autumn 1980): 5–60. Also see the discussion of her article that followed in subsequent issues: Keith Wrightson, "Critique: Household and Kinship in sixteenth-century England," *History Workshop* 12 (Autumn 1981): 151–58; Richard Wall, "Readers' Letter," *History Workshop* 12 (Autumn 1981): 199; Olivia Harris, "Debate: Households and their Boundaries," *History Workshop* 13 (Spring 1982): 143–52; Rab Houston and Richard Smith, "Critique: A New Approach to Family History," *History Workshop* 14 (Autumn 1982): 120–31.

4. For an exploration of the problem of the category of "woman" in historical scholarship, see Denise Riley, *Am I That Name?: Feminism and the Category of Woman in History* (Basingstoke, Eng.: Macmillan, 1988).

5. For a useful summary of the debates surrounding history's meaning(s), even its possibility, under postmodernism, see *The Postmodern History Reader*, ed. Keith Jenkins.

6. Natalie Davis, *The Return of Martin Guerre* (Cambridge: Harvard University Press, 1983).

7. Robert Finlay, "The Refashioning of Martin Guerre," *American Historical Review* 93 (June 1988): 553–71; Natalie Zemon Davis, "On the Lame," *American Historical Review* 93 (June 1988): 572–603.

Workshop Summaries 29–39: Pedagogy

Workshop #29: "Attending to Gifted Women (and Men) in the Pre-Collegiate Classroom: Teaching Early Modern Literature and Culture to the Young and Interested"

Organizers

Martha J. Craig, English, Bradley University, Peoria, Illinois; Robert Berry, Humanities, Greencastle High School, Greencastle, Indiana; Carrie Keesling, student, Smith College

Readings

Robert Berry, "Integrating Marguerite de Navarre into Existing Curriculum," a curriculum guide (Greencastle, Ind.: Greencastle High School, 1997); Martha J. Craig, "Gender Wars: Medieval and Renaissance Textual Politics," a syllabus (Muncie, Ind.: Indiana Academy, 1997); Craig, "Gender Wars," a course packet (Muncie, Ind.: Indiana Academy, 1997); Carrie Keesling, "Alice in Iceland: An Image of the Wife of Bath in Nordic Myth," a paper submitted for "Gender Wars" (Muncie, Ind.: The Indiana Academy, 1996); Kathleen D. Noble, "The Dilemma of the Gifted Woman," in *Psychology of Women Quarterly* 2 (1987): 367–78; Harry Passow, et al., *Differentiated Curricula for the Gifted/Talented*, a Committee Report to the National/State Leadership Training Institute on the Gifted and Talented (Ventura County, Calif.: Office of the Superintendent of Schools, 1982).

This workshop addressed the philosophy and problematics of attending to the needs of "gifted" learners, most specifically when introducing them to texts as historically marginalized as these students may feel themselves to be. When gifted teenagers encounter for the first time such works as Christine de

Pizan's *The Book of the City of Ladies,* Marguerite de Navarre's *Heptameron,* or Elizabeth Cary's *The Tragedie of Mariam* (written when she was only seventeen), and learn about the cultural environment that dictated silence and privacy for most women, they gain a view of the artist as solitary and unique—the same view many of them have of themselves vis-à-vis society at large, or among groups of more intellectually resistant peers. What can we learn from the enthusiasm gifted high school students demonstrate towards the ideology, language, politics, imagination, and courage of early modern texts by women? What do we learn from the occasional failures of these texts to appeal to them? Do these students' "fascinated antagonism as well as admiration" (see David Lee Miller's "The Death of the Modern: Gender and Desire in Marlowe's 'Hero and Leander'" in *The South Atlantic Quarterly* 88, no. 4,[Fall 1989]: 757) suggest that their age and environment, as well as their intellectual gifts, uniquely suit them for grappling with the importance of these early cultural artifacts?

Martha Craig described her pilot class, "Gender Wars: Medieval and Renaissance Textual Politics," at the Indiana Academy for Science, Mathematics, and Humanities, a school for gifted high school juniors and seniors affiliated with Ball State University. Coming to the Academy after teaching college literature classes, Craig was committed to preparing high school students for (enlightened) university humanities curricula by introducing them to women-authored noncanonical as well as male-authored canonical texts, and to the contexts in which these works often warred. Not knowing how young students would fare with the language and "politics" of unfamiliar classical and early modern works, she was astonished in the first week of class to find students in the lounges reading enthusiastically selections from Aristotle, St. Jerome, Jean de Meun, Christine de Pizan, and the English women tract writers to their disbelieving friends. Carrie Keesling, a student in that pilot class, discussed this enthusiasm for both the incendiary misogynistic texts included in the syllabus and the strong responses of the women authors. The elements of conflict inherent in these literary attacks and defenses particularly appealed to the students, as did the class's developing sense of the long history of gender debate.

Bob Berry, a visiting scholar at the Academy in 1994, subsequently developed and implemented for his high school a curriculum model outlining various ways to bring the history and writings of Marguerite de Navarre into social studies and literature curricula that had traditionally not included women. He was particularly struck by how eager his female students were to study a woman so long excluded from general scholarly discussion, but the males were enthusiastic also. Bob, an expert in gifted theory, was able to help clarify that the *need* gifted students have for differentiated materials and techniques behooves us to reveal to them the complexity of early modern textual politics Their positive response should be a signal that the many points of identification they find with early modern writers would be shared by many "average" teenagers as well.

The central question raised by the workshop is how best to bring these early texts and contexts to the classroom, a basic issue for college as well as high school teachers. Methods discussed were pairing women-authored with male canonical texts (*The Tragedie of Mariam* with *Othello,* for instance, or Aemilia Lanyer's *Salve Deus Rex Judaeorum* with *Paradise Lost*); involving the students in finding and reading primary documents on microfilm or in collections of early books; and encouraging Internet searches and creative interdisciplinary projects.

Additional Readings

Belenky, Mary Field, Blythe McVicker Clinchy, Nancy Rule Goldberger, and Jill Mattuck Tarule. *Women's Ways of Knowing: The Development of Self, Voice, and Mind.* New York: Basic Books, 1986.

Christine de Pizan. *The Book of the City of Ladies.* Translated by Earl Jeffrey Richards. New York: Persea Books, 1982.

Half-Humankind: Contexts and Texts of the Controversy About Women in England, 1540–1640. Edited by Katherine Henderson and Barbara McManus. Urbana: University of Illinois Press, 1985.

Loomba, Ania. *Gender, Race, Renaissance Drama.* Manchester, Eng.: Manchester University Press, 1989.

Marguerite de Navarre. *The Heptameron.* Translated by P. S. Chilton. London: Penguin, 1984.

Submitted by: Martha J. Craig

Workshop #30: "The Creative Spirit: Voices of Women in Philosophy, Music and Literature"

Organizers

Jacqueline Padgett, English, Trinity College, Washington, D.C.; Minerva San Juan, Philosophy, Trinity College, Washington, D.C.; and Sharon Guertin Shafer, Music, Trinity College, Washington, D.C.

Readings

Jane Bowers and Judith Tick, eds. *Women Making Music: The Western Art Tradition, 1150–1950* (Urbana: University of Illinois Press, 1986), 127–28, 143–46, 152–61; John Dryden, "To the Pious Memory of the Accomplisht Young Lady Mrs Anne Killigrew, Excellent in the two Sister-Arts of Poësie, and Painting. An Ode," in *The Works of John Dryden: Poems, 1685–1692* (Berkeley: University of California Press, 1969), 109–15; Anne Killigrew, "Upon the saying that my VERSES were made by another," in *Poems (1686): A Facsimile Reproduction* (Gainesville, Fla.: Scholars' Facsimiles & Reprints, 1967), 44–47; Karin Pendle, ed., *Women & Music: A History* (Bloomington: Indiana University Press, 1991), 64–65; Mary Warnock, ed., *Women Philosophers* (London: J. M. Dent, 1996), 3–5, 14–15, 19–23.

The workshop organizers offered an example of interdisciplinary pedagogy for the study of seventeenth-century women using a case study methodology. Readings were chosen as preparation for discussion of three women: Anne Conway in philosophy, Anne Killigrew in literature, and Bianca Maria Meda in music. Participants received material that included discussion of the lives of religious women in Italian convents who experienced severe restrictions on their study and practice of music; Anne Killigrew's poem "Upon the Saying that My Verses Were Made by Another"; John Dryden's ode to Anne Killigrew; and excerpts from Anne Conway's *The Principles of the Most Ancient and Modern Philosophy*.

Minerva San Juan opened the workshop by asking participants to consider why women are invisible in the histories of Western Europe, referring to *A History of Their Own*, in which the editors argue that the invisibility of women results directly from the forcing of women's lives and creative work into male categories. The women discussed in the workshop, however, *were* visible to their contemporaries; they performed well in male creative space while, by their very performance, they subverted the gendering of that space as male. What might it have been for these women to experience urgent creative voices so as to do the work of philosophy, music, and literature? Women who may not have had easy access to domains of creativity largely inhabited and governed by men or to the structures that provided formal training did write philosophy, compose music, and create literary texts. Specific examples were demonstrated in the workshop. Women philosophers, composers, and writers crossed over the border demarcating male authorship and women's unauthorized creativity. Often these creative women denied to themselves authority over their own production, seeing it as unworthy or diseased.

Following Jacqueline Padgett's presentation of Anne Killigrew's poem and Sharon Shafer's introduction to Bianca Maria Meda's music composition, "Cari Musici," workshop participants exchanged pedagogical strategies appropriate to the teaching of seventeenth-century women in an interdisciplinary and collaborative framework. Collaboration across discipline boundaries encourages an intensive questioning of assumptions within disciplines, including those at the foundation of disciplinary histories. Recent recordings, now widely available, of works by Bianca Maria Meda and Sor Juana de la Cruz that were played during the workshop, provide an inventive strategy for the study of early modern women. Participants shared their pedagogical strategies: asking students to be detectives in discovering (un-covering) women who have been written out of intellectual and cultural history, and assigning students the task of "inventing" a life for an early modern woman musician, writer, or philosopher based on available historical information.

Additional Readings

Anderson, Bonnie S., and Judith P. Zinsser. *A History of Their Own: Women in Europe from Prehistory to the Present.* New York: Harper & Row, 1988.

Hendricks, Margo, and Patricia Parker, editors. *Women, "Race," and Writing in the Early Modern Period.* London: Routledge, 1994.

Holland, Nancy. *Is Women's Philosophy Possible?* Savage, Md.: Rowman Littlefield, 1990.

Marshall, Kimberly, editor. *Rediscovering the Muses: Women's Musical Traditions.* Boston: Northeastern University Press, 1993.

Menages, Gilles. *The History of Women Philosophers (1690).* New York: University Press of America, 1984.

Submitted by: Sharon Guertin Shafer

Workshop #31: "Dissolving Disciplines and Constructing Models"

Organizers

Margaret Hannay, English, Siena College; Carole Levin, History, University of Nebraska; Susanne Woods, English, Franklin and Marshall College, and founder of the NEH/ Brown University Women Writers Project

Readings

Carole Levin, "Illuminating the Margins of the Early Modern Period: Using Women's Voices in the History Class," in *Teaching Tudor and Stuart Women Writers*, ed. Susanne Woods and Margaret Hannay (New York: MLA Press, forthcoming), and Leeds Barroll, ed., Forum on "Studying Early Modern Women," *Shakespeare Studies* 25 (1997): 19–87: Leeds Barroll, "Introduction," 19–20; Margaret L. King, "Women's Voices, the Early Modern, and the Civilization of the West," 21–31; Catherine Belsey, "Feminism and Beyond," 32–41; Maureen Quilligan, "Completing the Conversation," 42–49; Lena Cowen Orlin, "Women on the Threshold," 50–58; Susan Dwyer Amussen, "Studying Early Modern Women," 59–66; Susanne Woods, "Shifting Centers and Self-Assertions: The Study of Early Modern Women," 67–75; Margaret P. Hannay, "Constructing a City of Ladies," 76–87.

    The workshop addressed several questions. What methodological, theoretical, and interpretative issues are raised by our attempts to bring early modern women into the classroom? How do we incorporate materials and methodologies from disciplines other than our own? What impact do the new electronic forms of communication have on our interdisciplinary pedagogy? Participants were encouraged to bring a one-page handout for the group, responding to these issues. The readings, distributed with permission prior to publication, were chosen for their focus on creative pedagogy.

    Susanne Woods opened the session by locating the study of early modern women in a more general shift away from traditional disciplinary boundaries toward a reconfigured and cross-disciplinary sense of how we teach and learn. Because our material is "new" and largely free from the disciplinary categorizing of the male tradition, we have a fresh opportunity to think beyond boundaries, and we have found not only that we can, but that we must. As one example of a way to incorporate interdisciplinary materials into the classroom, Carole Levin discussed a highly successful course that she has taught for the past ten years, "Saints, Witches, and Madwomen," which focuses on women on the margins and how they have been labeled in different historical periods. The course considers how women's voices are mediated as they are transcribed by others, using such examples as the trial of Anne Askew and the speeches of Elizabeth I. Why have these particular voices been published rather than others? Margaret Hannay discussed the use of primary sources to pull students into the early modern period. Using as examples two holograph letters and two portraits representing Mary Sidney, Countess of Pembroke, we examined her self-constructions, first as a teenager overwhelmed by her new position as countess, and then as a self-assured woman petitioning the queen on behalf of her adolescent son. Once students have met the author in this way, they are ready to consider how she expresses her subjectivity in her poetry.

Most of the discussion period was devoted to pedagogical strategies. Anne Shaver shared her experience in guiding students to produce an edition of five dramas by Margaret Cavendish, Duchess of Newcastle. Fran Dolan explained how she begins her seminar on "women as writers and readers in sixteenth- and seventeenth-century England" by problematizing each word in the course title. Jodi Bilinkoff distributed a handout with three provocative paragraphs from St. Teresa of Avila, which demonstrate her shifting power relations with her confessor. Christina Malcolmson objected to the projection of feminism onto early modern writers. Suzanne Hull cautioned against spending all our time on the women who are visible according to traditional historical standards (e.g., queens, maverick writers, and martyrs) and encouraged more focus on the "common woman." Paula Woods described the resistance she has found when she attempts to incorporate women writers into standard period courses. The session ended with a lively discussion of political and economic contexts for studies of early modern women in an age of reduced funding for education.

Additional Readings

Dash, Irene G. "Single-Sex Retreats in Two Early Modern Dramas: *Love's Labor's Lost* and *The Convent of Pleasure*," *Shakespeare Quarterly* 47 (1996): 387–95.

Donawerth, Jane. "Teaching Shakespeare in the Context of Renaissance Women's Culture," *Shakespeare Quarterly* 47 (1996): 476–89.

Gutierrez, Nancy. "Why William and Judith Both Need Their Own Rooms," *Shakespeare Quarterly* 47 (1996): 424–32.

Hageman, Elizabeth H., and Sara Jayne Steen, editors. "Teaching Judith Shakespeare," *Shakespeare Quarterly* 47 (1996): 361–489.

Hall, Kim F. "Beauty and the Beast of Whiteness: Teaching Race and Gender," *Shakespeare Quarterly* 47 (1996): 461–75.

Hopkins, Lisa. "Judith Shakespeare's Reading: Teaching *The Concealed Fancies*," *Shakespeare Quarterly* 47 (1996): 396–406.

Kemp, Theresa D. "The Family Is a Little Commonwealth: Teaching *Mariam* and *Othello* in a Special-Topics Course on Domestic England," *Shakespeare Quarterly* 47 (1996): 451–60.

Matchinske, Megan. "Credible Consorts: What Happens When Shakespeare's Sisters Enter the Syllabus?" *Shakespeare Quarterly* 47 (1996): 433–50.

Roberts, Josephine A. "'Thou maist have thy *Will*': The Sonnets of Shakespeare and His Stepsisters," *Shakespeare Quarterly* 47 (1996): 407–23.

Stirm, Jan. "'For solice a twinne-like sister': Teaching Themes of Sisterhood in *As You Like It* and Beyond," *Shakespeare Quarterly* 47 (1996): 374–86.

Teague, Frances Teague. "Judith Shakespeare Reading," *Shakespeare Quarterly* 47 (1996): 361–73.

Submitted by: Margaret P. Hannay

Workshop # 32: "Early Women Writers and Postmodern Culture: Creating and Teaching with the Brown Women Writers Project Textbase"

Organizers

Paul Caton, English, Brown University Women Writers Project; Erika Olbricht, English, University of New Hampshire

Readings

Julia Flanders, "The Body Encoded: Questions of Gender and the Electronic Text," in *Electronic Textuality,* ed. Kathryn Sutherland (Oxford: Oxford University Press, 1997), 127–43; John Lavagnino, "Electronic Editions and the Needs of Readers," *Critical Survey* 9, no. 1 (1997): 70–77.

The organizers had a twofold intention: first, to show participants the electronic form in which the Women Writers Project (WWP) planned to make available its textbase of early modern women's writing in English, and, second, to raise questions and concerns about such resources: the different institutional and intellectual frameworks within which they arise, their accessibility and utility, and the role they will play in future pedagogy. The readings by Lavagnino and Flanders respectively complemented those aims. Paul Caton began the workshop by demonstrating the WWP's prototype Web-based resource and explained the imperatives—technical, pedagogical, and financial— driving its design and execution. Erika Olbricht followed by laying out some of the new intellectual opportunities and pitfalls presented by electronic environments, particularly in relation to the decoupling of text and book.

Two closely related concerns—cost and access—dominated the open discussion. Several participants thought that their institutions might balk at the projected licensing fee, or would be reluctant to invest in a resource that required repeated payments while never becoming an institution-owned tangible asset like library books or journal volumes. While the World Wide Web seems to promise democracy of access to resources, the reality of license fees means that established inequalities persist. The scholars who most need access are those at institutions unable to afford alternatives like the microfilm set of early English books—precisely the institutions least likely to buy into what they might perceive as an expensive electronic resource. Participants noted the ironic possibility that the long-inaccessible works being recovered by the WWP might remain inaccessible in electronic form, although it was generally acknowledged that the Project's print versions were inexpensive and readily available. Other issues centered on the promise and danger inherent in the electronic edition. The ability to quickly and easily manipulate digitized and encoded text (in searching, indexing, and collating) represents the medium's obvious advantage. However, as with any source, scholars need to know the right questions to ask about the provenance and creation of what they see. Scholars must transfer their familiar book-based skills to working in the electronic medium, and they must come to terms with new factors, such as text encoding and user interfaces. The workshop came to no conclusions and offered no final answers; rather, it reflected the moment in the development of electronic resources, with participants welcoming them in principle while reserving judgment on their implementation.

Additional Readings

Chernaik, Warren, Caroline Davis, and Marilyn Deegan, editors. *The Politics of the Electronic Text*. Oxford: Office for Humanities Communication, 1993.
Delany, Paul, and George P. Landow, editors. *Hypermedia and Literary Studies*. Cambridge: MIT Press, 1991.
Lavagnino, John. "Reading, Scholarship, and Hypertext Editions." *Text: Transactions of the Society for Textual Scholarship* 8 (1996).

Submitted by: Paul Caton

Workshop #33: "Listening for the Voices of Early Modern European Women"

Organizers

Chris Africa, History, University of Iowa Libraries; Luci Fortunato De Lisle, History, Bridgewater State College; Robert C. Evans, English, Auburn

University; Mary M. Gallucci, Italian, University of Connecticut; Jesse G. Swan, English, University of Northern Iowa

Readings

Aretino. *Aretino's Dialogues,* trans. Raymond Rosenthal (New York: Ballantine Books, 1971), 158–59, 175, 298–300, 302–303, 333, 434; Martha Moulsworth, *The Birthday of My Self,* ed. Ann Depas-Orange and Robert C. Evans, *Critical Matrix* special issue (1996), 1–18; Charlotte Otten, ed., *English Women's Voices, 1540–1700* (Miami: Florida International University Press, 1992), selections: *The Trial and Condemnation of Mervin Lord Audley Earl of Castle-Haven at Westminster, April the 5th, 1631:* Ann Audley's testimony, 34–37, and Elizabeth Hooton's letter, *In Pursuit of the King,* 110–13.

Since the printed book or document serves as the chief means of transmitting early modern women's experiences to current students, and since we all endeavor to communicate the quickening excitement we feel listening to the rich variety of women's voices, we organized this workshop to present five interdisciplinary pedagogies for helping students listen to the voices embodied by printed documents. Further, we selected facilitators who approach literary material historically and historical material literarily. Our focus was on how this mix of method and material worked in specific classroom circumstances.

We emphasized the fictional dimension of representations of female prostitutes in statutory records and judicial complaints in sixteenth-century Lucca; the interpretive techniques for describing multiple female voices generated by early modern English documents; the current opportunities for student work on early modern women; and the narrative structure and characterization of early modern formal documentary records of witches and their power. Throughout, ontological issues of the texts and methodological issues of interpretation were debated, with much vigorous comment from workshop participants.

The most important issues and questions we left with involved integrating our teaching of women's voices in a range of documents into courses other than the customary ones. A course on the history of the book may integrate women's voices, but the challenge is to do so without making "women" marginally "other." In the case of prostitutes or witches, we thought about accelerating the defeminization of the Western gendering of these categories in various, as yet to be determined, ways. Other issues included the reliability and accuracy of scribal records of women's voices, such as in court records, and the effect of the printing process on the transmission of these voices. Finally, we speculated about the relationship between voice and experience: what gaps, gendered or other, exist between experience and utterance?

Additional Readings

Chartier, Roger, editor. *The Culture of Print: Power and the Uses of Print in Early Modern Europe.* Princeton: Princeton University Press, 1989.

Kors, Alan C., and Edward Peters, editors. *Witchcraft in Europe, 1100–1700: A Documentary History.* Philadelphia: University of Pennsylvania Press, 1992.

Rosen, Barbara, editor. *Witchcraft in England, 1558–1618.* Amherst: University of Massachusetts Press, 1991.

Submitted by Jesse G. Swan

Workshop # 34: "On the Ancient Education of Gentlewomen, or Why Do the Same Issues Keep Recurring?"

Organizers

Fran Teague, English, University of Georgia; Judith Hallett, Classics, University of Maryland; Ruth Perry, Humanities and Women's Studies, MIT

Readings

Mary Astell, *A Serious Proposal to the Ladies,* 4th ed. (New York: Source Book, 1970), 139–60, 165–72; Alan K. Bowman and J. David Thomas, *Life and Letters on the Roman Frontier: Vindolanda and its People* (London: British Museum Press, 1994), 93; David Cressy, *Education in Tudor and Stuart England,* (New York: St. Martin's Press, 1975), 106–11; Linda Grant, "The Smarter Sex?" *The London Guardian,* reprinted in *World Press Review* (January 1995), 45; Judith P. Hallett, "Edith Hamilton (1867–1963)," *Classical World* 90, nos. 2–3 (1996–97), 128; Bathsua Makin, "Essay on the Antient Education of Gentlewomen," ed. Frances Teague, in *Bathsua Makin, Woman of Learning* (Lewisburg, Pa.: Bucknell University Press, 1997), 109–10, 128–50; Ruth Perry, "Bluestockings in Utopia," in *History, Gender, and Eighteenth-Century Literature,* ed. Beth Fowkes Tobin

(Athens, Ga.: University of Georgia Press, 1994), 159–78; Cornelius Tacitus, *The Annals of Imperial Rome*, trans. Michael Grant (Baltimore: Penguin Books, 1964), 132–34.

The readings for this workshop sampled commentary on women's education through the centuries: what struck the organizers as notable was how often the same issues recurred over the centuries. We asked members to come prepared to discuss these issues from their knowledge of women's history, from their own personal history as students, and finally from the perspective of their experience as teachers. In our preliminary mailing, we proposed several questions for the workshop to consider. From Richard Mulcaster to Makin to Astell to *The Guardian*, writers comment on women's bodies during discussions of education. How should we understand the body-mind split, and should biological difference affect the education of boys and girls? When we seek an earlier tradition of learned women, as did both Makin and Astell, does it matter if that tradition is redefined? Can we seek role models, without becoming trapped by identity politics? What are the ends of education for women? How does our answer affect both the subject and the method of our study? Is education predicated on living in an alternative community? If we think that the best education is in a world that is set aside, what are the implications of that assumption for those who cannot or will not enter the world set aside for education? We specified these concerns about educating women, for they have been part of the discussion at least since ancient Roman times and they remain a concern in our own classrooms.

Because the participants had studied or had taught at a variety of institutions, we spent some part of the workshop comparing our experiences. In our discussion of coeducation, two ideas became clear: first, that not all of us endorsed the sort of education that we had had ourselves, and, second, that a variety of institutions was necessary because different individuals need different systems. For example, whereas the separate and secluded community of women that Astell had insisted on in her *A Serious Proposal to the Ladies* had been important to some participants who had attended women's colleges, others would have preferred to learn (or teach) in a classroom that included both women and men. The separation of a student from her family may work well for a woman in her late teens or early twenties, as participants pointed out, but it serves to exclude older women students who must support and raise families. Makin's suggestions for incorporating women's education with domestic concerns seemed particularly useful to some participants, while others resisted the assumption that domesticity was an exclusively feminine subject.

The liveliest discussion centered on the usefulness of finding women—as Makin does—who can serve as intellectual models. Thus, we study Bathsua Makin, Mary Astell, or Edith Hamilton not only to understand their ideas, but also to discover parallels between our lives and theirs. One participant pointed out that we were not limited to model women: as a girl she had identified with male, as well as female figures, in the novels she read. Another commented that she felt some distance from early modern learned women because they generally were not working-class women or women of color. Most of us did like knowing about learned women who had faced problems like those we have in our own classrooms, however, and we all agreed that knowing the traditions matters (hardly a surprising conclusion given the sort of conference we were attending).

Additional Readings

Gardiner, Dorothy *English Girlhood at School: A Study of Women's Education through Twelve Centuries*. Oxford: Oxford University Press, 1929.

Hannay, Margaret Patterson, editor. *Silent but for the Word: Tudor Women as Patrons, Translators, and Writers of Religious Works*. Kent, Ohio: Kent State University Press, 1985.

O'Day, Rosemary. *Education and Society, 1500–1800: The Social Foundations of Education in Early Modern Britain*. London: Longman, 1982.

Warnicke, Retha. *Women of the English Renaissance and Reformation*. Westport, Conn.: Greenwood Press, 1983.

Submitted by: Fran Teague

Workshop #35: "Poetry, Publication, and Pedagogy"

Organizers

Jane Donawerth, English, University of Maryland; Grace S. Fong, East Asian Studies, McGill University, Canada; Ana Kothe, Comparative Literature, University of Puerto Rico

Readings

Anne Bradstreet, *The Works of Anne Bradstreet*, ed. Jeannine Hensley (Cambridge, Mass.: Harvard University Press 1967), 13–17, 221; Elizabeth Cary, title page and I.i.1–30, *The Tragedy of Mariam* (London, 1613); Elizabeth Cary, title page and I.i.1–35, *The Tragedy of Mariam*, ed. Christopher O'Callaghan, Dana Garris, Michele Beth Richman, Maureen Fern, Jennifer Sainato, Charles T. Gaush, Adele Steiner, Karen Homan, Nancy Suprenant, Julie Marino (desktop published, College Park: University of Maryland, 1990); Sor Juana Inés de la Cruz, "Prologo al Lector," and "Soneto a la excelentissima Senora," *Inundacion Castalida* (Madrid, 1689), with translations provided by Ana Kothe; Sor Juana Inés de la Cruz, *Poems*, trans. Margaret Sayers Peden (Binghamton, N.Y.: Bilingual Press, 1985), 12–15; Dorothy Ko, "In the Floating World: Women and Commercial Publishing," *Teachers of the Inner Chambers: Women and Culture in Seventeenth-Century China* (Stanford, Calif.: Stanford University Press, 1994), 26–27; Stephanie Jed, "The Tenth Muse," in *Women, "Race," and Writing*, ed. Margo Hendricks and Patricia Parker, 195–208 (New York: Routledge, 1994); Anne Lok, title page and "A Meditation of a Penitent Sinner," *Sermons of John Calvin, Upon the Songe that Ezechias Made* (London, 1560); Madeleine de Scudéry, "Of Conversation," cover, title page, and p. 1, *Conversations Upon Several Subjects*, trans. Ferrand Spence, ed. Kelly Blake, Kirk Bridygham, Jason Butler, Rebecca Coddington, Kimberly Kay Cutright, Charcy Evers, Mark A. Johnson, Jill Jones, Stephanie Lenkey, Mark Little, Amy E. McPartland, Jennifer Nicolosi, Linda Samuel, Deborah Smallenberg, Catherine Semple, James Thuman, and Catherine Worth (desktop published, College Park: University of Maryland, 1993); Isabella Whitney, title page of *The Copy of a Letter, Lately written in meeter, by a yonge Gentilwoman to her unconstant Louer* (London, 1567?); Isabella Whitney, title page and "To her Sister Misteris A.B.," *A Sweet Nosgay, or Pleasant Posy* (London, 1573); Mary Wroth, "In this strang labourinth," P77, *The Poems of Lady Mary Wroth*, ed. Josephine A. Roberts (Baton Rouge: Louisiana State University Press, 1983); Ji Xian, ten poems, "Preface" to Prose Collection, and "Record of Past Karma," 1600s, trans. Grace Fong (1998).

In this workshop we looked at early modern women's poetry and publishing across several cultures: England, China, and the American colonies. We chose materials to help participants examine how women "published" poetry in the sixteenth and seventeenth centuries, how such publication challenges the designation of "early modern," and how we publish their poetry in today's classrooms. From England we examined Anne Lok, who published, under her initials, poems in the end pages of her translations of religious works by men; Isabella Whitney, who published more openly an entire volume under a transparent shortening of her name (IS W); and Elizabeth Cary, who claimed that her verse drama was pirated. From across the Atlantic, we looked at Anne

Bradstreet and Sor Juana Inés de la Cruz, the two "first" women poets of the Americas to be published in print, both sponsored by more privileged patrons, and both printed in the mother country. We also included new material by Ji Xian, a seventeenth-century Chinese writer of poems and an autobiography, published under the auspices of the men of her family. We further aimed to consider the politics of translation for Sor Juana and Ji Xian, and the significance of today's publication of all these poets for our classrooms in photocopied packet, anthology, student edition, and scholarly edition.

The discussion centered on the Chinese writer Ji Xian (fl. 1650s), because the group was very small and this writer was new to all of us. Ji Xian came from a powerful family and was well educated in a China ruled by the Manchu dynasty, who made interventions to uphold traditions and Confucian values. She wrote only poetry, no novels, mixing vernacular and classical language, poetry, and formal prose. Women's writings (as art writings in general) were printed in small runs of a few hundred, and many middle-class family women published in this way. Her autobiography tells the story of her childhood, difficult marriage, and steady desire to become a Buddhist nun, which she achieves.

We discussed the genre of autobiography and ghost stories as possible influences. We considered what the autobiography tells us about Chinese family history: that her husband is called "free-spirited" suggests that perhaps Ji Xian managed the household and accounts while he was out of the house; as first wife, she continued to be in charge when a concubine temporarily joined the household, but wording implies distance in the marriage.

We were surprised by the similarities of Ji Xian's story to that of Margery Kempe's, especially in their desire for celibacy in marriage. Unlike Japanese women, early modern Chinese women did not write novels, or any prose— only poetry. So this tradition makes Xian's prose autobiography very surprising.

Additional Readings

Arenal, Electa, and Stacey Schlau. "'Leyendo yo y escribiendo ella': The Convent as Intellectual Community." *Journal of Hispanic Philology* 13, no. 1 (Autumn 1989): 214–29.

Hageman, Elizabeth, and Sara Jayne Steen, eds. "Teaching Judith Shakespeare" (Special Edition). *Shakespeare Quarterly* 47, no. 4 (Winter 1996).

Symposium on Poetry and Women's Culture in Late Imperial China" (Special Edition). *Late Imperial China* 13, no. 1 (June 1992).

Wall, Wendy. *The Imprint of Gender: Authorship and Publication in the*

English Renaissance. Ithaca: Cornell University Press, 1993.
Widmer, Ellen, and Kang-i S. Chang, eds. *Writing Women in Late Imperial China.* Stanford, Calif.: Stanford University Press, 1994.

Submitted by: Jane Donawerth

Workshop #36: "Portraits and Portrayals: A Multi-Media, Multi-Disciplinary Approach"

Organizers

William Pressly, Art History, University of Maryland; Catherine Schuler, Theatre, University of Maryland; and Marvin A. Breslow, History, University of Maryland

Readings

Court and Times of Charles I, ed. T. Birch (London, 1848), 2: 62–63; Lucy Hutchinson, *Memoirs of the Life of Colonel Hutchinson* (London, 1848), 1: 126; *Diary of Walter Yonge, 1604 to 1628,* ed. George Roberts for Camden Society (London, 1848), 77, 82–83; *The Autobiography of Sir Simonds D'Ewes, Bart,* ed. J. O. Halliwell (London, 1845) 1:. 257, 272–73; and *The Memoirs of Edmund Ludlow,* ed. C. H. Firth (Oxford, 1894), 1: 10.

In this workshop, faculty from, History, Theatre, and Art History who had previously taught in the multidisciplinary, multimedia humanities courses sponsored by the Center for Renaissance and Baroque Studies at the University of Maryland explored with the workshop participants the development of such a course and its focus on women in the early modern period. Henrietta Maria was selected as a case study for the use of multidisciplinary materials in a multimedia approach. There are abundant accessible materials in the visual arts, most famously the Van Dyck paintings; there are contemporary descriptions in letters and memoirs; and there are records of her patronage and participation in court performances, notably masques. Unlike Elizabeth I, where power and governance were joined, Henrietta Maria was, like her mother Marie de' Medici, in the more typical position of queen consort where there might be portrayals of power but not of rule. The commissioned portraits of a queen such as Henrietta Maria were to record important events, but they were also made to disseminate likeness, and to fashion ideas of status and cultural prowess. The images—painted, verbal, and theatrical—also reflected the interaction between the portrayed and the act of portrayal, between the creative work and its creator, and between the individual and the community.

The structure of the workshop allowed the organizers to demonstrate briefly ways in which they could use materials for a course much like the one they did in 1996. Breslow cited the previously distributed contemporary written accounts of Henrietta Maria to discuss Stuart politics and religion. Schuler used visuals from contemporary works to address Henrietta Maria and her relationship to theater and the and theatrical. Pressly used digital technology to show the workshop how a painting can be read and manipulated for a class.

Throughout the presentations, all the members of the workshop participated through the use of the technology available in the teaching theater. Examples ranged from summoning and manipulating images to writing responses in two-minute electronic essays. Discussions among the participants revealed a wide range of experience with the technology. The experiences brought out the limitations as well as the strengths of technology for humanities students. For example, where some had found that the anonymous two-minute essays that were collected on everyone's terminal provided a way to break the ice and to encourage participation, others reported that students who were weak in grammar and spelling often were reluctant to post even anonymous comments. Although there was general acceptance of the value of digital technology, enthusiasm was checked by the need to evaluate the use of these resources. When the best way to make an illustration available is through an overhead projector, does this need to be done in a fully equipped teaching theater? Is a teaching theater fully equipped when it has twenty terminals for forty students?

In the end, the participants shared not only their individual experiences with multimedia, multidisciplinary courses, but also a cautiously optimistic appreciation for the uses of technology in the humanities.

Additional Readings

Jones, Inigo. *The Theatre of the Stuart Court.* Edited by Stephen Orgel and Roy Strong. London: Sotheby Parke Bernet; and Berkeley: University of California Press, 1973.

Millar, Oliver. *Van Dyck in England.* London: National Portrait Gallery, ca. 1982.

Sharpe, Kevin. *The Personal Rule of Charles I.* New Haven: Yale University Press, 1992.

Starkey, David, et al. *The English Court: From the War of the Roses to the Civil War* (London: and New York: Longman, 1987.

Veevers, Erica. *Images of Love and Religion: Queen Henrietta Maria and Court Entertainments.* Cambridge and New York: Cambridge University Press, 1989.

Submitted by: Marvin A. Breslow

Workshop #37: "Renaissance Women Adrift in the World: Entering Unfamiliar Territories for Teaching and Writing"

Organizers

Deirdre McChrystal, English, Carroll College; Merry Wiesner-Hanks, History, University of Wisconsin-Milwaukee

Readings

Chandra Talpade Mohanty, "Under Western Eyes: Feminist Scholarship and Colonial Discourses," in *Third World Women and the Politics of Feminism,* ed. Chandra Talpade Mohanty, Ann Russo, and Lourdes Torres (Bloomington: Indiana University Press, 1991), 51–79; Tessie Liu, "Teaching the Differences Among Women from a Historical Perspective: Rethinking Race and Gender as Social Categories," *Women's Studies International Forum* 14, no. 4 (1991): 265–76.

The workshop focused on the methodological and philosophical problems involved in entering new intellectual and geographic territories for teaching and writing, particularly for teachers moving beyond Europe despite graduate training that concentrated on Europe. As department sizes shrink, many of us are asked to teach courses for which we have no graduate training, and these are no longer simply courses in a closely related field, but in completely different cultural traditions and historical periods. Discussion revealed that most workshop participants currently confront this situation in many disciplines, and that a disproportionate number of female faculty members are asked to teach such courses, both because they are concentrated at junior ranks and thus frequently given challenging teaching assignments, and because they are perceived to be more "sympathetic" to non-Eurocentric approaches.

We provided participants with a list of questions in advance, which included: How do we begin? What materials are available? Knowing that whatever we choose will become representative of a culture to our students or readers, how do we choose? How can we ask the right kinds of questions? How do we measure the credibility of a newly informed perspective? How do we balance difference and familiarity, both for ourselves and for our students, to avoid orientalizing and exoticizing and yet not erase otherness? How do we assess whether a text provides an indigenous perspective or one that has been acculturated? What are the problems particular to teaching about *women* in the non-Western world, and are these different from those created by teaching about *gender*? What are the special problems created by using a comparative framework, either one that compares Europe with an area outside of Europe, or one that compares areas within Asia, Africa, Latin America, or the Middle East? What are the problems peculiar to teaching and writing about the premodern world, when using written sources privileges certain cultures? To what extent can we escape our own cultural perspective or hegemony, especially one reinforced by graduate training? How should and can our teaching and writing about areas beyond Europe shape our approach to European topics?

At the workshop we also provided an annotated bibliography and copies of a series of woodcut prints by Guaman Poma, a seventeenth-century acculturated Christian Native American from Peru. (These illustrations may be found in the Silverblatt book noted below.) Our discussion of these woodcuts demonstrated more clearly than we had anticipated the layers of interpretive complexity and pedagogical problems raised when we cross boundaries. Participants disagreed about the literal translation of the Spanish texts included on the images, the extent of Poma's acculturation, the appropriateness of graphic sexual images in some classroom settings, and even the ethics of using materials far beyond one's expertise. We reached no consensus, but having articulated our concerns and experiences in an interdisciplinary setting, we feel less isolated. We also rediscovered the excitement for both us and our students of entering new territories.

Additional Readings

Restoring Women to History: Teaching Packets for Integrating Women's History into Courses on Africa, Asia, Latin America and the Caribbean, and the Middle East. Bloomington, Ind.: Organization of American Historians, 1990.

Ashcroft, Bill, Gareth Griffiths, and Helen Tiffin. *The Empire Writes Back: Theory and Practice in Post-colonial Literatures.* London: Routledge, 1989.

Hall, Kim. *Things of Darkness: Economies of Race and Gender in Early Modern England*. Ithaca: Cornell University Press, 1995.

Hendricks, Margo, and Patricia Parker, editors. *Women, "Race" and Writing in the Early Modern Period*. London: Routledge, 1994.

Silverblatt, Irene. *Moon, Sun and Witches: Gender Ideologies and Class in Inca and Colonial Peru*. Princeton: Princeton University Press, 1987.

Submitted by: Deirdre McChrystal and Merry Wiesner-Hanks

Workshop #38: "Teaching Early Modern Women Philosophers"

Organizers

Peter S. Fosl, Philosophy, Transylvania University; Deborah Nails, Philosophy, Mary Washington College

Readings

Margaret Atherton, "Introduction," in *Women Philosophers of the Early Modern Period*, ed. Margaret Atherton, 1–7 (Indianapolis, Ind.: Hackett, 1994); Elizabeth Kamarck Minnich, "From the Circle of the Elite to the World of the Whole," in *Educating the Majority: Women Challenge Tradition in Higher Education*, ed. Carol S. Pearson, Donna L. Shavlik, and Judith G. Touchton, 277–93 (New York: Macmillan, 1989).

Deborah Nails began the workshop with an exploration of why it has taken so long and been so difficult to attend properly to early modern women philosophers. The reasons she cited include the limited circulation of information regarding early modern women philosophers, early modern bias against women and their works as intellectually inferior, the lack of education or leisure for early modern women to write philosophy, the overlap of philosophy and theology in early modern times, the scarcity of texts for teaching the work of early modern women, the private nature of early modern philosophical inquiry, lack of interest on the part of contemporary philosophers, misunderstanding of the obstacles in the way of female philosophers, denigration of early modern women thinkers as nonphilosophers, and the remarkably stable canon of philosophical literature. In order to introduce early modern female thinkers who have received recent attention, Nails's remarks accompanied a slide presentation showing images of the following figures: Christine de Pizan, Marie de Gournay, Anna Maria van Schurman, Madeleine de Scudéry, Elisabeth of Bohemia, Margaret Lucas Cavendish, Queen Christina of Sweden, Sophia Electress of Hanover, Sor Juana, Mary Astell, Queen Sophia Charlotte, and Catherine Trotter Cockburn. Nails provided significantly more detailed biographical and bibliographical information about these and other figures in a set of "Thumbnail Sketches" she distributed prior to the session.

In order to raise pedagogical and interpretive questions regarding the work of early modern women thinkers, Peter Fosl initiated a discussion of ideas developed by leading contemporary theorists Erica Harth, Michèle Le Doeuff, and Nancy Tuana. Participants discussed Le Doeuff's notion that women's relationship to philosophy has generally been mediated by men. Harth's claims stimulated a discussion of the way in which philosophy was both attractive and threatening to early modern women philosophers as well as the way dualism and materialism affected considerations of the status of women. Tuana's text provoked questions about the manner in which reading philosophy differs for men and women and asked participants to investigate in their teaching the development of nonbinary ways of thinking in works by early modern female philosophers. Minnich's thesis that the very criteria governing what counts as genuine philosophy are biased required participants to consider to what extent early modern female thinkers challenged prevailing norms of "real" philosophy and to what extent contemporary norms are satisfactory. After interrogating a sample syllabus Fosl distributed, participants questioned the composition of the current curricular canon and the extent to which contemporary curricula are biased in their methods, their appeal to "false universals," and their topics of interest.

Additional Readings

Le Doeuff, Michèle. *Hipparchia's Choice: An Essay Concerning Women, Philosophy, Etc.* Translated by Trista Selous. Oxford: Basil Blackwell, 1989.
———. *The Philosophical Imaginary.* Translated by Colin Gordon. Stanford, Calif.: Stanford University Press, 1989.
Harth, Erica. *Cartesian Women: Versions and Subversions of Rational Discourse in the Old Regime.* Ithaca: Cornell University Press, 1992.
Tuana, Nancy. *Woman and the History of Philosophy.* New York: Paragon House, 1992.

Submitted by: Peter S. Fosl

Workshop # 39: "'There's Magic in the Web of It': Integrating the World Wide Web into the Women's Studies Curriculum

Organizers

Susan Jenson, Art History, University of Maryland; Karen Nelson, English, University of Maryland; Michele Osherow, English, University of Maryland

Readings

Nelson, Karen, Susan Jenson, and Michele Osherow, "Integrating the World Wide Web into the Women's Studies Curriculum," http://www.wam.umd.edu/ ~klnelson/integrating.html

In this workshop we began a conversation about ways we can and do use technology in the classroom. Instead of readings, we sent a questionnaire to participants so that we could tailor the discussion to the group, and we asked that each participant think of classroom situations that would be enhanced by internet research, web presentations, or computer projects. We also constructed a web site for the workshop, which included a sample syllabus, some lesson plan ideas, an art gallery exhibition, a mock-up of a student-edited web edition and production of Lady Mary Wroth's *Love's Victorie*, a simple how-to guide for constructing web pages, and links to some of our favorite resources on the web. We referred participants to that site and brought photocopied packets of the pages to the workshop.

In our presentations, we offered quick explanations of the web site we had constructed, and we talked about our reasons for advocating classroom use of web technology. Karen Nelson found that students began to write for a wider audience, which gave assignments in the literature classroom additional exigency and gave students an increased investment in their work. Susan Jenson articulated the advantages of designing a virtual gallery as part of an art history course. Students understood some of the reasons behind an exhibition, and they engaged more intensely with the artwork presented on the web than they did with slides or with reserve materials. Michele Osherow talked about how she used the web in the drama classroom and demonstrated how students could offer a virtual production of *Love's Victorie*. Her web pages included costume designs, student monologues and dialogues, set designs, and character interpretations, and she discussed her drama students' involvement in electronic publicity and marketing for a 1997 production of a newly authored play.

Participants then worked in small groups to articulate possible applications. Using either the sample syllabus or a scene from *Love's Victorie* featuring Venus and Cupid, they came up with suggestions on how to mark up, link, or explain these materials in their own classrooms. After the members of the small groups had talked for a few minutes, we assembled the whole group, gave them a ball of yarn, and asked them to share their ideas. Individual groups offered their findings in turn, while others identified connections between those suggestions and their own results. The yarn followed the conversation from group to group, and we literally constructed a web for the "class project." Participants suggested various ideas for textual interpretation, including links to research resources, classical and early English dictionaries, astrological information, museum collections, poetry, literary commentary, allusions, and pastoral drama such as William Shakespeare's *As You Like It*. One group proposed a virtual staging of the play in Mary Wroth's country house. We also discussed our questions and concerns about the new technology. Topics included access and logistics, quality control of images, student work, time management in already crowded syllabi, intellectual honesty, copyright concerns, and plagiarism.

Additional Readings

Fitch, Nancy. "History after the Web: Teaching with Hypermedia." *The History Teacher* 30, no. 4 (1997): 427–41.

Jones, Paul. "Whither Humanities and Advanced Technology?" *Educom Review* 33, no. 6 (1997): 26–29.

Kaplan, H. "Interactive Multimedia and the World Wide Web: A New Paradigm for Teaching and Learning." *Educom Review* 32, no. 1 (1997): 48–52.

Lanham, Richard A. *The Electronic Word: Democracy, Technology, and the Arts.* Chicago: University of Chicago Press, 1993.

Salomone, Ronald E., and James E. Davis, editors. *Teaching Shakespeare into the Twenty-First Century.* Athens: Ohio University Press, 1997.

Schneiderman, Ben. "Educational Journeys on the Web Frontier: Teaching your students where to go and how to get there." *Educom Review* 33, no. 6 (1998): 10–14.

Submitted by: Karen Nelson

Part Six
Performance

(En)Gendering Performance: Staging Plays by Early Modern Women

Alison Findlay, Stephanie Hodgson-Wright, and Gweno Williams
Theater

Prologue[1]

In 1994 we set up an interdisciplinary research project, Women and Dramatic Production, 1550–1670, in order to test and challenge the critical assumptions that drama in English by early modern women was not intended for performance, was unperformed, and therefore unperformable.[2]

First, we began by questioning the concept of "not intended for performance." The class and gender of aristocratic women of the early modern period may have precluded them from writing for the public stage in England, but the public playhouse was by no means the only site of dramatic production in the period. A major aim of our research project has been to destabilize conventional definitions of theater, to ask questions about what might have constituted a performance, and to consider ways in which women might have used theater in its widest sense as a means to empower themselves. Every early modern woman who wrote plays also wrote in other genres. In choosing to write a play, rather than a poem, prose fiction, or meditation, she made an active, informed, and deliberate choice of genre.

Second, we investigated the validity of "unperformed," a term that is often narrowly focused to mean "unperformed on the public stage." Historical accuracy is better served by the rephrasing, "as yet no records of performance have been discovered." The lack of material evidence is not entirely surprising here. The commercially driven public theater and the politically driven court masque were phenomena that by their very status and nature left records of their existence. A domestic performance taking place in front of a select audience is less likely to have produced such decisive evidence. We do not know that these plays were not performed; in the absence of conclusive evidence for or against performance, we must surely let the dramatists' choice of genre guide us.

Finally, we addressed the highly subjective term "unperformable," with its implicit grounding in historically and culturally determined concepts of aesthetic standards and dramatic fashion. After all, even plays with a record of success on the early modern stage may fail to engage a late twentieth-century audience.

The empirical process of staging these plays was for us the crucial test of their performability. We all learned much about our texts by translating them from the page to the stage in three very different venues: a public studio theater, a country house, and a converted Victorian wood-paneled drama studio. Our experiments were a resounding success, proving to us, our actors, and our audiences that the plays are indeed performable, and teaching us much about the types of performance their authors envisaged. Our illustrative photographs, taken from video recordings of the original productions, have been chosen to highlight important aspects of the plays' performativity.

The Tragedy of Mariam – Stephanie Hodgson-Wright

When I started work on *The Tragedy of Mariam*[3] with Tinderbox Theater Co. in 1994,[4] one of my first tasks was to create a set on which the action could take place, because the play itself, like many early modern play texts, does not indicate a specific location for each scene. Rather, it is set in the general location of Judea in the years immediately before the birth of Christ. However, the text does place the action in a clear social, political, and psychological framework. The power of Rome is strongly felt; it is Herod's obligation to explain his recent support of Mark Antony to the newly empowered Octavius Caesar that causes Herod's absence and supposed death at the beginning of the play. The recent deaths of Mariam's grandfather, Hircanus, and her brother, Aristobolus, at Herod's instigation, provide a psychological background to the fatal rift between Herod and Mariam.

The set was a physical manifestation of these ideas, offering a visual testimony to Roman imperialism and Herod's ruthless eradication of his rivals. Stage center, on the back wall, was a poster of Herod, defaced to indicate the liberated feelings of the Judean people. He was figured as a petty dictator of a "banana republic," an effective modern analogy for the historical Herod's position as a creature of the Roman Empire. Stage left, from the audience's perspective, was a site of public celebration, dedicated to Imperial Roman overlords living and deceased: Octavius Caesar, Mark Antony, and Julius Caesar. There was another bust waiting to be unveiled. In the first part of the play, Herod's absence causes patriarchal power to be demonstrably compromised. This was reinforced by the passivity of the images during the transgressive speeches and deeds that litter Acts 1, 2, and 3. Having regained Octavius Caesar's confidence, Herod returned; the busts took on a new significance, as they silently bore witness to his absolute power. On the other side of the stage was another public

Set for *The Tragedy of Mariam*, Alhambra Studio, Bradford, October 1994[5]

site, a graveyard where Hircanus and Aristobolus were buried. As human bodies decaying in the ground, they formed the topographical antithesis of the elevated celebratory busts on the opposite side of the stage. A third grave was under construction, and a covered gravestone waited to be used.

The set also functioned as rationale for the presence and characterization of the Chorus. Although the rehearsal process saw the named characters in the play making the transitions from page to stage with relative ease,[6] the Chorus needed some interpretation. Not actually in the play, yet also a key part of it, the Chorus needed a reason to be there. I decided to characterize the Chorus as two workers engaged in jobs on each side of the stage: on the left a Sculptor finished off the new bust, and on the right a Gravedigger dug the new grave. The opposing positions of the Chorus on the stage, and the differences in their work, suggested a tension between the two, underscored by Paula M. Wells's arrangement of Chorus 1, 2, and 4 into two-part songs. Following Act 3 the problematic nature of the Chorus offered a particular challenge: it apparently enjoins women to silence, yet it is part of a female-authored play in which female speech is a crucial feature. In rehearsal, it became apparent that Chorus 3 is comprised of two contradictory voices struggling for supremacy. As a result, the lines were divided between the two performers, the Gravedigger expressing protest at the impositions placed upon wives, and the Sculptor articulating a more conservative position. For example, stanza 3:

Sculptor: That wife her hand against her fame doth rear,
That more than to her lord alone will give
A private word to any second ear.

Gravedigger: And though she may with reputation live
Yet though most chaste

Sculptor: She doth her glory blot
And wounds her honour

Gravedigger: Though she kills it not.[7]

Despite Nancy Gutierrez's observation that *The Tragedy of Mariam* is very unlike the Sidnean closet dramas with which it is so often associated,[8] the play continues to be classed as a closet drama, intended only for reading aloud. However, the sword fight in Act 2 contradicts this classification.[9] In my production, the sword fight was played for maximum effect, pitting the unimaginative Constabarus against the flamboyant, leather-clad Silleus. The scene itself

Salome (Suzannah Rogers) and Herod (Dave Newport), 4.7

is unsettlingly comic, especially as the victory goes not to the posturing gallant defending his mistress's name, but to the jilted husband, and it is swiftly followed by an incongruous demonstration of male bonding between the pair. The rehearsal process led to a crucial discovery about this scene: despite its intrinsic function as a well-constructed critique of masculine values, it does not move the plot forward in any way.[10] The digressive nature of the action in this scene underscores the performativity of the play.

The overtly physical "action" of the play constitutes only one small aspect of its performance potential. The encounter between Herod and Mariam offered the actors plenty of scope for expressing physically their strained relationship.[11] The textual indication that Mariam be dressed in a sombre fashion (4.3.3–6) to reflect her mood provided the catalyst for Herod's anger. The scene culminated in physical violence, as the soldiers hauled Mariam back and forth in response to Herod's changing orders. The gestures inspired by Salome's dialogue with Herod in 4.7 were entirely different. Armed with strong drink, soft words, and sensous caresses, Salome gave Herod the care and attention he actually craved from Mariam. The actors played up the semi-incestous undertones, though Salome's costume indicated the real object of her desire: her brother's power.

Salome's costume was designed as a silky, feminized version of Herod's military garb, incorporating the essential signifiers, such as lanyards and epaulets, of political power. Although the play's main theme is conflict between the sexes, confrontations between women provide the play with much of its dramatic power. As such, even minor characters like Mariam's mother Alexandra, who makes a single appearance in 1.2, and Herod's vengeful first wife, Doris, who appears only in 2.3 and 4.8, are drawn with clear dramatic purpose. As Naomi J. Miller has recently pointed out, "their spirited engagements with one another often serve to sharpen their respective positions as subjects able to claim voices for themselves apart from the otherwise overdetermined social roles afforded them by male authored codes of feminine conduct."[12] The confrontation between Doris and Mariam took place in Mariam's prison cell, created onstage as a dark, feminized private interior.

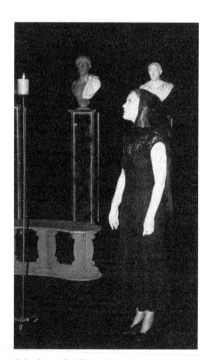

Mariam (Jo Dyer), 4.8

The actor playing Doris used physical contact, ranging from gentle and intimate to aggressive and threatening in order to maximize the confusing and demoralizing effects of the confrontation upon Mariam. Salome's monologue in 1.4, clearly a public oration rather than a private meditation, assumes the presence of an audience. Furthermore this speech contains a feature typical of the play's dialogue: an internal stage direction. Where stage directions are not given separately, the entrance or exit of a character inheres in the dialogue, thereby supplying a comprehensive apparatus for moving the characters on and offstage. It is surely of the greatest significance that, precisely at the end of Salome's most subversive oration in Act 1, the text draws the most overt attention to an entrance cue:

> Silleus said
> He would be here and see he comes at last.
> Had I not named him, longer had he stayed.
>
> (1.4.62–4)

These lines clearly refer to the crucial function, not of Salome the character, but of the actor playing Salome to summon the actor playing Silleus into the playing space. Until he gets his cue, he cannot make his entrance. Salome's dialogue, in breaking the theatrical frame, draws attention to its very existence. Only by acknowledging the presence of this theatrical frame can we, as critics, appreciate the full value of *The Tragedy of Mariam*.

The Concealed Fancies – Alison Findlay

The Concealed Fancies by Jane Cavendish and Elizabeth Brackley was certainly written with a multidimensional production in mind, as the script demonstrates. Even more important than its intrinsic theatricality, however, is the specific arena and audience for which it was composed: the Cavendish family circle. Taking into account the possibility that the play may have been produced at one of the two Cavendish homes—Welbeck Abbey and Bolsover Castle—is vital. *The Concealed Fancies* dramatizes those arenas in its two household settings and is intimately linked to the real and imagined lives of the authors during the English Civil War.

Our production tried to create the ambience of a domestic performance[13] by presenting the play to a knowing coterie of conference delegates and by staging it in a nonofficial performance space: one of the large rooms at Bretton Hall, originally a country house with Royalist connections.[14] The Cavendish context for the play can be seen as imposing certain limitations to its performability.[15] *The Concealed Fancies* is designed for a particular, noncommercial "playing" arena but, excluded from the public stage, Cavendish and Brackley deliberately employ the domestic context to raise disturbing questions about the position of women in the family. They write a play for and about the household, which manipulates that typically feminine space to demonstrate the instability of gender constructs.

The authors use theatrical techniques to undermine male supremacy in the home. Throughout *The Concealed Fancies* the heroines Luceny and Tattiney are determined to remain mistresses of themselves. Both sisters vow that they will not alter at the altar, and they use performance to show the illusory nature

of wifely submission. In 2.3 Luceny gives a parodic rehearsal of wifely deference, and on her wedding morning she has a remarkable song, as she looks in
a mirror and literally reflects on what it will mean to be married. She asks,
"What is't they say, must I a wife become?" and determines,

> Why then, a wife in show appear,
> Though monkey I should dare;
> And so upon the marriage day
> I'll look as if obey.[16]

She prepares to mimic the role of a dutiful wife, rather than truly submitting
to the authority of her husband.

Playing the role of obedient wife pushes the boundaries of performance
beyond the script or the stage and gives the play its limitless subversive potential. Through moments like this, Cavendish and Brackley extend the idea of
acting beyond their play to raise the possibility that gender itself is performative, an endless citation. In seventeenth-century England, insincere mimicry of
the wifely role was perceived as dangerous, because, if women were such good
performers, how was any man to know whether his wife's decorous behavior
was a genuine act of submission or just a mimicry? If, as I believe, Cavendish
and Brackley wrote the roles of Luceny and Tattiney for themselves and possibly played them, then the heroines' ideas about marriage take on an added
dimension. *The Concealed Fancies* may have given the authors opportunity to
negotiate marital relationships through "play" since numerous metatheatrical
references elide the identities of characters, writers, and actors.[17]

Songs are an important tool that Luceny and Tattiney (and the authors who
stand behind them) use to theatricalize conventional gender roles in courtship
and marriage. The heightened artifice of song "empties" such roles, while its cita-
tionality protects the performer, whether character or actor, from direct association with the subversive sentiments expressed. In Act 2 scene 3, Luceny addresses
an unwelcome, arrogant suitor called Corpolant, in song rather than speech.
Singing allows her to win a bet with Tattiney that she will not speak to Corpolant
but, more importantly, it gives her license to insult him unmercifully:

> I prithee fool, not speak no more
> For I can not thee like,
> Thy folly hath been great enough
> For me to laughing slight;
> Thy face a black, bruised honeycomb,
> Thyself, an ugly sot,
> Besides, you are a clog of dun[g],
> So I'll not be your lot.
>
> (2.3.70–77)

Luceny (Lesley Sharp) and Corpolant (Rhys Williams), 2.3

The formality of song distances Luceny from the insults: when she calls Corpolant a "clog of dun[g]" the words are both hers and not hers because the lyric makes them a citation. Corpolant's patient attention to three full verses suggests that it takes some time for the unpleasant meaning to penetrate. In our production the harp accompaniment was designed to highlight the discontinuity between romantic form and harsh message. As if in mockery of courtly serenades, Luceny circled Corpolant with gestures of affection, while insulting him.

During the course of the play, Luceny and Tattiney mock their suitors and retire to a nunnery. They are likely to be converted to marriage only by a miracle, so Courtley and Presumption stage one, appearing disguised as gods and promising to bring the heroines' father, Lord Calsindow, back from exile. The betrothal scene offers the most striking textual evidence in favor of a performance. The masquelike interlude is designed to assault the audience's senses from all sides. It relies on music, spatial, temporal, and visual effects.

Detailed stage directions in the manuscript state that Courtley and Presumption enter with "A Song sung by 2 gods coming downe out of the sky to the nunns."[18] The "gods" bring Luceny and Tattiney "garments" to substitute for their nuns' habits; these new clothes clearly symbolize the heroines'

Presumption (Matthew Chambers), 5.2

shift from withdrawal to betrothal.[19] The new harmony between the lovers is also signaled through music. The protagonists unite in a four-part song, which hastens them to their "happy day" of marriage:

> Courtley: Now let us cut each way away.
> Presumption: And make rude winds us to obey.
> Luceny: To bring us to our happy day.
> Tattiney: Then blessings will be our rich pay.
> (5.2.43–6)

The song is "sung over soe often 'till they bee drawne up."[20] Precisely what kind of device was envisaged to draw actors up from one level to another is not known, but the arrangement of the scene shows how the authors rely on space to achieve an effect. The distance between floor level and the entrance above necessitates a fairly slow exit, thus allowing the blending of the four voices to advertise the new cooperation between the characters.

The appearance of the godlike patriarchs, including the heroines' father, transforms Luceny and Tattiney from domineering mistresses into silent

Presumption (Matthew Chambers), Tattiney (Jessie Dawson), Luceny (Lesley Sharp) and Courtley (Tony Gilsenan), 5.2

wives, yet this conservative message about male authority is rendered deeply ambiguous in performance. On one level, the authors are self-consciously imitating the court masque to persuade the audience to celebrate the traditions it upholds: the supremacy of the paternal governor in the home and the kingdom. Conversely, the scene highlights the artifice of that illusion. The audience (and the heroines) know that the "gods" are just Courtley and Presumption, dressed up in a final attempt to win their mistresses. There is at least a hint of parody when Luceny and Tattiney ask "Are you god-cheaters? / Or are we not ourselves?" (5.2.9–10). The "gods" are spectacular but very obviously theatrical cheats whose divine authority is only a construct of performance. This implies that the power of the husband, as divinely appointed head of the family, is as artificial as Courtley and Presumption's disguises, a shadow of authority without any natural substance.

Domestic performance conditions accentuate this subversive message. In our production, we attempted to stage a spectacle, using dry ice, music, glittering costumes, and a balcony, but the cast were not professional actors or musicians and the props were mostly domestic items. Presumably for a performance at their home, Cavendish and Brackley would also have had to draw on the resources immediately available to them. I think that they deliberately exploit this apparent deficiency: the overambitious attempt to stage a divine spectacle within the household is precisely what they are dramatizing—parodically destabilizing patriarchal authority while seeming to celebrate it.

In a domestic venue, where acting on and off stage happens in the same place, boundaries between performance and being are fascinatingly blurred. By re-creating themselves in the characters of Luceny and Tattiney, Cavendish and Brackley can distance themselves from radical ideas and simultaneously advertise their own skill as subversive performers—within the script and beyond it. In this sense, as much as in the practical hints we are given in the text, it is obvious that *The Concealed Fancies* was written with a performance in mind. Only in a three-dimensional production could its persuasive message about gender and status be realized.

The Convent of Pleasure – Gweno Williams

In 1995 I devised a stage production[21] of Margaret Cavendish's 1668 play *The Convent of Pleasure*, at the University College of Ripon and York St. John.[22] The production was designed as a case study to demonstrate the intrinsic performability of Cavendish's plays and to challenge three centuries of dismissive critical comments on her plays as performance texts.[23] I selected *The Convent of Pleasure* from Cavendish's oeuvre of more than nineteen plays because it illustrates her competence as a dramatist in a number of ways. It is one of her most self-consciously theatrical plays, demonstrating a finely nuanced awareness and understanding of dramatic genre, including, for example, comedy, masque, and pastoral. In *The Convent of Pleasure*, Cavendish displays her familiarity with the male canonical dramatic tradition in a number of ways, such as her exploitation and exploration of the device of cross-dressing used in plays for the public stage, such as *Epicoene*, *The Taming of the Shrew*, *Twelfth Night* and *As You Like It*. The play effectively deploys a wide range of spectacular theatrical effects, including movable scenery and multiple changes of costume. In case Cavendish's conception of the play as a potential performance text is in any doubt, the Epilogue specifically refers to the mechanics and conventions of the contemporary theater, including lighting and applause.[24]

I invited my colleague Bill Pinner[25] to direct the play for the stage. His commitment to searching out the physical logic of a dramatic text ensured a rigorous test of the play's performability. The actors were second-year undergraduates studying drama, and the play's lack of recorded stage history provided the impetus to encourage extensive actor involvement in production decisions, in order to develop as many readings of the stage text as possible. In addition to its strongly theatrical dimensions, the intriguing enactments of the fluidity of gender identity and sexual relationships in *The Convent of Pleasure* made it an appealing production choice.

The plot is quite straightforwardly structured around two main events. The first is the decision of the newly independent heiress, Lady Happy, to use her considerable inheritance to found an enclosed separatist all-female community dedicated to lifelong pleasure. In a creative and provocative reversal of early modern social expectations of women's roles and duties, whereby all women "are understood married or to be married and their desires are subject to their husband,"[26] she uses her potential dowry to fund a hedonistic single-sex alternative to heterosexual marriage for women. Alternating early scenes comically dramatize the frantic disappointment and anxiety of those who are excluded from the Convent and its pleasures—i.e., men and married women. Cavendish then skillfully complicates the political premises of this intriguing new society's existence by the second major plot event—the entry of the enigmatic "great Foreign Princess" to the Convent. S/he is visually and verbally ambiguous, a cross-dressed "Princely brave Woman truly, of a Masculine Presence" (2.3). Our student actors were unproblematically united in their decision to cast a male actor as the Princess, thereby creating some of the most complex and erotically charged moments in our production.[27]

The Convent is an ideal community with protofeminist values. The inmates have a lifelong commitment to varieties of pleasure, together with complete freedom from men, "the only troublers of Women" (1.2), and the burden and dangers of reproductive labor. This women's world of imaginative and creative play also appears to offer the possibility of same-sex eroticism; it is a common practice in the Convent for women to dress as men and "act Lovers parts" (3.1). The sexually charged doubly cross-dressed courtship that quickly develops between the Princess and Lady Happy is replete with double entendres and dramatic irony, due to her ignorance of his male identity. An exploration of same-sex love between women masks a heterosexual seduction recognizable as such only to the theater audience. This privileged perspective on the literally multilayered sexual opportunities[28] and fluid gender positions developed in the play offers the theater audience a range of informed pleasures.

The performing and watching of plays is a principal activity within the Convent, and Cavendish repeatedly deploys the sophisticated and complex dramatic device of the play-within-a-play with confidence and success. Her skillful and varied use of this device with its established theatrical pedigree is further evidence of her familiarity with mainstream dramatic traditions and techniques. Indeed, she was arguably the first woman dramatist to write a play that includes a formally staged play-within-a-play.

Lady Happy (Sarah Davies) and the Princess (Steph Boyd), 3.1

The first of these is tellingly positioned at the exact structural center of *The Convent of Pleasure*. This play-within-a-play is a challenging, even shocking choice of entertainment for a community manifestly dedicated to female pleasure, for it consists of an explicit catalogue of physical and psychological horrors attendant upon marriage and childbirth. The dramatic focus is on women under stress at moments of crisis and disaster resulting from hetero-sexual relationships. There is a particular, graphic emphasis upon the distress induced by childbirth, especially the risks of infant and maternal mortality. This inner play functions as a moral object lesson to illustrate the sufferings of women of all classes in society and to remind the enclosed convent audience of what they have escaped. It also places the theater audience in an interesting and complicated position as they observe the psychological dilemma of the cross-dressed Princess, whom they alone can perceive as a "guilty creature sitting at a play."[29]

This play-within-a-play is also remarkable as the first known example in English drama of a woman dramatist depicting a formally structured play

staged entirely by women. It is a crucially important clue to Cavendish's positive attitude to women as actors. Here, aristocratic women are shown imper-
sonating women and men of a range of social classes in a dynamic and demand-

**Women Actors in the Convent of Pleasure (Claire Wiggins, Vivien Routledge,
Sarah Hill, Esther Jones, Claire Donaldson), 3.9**

ing acting situation. In this short play-within-a-play the pace is extremely
rapid, the action is physically vigorous and noisy, and there are sudden changes
of scene and mood. By implication, the convent actors must therefore be skillful, versatile, and resourceful, in direct contrast to the self-confessed (2.4) lack
of acting ability of the men outside. Significantly, at a historical moment when
women's presence on the English stage was new and controversial,[30] Cavendish
claims acting as a skill that women possess in full measure.

Because the Convent inmates appear to spontaneously author their own
acting texts, female creativity and ingenuity are being exploited to demonstrate the dark and dangerous side of heterosexual relationships. In a particu-

larly effective mise-en-abime that underscores the troubling subtextual rape plot of *The Convent of Pleasure,* the play-within-a-play concludes by dramatizing entry into a nunnery as a woman's only means of escape from imminent rape.

Cavendish's plays are often dramatically innovative in confining the majority of the male characters to limited and subsidiary roles. In *The Convent of Pleasure* men are depicted solely as suitors preoccupied with efforts to penetrate the all-female stronghold of the Convent and gain access to the women. Only the disguised Princess finds a way to succeed. Much comedy in the play is derived from the ludicrously unsuccessful group efforts

Monsieur Adviser (Paul Giddings), Monsieur Facil (John Matthews), Monsieur Courtly (Stuart Ratcliffe), Monsieur Take-Pleasure (David Tucker), 2.4

of the other male characters to invade the women's space. They prove to be ineffectual, incompetent, slow-witted, and contentious. They dissipate their energy in futile and disorganized plotting, and they are readily distracted by bawdy innuendo and drink. The performance allowed full scope to realize the strong visual and verbal humor of these scenes and generated much audience enjoyment and laughter. The disorderly drunkenness of these men and their inability to carry through any plan is a powerful and humorous dramatic contrast both to the women's tranquil and harmonious creation of an orderly alternative community within the Convent walls and to the discreet maneuvers of the disguised Princess.

This successful production of *The Convent of Pleasure* clearly revealed the performance potential of Cavendish's plays, and it has repeatedly received an enthusiastic reception from both live and video audiences. In performance, the play proves engaging, provocative, humorous, subtle, and surprising.

Epilogue

A fourth production was added to our project in January 1997.[31] Jane Lumley's version of *Iphigenia at Aulis* (ca. 1555)[32] directed by Stephanie J. Hodgson-Wright, was successfully staged at the University of Sunderland.[33] The play deals with a central question: should Agamemnon let his daughter Iphigenia be sacrificed to the goddess Diana in order to enable the Greeks to sail to Troy and conquer it? The rehearsal process and the final realization in performance demonstrated that the text, rendered as it is in pithy and strikingly naturalistic prose, offers a whole variety of stageable moments.[34] Ritualized encounters between characters of differing status contrast with scenes of high emotion in which all decorum is abandoned, thus emphasizing the two sides of the central dilemma. This dilemma is resolved when Iphigenia agrees to die, apparently prompted by the alternative of internecine warfare among the Greek army, together with the rebellion of her mother, Clytemnestra, against Agamemnon. The scene in which Iphigenia is taken to her death especially provided a rich opportunity for the employment of ritualized staging. Iphigenia's exit is accompanied by commentary from the Chorus, which, the text suggests, should be set to music: Iphigenia instructs the Chorus to "sing some song of my death" (fol. 94^v).[35] In order to emphasize Iphigenia's full complicity in her sacrifice, the references to her exit were interpreted literally. She says, "Who is this that will carry me hence so soon?" (fol. 94^r) and "bring me therefore unto the altar of the temple" (fol. 94^v). In our production, Iphigenia was borne off on a wooden bier, carried by four men in stylized masks, whose movements were, of necessity, highly formalized.

The use of this wooden bier, coupled with the blue costume of Iphigenia, was designed to emphasize Jane Lumley's early modern refiguring of the character as both a type of Mary and a type of Christ.[36] The production process thereby constituted the fullest method of exploring the literal and symbolic layers of the play.

Our investigations thus far indicate strongly that early modern English-women were entirely capable of writing plays for performance. In addition, Jean Howard has demonstrated that the English playhouse was a place of particular freedom for women: they bought their right to operate a critical gaze on equal terms with men.[37] English women playwrights had sisters abroad, and the European influence of Anna of Denmark and Henrietta Maria meant increased access for aristocratic women to the site of dramatic production at court. This dynamic cultural context seems unlikely to have produced women dramatists who felt constrained to write plays "not intended for performance, unperformed and therefore unperformable." Viewed in the light of our empirical evidence, the early modern plays by women under discussion here were clearly written with an informed, sophisticated, and original sense of theater.

Iphigenia (Rebecca Brown), fol. 95

Notes

1. For a fuller discussion of the issues treated here, see Alison Findlay, Stephanie Hodgson-Wright, and Gweno Williams, "'The Play Is Ready to Be Acted': Women and Dramatic Production, 1570–1670," *Women's Writing: The Elizabethan to Victorian Period* 6, no. 1 (1999).

2. Some of the early material supporting this view is reprinted in *Readings in Renaissance Women's Drama: Criticism, History, and Performance, 1594–1998*, ed. S. P. Cerasano and Marion Wynne-Davies (London: Routledge, 1998).

3. For a fuller account of this production, see Introduction to *Elizabeth Cary: The Tragedy of Mariam*, ed. Stephanie Hodgson-Wright (London: Broadview Press, forthcoming 2000).

4. Cast: Sian Meyrick (Chorus Sculptor), Paula M. Wells (Chorus Gravedigger), Jo Dyer (Mariam), Lou Ford (Alexandra/Ananell/Butler), Suzannah Rogers (Salome), Paul Walker (Silleus), Anthony Bentley (Constabarus), Orazio Rea (Pheroras), Lyndsey Smith (Graphina/Nuntio), Andrew Maher (Baba's 1st Son/Sohemus), Graeme Watson (Baba's 2nd Son), Elizabeth Stannard (Doris), Robyn Howarth (Antipater), and Dave Newport (Herod). Video produced with the help of Media Services at Trinity and All Saints College, Leeds, United Kingdom, and the University of Sunderland, United Kingdom.

5. Photography for *The Tragedy of Mariam* by Stuart Ellis.

6. All of the cast, without exception, praised the play for its clearly drawn characters, exciting dramatic dialogue, and psychologically complex soliloquies. Much to my surprise, they found *The Tragedy of Mariam* more accessible and interesting than the Shakespearean plays they had worked on previously.

7. Chorus 3: 13–18. All quotations are taken from *Elizabeth Cary: The Tragedy of Mariam* (1613), ed. Stephanie J. Wright (Keele, Eng.: Keele University Press, 1996).

8. Nancy Gutierrez, "Valuing *Mariam*: Genre Study and Feminist Analysis," *Tulsa Studies in Women's Literature* 10, no. 2 (1991): 233–51, 242.

9. Richard Levin, "A Possible Source of *A Fair Quarrel*," *Notes & Queries* 228 (1983): 152–53 argues that a section of *A Fair Quarrel* is based upon this scene.

10. For example, it is not there to motivate Salome to act against Constabarus, because by the time she hears of Silleus's injuries (3.3), she has already determined her intrigues against Constabarus.

11. R.V. Holdsworth, "Middleton and *The Tragedy of Mariam*," *Notes & Queries* 231 (1986): 379–80, points to the influence of this scene upon *The Second Maiden's Tragedy*.

12. Naomi J. Miller, "Domestic Politics in Elizabeth Cary's *The Tragedy of Mariam*," *Studies in English Literature* 37 (1997): 367.

13. Cast: Lesley Sharp (Luceny/Lady Tranquillity), Jessie Dawson (Tattiney), Tony Gilsenan (Courtley/Mr. Divinity), Matthew Chambers (Presumption), Ross Burgess (Lord Calsindow/Col. Free /Elder Stellow), Rhys Williams (Corpolant/Younger Stellow/Gravity/Mr Friendly), Rebecca Thomas (Toy/Action), Jude Hebden (Pert/Mr Proper/Moderate), Dana Turell (Elizabeth/Angel/Care), Jean Bufton (Cicilley/Jack), Caroline Green (Grave/Sage). Production co-directed by Alison Findlay and Jane Milling; video produced by Andrew Muscroft; photographs captured from video.

14. For further discussion of the domestic context, see Alison Findlay, "'She Gave You the Civility of the House': household performance in *The Concealed Fancies* in Cerasano and Wynne-Davies, 259–71.

15. Dale B. J. Randall, *Winter Fruit: English Drama, 1642–1660* (Lexington: University Press of Kentucky, 1995), 326, argues that *The Concealed Fancies* is "not altogether satisfying art, but perhaps it was not a bad game for a couple of beleagured young women to play."

16. Jane Cavendish and Elizabeth Brackley, *The Concealed Fancies* in Cerasano and Wynne-Davies, 5.6.3–6. All quotations are taken from this edition, unless otherwise stated.

17. For further discussion of this idea, see Alison Findlay, "Playing the 'Scene-self'; and Jane Cavendish and Elizabeth Brackley's *The Concealed Fancies* in *Enacting Gender on the English Renaissance Stage*, ed. Viviana Comensoli and Anne Russell (Urbana: University of Illinois Press, 1998), 154–76.

18. *The Concealed Fansyes*, Bodleian Library MS Rawl. Poet. 16, 141.

19. In our production, the "garments" were wedding garlands and veils.

20. *The Concealed Fansyes,* Bodleian Library MS Rawl. Poet. 16, 142.

21. For a fuller account of this production, see Gweno Williams, "'Why May Not a Lady Write a Good Play?' Plays by Early Modern Women Reassessed As Performance Texts," in Cerasano and Wynne-Davies, 95–107.

22. Cast: Steph Boyd, Sarah Davies, Claire Donaldson, Vicki Elsdon, Joanne Eyre, Paul Giddings, Debi Haworth, Sarah Hill, Esther Jones, John Matthews, Stuart Ratcliffe, Vivien Routledge, Sarah Salholm, Melissa Shorten, Claire Summerfield, David Tucker, and Claire Wiggins. Production directed by Bill Pinner; video produced by Louis Purver, Richard Berry, and Jane Moore; photographs captured from video.

23. See, for example, Randall, 339; Henry Ten Eyck Perry, *The First Duchess of Newcastle and her Husband as Figures in Literary History* (Boston and London: Ginn, 1918), 214; *Dictionary of National Biography,* 356–57.

24. Margaret Cavendish, *The Convent of Pleasure,* 53. All quotations are taken from the University of Leeds Brotherton Library Special Collection's copy of *Plays, Never Before Printed* (London, 1668). N.B. plays are individually paginated and line numbers are not given.

25. Bill Pinner is Senior Lecturer in Performance Studies at University College of Ripon and York St. John, United Kingdom. His professional theater credits include designer for Mary Pix, *The Innocent Mistress,* Derby Playhouse, 1986, directed by Annie Castledine.

26. T. E., *The Law's Resolutions of Women's Rights* (1632), quoted in Joan Larsen Klein, ed., *Daughters, Wives and Widows: Writings by Men about Women and Marriage in England, 1500–1640,* 32 (Urbana and Chicago: University of Illinois Press, 1992).

27. Sophie Tomlinson, in "'My Brain the Stage': Margaret Cavendish and the Fantasy of Female Performance," in *Women, Texts and Histories, 1575–1760,* eds. Clare Brant and Diane Purkiss (London: Routledge, 1992), 134–63, argues that the list of "the Actors Names" placed at the end of the play suggests that "in Cavendish's mind 'the Princess' was not an actor but an actress"(157).

28. A number of characters, including Lady Happy and the disconsolate male suitors, refer to women's underwear in the course of the play, thus drawing the audience's attention to the ways in which layers of costume and disguise offer different erotic possibilities. See, for example, 2.2 and 2.4.

29. William Shakespeare, *Hamlet,* ed. Harold Jenkins (rpt. London & New York: Routledge, 1993), 2.2.585.

30. See, for example, Ann Thompson, "Women/'Women' and the Stage," in *Women and Literature in Britain, 1500–1700,* ed. Helen Wilcox (Cambridge: Cambridge University Press, 1996), 100–16; Elizabeth Howe, *The First English Actresses: Women and Drama, 1660–1700,* (Cambridge: Cambridge University Press, 1992); Rosamund Gilder, *Enter the Actress: The First Women in the Theatre* (New York: Theatre Arts Books, 1931), 132–72.

31. Due to time constraints, a full discussion of the production was not possible, and the paragraph here reflects the format of the live presentation.

32. Performance text taken from British Library MS Royal 15 A ix.

33. Cast: Dorette Clarke (Chorus), Helen Angus (Chorus), Guy Rushworth (Agamemnon), Dave Brown (Senex), Gary Kitching (Menelaus), Katerina Petersen (Nuntio), Joy Sanders (Clytemnestra), Rebecca Brown (Iphigenia), Chris Smith (Achilles).Video recorded by University of Sunderland Media Studies students and produced with the help of Media Services at the University of Sunderland; photograph captured from video.

34. The production was undertaken by Creative Arts students, who decided that, as the final product would be a late twentieth-century staging of an early modern version of a Classical Greek play, the costumes, set and music should reflect this unique mix.

35. Chris Smith composed original music for the Chorus's song (fol. 95) as Iphigenia is taken to the altar.

36. For a fuller discussion of the early modern context of the play, see Stephanie Hodgson-Wright, "Jane Lumley's *Iphigenia at Aulis: multum in parvo,* or, Less Is More" in Cerasano and Wynne-Davies (1998), 129–41.

37. Jean E. Howard, *The Stage and Social Struggle in Early Modern England* (London: Routledge, 1994), 75–80. Furthermore, Stephen Orgel suggests that the male exclusivity of the public stage in England was exceptional in early modern Europe; see *Impersonations: The Performance of Gender in Shakespeare's England* (Cambridge: Cambridge University Press, 1996), 10.

Contributors

ELECTA ARENAL, Latin Americanist, professor of Hispanic literatures, and translator, has published three books: *Untold Sisters: Hispanic Nuns in Their Own Works; Cultura conventual femenina: Obras completes de sor Marcelade San Felix, la hija de Lope de Vega* [Women's Convent Culture: Complete Works of S.M.S.F., daughter of L. de V.]; and the bilingual, annotated edition of Sor Juana Inés de Cruz, *The Answer/La Respuesta.* She has also published essays on Sor Juana and other monastic women, and on the work of twenti-eth-century Central American writers Claribel Alegria, Gioconda Belli, and Carmen Naranjo. She has been a peace and social justice activist since the 1950s, and helped found women's studies at Richmond College (now the College of Staten Island of the City University of New York). From 1992 to 1994 she was director of research at the Center for Feminist Research in the Humanities at the University of Bergen, Norway. Since 1997 she has directed the Center for the Study of Women and Society and the Women's Studies Certificate Program at CUNY's Graduate School. Her play, "This Life Within Me Won't Keep Still," based on the life and work of Anne Bradstreet and Sor Juana de la Cruz, was premiered in San Francisco. She is working on a book and CD-ROM project, *Sor Juana's Arch/El arco de Sor Juana.*

ANNE LLEWELLYN BARSTOW is a retired historian from SUNY College at Old Westbury. She is the author of *Witchcraze: A New History of the European Witch Hunts* and *Joan of Arc: Heretic, Mystic, Shaman.* Barstow is still inter-ested in working on ways in which the story of Joan of Arc has impact on women's lives today.

JODI BILINKOFF earned her Ph.D. from Princeton University in 1983. She is the author of *The Avila of Saint Teresa: Religious Reform in a Sixteenth-Century City* (Ithaca: Cornell University Press, 1989; paperback 1992, Spanish edition 1993) and of a number of essays and articles exploring religion, gender, authority, and the construction of identities in early modern Spain. She is associate professor of history at the University of North Carolina at Greensboro. When not teaching, researching, or plotting how to get back to Spain, she enjoys music, films, cooking, and listening to her daughter Amanda at play.

SUZANNE G. CUSICK teaches music history and criticism at the University of Virginia, where she directs graduate studies in music. Her essays on aspects of gender and sexuality in relation to music have appeared in *Early Music, Musical Quarterly, Il Saggiatore musicale*, and the *Journal of the American Musicological Society*, as well as in such anthologies as *Musicology and Difference* and *Queering the Pitch*. Her monograph on Francesca Caccini, *A Romanesca of One's Own*, is forthcoming from the University of Chicago Press.

FRANCES E. DOLAN is professor of English and an affiliate of the History Department and the Women's Studies Program, at Miami University in Ohio. She is the author of *Dangerous Familiars: Representations of Domestic Crime in England, 1550–1700* (Ithaca: Cornell University Press, 1994) and *Whores of Babylon: Catholicism, Gender, and Seventeenth-Century Print Culture* (Ithaca: Cornell University Press, 1999). She is the editor of *The Taming of the Shrew: Texts and Contexts* (Bedford Books, 1996) and of five plays for the New Pelican Shakespeare series.

JANE DONAWERTH is professor of English and affiliate in Women's Studies at the University of Maryland. She has authored *Shakespeare and the Sixteenth-Century Study of Language* (Illinois University Press) and co-edited *Women, Writing, and the Reproduction of Culture in Tudor and Stuart Britain* (Syracuse, N.Y.: Syracuse University Press). She has also published two books on science fiction by women, and essays on Shakespeare, feminist pedagogy, and history of rhetorical theory. She has won seven teaching awards. She is currently working on an anthology of rhetorical theory by women before 1900, and a book on Renaissance women's reading and writing.

ALISON FINDLAY is a Senior Lecturer in English at Lancaster University where she teaches courses on Shakespeare, Renaissance drama and women's writing. She is author of *Illegitimate Power: Bastards in Renaissance Drama* (Manchester: Manchester University Press, 1994) and *A Feminist Perspective on Renaissance Drama* (Oxford: Blackwell Publishers, 1999), and has published several articles on Renaissance drama. She is co-director, with Stephanie Hodgson-Wright and Gweno Williams, of the interdisciplinary research project, Women and Dramatic Production 1550–1700, and co-author of a forthcoming book of the same title to be published by Longman's in November 2000.

STEPHANIE HODGSON-WRIGHT is Senior Lecturer in English Studies at the University of Sunderland. She has published widely on Early Modern women's writing, including an edition of *The Tragedy of Mariam* for Keele University Press and Broadview Press, a volume in the Early Modern

Englishwoman facsimile library of essential works and a forthcoming anthology of women's writing 1588–1688 for Edinburgh University Press.

MARTHA HOWELL is professor of history at Columbia University, where, from 1989 to 1994, she directed Columbia's Institute for Research on Women and Gender. Professor Howell is a specialist in the urban history of the late medieval and early modern Low Countries, northern France, and Germany, and she focuses in particular on the gender system of those cultures. She is the author of two monographs, both published by University of Chicago Press: *Women, Production and Patriarchy in Late Medieval Cities* (1986) and *The Marriage Exchange: Property, Social Place and Gender in Cities of the Low Countries,1300–1550* (1998). Presently she is working with Professor Walter Prevenier of the University of Ghent on a book concerning historical methodology, which will be published by Cornell University Press.

BARBARA F. MCMANUS is professor of classics at the College of New Rochelle in New York. An interest in feminist theory, feminist cultural studies, and feminist pedagogy provides a unifying foundation for her work in apparently diverse areas, ranging from classical antiquity to Renaissance England to the humanistic potential of computers. She has published two books, *Half Humankind: Contexts and Texts of the Controversy about Women in England, 1540–1640* and *Classics and Feminism: Gendering the Classics*, and she is currently assessment director of the VRoma Project, funded by a National Endowment for the Humanities Teaching with Technology grant.

KAREN NEWMAN is University Professor and professor of comparative literature and English at Brown University. Her books include *Shakespeare's Rhetoric of Comic Character*, *Fashioning Femininity and English Renaissance Drama*, and *Fetal Positions: Individualism, Science, Visuality*, as well as numerous articles on early modern culture and literary theory. This essay is part of a new book on cultural production in early modern London and Paris.

KATHARINE PARK is Zemurray Stone Radcliffe Professor of the history of science and women's studies at Harvard University. She is the author of *Doctors and Medicine in Early Renaissance Florence* (Princeton: Princeton University Press, 1985) and *Wonders and the Order of Nature, 1150–1750* (Zone Books, 1998), co-authored with Lorraine Daston. Her recent research focuses on the history of medical and philosophical constructions of sexuality and sex difference in medieval and Renaissance Europe. The article in this collection is related to a her current book project, *Visible Women: Gender, Generation, and the Origins of Human Dissection*.

ANNE LAKE PRESCOTT is the Helen Goodhart Altschul Professor of English at Barnard College. She is co-editor of *Spenser Studies* and has recently published *Imagining Rabelais in the English Renaissance*. Together with Betty Travitsky, she has a forthcoming anthology entitled *Female and Male Voices* that juxtaposes texts by early modern women and men.

ADELE SEEFF is the director of the Center for Renaissance and Baroque Studies at the University of Maryland where she develops interdisciplinary postgraduate programming for a campus and a national audience. She is co-editor of the center's volume series–eight volumes are in print. She has written on Shakespeare and issues in higher education, and has authored scripts for public television, two of which won national awards. In 1997 she was the recipient of the President of the University of Maryland's Award for Outstanding Work in the Schools.

GWENO K. WILLIAMS is Senior Lecturer in Literature Studies at the University College of Ripon and York St. John in York, England. She is engaged in interdisciplinary research into Margaret Cavendish's plays, consisting of a series of productions recorded on video, and has published a number of articles on aspects of Cavendish's dramatic oeuvre. She is co-founder, with Alison Findlay and Stephanie Hodgson-Wright, of the collaborative interdisciplinary research project into female-authored early modern drama Women and Dramatic Production 1550–1700.

JUDITH T. ZEITLIN is associate professor of Chinese literature in the Department of East Asian Languages and Civilizations at the University of Chicago. The author of *Historian of the Strange: Pu Songling and the Chinese Classical Tale* (Stanford, Calif.: Stanford University Press, 1993), she is currently completing a book on ghosts and gender in the late imperial Chinese imagination and working on a study of the doctor's casebook and the literary construction of medical authority in sixteenth-century China.

Index

Edelman, Nathan, 222n. 6
Eden, 146
education, Renaissance reform of, 254
effigy portrait, 48–79
Egypt, 187
electronic technology, 23, 236, 268, 270–71, 278–79, 284–85
elegy, 49, 51–54
Elisabeth of Bohemia, 283
Elizabeth I, Queen of England, 19, 111, 114–15, 141, 146, 203–4, 268, 278
Elliott, Dyan, 113
Ellis, Robert Leslie, 43n. 1
Ellis, Stuart, 306n. 5
Elsdon, Vicki, 307n. 22
Elsner, Jas., 44n. 8
Elyot, Sir Thomas, 231, 238n. 9
emblems, 181, 184–85
empiricism, 215
England, 17, 21–23, 32, 101–2, 106, 116, 124–26, 140–42, 146, 150, 156–57, 203–4, 213, 219, 227, 233, 276
English Civil War, 294
Enikel, 32
Enlightenment, 211
epic, 146, 237
epigram, 100, 179, 231
epigraph, 180
epitaph, 231
Equiano, Olaudah B., 200
Erasmus, Desiderius, 259
Erickson, Amy Louise, 111, 151, 246–57, 251
Eriksson, Ruben, 46n. 44
eroticism, 14, 16, 66, 92, 104, 123, 142–43, 233, 307n. 28
Este, Giulio d', 94n. 6
Este family, 94n. 6
ethnicity, 247
euphemism, 51
Evans, G. Blakemore, 45n. 26
Evans, Katharine, 200
Evans, Robert C., 24n. 3, 271–73
Eve, 146
Evelyn, John, 111
Evers, Charcy, 276
evidence, 241–46, 254–56, 259, 281, 289

Eworth, Hans, 156
execution, public, 131, 144
exegesis, 184, 242
explication: See exegesis
Eyre, Joanne, 307n. 22
Ezell, Margaret, 101–3

fabliau, 22, 259
Falloppio, Giovanni, 87, 97n. 25
falsetto, 85, 97n. 19
family, 80–98, 247, 253–58
Farago, Claire, 105–8
Farge, Arlette, 120
Farrington, Benjamin, 47
farthingale, 125
fashion, 213
fasting, 163
Fein, Ellen, 251n. 8
female ruler, 204
feme couvert, 150
feminism: and pedagogy, 12–13, 21–23, 227–85; and theater, 23, 289–308; theory, 227–40
Feng Menglong, 75n. 18, 78–79
Ferdinand I, Duke, de' Medici, 81, 90
Ferdinand II, 92
Ferguson, Margaret W., 46n. 42, 117, 205, 207, 223n. 21
Ferguson, Moira, 195–96
Fern, Maureen, 276
Ferrari, Giovanna, 46n. 34
fetus, 33–39, 45n. 21, 123–24, 187
ffolliott, Sheila, 205–7
Fielding, Henry, 148–49
Fildes, Valerie, 107
Filteau, Claude, 223n. 23
Findlay, Alison, 23, 289–308
Findlen, Paul, 191n. 13, 192n. 32
Finke, Laurie, 229, 232, 236, 238n. 12
Finlay, Robert, 262n. 7
Finucci, Valeria, 147
Firth, C. H., 278
Fisher, Sheila, 232, 239n. 13
Fissell, Mary, 115–17
Fitch, Nancy, 285
Flanders, Julia, 270
Fletcher, Anthony, 138n. 14, 248, 251n. 11